Witchcraft

4 in 1

How to Become a Modern Witch and Live a Magical Life Using Wicca Spells, Magic Candles and Crystals, and Tarot Cards. Includes Wiccan Religion, Astrology and Tarot for Beginners

Lisa Woods

© COPYRIGHT 2020 ALL RIGHTS RESERVED

This document is geared towards providing exact and reliable information with regard to the topic and issue covered. The publication is sold with the idea that the publisher is not required to render accounting, officially permitted or otherwise qualified services. If advice is necessary, legal or professional, a practiced individual in the profession should be ordered.

From a Declaration of Principles which was accepted and approved equally by a Committee of the American Bar Association and a Committee of Publishers and Associations.

In no way is it legal to reproduce, duplicate, or transmit any part of this document in either electronic means or in printed format. Recording of this publication is strictly prohibited, and any storage of this document is not allowed unless with written permission from the publisher. All rights reserved.

The information provided herein is stated to be truthful and consistent, in that any liability, in terms of inattention or otherwise, by any usage or abuse of any policies, processes, or directions contained within is the solitary and utter responsibility of the recipient reader. Under no circumstances will any legal responsibility or blame be held against the publisher for any reparation, damages, or monetary loss due to the information herein, either directly or indirectly.

The presentation of the information is without a contract or any type of guarantee assurance. The trademarks that are used are without any consent, and the publication of the trademark is without permission or backing by the trademark owner. All trademark and brands within this book are for clarifying purposes only and are owned by the owners themselves, not affiliated with this document.

Table of Contents

BOOK 1: WICCA FOR BEGINNERS 9
Introduction 10
Chapter 1: What Is Wicca 12
Chapter 2: Wiccans And Their Beliefs 16
Chapter 3: What is Witchcraft 54
Chapter 4: Wiccan Tools for Spells and Rituals 59
Chapter 5: Wicca Meditation and Visualization 77
Chapter 6: Wiccan Crystal Magic 81
Chapter 7: Candles Magic 91
Chapter 8: Witchcraft Symbols and sign 98
Chapter 9: What are runes? 103
Chapter 10: Wicca Spells 124
Chapter 11: Herbs and Essential Oils 131
Chapter 12: Shamanism and Wicca 141
Conclusion 149

BOOK 2: TAROT FOR BEGINNERS 151
Introduction 152
Chapter 1: Tarot Through the History 156
Chapter 2: The Modern Tarot Deck 159
Chapter 3: How to Begin 161
Chapter 4: Method for Discovering Card Meanings 164
Chapter 4: Meaning of The Cards and Cards Interpretation Part 1 166
Chapter 5: Meaning of The Cards and Cards Interpretation Part 2 171
Chapter 6: Meaning of The Cards and Cards Interpretation Part 3 177
Chapter 7: Meaning of The Cards and Cards Interpretation Part 4 181
Chapter 8: Meaning of The Cards and Cards Interpretation Part 5 185
Chapter 9: Meaning of The Cards and Cards Interpretation Part 6 187
Chapter 10: Meaning of The Cards and Cards Interpretation The Swords 192
Chapter 11: Meaning of The Cards and Cards Interpretation The Pentacles 196

Chapter 12: Meaning of The Cards and Cards Interpretation Wands 203
Chapter 13: Reading for Yourself and For Others 210
Chapter 14: Techniques for Reading Tarot.. 213
Chapter 15: Choosing Your Cards or Letting the Cards Choose You.................................. 217
Chapter 16: The Most Effective Method to Read Tarot Cards – Your Step-By-Step Guide 221
Chapter 17: Selecting A Tarot Deck 228
Chapter 18: How Tarot Cards Connects to Astrology and A Zodiac Signs 231
Chapter 19: Tarot Spreads: Three Simple Spreads for Starting Out and Strengthening Your Intuitive Power 239
Chapter 20: Types of Tarot Decks 243
Chapter 21: Taking the Next Steps...246
Chapter 22: Other Uses for Tarot 248
Chapter 23: What to Do When You Get A "Bad" Card 254
Chapter 24: Is It Possible to Make Your Own Tarot Cards?..256
Chapter 25: How to Clean Tarot Decks?..258
Chapter 26: Putting It All Together 262
Chapter 27: The Art of Storytelling..264
Chapter 28: How to Make Your Cards Cranky?..270
Chapter 29: Shuffling Your Cards...272
Chapter 30: The Tarot and Secret Tradition 274
Chapter 31: Risks of Tarot 276
Chapter 32: Insight and the Tarot 278
Chapter 33: Teaching Yourself Tarot Mastery 281
Chapter 34: Starting Out Your Journey To Tarot Reading..284
Conclusion 288

BOOK 3: ASTROLOGY FOR BEGINNERS 291

Introduction..292
Chapter 1: Astrology Throughout the Ages (History)...294
Chapter 2: Astrology and the Planet..297
Chapter 3: Horoscopes...301
Chapter 4: The 12 Zodiac Signs and their Meanings 305
Chapter 5: The Birth Chart 309

Chapter 6: The Ascendant 313
Chapter 7: Tarot the History.. 318
Chapter 8: Tarot Cards and their Meanings 322
Chapter 9: Numerology, what is it? 327
Chapter 10: How to Calculate your Numerology and What it Means? 331
Chapter 11: The Significance of Names... 334
Chapter 12: Fibonacci Numbers 337
Chapter 13: What is Enneagram– Harmony Triads and Nine Types 341
Chapter 14: How to Master the Spiritual Growth 346
Chapter 15: Aquarius, Pisces, Aries and Taurus 349
Chapter 16: Gemini, Cancer, Leo, Virgo, Libra, Scorpio, Sagittarius and Capricorn 353
Chapter 17: Celestial Sphere 360
Chapter 18: How each Planet's Astrology Directly Affects every Zodiac Sign..... 363
Chapter 19: Oracle Cards and Psycards 368
Chapter 20: Performing Tarot Readings 371
Chapter 21: Note for Readings for Others 374
Chapter 22: Tarot 101- Getting Started 377
Chapter 23: Decks for Experienced Readers, Collectors, and Tarot Lovers......... 381
Chapter 24: The Effect of Numerology on Your Life 386
Chapter 25: How to Read Astrological Chart 389
Chapter 26: True Purpose of the Zodiac Sign in Life... 393
Chapter 27: Expression Number 398
Chapter 28: Life Paths 402
Chapter 29: Kundalini 407
Chapter 30: Kundalini Yoga Poses 412
Chapter 31: The Language of Energy... 415
Chapter 32: The Test Enneagram Instructions 417
Chapter 33: Decoding the Nine-Value Code.. 422
Conclusion 426

BOOK 4: ASTROLOGY 429
Introduction.. 430

- Chapter 1: The Beginning of Astrology 433
- Chapter 2: Astrology and the Planets 436
- Chapter 3: Understanding the Zodiac Signs 444
- Chapter 4: Horoscope 450
- Chapter 5: Birth Chart 455
- Chapter 6: The Ascendant 459
- Chapter 7: Astrology for Relationships - Sun Sign Compatibility, Rising Sign Compatibility 464
- Chapter 8: Tarot Basics 468
- Chapter 9: What is Numerology? 472
- Chapter 10: What is Wicca – Magic, Tools, Exercise and Magical Techniques 475
- Chapter 11: Astrology vs. Astronomy – What is the Difference? 480
- Chapter 12: The Basics of Astrology 485
- Chapter 13: What is Chakra? 488
- Chapter 14: Choosing Your Candles 493
- Chapter 15: Horoscope Matches – Why is it Important? 498
- Chapter 16: Kundalini Rising 502
- Chapter 17: Eclipses 507
- Chapter 18: Tarot and Western Astrology 512
- Chapter 19: Wiccan Beliefs 517
- Chapter 20: Personal Growth and Self Esteem 520
- Chapter 21: Opening Your Numerology Center 523
- Chapter 22: Lucky and Unlucky Numbers 526
- Chapter 23: How to Embrace Your Gift 528
- Chapter 24: Tarot Cards and Their Association to Specific Subjects 532
- Chapter 25: Wiccan Tools 541
- Chapter 26: Wiccan Moon 547
- Chapter 27: The Elements 552
- Chapter 28: Getting Started with Meditation 556
- Chapter 29: Forecasting 561
- Chapter 30: Geographical House Divisions and the Four Elemental House- Also Called Trinities 565
- Conclusion 567

Book 1

Wicca for Beginners

INTRODUCTION

Magic spells fascinated us for centuries. People are fascinated and obsessed with how spells could work in favor and against the interests and desires of an individual. Not only are magic spells done to achieve personal benefit, but they are also often practiced as part of a religious belief system like Wicca.

Wicca is profoundly rooted in ancient pagan traditions that originated hundreds of years ago. Gerald Gardner argued that Wicca's rituals and values were based on a hidden society that had welcomed him as a member. Wiccan spells are often referred to as "magic," rather than the common "magic," which distinguishes real magic from common tricks of conjuring and illusion practiced in shows by stage performers.

The revival and modern survival of the Ancient Earth-based Religion and its manifestations. This is what Wicca is, and its spiritual roots are in the European Neolithic and Paleolithic period, a time when the primitive peoples worshiped the feminine, the Mother Goddess as the great creator, nurturer, and sustainer of life.

The cult of the Goddess predates the Age of Taurus, which dates from 4000 to 2000 BC In this period, men basically survived from hunting and fishing and worshiped the forces of nature and especially the Great Mother, who was the breadwinner.

Another deity, the Cornish God, considered the masculine principle of creation, was also revered and worshiped to provide abundant fighters and at the same time protection.

For thousands of years, the ancient European peoples continued to reverence the Great Mother as their main deity, until in the middle of the 400 AD century a new religion emerged and dominated Europe, Christianity, first introducing in Rome, spread while the Empire expanded and conquered several countries around the world. Gradually the Christian faith was gaining adherents and conquering the political classes.

CHAPTER ONE
What Is Wicca

The word Wicca designates a religion of Neopagan originating in England during the first half of the 20th century. Its name is synonymous with the modern English word witch, a derivation of the medieval term Wicca that can mean 'evil' or 'wise.'

The Wiccan faith is associated with white witchcraft rituals and with other concepts of ancient polytheistic religions. Monotheistic religions, therefore, frequently equate them with satanic practices. But Satan's image is not part of Wicca's mythological fantasy.

The Wiccan faith was founded in 1954 by the British Gerald Gardner, and continued by Doreen Valiente, who became a priestess of this faith after becoming a member of a coven established by Gardner.

It is a dualistic religion as it recognizes two gods: a female goddess known as the Moon Goddess, or Triple Goddess, and a male deity known as the "horned king."

The Moon Goddess or Triple Goddess represents the daughter, the mom and the old Woman. These, in effect, symbolize the phases of the Moon and the divine, celestial, and earthly rule.

The horned God synthesizes a number of ancient mythological figures, including the Egyptian God Osiris, the Greek demigod Pan, or the Roman Faun, all of whom bear horns in their iconography and are linked to nature.

There is no overarching structure in this religion, which has created numerous trends. Traditional British Wicca, strictly regulated by the Gardner and Brave guidelines.

Eclectic Wicca originated in the '70s, where new concepts are added according to group characteristics. Every variety is named after its leading inspiration. WICCA comes from the Anglo-Saxon word "wicce" (to bend, to shape nature to one's liking) and refers to the practitioner's ability to use magic, under certain conditions, of course. It is also known as the popular practice, the magic of the people. It is a contemporary pagan religion with spiritual roots in the first expressions of nature worship.

Wiccans do not provide details about the Craft because they are not looking for new members; they are not proselytizing. Despite this, in countries where religion is recognized, the number of practitioners is constantly growing. The situation is viewed with dissatisfaction by traditional religious structures.

Many people seek a personal religion, in which reality is worshiped, both physical and spiritual, in which one's own agreement (physical and spiritual) with divinity is also achieved with the help of magic (ceremonial magic used especially in religion), The Craft including this aspect.

I know some will say that we do what we do, and we keep talking about magic. Here I referred to the ceremonial, which you should know is studied even in theological institutes, for example. I don't think there is a religion that doesn't use magic. It's true, Wiccans don't turn water into wine, and no one's body into Easter, not to mention other magical acts (necromancy - in the Christian religion). Besides, not all Wiccans practice the Craft, but for priests or the great Priests are absolutely necessary to know the Craft. More about magic, but a little later.

Wicca is precisely such a religion, based on the importance of love, reverence for nature, which is, in reality, the Woman (the Woman) and the Horned Man (the man), reflecting the feminine and masculine elements that exist in nature, without which the creation cycle is not possible.

The Goddess is identified with the Great Mother (Earth), and the Moon, and the Creator, the Sun, Nature, forest, Fertility, hunting, and life cycle. Some times the Lord is regarded as the Green Man, a common character in European architecture and sculpture. That is often associated with nature in this situation. He is also seen as the God of the Sun, particularly during the summer solstice.

God appears in a separate way as King Oak, who is the Lord of spring and summer, and then as King Laurel, the Lord of autumn and winter. The Goddess typically appears in the form of the Triune Goddess, assuming the form of the Virgin, the Mother and the Old Woman successively, being synonymous with beauty, fertility, or wisdom, respectively. Sometimes, the three forms correspond to the Moon's phases, and hence the Goddess is seen as the Moon's deity.

The recognition (as being real) of nature's magic and mystery, has its origins firmly embedded in the beginnings of human culture, made it have a special charm. Until recently, the lack of knowledge about Wicca and its perceived exclusivity created many disappointments for those interested and misinterpretations by the general public of Wiccan's behavior and practices.

Wicca is a religion of happiness, harmony and love that springs from the intimate bond between us, humans and nature; it is a communion between us and Goddess or Gods, between us and the divine forces that formed All. It is a personal experience, a meaningful and lasting Life celebration.

The Wiccan Code of Ethics is found in The Wiccan Rede: 'harm it none, do as you will, mean in Old English language' If no one is harmed, do what your heart desires.' People do not harm others, do not harm others except themselves. Another feature of the Code of Ethics is the Triple Return Rule, in which every good or bad act must return to the person who did it three times more powerfully. Gerald Gardner introduced those laws when he established the cult of Wicca.

Many Wiccans often follow the direction of Doreen Valiente in pursuit of the Goddess listed virtues. Love, gratitude, honor, humility, power, grace, and compassion are these. Valiente orders these virtues in parallel pairs, thereby representing the dualism that is often found in worship at Wiccan. A collection of 161 Wiccan Rules is found in some older cultures, also called the Craft Rules or Ardanes. Valiente, one of the first High Priestesses in the Gardnerian tradition, speculated that such rules were most likely conceived in ancient language by Gerald Gardner himself, as a result of internal disputes in his Bricket Wood Coven, which he tried to control. This way.

The notion of absolute evil or absolute good, like hell or heaven, is unknown to Wiccans. Of this purpose, we have no way to worship Satan, who is nothing more than a Christian invention they wanted. In reality, a little later, I will resume this subject, trying to show you how this Christian character appeared, and what its significance was.

To Wiccans, ecological concerns are of considerable significance, and for this, they have gained a reputation for caring for nature and trying to protect the environment. Wicca is a nature religion, and adherents see the Goddess in all things, praise her in all things, live in accordance with her.

CHAPTER TWO
Wiccans And Their Beliefs

Wicca is a peaceful and harmonious way of life that encourages harmony with the divine and everything that exists. Unlike common beliefs, people only have to persecute or lie about Wiccans. This is a belief system and lifestyle focused on the restoration of pre-Christian values. The Wiccans seek to rebuild those values from what the Christian church has not yet washed out.

Many of Wiccan's features lie in nature's deep love, such as seeing the sunrise or atmosphere. Each has its spiritual course, as shown by tarot cards. We believe that being a witch is associated with being a healer, teacher, seeker, giver, and the guardian of all things.

Archeological findings point to the Paleolithic people, who worshiped a hunter god and a fertility goddess, the root of Wiccan beliefs. The finds were cave paintings (about 30,000 years old), showing a man with a stag's head and a pregnant woman standing in a circle with eleven others. This also provides the basis for believing that witchcraft activity is one of the world's oldest recognized practices today.

Witchcraft and the past People who practiced the path of witchcraft in the past were in harmony with the forces of nature, had knowledge of herbs and their medicinal principles, provided guidance and were a significant part of the group as shamanic healers and members, and that's why it was known in ancient history as the 'Craft of the Wise.' We recognized the value of nature, not thinking that Man is superior to it, but only a part of it. Nevertheless, the modern man, with his advanced technology, has lost reverence for nature and its importance, and this is the cause of growing problems such as global warming caused by these activities.

The picture of witchcraft for the past few hundred years and also in the present is tainted with evil, heathenism and misconduct, a myth claimed by Wiccans to have arisen from the medieval church's actions in the 15th through 18th centuries. They made the witch a diabolical figure and converted the old pagan divinities into demons and evil spirits to instill fear in men, making the missionaries' work in the process of conversion a little easier.

1. Wicca - The Horned God

The consort of the Goddess is normally called The Horned God by those who follow his cult (whether Wiccan or not). The real name of God, used by the Wiccans, is secret and is revealed only after initiation. Not knowing the name of the Horned God, however, does not prevent people from knowing him and understanding the role he can play in life.

Who Is The Horned God?

The character of the Horned God was inspired by the myths of many Gods, as well as by various fantasy works, which are often milestones in modern Paganism.

Mythology has several horned gods, gods who wear a horned headdress, or have horns as their representative symbol. The Horned God of Wicca follows this tradition. Still, it must be noted that this divinity can be considered as God from the Deer Horn, making it synonymous with the noble animal but also with the path by which the deer grows and changes its horns with the changing seasons.

The Horned God has two primary aspects: God of Life and God of Death. These two identities are different sides of his essence, but rather aspects of his essence, which become evident with the changing seasons, which God moves in his continuous cycle of life, death, and rebirth.

Just as its essence is divided into dark and luminous aspects, so the Horned God adopts different roles that reflect his dualism in the changing seasons of the world. To make these roles easier to understand, they have been divided into two categories: who He is for the four major Sabbaths and who is in the imaginary of the Solstices and Equinoxes.

2. The Sun God

Who is the Sun, God? That is different from religion and tradition. In ancient cultures, where deities with specialized functions can be found, you'll probably find the sun god or Goddess, or several in the same religious tradition.

Sky ride

Many sun gods and goddesses are humanoid and ride or lead a ship of some sort in the sky. It can be a boat, a chariot or a cup. The sun god of the Greeks and Romans, for example, rode four chariot horses (Pyrios, AEO, Aethon and Phlegon).

In Hindu traditions, the sun god Surya wanders the sky in a chariot pulled by horses or a seven or one seven-headed horse. The coachman is Aruna, the personification of the dawn. In Hindu mythology, they fight the demons of darkness.

There cannot be more than one sun god. The Egyptians varied among aspects of the Sun and had several gods associated with it: khepri for the rising Sun Atum the Sun and again until midday the Sun that rode the sky in the Sun's cortex. The Greeks and Romans also had more than one Sun, god.

Female Sun Deities

You may notice that most of the sun deities are male and act as equivalents of the female moon deities, but don't take it for granted. Sometimes roles are reversed. There are sun goddesses just as there are male moon deities. In Norse mythology, for example, Sol (also called Sunna) is the Goddess of the Sun, while her brother Mani is the moon god. Sol rides a chariot that is pulled by two golden horses.

Amaterasu's other sun goddess is the main deity in the Shinto religion of Japan. Her brother, Tsukuyomi, is the moon god. It is from the sun goddess that the Japanese imperial family is believed to have descended from.

3. The Goddess and God

We see the Goddess embodied in the Earth and the Moon and the God we see in the fruits that the earth produces. God is also the one who fertilizes the earth and initiates the annual cycle. Without God, Earth would be barren and dead. Without the Goddess, there would be no Earth at all. The Goddess and God form a polarity of complementary forces. In the pagan religions of Antiquity, many Goddesses and Gods were worshiped. Often a Goddess and God were originally worshiped in a certain place. Their names simply meant Lady and Lord. When large areas were conquered and merged during the Bronze and Iron Ages, the local Gods and Goddesses were often included in the pantheon of the empire concerned. The titles from the older languages became proper names. Most Wiccans return to the old ways of worshiping only one Goddess and one God in religion, covering all facets of life.

For us, the Goddess is especially the Great Mother, who brings fertility and new life but also has to do with deterioration, the death of nature, and the care for the deceased. God is, above all, a Vegetation God for us. He impregnates the Goddess, whereby nature bears fruit every year and dies with the harvest - to be reborn in the new vegetation the following year. You should not see the death of God. It is a symbol of the cycle of nature, which makes life possible (see below). The Wine God Dionysos is a manifestation of the Vegetation God that particularly appeals to us. He was called Bacchus by the Romans.

For many Wiccans, God is primarily a symbol of primal Strength and Fertility. With the Greeks, Pan, with his uninhibited nature and his goat's legs, tail, and horns of a goat, represented this side of God. Pan also brought ecstasy, particularly through his music, and fertility. He was therefore associated with Aphrodite, the Goddess of love and beauty, whom the Romans called Venus.

The Goddess and God form a polarity of complementary forces. Polarity creates a field of tension from which our rituals derive their expressiveness. The Goddess and God are not far away, below or above the earth - they are the world around us and within ourselves.

When we talk about God, we usually use masculine words. This is a simplification because the creator cannot be defined as male or female.

Water can be in the form of ice, snow, or steam, but it never ceases to be water. Likewise, God can reveal both His masculine and feminine aspects, without thereby altering His unchanging and neutral essence.

By participating in His creation, God can present Himself as male or female. We call "The Goddess" the feminine part of God, while we call "The God" Her masculine part, without this meaning that there are two creators: the God and the Goddess are manifestations of the only God, they are the masculine and feminine part of Him.

To begin to understand them, we can see that God is connected to the day, the Sun, the heat, the fire, the air, and everything that represents movement, energy, work, courage, advancement, strength, confidence, and other characteristics commonly seen as masculine. The Goddess is linked to the night, the Moon, water, land, and everything that represents love, fertility, intuition, creativity, mystery, beauty, protection, softness, and other typically feminine characteristics.

We realize, then, that God is seen as the symbol of the Father, while the Goddess is seen as the mother. Here, it is important to remember that the creator is unlimited and, therefore, does not follow any model that we can imagine as acceptable or right. We should not imagine, for example, that beauty is only feminine, or that strength is only masculine. Both God and the Goddess are omnipotent, so each of them can present all aspects of the Sacred.

We need to understand that the following explanations do not mean that the God and the Goddess are divided or that these ages represent a physical age (the God and the Goddess as well as the one God are eternal and ageless). The God and Goddess, young, adult, or elderly, are only facets of the Creator, His representations, His presence manifested in nature.

The Goddess is always connected to water. Like a Girl, She is very present in the mists that cover the earth, hiding objects and beings. Like a Woman, Her energy is present in rivers, seas, waterfalls, and in all flowing waters. When Elderly, She is connected to still waters, to the mud of swamps and mangroves, where so many beings are born and live. It is present in the water that surrounds babies about to be born, in the sap of plants, in the blood of animals.

We can also find manifestations of the Goddess in other elements of nature. It is present in the fertile land, suitable for cultivation, as well as in the land that welcomes lifeless bodies. We can still perceive His gracious presence in the protection and comfort we receive from the fire. In the air, she shows all her multiplicity, revealing both the freshness of the breeze and the irresistible strength of the winds. Ultimately, the Goddess is in everything that allows life to begin and continue - but also in everything that determines the end of each cycle.

God is also manifested in all-natural elements. Present in the energy of fire and earth, He allows matter to be transformed according to His determinations. It is also present in the air, an element that represents the very intelligence that allows evolution, carrying the gases that maintain the life of beings. In water, in union with the Goddess, He allows life to spring in abundance.

The Goddess and God are also present in natural phenomena that we do not understand or accept. They are omnipresent, so their energy is also in what we consider to be calamities, but which are essential for the renewal of what was created.

The Young Goddess and God

The God and the Goddess are the very essence of creation in His youthful forms. They are the promise of fertility, of continuity of existence, of possibilities for the infinite future. Young beings receive their protection at the beginning of their lives so that they can grow, learn, and become stronger. They are the great compañeros of all that begins to live.

The Young God and Goddess are in total harmony, balancing everything that was made. The Lord and the Goddess are embodied in human creations (which we would call "sub-creations" because only Lord has the true power to create), particularly in the arts and in all activities in which beauty and harmony are important.

We can perceive characteristics of Him in all exquisite and uncommon species, exuberant plants and flowers, peculiar natural phenomena, poetic discourses, and in all that is special and desirable, reflecting the joy and vigor of the creator.

The Young Goddess, more mysterious than Him, concentrates Her energy on the beauty of galaxies, nebulae, northern lights, sky colors at dusk and all that is charming and untouchable. It is Her energy which keeps the planets in orbit, allowing life to remain. When the Moon causes the tide to rise or fall, the eternal equilibrium is governed by Her energy.

When we read that God and Goddess can become warriors, we must not imagine that this means that as any human soldier would, they can go to war. We must note we are talking about the creator Himself's female and male halves, who would never take the slightest joy in killing His children. In this case, when we talk about fighting, we don't say they kill anybody, bring guns and nothing like that. That is a metaphor for the spiritual evolution war. It is also a way to praise the unlimited power of God and Goddess (and, consequently, of the one God), which no created being ever surpasses.

The Adult Goddess and God

The Goddess and God require beings to attain fertility in their adult form and make life perpetuated. Not only do they make fertility there, but they are also fertility itself.

As adults, their imagination enables all material life to exist. Everything that occurs originates from the symbolic union of God and Goddess.

The Adult God and Goddess force are present in all settings where there are abundance and reproduction. They are manifested in the trees with ripe fruits, in the flocks of animals that go out to seek food, in the schools that swim free, in the celebrations where people come together to share food and company, in the hives that produce honey, in the fields covered with fresh flowers and in all the groups where there is joy in life and abundance.

The Adult Goddess may also pose herself as a valiant warrior like the Girl Goddess, protecting Her children from all evil. She is still the feminine 's beauty, but in any fight, Her power is unstoppable.

The adult God is the creator of all creation, behaving in such a way that His children always have all they need in their paths to progress. Nevertheless, as the Goddess, He is wise and always chooses not to offer material riches but the lessons that come from the experiences of life. We have to be patient in recognizing that what we want for our creation is not always the best. We 're here to learn, not enjoy facilities that would only make us feel relaxed. As even a human father knows, if he leads a life without challenges, nobody matures.

The Adult God (but often also the Goddess) is commonly represented as an infallible hunter or a skilled farmer and is always determined to get the food to support His children, but always following the logic of His own laws: watching for knowing when to sow or which animal to choose from, waiting for the time to harvest or hunt. Although miracles are entirely possible for God and Goddess, it is inspiring for all of us that the creator will always follow His own laws and keep them.

The Elder Goddess and God

After reaching this stage, the most utter wisdom is revealed by all embodiments of God and Goddess. They've already been through the processes of conception, growth, and reproduction, they've been through all the steps needed to maintain life, and now there's nothing else they can't understand and talk about. To the elder God and Goddess, there are no secrets or mysteries, and they are our greatest source of knowledge.

The elder God and the Goddess have an extreme love for all that is there. Its energy makes everyone peaceful, renews all hopes, and forgets all fears. They bring us the tranquility of being able to feel how everything is in the right place, how everything always follows the laws of God, and how natural happiness is.

At this stage, the Goddess is the Great Lady of all the life and death mysteries. Her imagination and fertility, which previously created living beings' bodies, now create the visions, the intuitions that direct Her children's steps.

When an elder, God ceases to be a warrior, adopting a conciliatory and compassionate nature. Now, He is no longer seeking to fight what he finds wrong, but to educate, reassure, and always make peace prevail.

The ancient Goddess expresses herself in all that is part of the spiritual life. It is present for the incarnate in the religious sentiment, in the organization of mystical symbols, and in everything that brings us closer to the sacred. Both the elder God and the Goddess manifest themselves in the use of oracles, offering their children bases for a better understanding of the situations in life and thus making wiser choices.

To conclude these remarks about God and Goddess, it's important to remember that they are manifestations of the one God and not isolated gods. They are far more complex than any explanation we can find, and because they have no limitations, there are no words that can define them.

4. The Triple Goddess

The Wicca phenomenon has a rather complex character, which is why it can not simply be represented. To put it plainly, this is the modern art of sorcery, which is closely linked to the Neopagan movement.

Triple Goddess - what does it mean?

The Triple Goddess symbol represents the Moon rising, full, and falling. The purpose of this definition is to present three distinct female figures. Of course, we're talking about the Bride, Mother and Old Woman figure that, as you may imagine, corresponds to human life cycles and moon phases. It is also worth noting that many pagans believe Robert Graves created the Triple Goddess.

In their adoration of the Goddess, the Wiccan will see that they still call the Triple Goddess, but to whom these three female archetypes or female trinity refer to the Wicca.

The Goddess, as we well know, represents all that has to do with the feminine in life, often as Mother Earth, and is also depicted as a woman in its three stages or phases in which each Woman passes, this being a cycle without end. These three phases of the Goddess are the aspects of: "The Maiden," "The Mother," and the "The Elder" aspect, each representing an aspect or stage of the Woman's life cycles and representing the Moon's Three main phases.

Across some parts of the best-known pagan religion, you will find the archetype of the Triple Goddess, for example, the three Roman Paracas (Nona, Tenth and Moira), the three Moiras of the Greeks (Clotho, Lachesis and Atropos), these are the ones that rule human destinies and, in several instances, as in Greek myths, those of the Gods, who like Zeus do not resist the plans of nature.

Let's see then what are the characteristics of the Triple Goddess in each of the three stages or phases.

- **The Mother**

The mother symbolizes the strength, the vitality, the maturity of the femininity, and they typically represent her as a woman in the prime of life and at the cusp of her power, the abundance of creation; represented by the Celts by Badb or Arianrhod, her color is red, blood color and vital energy, green and copper as well.

The Mother in Nature is represented by the summer season, the moment of a day's greatest splendor at noon represents the energy, the instructor, and the Moon's phase that represents it is the full Moon.

What is it invoked for, or what can a ritual or spell ask for?

The mother is called to understand things with specific energy for all that constitutes a vital moment in our life. Fertility, maximum protection, and justice, all that relates to marriage and family.

- ## The maid

The Maiden represents youth, new life, adolescence, childhood simplicity, described by the Celts as Anu or Danu; this one has no match, the colors representing it are all light and soft tones such as white, pale pink or light yellow, all pastel tones. It is important for the continuity of life, the season representing it in Nature in Spring, it is also depicted at dawn.

What is it invoked for, or what can a ritual or spell ask for?

Since the Maiden reflects or symbolizes the Goddess's virginal nature, she is called for everything that symbolizes the quest for happiness, wishes, new ventures.

- ## The old Woman

The Elder dimension, symbolized by the Waning Moon period, depicted by the Celts as Macha, the Harpy, or Cerridwen, shows us the end of a life cycle, showing us the picture of an older woman who is intelligent, wise, and skilled in understanding his life's achievements and mistakes.

The Elder also called the Dark Mother or the Witch; in this context, the Goddess is described as part of the day that reflects her by the winter season and by the Moon.

What is it invoked for, or what can a ritual or spell ask for?

This Triple Goddess fascist is called to receive guidance, knowledge, face death and reincarnation.

In this Triple Goddess process, we look back to examine and uncover our errors, protect ourselves against them and fix them where possible.

Here is a brief description of what is portrayed by the triple Goddess for the Wiccan and the pagans.

5. The Wheel of The Year

The Wheel of the Year is what symbolizes the idea of the so-called pagans' period and, in particular, that of the Celts (Druid festivals), and which was very different from the present one. They saw time not linearly but cyclically, circularly. Our calendars took into account not only the solar cycle as is ours, but the lunar cycle as well.

They originate in the Celtic tradition and occur eight times a year, taking into account the location of the earth in relation to the Sun: the equinoxes and the solstices. Two deities are revered on these occasions: the Mother Goddess, or simply the "Goddess," which symbolizes the land itself, and the Lord (companion and son).

They are recognized today as Sabbaths and have been adopted and reissued. He is the creator, O Gamo Rei, guardian of cattle, herds, and wildlife in some ancestral cultures. Many Gods are decorated in many forms of Paganism,

The Wheel of the Year is the celebration of several annual seasonal festivals, today is known as Sabás. It celebrates the annual seasons and their harvests. Some more diverse groups celebrate a set of eight days, while they only celebrate four in other groups, but the four Sabbaths common to all of these groups are known as the cross-quarter day and are commonly called the Great Sabbaths.

Its origin is from the ancient Celts of Ireland, and possibly from other western European regions. In Egyptologist Margaret Murray 's books The Witch-Cult in Western Europe (1921) and The God of the Witches (1933), interested in the ancient Witch Worship, she argues that those four Christianization festivals had survived and were celebrated in the pagan witchcraft faith. Consequently, when Wicca began to develop in the 1930s and 1960s, many groups, such as Gerald Gardner, adopted the Murray-described celebration of these four Sabbaths.

For these holidays, Gardner used the English names, saying that "the four great Sabbaths are Candlemass, May Eve, Lammas, and Halloween; equinoxes and solstices are celebrated too. "These festivals, however, had some differences in their origin from what's being celebrated today, mostly Samhain, which has become Halloween.

The other four celebrated festivals are known as Minor Sabás, which consists of solstices and equinoxes, were only introduced by members of the Bricket Wood Coven in 1958, before being inspired and embraced by other members of the Gardner family, and finally the Alexandrina Family.

And Dianism, that is. The present names of such holidays have been taken from the Germanic Paganism and Celtic polytheism festivals. Festivals, however, are not of a reconstructive nature, nor often resemble their historical counterparts, rather than displaying a form of universalism. Ritual observations can show the festivals' cultural influence from the names they've taken, as well as the influence of other independent cultures.

The Wheel of the Year-represented by the Eight Sabbath aims to synchronize our energies with the Seasons, that is to say, with the life cycle, Planet Earth and the Universe cycles. During the year, she describes the Sun 's Path representing the different faces of God (of the personality/ego/projection of the true Self):-Her birth, growth, union with the Goddess, and finally, her decline and death. Just as the Sun rises and sets every day, and just as spring makes the earth reborn after winter, God teaches us that death is just a point in our evolutionary Infinite Cycle so that we can be reborn from the womb of the mother.

The year begins on the Winter Solstice for some Rituals or the one known as Halloween or Halloween, but its common name is Samhain, meaning "Without Light," referring to the winter season. This time, too, corresponds to the New Year for Jews.

Eight festivals

- **Samhain**

October 31 (Northern Hemisphere) and May 1 (Southern Hemisphere).

This festival marks the Celtic New Year, as well as the beginning of a new Wheel of the Year. Samhain, the festival of the dead, was Christianized as Halloween. This is a time of meditation and reflection on the cycles of nature, life and death. Time to connect with the energy of our ancestors and all those spirits and beings who helped us on our journey, as it is a time when, according to pagan culture, the "veil between the worlds" becomes more tenuous.

Samhain (in Irish Samhain, Scottish Gaelic Samhuinn, Manu Satin and Gaul Samonios) was the festival that celebrates the passage of the Celtic Year. It marks the end of the old year and the beginning of the New Year. Samhain starts winter, one of the two seasons of the Celts.

The beginning of the other season, summer, is celebrated at the Beltane festival. This Festival, Samhain, is called Samonios in Gaul. According to some authors, much of the tradition of Halloween, All Saints' Day and the Day of the Dead can be associated with Samhain. Samhain was the time when it was believed that the souls of the dead returned to their homes to visit family members, to seek food and to warm themselves by the fire in the fireplace.

Some authors believe that there is no evidence to link Samhain with the cult of the dead and that this belief became popular in the 19th century. According to the ancient sagas, Samhain was the time when tribes paid tribute if they had been conquered by another people. It was also the time when the Sidhe foresaw the other world. The faith-spin, the magical fog that made people invisible, dispersed in Samhain, and the elves could be seen by humans. The boundary between the Otherworld and the real world disappeared. One of the dates in Coligny's Celtic lunar calendar can be associated with Samhain. On the 17th day of the Samon lunar month, the reference *trinox Samoni sindiu is interpreted as the date of the celebration of Samhain among the Gauls.

The word Samhain means the end of summer and is derived from two words "samh," summer, and "fuin," end. The month of November is called in Irish "Mí na Samhain."

- **Yule**

December 21 (Northern Hemisphere) and June 21 (Southern Hemisphere).

Yule is the time of the Winter Solstice, when the Child of the Sun is reborn, which is an image of the return of all new life through the love of the Gods. Scandinavians had a God called Ullr, and within the Nordic Tradition, Yule is considered the New Year. In the other tribes and peoples of pre-Christian Europe, the winter solstice was the oldest seasonal feast, and, given its importance, it was syncretized with the Christian Christmas festivities.

Yule is a celebration of Northern Europe that exists from pre-Christian times. Germanic pagans celebrated Yule from late December to early January, covering the Winter Solstice. It was the first seasonal festival celebrated by the Neolithic tribes of northern Europe, and it is still considered the beginning of the Circle of the Year by many Pagan traditions. At the moment, it is one of the eight solar holidays or Sabbatsdo Neopaganism. In modern Neopaganism, Yule is celebrated on the Winter Solstice, around December 21, in the northern hemisphere and around June 21 in the southern hemisphere.

Yule - Winter Solstice - HN - (December 21) - HS (June 21) - It is from this ancient date that Christian Christmas originated. At that time, the Goddess gives birth to God, who is revered as a Promised Child. In Yule, it is time to rediscover our hopes, asking the Gods to rejuvenate our hearts and give us the strength to free ourselves from old and worn out things. It is time to discover the Child within us and be reborn with its purity and joy. Place flowers and seasonal fruits on the altar. If you like, you can make an ornamented tree, as this is the ancient Pagan tradition, where the tree was sacred, and the months of the year were named after the trees. As it is the longest night of the year, where the Goddess is revered as the mother of the Promised Child or of the Sun God, who was born to bring light to the world. Similarly,

As in the summer solstice, pre-Celtic megaliths are aligned at sunrise, as in Stonehenge, so is the winter in Newgrange, Ireland.

Decorate your altar with fig, holly or oak leaves, as well as the pine tree that symbolizes renewal and growth, as well as elements that resemble winter. Light some candles, to symbolize the Sun and to lift spirits. Honor Mother Earth and the rebirth of solar power, as the hope of the return of light.

From the Winter King to Santa Claus!

Some Celtic tribes nurtured the belief that at the time of the Winter Feast, the exotic figure of a supernatural being emerged, described as a man of very old age, armed with a large oak staff, always expressing on his face a pleasant air that was framed. With a large beard and hair as white as snow that reached the ground and mingled with his clothes with a spectral air that had the magical power to enter the houses without being seen or heard, where he arrived to give gifts to the children.

Ledo mistake if you thought I'm talking about Santa Claus, not really who I'm describing is a character called by the Celts as the "King of Winter" who was present at the time of winter.

In fact, not only the Celts but also other contemporary peoples of their time celebrated what the Winter Festival ritualistically represented, namely, the arrival of the winter solstice in the Northern Hemisphere. Thus, in addition to the Celtic celebration of winter, the "Natalis Solis Invicti" (Birth of the Invincible Sun) of the Mithraists, Saturnalia by the Romans and so on.

- **Imbolc**

February 1 (Northern Hemisphere) and August 1 (Southern Hemisphere).

Imbolc, also called Oilmec and Candlemas ("Candelária"), celebrates the awakening of the earth and the growing power of the Sun. The Goddess is venerated in her aspect as Virgin of Light, and her altar is decorated with gallant, which announces spring. It is the feast of lactation, of the blessing to newborns, because the Goddess breastfeeds the reborn God in the form of her Child.

Northern Hemisphere: February 2

Southern Hemisphere: August 1

Also known as Imbolc, Oimelc, and Lady's Day, Candlemas is the Festival of Fire that celebrates the arrival of spring. The invoked aspect of the Goddess on this sabbat is that of

Brígida, the Celtic Goddess of fire, wisdom, poetry, and sacred sources. She is also a deity associated with prophecy, divination, and healing.

This sabbat also represents new beginnings and individual growth, being the "departure from the old" symbolized by the sweeping of the circle with a broom, or witch's broom, traditionally carried out by the High Priest of the Coven, who wears a brilliant crown of 13 candles in top of your head.

In Europe, Sabbat Candlemas was celebrated in ancient times with a torchlight procession to purify and fertilize the fields before the season of planting seeds and to glorify the various deities and spirits associated with this aspect, thanking them.

The Christianized version of the Candlemas procession honors the Virgin Mary, and, in Mexico, it corresponds to the Aztec New Year.

Incense: basil, myrrh, and wisteria. Candle colors: brown, pink, red. Sacred gemstones: amethyst, garnet, onyx, turquoise. Traditional ritualistic herbs: angelica, basil, laurel, benzoin, Chelidonium, heather, myrrh, and all yellow flowers.

Imbolc or Oilmec (or Lunasa) It is the festival in honor of the Goddess Brigida (Briga, Brigidh and its variations). It is when the earth is recovering from winter, and the Sun is strengthening for spring. Season of joyful parties, torches and fogues, spicy foods and juices and wines with remarkable flavors. It is traditionally celebrated on February 2, in the Northern Hemisphere, and August 1, in the Southern Hemisphere. It is also called Festival of the Bride, and it is the time of the beginning of the process of plowing the land and planting.

Candlemas - Feast of Fire or Night of Brigit - HN - (February 02) - HS (August 01) - This Sabbat is dedicated to the Goddess Brigit, Lady of poetry, Inspiration, Healing, Writing, Metallurgy, Martial Arts, and Fire. That night, the Witches put orange candles around the circle, and a candle lit inside the cauldron. If the ritual is done outdoors, torches can be made and rotated around the circle with them. The youngest witch of the Assembly can represent Brigit, entering the circle last, to light, with her torch, the candle of the cauldron, or the bonfire, if the ritual is in the Open, which would represent the inspiration, being brought to the circle by the Goddess.

Coven members must read poetry, or sing in honor of Goddess Brigit. Requests, thanks or poetry, must be burned at the bonfire or in the cauldron, as an offering, at the end of the ritual. God is growing and becoming stronger to bring light back to the world. It is time to ask for protection for all young people, especially those of our family and those of the coven. We must realize that God is always keeping alive within us the flame of health, courage, boldness, and youth. The altar must be decorated with yellow, orange, or red flowers. Consecration must be done by the youngest members of the coven.

- **Ostara**

March 21 (Northern Hemisphere) and September 21 (Southern Hemisphere).

Now night and day are the same. In Ostara, the Sun increases in power, and the earth begins to flourish. At the time of the spring equinox, the powers of the storage phase of the year are the same as those of winter darkness and death. For many pagans, the young God, with his hunting call, shows the way with dance and celebration. Others dedicate this time of Year to Eostre, the Anglo-Saxon Goddess of Fertility.

Ostara is related to festivities that are celebrated during the spring equinox. The modern celebration has a strong relationship with other ancestral celebrations.

Ostara is the first day of spring, occurs around September 21 in the southern hemisphere and March 21 in the northern hemisphere. The beginning of spring also marks the return of the Sun and time of year when day and night are the same duration after winter. It is the awakening of the earth with feelings of balance and renewal.

Ostara, also known as Eostre (Anglo-Saxon Goddess, meaning Goddess of Aurora - see link here) or Easter(Easter, in English), because Easter in the northern hemisphere takes place at this time, they are goddesses of spring, resurrection and rebirth and have the Rabbit as their symbol. One of the main traditions of this festival is the decoration of eggs. The egg represents the Fertility of the Goddess and God. Another very old tradition is to hide the eggs and then find them. (Perhaps the North Americans' habit of hiding chocolate eggs on Easter Day so that children can find them.) It is time to start planting, a time of love, of promises and decisions because Earth and Nature awaken to a new life.

Spring Equinox - Ostara - HN - (March 21) - HS (September 21) - Ostara is the festival in honor of the Goddess Oster, Lady of Fertility, whose symbol is the Rabbit. It was from that old Festival that Easter originated. Coven members wear garlands, and the altar must be adorned with the flowers of the season. It is a very old custom to lay painted eggs on the altar. They symbolize abundance and renewal. Eggs can be painted raw and then buried, or cooked and eaten while mentalizing our desires. In this case, use non-toxic paints, as they can cause health problems if ingested. Use cake anilines, or cook the eggs with the onion skin in the water, which will give a golden color.

Before eating them, members of the coven must turn hand in hand around the altar, to energize their requests. Eggs should be decorated with magic symbols, according to your creativity. Orders must be turned to "Fertility" in all areas.

At that time, it is customary to bless the land by placing painted eggs on the altar, symbolizing the fruitfulness of dreams and the rebirth of hopes. Eggs can be painted raw or cooked, with Celtic symbols and then buried or eaten while mentalizing our requests and wishes.

Ideal stage to harmonize inwardly in love, in the profession or in all areas of life. Take the opportunity to meditate near the green fields. So be it!

- **Beltane**

May 1 (Northern Hemisphere) and October 31 (Southern Hemisphere).

The powers of light and new life now dance and move through all of creation. The Wheel continues to rotate. Spring gives way to the first full bloom of summer, and Pagans celebrate Beltane with the ribbon dance, symbolizing the Sacred Marriage between Goddess and God.

Beltane, Beltain or Bealtaine is a Celtic festival, still celebrated today, recognized in the celebrations of the Spring Festival, but which originally marked the summer. We must, however, make it clear that there is a big discrepancy between contemporary celebrations (which prioritize human sensuality) and commemoration in remote times (which had a greater focus on Earth's Fertility). Beltane is the most joyful of the Celtic Festivals, where the participants dance and rejoice in the campfire.

Opposite the Samhain festival, Beltane is a fertility festival, symbolizing the union between male and female energies, the Fertility of the Earth and the fires of the Celtic God Belenos, and all his energy and Light.

During the festival, bonfires were lit on the tops of hills and places considered sacred, which is an important ritual in the Celtic lands. And as a tradition, people would burn offerings like, for example, totems so that the power of the fire could be passed on to the flock and, they would jump over the fires so that they would be filled with the same powerful energies.

It represents the beginning of summer and marks the death of winter, is celebrated with dances and banquets.

It occurs on May 1 in the Northern Hemisphere and November 1 in the Southern Hemisphere.

In work "The Mists of Avalon" by Marion Zimmer Bradley, the festivity is reported, but it must be remembered that in remote times sexuality had a prominent place and nothing shameful, because as mentioned in many texts, it is the celebration of fertility.

Fertility in this celebration is like the blossoming of spring, with the opening of flowers, seeds and the life of the offspring considered in the Animal Kingdom. A party that should be showered with great joy, with dances, wreaths and a banquet that values the food of the time and especially the bonfire, or something representing the fire. So that we can let this element free us from diseases and restart life in the primordial, simple and pure form.

Many groups that follow Celtic spirituality still celebrate this festival, as well as the other.

Beltane - The Balenos campfire - Spring Festival - HN (May 1) - HS - (October 31) - Beltane is the most joyful and festive of all Sabbaths. The God, who is now a young man at the height of his fertility, falls in love with the Goddess, who in Beltane, presents herself as the Virgin and is called "Queen of May."

In Beltane, the love that gave rise to all things in the universe is celebrated. Beleno is the radiant face of the Sun, which returned to the world in the spring. In Beltane, two bonfires are lit, as it is customary to pass between them, to get rid of all diseases and negative energies. In ancient times, cattle and domestic animals were used to pass among Bonfires for the same purpose.

Then came the custom of "Skipping the Campfire" at the Juninas party. If there is no space, two Torches or even two Candles can have the same function. Great care must be taken to avoid accidents! One of Beltane's most beautiful traditions is MAYPOLE or MASTRO DE TAPAS. It is a mast decorated with colored ribbons. During the ritual, each member chooses a ribbon of their favorite color or linked to a wish. Everyone must spin by braiding the ribbons, as if they are weaving their own destiny, placing us under the protection of the Gods.

The great bonfires also mark a time of purification and transition, announcing the hope of good harvests and the blessings of creation in our lives. A typical Beltane custom is to pass between two fires, and the fire can be represented by candles or torches. Continental Celts celebrated in honor of Belenos at this time of year.

This is a very joyful ritual, celebrated with dances and music!

This is an excellent time to make enchantments of healing, love and prosperity, in addition to harvesting dew in the dawn of Beltane to wash your face and, with that, receive your blessings of beauty and youth.

- **Litha customs**

There is a multitude of legends and rites that involve the summer solstice night: One of the most popular customs in Europe and North Africa is the harvest of medicinal and magical herbs on that day. It is believed that the fullness of God's Strength is impregnated in these herbs and contains all the healing and magical power to cure diseases. Mistletoe and basil, like many other herbs, are harvested ritualistically and used to preserve energy in cold times in spells and spells.

Purifying baths and miracle cures are performed on magical nights in fountains, rivers, and waterfalls. It is also believed that whatever is dreamed, desired, or requested on Litha's night will come true.

The ancient Peoples of Europe believe that, on that night, magical creatures are running through the fields and forests and could easily be seen and contacted.

On that day, the charms of the previous year are burned, and new protective talismans, potions for prophetic dreams, and filters are made to take advantage of the great moment of power.

It is customary to continue Beltane's great bonfire, as well as to jump out of misfortune and negativity. Traditionally, this fire is lit with fir and oak sticks, two trees considered Dates and related festivals

- Summer Solstice.
- Coamhaim.
- Feil Seathlain.
- The Dell' Estate party.

Litha-Summer Solstice-HN (June 21)-HS (December 21)-The Sun hit its fullness that day. It is one of the longest days of the year. God is at the height of his might. It is the only Sabbath on which often spells are made because their magic power is very powerful. It's time to ask for strength, courage and safety. But we must not forget that while God is in his fullness, he is starting to fall at this point in time. Soon, He will send his wife, the Goddess, the last kiss and set off on the Boat of Death, in search of the Summer Land. Likewise, we must be patient so that the brilliance of achievement and strength will not blind us. All in the Universe is cyclical. Not only must we link to the fullness, but we must also embrace decline and death. For that day, making a Ring of Stones or Red Candles is customary.

At this period, the ancient druids honored the oak, especially with the sacrificial cutting of the sacred mistletoe. Many stone circles and pre-Celtic megaliths lie associated with the day's sunrise, like Stonehenge. On the Isle of Mann, it is traditional for people to go to the top of the highest hill to pay the rent for their island on the Summer Solstice, giving a tribute in memory of Manannán Mac Lir, the Lord of the Portal between the Worlds.

Using this rite to make offerings, and speak with the "People of the Fairies," asking them for knowledge, guidance, and wisdom. Decorate your altar with sunflowers, fresh fruit, and dried herbs like lavender, chamomile, verbena, or any special mid-summer herb.

Seek to sense all of nature's elementary energy flowing through your body. This festival is conducive to renewing all the vibrations from home as well as from people. The tradition of outdoor sports and family picnics is in addition to being an ideal way to trigger prosperity.

Period of materialization of all our aspirations, in which ventures, visions and wishes initiated at the time of planting begin to bear fruit as the awakening of consciousness becomes a reality. Celebrate the Gods and praise them for yet another expansion cycle. And let it be!

- **Lammas**

August 1 (Northern Hemisphere) and February 2 (Southern Hemisphere).

Lammas, also called Lughnasadh, is the time of harvesting wheat when Pagans reap what they have sown when they celebrate the fruits of the mystery of nature. In Lammas, the Pagans give thanks for the generosity of the Goddess in her aspect as Queen of the Earth.

Lughnasadh is also known as Lammas (it reads "lamas") or Festival of the First Harvest. Sacred day in Paganism, having a mainly Celtic origin. Celebrated on February 2 in the southern hemisphere and on August 1 in the northern hemisphere.

It is important to remember that Sabás do not originate from Wicca. They are celebrations that are much older than this religion that appeared in the mid-50s, which added these, and other characteristics to its doctrine.

This Sabbath, which takes place between the Summer Solstice (Litha) and the Autumn Equinox (Mabon), the feast of the first harvest, a time of thanks to the Gods for all that we have harvested. We are grateful for what was good and also for what seemed bad because it is believed that everything that happens in life is part of the evolutionary path of each one.

The name Lughnasadh came from a typical Celtic agricultural festival. A harvest festival in honor of the Celtic God of the Sun: Lugh (the greatest warrior among the Celts, as he defeated the giants who demanded human sacrifices).

The name Lammas means "Bread Mission (loaf Mass)," which represents the food (usually bread or cake or any other mass) made with the grains, which represent the harvest, and shared (as sacred food) among the members of the coven or family or even among friends. This name comes from the medieval custom of taking the first bread (cakes, etc.) for a celebration.

Lammas - Lughnasad or Harvest Festival - HN (August 1) - HS (February 2) - Lughnasad was typically an agricultural festival, where one thanked for the first harvest of the year. Lugh is the Sun God, in Celtic Mythology, he is the greatest of the warriors, who defeated the Giants, who demanded Human Sacrifices from the people.

Tradition calls for dolls to be made of ears of corn or branches of wheat representing the Gods, who at this festival are called Senhor and Senhora do Milho. On that date, we should thank all that we harvest during the year, be it good or bad, because even problems are vehicles for our evolution. Sabbat's other name is Lammas, which means "Lugh's Mass." This is due to the custom of harvesting the first grains and making community bread, which must be consecrated with the wine and shared within the circle. The first sip of wine and the first piece of bread must be thrown into the cauldron, to be burned along with the papers, where thanks are written, and grains of cereal. The Doll representing the God of the Corn is also burned, to remind us that we must get rid of everything that is old and worn out so that we can reap new life.

The altar is decorated with seeds, wheat branches, ears of corn, and seasonal fruits.

Lughnasadh literally means "Lugh Games," this is due to the ancient Celtic custom of promoting tribal meetings, fairs, and sports competitions, called "Oenach," when the clans met in peace, to honor the sovereignty of the land and to resolve legal issues. In this ritual, the first sip of wine and the first piece of bread must be thrown into the cauldron, along with papers, where your thanks will be written.

During this festival, we also honor Lugh's adopted mother, Tailtiu, who died after the great effort she made to clear the central plain of Ireland, preparing the land for cultivation, a metaphor for the sacrifice that Mother Earth makes every year so that the harvest cycle is perpetuated.

Ancient amulets and talismans must be burned in this ritual; symbolically, we get rid of everything that is old and worn out because life becomes death and death becomes life, the cycle of creation.

Even if you don't plant or harvest our food anymore, remember that everything was sown and produced in the fields and on the land. So, always thank the gods for the abundance and abundance of our lives. At this festival, decorate your altar with seeds, wheat branches, corn cobs and seasonal fruits.

• Mabon

September 21 (Northern Hemisphere) and March 21 (Southern Hemisphere).

In Mabon, the autumnal equinox day and night become the same. As the shadows increase, Pagans see the darker faces of God and Goddess. For many, this rite honors old age and the approach of winter.

Mabon (pronounced Mêibon) is also known as Autumn Equinox or Harvest Home or the Second Harvest Festival. Celebrated on the day of the autumn equinox, which corresponds to approximately March 20 in the southern hemisphere and September 22 in the northern hemisphere (the dates of the equinoxes may vary by up to 3 days according to the year).

This sabbat (Sabbat in most countries), which takes place between the First Harvest Festival (Lughnasadh) and the Pagan New Year (Samhain), marks the beginning of autumn, a pagan holy day of harvest rest and celebration, a time of thanksgiving to the Gods for all that was collected and hunted. It is a time of balance, where day and night have the same duration.

This is the thanksgiving day of Paganism. Date where pagans honor God in their seed aspect and the Great Mother in their Provider aspect.

The name Mabon came from a Celtic god (also known as Angus), the God of Love. This is the ideal time to ask for all those we love, as well as all who are sick or old.

Mabon-Autumn Equinox-HN (September 21)-HS (March 21)-Mabon, also known as Angus, was the God of Love in the Celtic Pantheon. Tonight we will ask the people we love for peace and security. It is the year's second harvest. The altar must be decorated with the seeds to be reborn in springtime. Dry leaves need to line the floor. The Lord is dying and is going to die soon. This is the festival in which we must ask for the sick and the elderly, who need our help and comfort. It is also at this festival that we praise our Female Ancestors, burning papers in the cauldron with their names and offering words of thanks and blessings! To them.

This festival pays homage to the Welsh god Mabon, which reflects the coming fruit harvest, summer farewell and winter preparation. Mabon is Modron 's mother, the Welsh Mother Goddess, who is associated with fertility and field crops. Modron was often associated with Morrighan and the Arthurian myths of Morgana Le Fay.

Ideal phase for the people we love, for healing, harmony, love and protection. Take advantage of this ritual 's energy to walk in the woods, and harvest dry seeds and leaves, reflecting on the harvest received during the autumn height. Portals in between Samhain and Lughnasadh. Awen's Wind!

Remember also those who are sick and older people who need our help at the Autumn Equinox, address them with words of love and affection, before crossing into the Other World.

Decorate your altar with the remaining grains and seeds from the first harvest, potatoes, pumpkins, apples and other autumn fruits. And, once again, thank you, Mother Earth, for the blessings she received during her personal harvest.

6. Wicca: The Elements and the Elementals

The four elements, Fire-Earth-Air-Water, were of great importance in the ancient religions of nature, from which it was thought that our earth and indeed the entire universe was built. The secret, to life in general and to earth in particular, was believed to lie in the appropriate composition/balance of these four elements.

Natural magic has also been seen in both the physical and spiritual world, in terms of the harmonious partnership of the four elements, each with its own characteristics and mystical powers. Understanding these primal forces then leads to a greater understanding of life itself and of the world around us.

The Elements of Mother Earth

Volumes can be written regarding the earth's four elements. Every dimension is a kind of Mother Earth archetype, nature and our life. Those four elements of nature have been revered and studied carefully long before our era. Not only in nature, but in humans too, and maybe particularly. A good balance of the four elements in character was believed to lead to a good and dignified person, and also to a powerful and just leader. Some brief descriptions of each element's qualities are given below.

- **Fire**

Fire is great and powerful, dynamic, and changeable. But inspiration and temperament also fall under the element of fire; without it, life would stagnate and become monotonous. The typical Fire qualities include terms such as 'a fiery temperament' or 'have fire in the heart.' Fire brings determination and bravery, and thus action. It is hard to keep in check and can run rampant, but it brings light and warmth when used wisely. Keywords also include inspiration, excitement, transformation, change, energy.

Fire is the element of luck, will, and passion. In a sense, it contains all forms of magic within, since magic is a change process. The magic of fire can be frightening. The results quickly and spectacularly manifest themselves. It is not a fearful element. However, it is the main one, and it is widely used for this reason. That is the realm of passion and sexuality.

Not only is it the sacred fire of sex, but it is the spark of divinity that shines in us and in all living things. It is the most physical and the most spiritual of the elements at the same time. Usually, their magical rituals involve energy, authority, sex, healing, destruction (of negative habits, illness), purification, evolution, etc.

Usually, a fire ritual involves smoking or burning an image, grass, or any other flammable object, or using candles or little fires. Its magic is usually practiced either by the fireplace, or by fires burning in wild spaces, or by a simple candle flame. Fire is human-made. The South, the hottest place, the color red and the summer season are regulated. The candles' all magic is under the powers of fire.

- **Soil**

Earth is the material dimension of the universe. It provides the rocks as soil, fertile ground for planting, and food for humans, animals, and plants to live on. The element also stands for level-headedness and reliability. Expressions such as 'a rock in the surf,' 'the salt of the earth' (about people who are steadfast and helpful) and 'standing on the ground with both feet' offer the product a positive impression. Earth teaches that all living things must be founded on solid foundations. But it can also be too cautious, too sluggish, and sometimes risk-triggering. Also, the keywords are anchor, safety, stability, common sense, level-headedness.

This is the element with which we are closest to the home since it is our home. The earth does not necessarily represent the physical earth, but that part of it that is stable, solid, secure. Earth is the foundation of the elements, the base. It is in this domain that most of us live a good part of our lives. When we walk, we sit, we get up, we crawl, we eat, we sleep, we do our jobs, we take care of our plants, we examine our checkbooks, or we try salt we are working with the Earth element.

Earth is the kingdom of abundance, prosperity and wealth. Although it is the most physical element, this is not negative, because the other three rely on the earth. Without the earth, the way we know it would not exist. In magical tasks, Earth "regulates all spells and rituals that involve business, money, employment, prosperity in all its forms, stability, fertility, and so on. A ritual of this element could be to bury an object representative of your need in a virgin plot of land, walk through miles of countryside visualizing your need, or draw images in the mud. Earth is a feminine element. It is nutritious, moist, fruitful, and these are qualities that make her feminine. Such attributes have prompted countless civilizations to consider the earth as a great Mother Goddess, the all-fertile Creator of Nature. The earth regulates the north point of the compass because it is the place of greatest darkness and winter. Its color is the green of the fields and plants. It governs the magic of stones, images, trees, and knots.

- **Sky**

Air is intangible, but essential for life on earth at the same time. Wind can be a gentle breeze or a great hurricane. It reflects organized thought, reason, mind. Air holds emotions at bay; it gives everything you need, not what you want. Air can refresh and clean up problems, and even blow them away, leading to a new thought or solution. Examples of that are the phrases 'a breath of fresh air' and 'blowing away the mice.' At a certain degree, though, reasoning and rationalizing just works. A time will come when steps have to be taken; otherwise, in the air, feelings, wishes and dreams will remain. Also, keywords are attitude, calmness, perspective, pace, volatility.

Air is the intellect element; It is the realm of thought, which is the first step towards creation. In relation to magic, the air is the clear, orderly, pure visualization that is a powerful instrument for change. It is also movement, the impetus that sends the visualization outward, towards the manifestation. Regulates spells and rituals that involve travel, instruction, freedom, obtaining knowledge, discovering lost objects, revealing lies, and so on. It can also be used to develop psychic faculties. Spells that involve the air usually include the act of placing an object in the air or dropping something from the edge of a mountain or other elevated place so that the object physically connects with the element. Air is a masculine, dry, expansive, and active element. It is the element that stands out in places of learning, and that acts when we theorize, think or ponder. The air regulates the East because this is the direction of greater clarity and that of wisdom and knowledge. Its color is yellow, the yellow of the Sun and the sky at dawn, and its season is spring. The Air governs the magic of the four winds, most of the divinations, the concentration and the magic of visualization.

- **Water**

Water is more fluid than air but elusive as well. It doesn't have set form, and it adapts to the climate. Water is essential for life on earth, too; life without water is not possible. The element represents the sea, the rivers, the tide and the emotions as well. It gives the possibility of life, but it can also take it away, something that was all too aware of (sea) sailing peoples. You can float or sink into it, after all. Water can be calm or stormy, just like emotions. A calm mind, in balance with the emotions, gives a sensitive and empathetic person "with the heart in the right place." Nevertheless, in too many emotions, you can 'drown,' in fact get lost, so that with both feet you can no longer come to earth, the mind no longer gets air, and you no longer have Fired for action; a very unwanted situation. Also, the keywords are emotions and thoughts, sympathy, heart wishes, affection, versatility.

Water is the element of purification, the subconscious mind, love, and emotions. Just as it is a fluid, constantly changing, flowing from one level to another, so our emotions are in a constant state of flux. Water is the element of absorption and germination. The subconscious is symbolized by this element because it is spinning, always moving like the sea that rests neither night nor day. Water magic involves pleasure, friendship, marriage, fertility, happiness, healing, sleeping, dreaming, physical acts, purification, and so on. A water ritual usually ends up throwing or placing an object in the water. This is a feminine element, and its color is the deep, deep blue of the water. It regulates the West and the autumn months when the showers wash the earth. The magic of water is done with mirrors, the sea, the fog, and the rain. These, then, are the four elements. A complete study of them can take a lifetime, but these are the bases. Although it is not necessary to invoke these elements or work with them directly, it is beneficial to be aware of them and remember them when magic is practiced.

Pentagram and Pentacle

The Pentagram is a five-pointed star (pointing up) and represents the four elements of Mother Earth plus, as the fifth point, the element of ether or spirit. The latter element was seen as inaccessible to man and was traditionally reserved for the (heaven) gods, heaven itself, or, even further, the universe.

Wicca uses the Pentagram in honor of the elements but usually use the symbol with a circle around the star. The Pentagram in the circle then becomes a new symbol called the Pentacle. The Pentacle symbolizes the element earth on the Wiccan altar.

The Elementals of Mother Earth

Life consists of various dimensions, and each has its own vibration. Whoever lives in the same world can see, hear, smell, and feel one another. There are also measurements, however, which are higher in vibration than that in which man resides on Mother Earth. You come across legends of supernatural beings everywhere in the world, dwelling in unseen realms, and being benevolent or evil to humans.

The Empire of Elementals was a natural force for our distant ancestors to reckon with. The Elemental Kingdom was historically formed to represent, support, and preserve Mother Earth's four elements. -- element had a hierarchy of its own servants, who were at times friendly, but at times also hostile to man, particularly if it had conducted an unreasonable attack on an element (for example, cutting down trees, damming or drawing water from lakes or rivers, or polluting air). Therefore, the Elementals could be felt tangibly but remained invisible. They inhabited a higher dimension after all, and could only be seen if they wanted to descend to our lower dimension themselves or if a human could travel through magic to their dimension. Caution was also recommended when crossing forests or when crossing lakes or rivers. The Elemental archetypes are still found today in fairy tales, legends, and myths, as well as in modern fantasy literature.

- **Fire Elementals**

The fire salamanders are the keepers of the fire and can keep this in check without any effort. They are long and large and have a majestic appearance. Fire salamanders are the largest elementals of the four groups and, at the same time, also the most powerful. They are found in electricity (lightning), hobs, candles, and wildfires. Another mythical creature, which is strongly linked to fire, is the Phoenix. This particular bird catches fire and burns at the end of its life, after which it is born again from the ashes.

- **Earth Elementals**

The gnomes, also called gnomes or goblins, are the guardians of the element earth. They take care of everything that has to do with earth. Dwarves are experts in precious stones and metals and can, therefore, be found in mines deep in the mountains. They are not on friendly terms with humans, because in their eyes, they steal their valuables. Little fairies (or English fairies) can be found in the realm of almost every element. The Earth elves often care for specific wild plants or flowers. According to Celtic / Irish stories, they can get you lost in a forest if you pick or damage their plants or flowers.

- **Air Elementals**

The guardians of the element Air are the sylphs. They provide clean and healthy air for all organisms. Sylphs or elves have thin and delicate bodies but do not always have to be small. Sylphs have beautiful wings, which often resemble transparent butterfly wings. They are particularly elegant and graceful creatures and symbolize the beauty of the Elemental Kingdom. They are the Elementals of the mind.

- **Water Elementals**

This group includes the predominantly gentle water nymphs (Ondine or undine), who are the guardians of the element of water. They have no soul and can only obtain it if they marry a mortal. Furthermore, there are the usually evil water spirits or kelpies that can drown you, and the sea is the site of the mermaids, who lure seafarers to their death as true temptresses. An aquatic animal that is very close to the (benign) Water Elementals is the dolphin.

7. Reincarnation

Reincarnation is one of Wicca's most treasured lessons. The realization that this life is only one of the others, that when the physical body dies, we do not cease to exist, but rather we are reborn in another body, addresses a great number of questions, but creates many others.

Why? For what? Why is it that we reincarnate? Like many other religions, Wicca teaches that reincarnation is the instrument that perfects our souls. Therefore, consciousness (soul) is reborn countless times; each life was encompassing a particular set of lessons before perfection is attained.

No one can tell how many lifetimes it takes before it is accomplished. We're human, and non-evolutionary habits are easy to stick to. Greed, anger, jealousy, obsession, and all our negative emotions are inhibiting our growth.

We strive at Wicca to strengthen our bodies, minds, and souls. Sure, we live earthly lives complete and successful, but we seek to do so without hurting others, the antithesis of rivalry, coercion, and the quest for first place.

The soul is without age, sex, or physical, possessing the Goddess and God's holy light. Each representation of the soul (e.g., each body inhabiting the earth) is different. No two bodies or lives are exactly the same. The soul would stagnate if this were not so. Sex, race, place of birth, economic status, and all other individualities of the soul are decided in past lives by their actions, and by the necessary lessons of the present life.

To Wiccan's philosophy, this is of utmost importance: we decide the creation of our lives. There is no god, curse, mysterious force of fate on which to shoulder responsibility for the facts of our life. We determine what we need to know to develop, and then we are supposed to work in the quest for this advance during that incarnation. Otherwise, we'll get back into the dark.

There is a concept that serves as a support in learning the lessons of through life, called karma. Karma is usually nonsensical. This is not a reward and punishment scheme, but a mechanism that directs the soul through evolutionary behavior. Therefore, if an individual engages in negative actions, he will receive negative actions in return. Better pulls better. With that in mind, there are few grounds for behaving negatively. Karma means action, and it works like this, as an instrument, and not as a punishment.

There's no way one can "erase" karma, just as not all of our life's apparently horrible events are its byproduct. We only learn from Karma when we are conscious of it. In their past lives, many looks to discover their mistakes, to solve the problems that inhibit their progress in this life. Trance and meditation methods may be useful, but the best way to achieve this goal is true self-knowledge.

Regression to past lives can be risky because the possibility of self-deception is present. In looking for past incarnations, our conscious minds quickly cling to those romantic ideals.

Observe this existence if this becomes a problem, or you don't want to know your past lives or lack instruction on how to do it. Through witnessing this life, you can discover some interesting information about your past lives. If you have solved your issues in past lives, this isn't going to be an issue for you today. Otherwise, the same things will come up again and again; therefore, emphasis on this life.

Analyze your day's actions at night for both positive actions and thoughts and negative ones. Analyze the past decade, the week before, the year. Check your possessional agendas, diaries, or old letters to refresh your memory. Will you make the same mistakes all the time? In a good event, in a ritual created by you, promise never to replicate them again.

You might write such errors on a piece of paper at your altar or sanctuary. His notes may include negative emotions, fears, excessive pleasures, allowing others to control his or her life, endless obsessions of love with men/women indifferent to their feelings. As you write, visualize yourself in the past, not in the present, acting this way.

Lighten a red candle then. Brighten up the paper over the flame and put it into a fireproof jar or cauldron. Shout-or just asserts to yourself-that past actions like this are no longer part of you. Visualize your future life free from such harmful conducts, limitations, inhibitors. Repeat the ritual as necessary to end the destruction of those aspects of your life, perhaps on waning moon nights.

If your determination to progress in this life is ritualized, your oath will vibrate strongly. When in your old ways of acting or thinking, you feel tempted to backslide, remember the ritual, and overcome that need with your power.

What happens after they die?

Just the body dies. The Survival of the Soul. Some Wiccans say that she is traveling to a kingdom known as Fairyland, Bright Land, and Young Land.

This Kingdom is neither underworld nor paradise. It is literally-a non-physical reality, much less complex than ours. It is defined by some Wicca traditions as the land of everlasting summer, with grassy fields and sweet rivers, perhaps as the land before the advent of humanity. Others vaguely see it as a place without forms, where energy flows coexist with the major energies-the Goddess and God in their celestial identities. It's said the soul sees the last life with the deities again, maybe in a mystical way.

This is not a judgment, or weighing of the soul of the human, but rather an incarnate revision. Light is shed upon learned or missed lessons. When the Earth's conditions are favorable, the soul reincarnates after an appropriate period, and life recurs. It's said the soul sees the last life with the deities again, maybe in a mystical way.

This is not a judgment, or weighing of the soul of the human, but rather an incarnate revision. Light is shed upon learned or missed lessons. When the Earth's conditions are favorable after an acceptable time, the soul reincarnates and life recurrences.

The final question: After the last incarnation, what happens?

Wicca's teachings have always been free on that point. Basically, the Wiccans say that after climbing the spiral of life, death, and rebirth, the souls that have attained perfection are released from that cycle forever and cohabit with the Goddess and with God. Nothing perishes forever. The energies found in our souls are returning to the divine source they originally emanated from.

By embracing reincarnation, the Wiccans do not fear death as a loss in oblivion, with their mortal life days in the past forever lost. Death is known as the doorway to life. Our own lives are thus symbolically linked to the infinite cycles of the seasons that shape our planet.

Try not to force yourself into believing in reincarnation. Knowledge is far superior to belief because believing is a malicious way of thinking. Accepting a theory as relevant as reincarnation without researching it extensively is not very wise to know whether she is actually telling you something.

Also, although there may be strong connections with those we love, be careful about the notion of soulmates, such as people you have loved in other lives and believe that you are destined to love again. Though sincere, your feelings and beliefs are not always based on facts. In the course of your life, given your current involvement, you will find five or six people who you share the same connection with. Is it possible they're all soulmates?

One of the difficulties of this concept is that if we are all intrinsically connected to the souls of other people, we will not learn anything by continuing to incarnate with them. Announcing that you have found your soulmate, therefore, has the same effect as saying you are not progressing in the spiral of rebirth.

One day, you'll learn, and not only believe, but that reincarnation is as true as a plant that sprouts, blooms, spreads its seed, shrinks, and in its picture produces another. Ancient cultures undoubtedly intuited the reincarnation as they studied nature.

The Belief in Reincarnation

From ancient times the ancient civilizations had a constant observation of their surroundings: how day and night were constantly taken as the sun's rebirth and death, and the lunar cycles being the crescent moon childhood, full adult and waning sunset in nature were seen as the cycles of eternal rebirth. Like the tree that loses its leaves in winter, giving the appearance of dead, but in reality, it only directs all its energy to the roots. All religions are given a specific visualization of what happens after death. Several hypotheses exist about what happens after our soul leaves our physical body. Like many other spiritual paths in Wicca and Paganism, we believe in reincarnation.

This belief popularly brings together various terms:

- Transmigration.
- Reincarnation.
- Renaissance.
- Re corporation (return to your body).

Reincarnation, as observed in nature, is a cyclical process of life, death, and rebirth. This theory describes an individual's continuous rebirth, because each time the soul returns to the physical world, it returns with a clear motive. During that process, I seek to achieve perfection in our soul or spiritual, amending errors or achieving goals that could not be achieved in other lives.

After physical death, Wiccans don't believe in hell or any place of torture, and we believe that there is a place known as the Summer Land or Summerland, which is eternal summer land. If we see it from this perspective, we could say that the Wiccan sky is the Summer Earth. It is a place of rest for our soul where it will remain until it decides to return to the physical plane. We are reviewing what we did and what we still have to do in the Summer Field. We can pick who we are going to be in our next incarnation too.

The soul or spiritual self is energy, and it is impossible to destroy energy, which is why we remain in a continuous rebirth. Though, of course, once a soul reaches the level of perfection it needs, if it prefers, it can permanently remain on the Summer Land or be reborn.

8. Animism, The Human Being, And Creation

When talking about animism, it should be borne in mind that this concept includes a wide variety of beliefs in which everything from everyday objects, special and particular, to elements that are part of nature, such as animals, rivers, rocks, plants, trees, among others. This set of elements is characterized by the fact that each of them in animism is endowed with a type of consciousness of their own or of soul.

Animism is, therefore, a primitive religion in which its followers, called animists, regard each of the souls as both a spirit capable of good, producing good or evil. This should be adorable but feared at the same time. Given the antiquity of its existence, this religion has deified a great variety of elements through practices such as magic, enchantments, spells, amulets, superstitions, and all kinds of forms that are considered means of protection against positive or good-spirited Negative spirits.

Origin of animism in history

Although it is a primitive religion, its origins have been traced in the African continent, specifically in the South of the Sahara, although other places such as Oceania, Australia, Central, and Southeast Asia and in general in the American continent are also dated. Another aspect that accounts for its development in the different regions is archeology and anthropology, key disciplines that have allowed finding evidence within indigenous cultures.

The term animism is granted by Edward Burnett Tylor, an anthropologist who is 1871 called the set of beliefs to shape a theory of religion, which appears in his book Primitive Culture.

In the African territory, it is considered that animism has the most complex version since it includes a series of aspects among which the concept of magara stands out, which refers to "universal life force" and that allows the connection of animated beings, a process that constitutes one of the fundamental beliefs of this religious group.

Beliefs and principles of animism

The principle of animism at a general level can be defined as the belief in the existence of a soul or substantial life force that is found in animated beings and which allows the relationship and connection of the world of the living with the world of the dead, aspect which evidences the recognition of the existence of several gods with which it is possible to interact. Thus, the following beliefs appear:

The being and the creation

One of the main characteristics of animism is the relationship that the human being has with all the elements that are part of the creation so that all aspects that belong to the tangible world are attributed with aspects of great spirit that are interconnected with spiritual form, which is why everything is conceived as a single-family.

Starting from this direct relationship of being with creation, indigenous groups consider the earth to be their mother, as they have also chosen to be guardians of it. Objects that are considered inanimate by other beliefs, in animism they take a fundamental role within the creation and are personified as living beings, such as mountains, rocks, bodies of water (rivers, seas, oceans), the trees, the plants, among others.

Animism is a religion

The origins of animism are hardly concrete, contrary to what happens with the vast majority of religions. Since it is considered one of the oldest beliefs in human history, it reaches the point where there is evidence that the Ancient Egyptian religion already has animism foundations.

Throughout the time, different theories have been developed, which point to animism as the germ of current mystical religions and beliefs, as it associates the beginnings of religions with the characteristic cult of the dead.

A second theory states that animism can be seen as the foundation of all religion. Despite the fact that another religion has overlapped or revised the veneration of a vast number of gods, as well as of the dead, the impact animism has on them is evident.

Lastly, while animism has been seen throughout history as a religion, modern religions fail to interpret it as such. Rather, it is considered a type of philosophy that influences and is found in various religions, which attempts to create an explanation for spiritual mysteries and expresses an emotional attitude or disposition towards those mysteries.

9. Life after death

One of the features the set of animistic beliefs coincides with is the belief that the soul exists, and that it survives when the body dies. Thus, the soul is considered to go to a quiet space, where you can find plenty of activities and food for your stay. Other beliefs, however, such as the Navajo, an American nation, consider that the soul does not leave Earth but stays with the ghost figure in it, and may or may not be evil. In the face of this assumption, a third viewpoint tends to try the combination of the two previous ones, in which they confirm that the soul escapes from the earthly plane and that it would not pass away because this would mean that it wandered in the form of a ghost without intent.

To guarantee the relationship and connection between the two worlds, grieving funerals and worship of ancestors must be performed. Some animistic beliefs, however, do not perform rituals by private individuals but instead perform them in veneration for priests or religious leaders, or shamans, considering them as possessors of spiritual powers which are in a higher degree in relation to the overall human experience.

The reduction of heads was a practice that was practiced mainly in South America, derived from the animistic belief that the enemy's soul should be locked, for if not, it would escape from its skull, so that the enemy would transmigrate to the womb of a predatory animal's female, from which it could be reborn to commit its revenge.

The importance of dreams and hallucinations

Dreams are very common in some communities, which is why they are mostly interpreted as travel species and the encounters that the sleeper lives, which can be both humans, animals and environmental objects. As for visions, this assists in improving dream perception. At the moment when the being wakes up to offer a justification for the visits he made, the assumptions are generally related to the fact that traveling is not exactly the body.

An important feature of the dream experience has to do with the fact that it takes on tremendous significance in the prehistoric development of the collection of values, which is why it continues to evolve in such a way that it is integrated in relation to reality as a theory of nature.

Inanimate objects

While part of cultures considers a soul's existence in inanimate objects, there are others who do not distinguish animated objects from inanimate objects. In this sense, aspects like natural phenomena, conditions of geography, everyday objects, and manufactured items may or may not have souls.

An example of this animism belief system in China, northern Europe, and ancient Greece because they believed the water spirit to be a bull-shaped entity. So, the water monster may take the form of another being, like the snake, which is usually the most commonly used. However, it must be stressed that this is not strictly a water spirit. Syncretism manifests itself through this position of the animist system to complement this position so that the immanent spirit can be changed to that of a local god in force.

The conception of death

Many cultures are setting different positions regarding their conception of death. On the one hand, the human body is the soul's container in several parts of the world of animism. It is conceived in four ways, for example, on the Island of Nías: the first and the second is the shadow and intelligence that die when the body dies, while the third and fourth are the guardian spirit and the spirit that is inside the head.

Many other groupings say that as part of European animism claims, the ghost of a person who died sometimes travels through the location where the being died or even the location where the body was buried. Other cultures place dwellings that are different from souls according to the multiplicity that exists in such a way that they consider that the human being has several souls. One of them remains in the corpse, another in the city, the third spreads with the air, and the fourth goes to the soul land.

Survival of the Dead

Based on this belief, the numerous peoples that practice animism, among others, have carried out a series of activities, including offering food, as well as lighting fires to provide heat in the grave. It is done in relation to the importance of the ancestors as a form of a fellowship or filial piety with the being who has died after an act of worship. Many others still deliver bloodshed on the grave under the presumption that it will evolve after a scheme of sacrifice.

Accordingly, even where the ancestor is not conceived, these practices are performed with the intention of offering comfort to the being who died in the future life, which is also often provided through the sacrifice of slavery, the sacrifice of animals, the sacrifice of wives, among others. This is done successively until the objects are buried in the grave or when the break comes, but the payment of the passage provided to the soul to reach the land of the dead does not end.

The soul is considered to be able to return, if it wishes, to avenge itself for its death through processes that allow us to find the individual responsible for its death or even to take revenge directly upon it. It fits with the idea that evil spirits are the entities who have experienced a violent death, and they have put the lives of those connected to their condition in danger. To combat this, many believers go to religious outlets to shield themselves from the threats of the evil spirit.

Sacred Actions

There are many rituals and behaviors considered sacred, among which are animal or plant sacrifices for the purpose of worshiping deities. In this sense, the sacred rites are added, which are directed by shamans or priests.

Many sacred acts, on the other hand, are omens, from which comes the practice of saying "Cheers!" when a person sneezes, as it is assumed that this is how it is possible to keep the spirits from leaving and going beyond a person deemed weak and near. Many actions of great significance within animism have to do with acts such as signs in the sky and also with animals, for example, the crossing of a black cat indicating bad luck, among other acts capable of predicting the human being's future or Destiny.

Figures and sacred people of animism

There are people who are considered sacred within this religious practice that covers a wide variety of cult systems, traditions, rites, and cultures. Among the most important figures are:

- Brujas: they are considered one of the most important sacred people since through their powers they can either use them to generate good, or to generate evil, so their powers are specially required by communities that want to protect themselves from their enemies, as well as establish communication with the spirits of their ancestors and with the gods. However, in some places, the witches are very feared because there is a belief that in addition to performing spells, they can kill at a distance, dominate the demons and can travel great distances in substantially short times, as well as cause diseases and generate evil in the body.
- Shaman: also called sorcerers, they are sacred since they have the power to cure diseases in humans. Often the shamans are the ones who direct the rituals, just as they watch the sacrifices and even act as escorts of the souls on their journey to the afterlife. Within their powers, according to animism, shamans can leave their bodies at times to observe situations and events at a distance.

- Subhumans: it is a kind of elves that are also known as "water spirits." They are also known as Leprechaun, a dual being of nature that combines the material and the spirit of the masculine gender. They are creatures that take the figure of older men who make mischief to people, make shoes, and guard the earthen vessels containing treasures buried in times of war.
- The illness
- In animism, the disease is seen as the absence of the soul in the body and on some occasions, for this, actions are carried out that allow measures to be taken through which the being can attract the wandering soul again.
- In regions like China, tradition suggests that when a person is close to dying from an illness, the soul leaves the physical body, so the patient is subjected to a long bamboo pole in which his coat is located there while The priest puts into practice his powers and techniques to return the spirit back to the shelter, often using spells for it. In case the bamboo turns in the person's hands, it is a sign that the soul returned to being.

The conception of the future

Within animism, the being wishes to know the future based on knowing the intentions of the spiritual powers, but also the dispositions of these, a process that is carried out from the practice of rituals and techniques by sacred people. This knowledge about the future is achieved with the reading and interpretation of omens present in various aspects and situations, such as the flight of birds and birds, the sound of thunder, the alignment of planets and stars, the appearance of comets, accidents, sudden deaths, interpretation of dreams, visions, among others. The horoscope is also very important. The fundamental interest of being in animism is the knowledge of future life or even the continuation of life after death.

General characteristics of animistic beliefs:

- Animists believe that the life of their ancestors continues even after their death.
- Living humans have the ability to interact directly with the spirits of dead beings.
- Animists often make offerings that comprise a wide variety of practices and atoning sacrifices.
- The soul has the ability to leave the body of the being during the moment of sleep or even in trance processes.
- The animist recognizes that there is a great variety of existing gods, just as there is a great variety of spirits.
- Within this set of beliefs, concepts such as the present and the past, the individual and the community, the object and the symbol are mixed.
- Animists believe in the mediation processes of shamans or sorcerers who take the role of intermediaries, as they are considered sacred people.

Initiation Rites

The initiation rites are carried out in order to generate access to a being towards secret knowledge or the entrance to an esoteric type of teaching, so it implies the use of a series of symbolic acts through which aspects are represented such as rebirth in a new state, death, the continuation of life, etc. It is believed that in prehistory, the shamans were responsible for directing the rites of initiation, for which they practiced it with a person entering their secrets. One of the initial practices that are known is the rites of initiation in the Amazon rainforest, where young people had to consume hallucinogenic drinks within the thicket of the jungle. Other initiation practices included hunting for animals alone.

CHAPTER THREE
What is Witchcraft

Witchcraft is a craft that is commonly misunderstood. In ancient times, witches are accused of all sorts of demonic and despicable acts that seem to ignite the flames of thousands of people's imagination as the villains. During the 20th century, it gained popularity and is usually blamed for harming properties and individuals. In addition to the known witch vehicle (which is a moving broomstick), the general public tends to misinterpret the witchcraft as satanic practices and rituals

It is believed that witchcraft is the practice of supernatural and magical forces to affect an individual, place, event or property in either a good or a bad manner. It is said to have historical, social, and anthropological meanings. It is usually viewed as "evil" or "death" by the public, and this is possibly due to the fact that it is primarily blamed for the many unexplained events that occur during the 20th century. In fact, witchcraft is simply at its best a magic of nature, and there is nothing wrong with learning how to be a witch and witchcraft spells as long as you wish to do it for personal purposes for the right reasons.

There's been a lot of discussion about both ancient and modern witchcraft, and in this book, it's going to put in your hands what we think is useful to understand better what we're talking about when we're talking about witchcraft.

The witchcraft is exercising or invoking supernatural powers to control people or events, practices that typically involve magic or witchcraft. While described differently in various historical and cultural contexts, witchcraft has always been seen, particularly in the West, as the work of witches who meet secretly at night, enjoy cannibalistic and orgiastic rites with the Devil, and practice black magic.

Thus, defined witchcraft exists more in the imagination of contemporaries than in any objective reality, although it is still true that very little is practiced. This stereotype, however, has a long history and, for many cultures, has been a viable explanation of evil in the world.

At the heart of neo-paganism, scholars prefer to condemn modern witchcraft (known as "Wicca"), as a dumb fad. Wicca adherents worship the goddess, nature, practice ritual spells, seek the gods' aid and observe Halloween, the summer solstice and the winter equinox.

During the early twenty-first century, only a few hundred thousand people (mostly in North America and Great Britain) practiced Wicca and Neo-paganism, a modern Western reconstruction of pre-Christian religions focused on the plurality of polytheistic religions around the world to establish a new and egalitarian religious step.

The rise in contemporary witchcraft or Wicca and Neo-paganism is partly due to the increase of religious acceptance and syncretism, the understanding of the symbology of the unconscious, the decline of Christianity, the popularity of fantasy and science fiction, the growth of feminism and relativistic philosophy and the emphasis on individuality and subjectivity in the face of intellectual cohe

Although Neo-Paganism integrates with its tradition the emotional connection and ceremonial rituals associated with religion, many Neopagans tend to see themselves as the practitioners of magic rather than religion, and while their focus is on opening up to unseen powers through rites and songs or charms, most of them do not consider themselves "sorcerers."

Both Wiccans and neo-pagans also have strong environmental and ecological values, goddess worship and other deities and celebrate the seasonal change with elaborate ceremonies. Whether magic or religion, in favor of personal experience, these groups reject intellectual coherence and objectivity and reject traditional science and religion.

While some Wiccans claim to be part of the "traditional ways" and "old culture," there is something modern about religion. Wicca is creative, imaginative and entirely a twentieth-century creation, with no connection to ancient paganism or the witch hunt 's supposed "witches."

No cult of the "Goddess" between antiquity and the twentieth century played a significant role in Western culture. In fact, contemporary witchcraft or Wicca emerged around 1939 from the works of the magician Aleister Crowley, the "old" Aradia text (1899), the Hermetic Order of the Golden Dawn, and other movements of the late nineteenth and early twentieth centuries, by an Englishman, Gerald Gardner. Murray Margaret The Witch-Cult in Western Europe (1921) and the essay "Witchcraft" in the 14th edition of the Encyclopedia Britannica (1929), which put forth in its most common form its hypothesis that the witches of Western Europe were, in fact, enduring adherents of a pagan faith that had once been replaced by Christianity, albeit not exactly so.

Magic and Science

Religion-science relationship has been a topic of study since classical antiquity, approached by philosophers, theologians, scientists, etc. Various viewpoints from various geographical regions, cultures, and historical epochs, some classify this relationship as one of confrontation; others define it as one of peace, while others entail only a small interaction between religion and science. The degree to which science and religion can attempt to understand and explain similar phenomena can often be stated in the demarcation question.

Science and religion typically seek universe knowledge using specific methodologies. Science recognizes reason, empiricism, and proof, while religions recognize revelation, faith, and holiness. Despite these disparities, most scientific and technological advances were produced by religious traditions-organized communities before the scientific revolution. Islamic scientists first developed much of the scientific method, and later Christians. Hinduism promoted historical motivations and empiricism, claiming science offers true yet imperfect knowledge of the (surrounding) universe. Confucian philosophy has interpreted science differently over time. Most Buddhists find science complementing their beliefs.

Difference between Whitch and Wicca

The Wiccans are those people belonging to the polytheistic religion that was founded in 1950 by Gerald Gardner.

It is a mixture of ancient reconstructed pagan beliefs and modern magical practices. Wiccans celebrate the eight sabbats and use the energy of nature for their spells.

Wiccans believe that all things are interconnected and that all thoughts and actions can have a positive or negative influence, which in turn is reflected in the triple belief that all things you do are returned by three.

They also believe in the duality of the Deity, which means that it is both male and female (God and the Goddess). You can refer to the Deity through many names, this depending on a person's preferences or the tradition that follows.

There is also the belief that divinity is imminent, which means that the God / Goddess is within everyone and in all of nature. Wiccans do not accept the existence of Satan (which is seen as a Christian creation), or in the forces of evil. They know the existence of negative energy, but recognize that it is part of nature and I think there are valuable lessons to learn from both positive and negative energy.

Wiccans practice magic, but it is not done to manipulate or harm anyone or anything. It is a delicate art that requires knowledge, practice, and patience.

Witches:

Witches practice magic and venerate their gods and goddesses in their own way, and do not usually practice the ritual in very precise ways (typical of Wiccans).

There are many varieties of witches, and those who seek the true magic of witchcraft can study for years before being called a witch or sorcerer, this indicates that both study and a high level of practical knowledge are needed.

Many people who are witches are hereditary witches, which means that their knowledge and skills have been taught by a family member who is a witch. However, a person is not automatically a witch just because a family member is.

People who are witches are knowledgeable about the properties of healing herbs, spells, divination, work with spiritual and natural energies, and many other things. The practice of witchcraft is not associated with any religion, so a person can be both a witch and a practitioner of any number of religions, or not practice a religion at all.

CHAPTER FOUR
Wiccan Tools for Spells and Rituals

The Wicca is a neo-pagan religion with various practitioners who stand out in their ceremonies for using magic. And that is because the magic of Wicca is very strong and effective. Wicca Magic practitioners may change and alter events by different spells as long as they do not behave against any living being and claim the favor of either the goddess or the deity of the Estado. We do have to follow the maxim of the Three Years and do just nice.

A series of Wicca tools or magic elements that facilitate the performance of rituals are needed to practice Wicca magic. They invoke divinities with these Wicca instruments, banish evil and guide energy by contact with the magician. You definitely know all of these devices, as they also appear in tv shows and films. They are part of present-day legends as well. I am talking about the broom the witches will sit on, from among others the cauldron for potions and the magic wand.

In fact, the use of these elements in Wicca has nothing to do with what stories, movies, are saying about them. They are mystical objects of great strength, it is true, but not as they are depicted in common imagery. You will need some of those tools if you want to practice Wiccan magic. Most of the antique stores, markets, and esoteric stores can be found in.

Before using Wicca tools

All Wicca magic devices have to be cleansed and consecrated when first learned or used. Bear in mind that the components used in a Wicca ritual are proprietary extensions. That means they store a part of the owner 's resources. This also means that someone who manipulates them in the Wicca tools leaves a residue of their own strength. And they have to be washed before they are used. This way, the energies of any other beings, and harmful energies that was able to contaminate them, would be eliminated. It will be consecrated until the negative waste devices have been washed. And, what's the same about the Wiccan gods' ability to protect them.

Because the Wicca tools store the feelings of their creator, it is best not to contact or use another officer's magic devices. If anyone approaches their tools with a specific energy vibration from the creator, they will no longer be successful until they are purified and consecrated again. To avoid carbon waste, all Wicca methods need to be used solely and strictly for spells and ceremonial celebrations.

Main Wicca Tools

In order to perform a Wicca magic ritual, there are many elements required. Each one represents one of the elements that the Wiccans venerate: Air, Water, Earth and Fire. The Guardians of the Elements are commonly invoked in their ceremonies as a propitiatory power of energy.

As I have already said, all Wicca tools can be purchased, but if you don't have a lot of money or prefer to be fully charged with your energy, you can make them yourself. A spell will not work better, because you're spending a lot on the tools you 're using. The main thing is that they are clean, consecrated and that in their efficacy, you put your faith. The most commonly used Wicca tools are Pentacle, Athame, Incense, Wand, Shadow Book, Cauldron, Bowline, and Bowline.

The pentacle is one of the most representative and popular elements. It's always for a Wiccan the source of more divine interest. The pentacle is shaped by a five-pointed star with a circle around it. Each of its tips constitutes one of the Four Elements. The fifth point reflects the Essence or Spirit that many find to be the fifth dimension. This figure represents the Earth element, is a protective symbol and is often used for centering energy. This will enshrine all that is put on the pentacle. The pentacle's main objective is to contain and support other energy-concentrating elements. So, it doesn't disperse, and the magic becomes more effective.

You can buy your pentacle ready-made, or you can do it by yourself, drawing it on a plate or piece of wood. Every time you go to do a ritual on your altar, you can draw it too, for example, with a little salt.

➢ The Athame

Another element used in Wicca magic that is quite well known is the Athame. The athame is a double-edged ritual dagger that represents the element Air. It is used to direct the inner energy of the officiant outward. It is also used to consecrate and bless water and salt, fire and air and ritual wines. In many spells, it is used to trace the pentacle and attract energies for evocation and invocation rites. It also helps to "cut" the energy or separate it when necessary. None of its uses involve harming or physically cutting something. Only symbolically. It is a great protector of the Wiccan altar.

The athame has to be of a natural matter, metal, wood ... but never plastic. With the black handle and always double-edged. Although the edges do not cut, they have to be profiled. If you don't have an athame, you can use an old letter opener or a knife, as long as you clean and consecrate them.

➢ The wand

The instrument used in Wicca magic to send power to the desired purpose is the rod or wand. This tool symbolizes the Fire element and opens the way to energies. Wands can be purchased made, but many Wiccans prefer to cut a tree's wand directly. The best wood to make a wand is willow, oak, apple, cherry or hazelnut. See a forest and look for a branch you like on the ground, remove twigs, leaves and bark and polish it. If you can't find it on the ground, ask the tree that has the branch you like and let it thank you. Do not tear it, cut it so as not to damage the tree.

Some Wiccans recommend that the length of the wand be from the elbow to the tip of the index finger. Although I think it is best that you like it, both in length, thickness, and color.

> **The incense**

An almost essential element in any Wiccan magic ritual is the incense that, at the same time, perfumes, purifies the area where the ritual is going to be performed, removes negative energies and helps to meditate. P or that is necessary to have a censer in addition to burning incense burn herbs in honor of the Goddess and God.

The censer must be a large concave vessel, if possible, made of metal and with an engraved crescent and pentacle. If you do not have and do not want to buy it, you can serve a large metal bowl or even a seashell. You can make the recorded elements yourself with a pin. You can also use a cup full of salt or sand. That way, putting the incense will prevent the cup from breaking. If you are outdoors, you can use incense sticks and stick them in the ground.

One of the most iconic and well-known Wicca ritual tools is the **cauldron**. It is the tool of the sorcerer par excellence. The cauldron is a container, preferably of iron and shaped like a vessel in which magicians cook, prepare drinks and mix the ingredients of their spells.

This is a three-legged tripod under which, formerly, it was set on fire to heat the contents of the cauldron. The three legs of the trébede symbolize the three aspects of the Mother Goddess: maiden, mother and older woman.

And this Wicca tool symbolizes the Goddess, representative of femininity and fertility. The cauldron welcomes the elements of the ritual as if it were the womb of a mother. It is a symbol in addition to the water element, reincarnation, and inspiration.

A smaller and more manageable version of the cauldron is found in the calyx. Which also represents the eternal feminine and the water element. The calyx is a normal round and metal cup. It is usually used to contain the water that is required in some rituals, although sometimes it can contain wine and even be used instead of the cauldron.

The broom is, next to the cauldron, the most famous tool associated with witches and magic. Brooms are a symbol of the union of masculine and feminine principles. It is used for the ritual cleaning of the workspace and for some rituals of protection and fertility. When in the Middle Ages, witches or any practitioner of magic were persecuted, brooms were used to hide the typical wand of Wicca magic, thus disguising it as an element of everyday use.

The bolline and the Book of Shadows

The bolline is a white-handled knife used to cut wands and sacred herbs. Also, to inscribe symbols on candles, wood or wax and to cut strings for magical use. It is similar to Athame but with the white handle. It differs from this because the bolline has a practical use, and the Athame is merely a ritual.

Another instrument for Wicca magic rituals is the Book of Shadows. P that to such a sinister name is a practical tool that each Wiccan personalizes in its own way. The book of shadows is a workbook in which the Wicca magic practitioner includes everything important to his magical practices. As invocations, ritual patterns, spells, runes, rules governing magic, etc. Each coven has his own book of shadows, written by hand and passed from the oldest to the youngest members. Many Wiccans prefer to call it Grimoire, which is the name traditionally assigned to magic books used by magicians and witches.

Although each Wicca magic practitioner can customize the Book of Shadows in his own style, there are some characteristics that he must have in order to be called the book of shadows. It must be of standard size, comfortable and easy to transport. It should not contain crossed out paragraphs or torn sheets. Therefore, it is recommended to use a notebook as a draft or a folder to which sheets can be added. Once the content is clear, it can be copied in the Book of Shadows.

Wicca tools for ritual

Many tools are used in Wiccan rituals. And you can't always buy all the new ones. Sometimes they get second hand, or a friend can leave you some. In any of these cases, before using them, you must clean them.

Cleaning tools for Wiccan rituals

The cleaning consists of two parts. You must first perform a physical cleaning. That is, you must clean the tool with a cotton cloth and remove any dirt or dust that may have accumulated. You will also have to try to correct any manufacturing defect that is detected. While this first part of the cleaning is being carried out, all the negative energy that the object could possess must be visualized in order to expel it through the cleaning.

The second part of the cleaning will be what is usually called ritual cleaning. To carry it out, you will need a candle that will represent the fire element, an incense stick that will represent the air element. Also, a handful of consecrated salt that will represent the earth element and a container with consecrated water that will represent the water element. In the place where you usually enhance ritual rituals, prepare a table with a white cotton tablecloth (or without it, it is not essential). This table will be your altar, and you will always use it for your Wiccan offerings and rituals.

Wait for a full moon night and place the tool you want to clean in the center of the table. Around it, the objects that represent the four elements. Once placed, light the candle and the incense stick. Take the tool and touch it everywhere. In this way, you will transmit your heat and charge it with your personal energy. Then pass it over the candle, incense, water, and salt. At the same time, offer it to the Gods.

The offering to the Gods

To make the offering of the tool, you must recite an offering prayer. You can create it yourself. As you know, in Wiccan rituals, each practitioner is allowed to create their own prayers. The most important thing is to offer the tool to the gods and pass it through the four elements to leave it clean and charged with positive energy.

If you can't think of any prayer, you can use this: «In the name of the God and the Goddess, with the fire element I am going to clean you, and thus all dirt and negativity from you I will eliminate. With the force of the earth, the air, and the water, I am going to clean you. Pure for these elements you have remained, for the Gods; thus, it is decreed.»

Consecration of tools for Wiccan rituals

Normally, just after cleaning the consecration is done because the elements that are needed are the same by adding the pentacle and tracing the magic circle. You can make it on your table that is now your altar. Although if you prefer, you can perform the consecration outdoors. In a forest, a beach, in a park or your garden, for example. If you do it outside, try to make the place bathed in the moonlight. The most important thing is that you do it in a place that you feel comfortable with.

In addition to the place, the date on which the consecration will take place is important. It is advisable to do it on a date that is special for you. The date of your birthday, the wedding anniversary, your favorite holiday, etc. The tools can be consecrated together or one by one. Not so the cleaning in which the tools must be cleaned individually.

Wiccan Ritual Preparation

To perform many rituals, it is sometimes helpful to have some sort of model on which to rely.

Steps.

1. Decide which ritual you want to perform. There are various common Wiccan rituals, many of which are found in books dedicated to the Wiccan religion. One of these, very famous, is called Drawing Down the Moon (literally, "pulling down the moon"). Find some information on this ritual.

2. Plan. If more than one person is present, establish the various roles in advance: who will call the quarters, who will lead the different parts of the ritual, etc. This will prevent confusion, which could disturb the atmosphere and the concentration of energy.

3. Prepare the space.
    - If you do the ritual indoors, clean and purify the room by doing a good cleaning.
    - If you do it outdoors, clear the space of any waste or debris. Make sure participants can freely walk barefoot if necessary. Prepare any practical details such as a fire pit, firewood, lanterns or an altar.

4. Purify yourself by taking a bath or shower and using bath oils that you only use when preparing to do a ritual.

5. Start balancing yourself. Find your inner peace, be well disposed and relaxed. Turn off all the thoughts of daily life that distract you.

6. Gather everyone who will perform the ritual with you and create the magic circle.

7. Call the elements so that they are present in your space; clockwise, starting from the east:
    - East, Aria
    - South, Fire
    - West, Water
    - North, Earth
    - Everyone, Spirit

8. Take a moment to honor your divinities. A symbolic image or statue helps to focus the mind, especially during group rituals, so that everyone is focused on the same thing.

9. View your goal and meditate on it. Take some time to cast the spell.

10. Thank the gods.

11. Thank the elements and release them in reverse order.

12. In the end, open the magic circle. This will release any residual energy. Some prefer to do this while releasing the elements.

13. Take some time to return to the present and balance yourself again. You can also do this by eating and drinking something, hugging a friend, caressing your whole body or visualizing roots that penetrate the ground in order to keep you upright.

Both individual and group rituals benefit if you share wine and sweets at this point to rebalance yourself and bless each other. Pass the wine and cake or bread clockwise, so that the person before you bless you and you do the same with those who come next. When everyone feels okay, it's a great idea to discuss and express their opinions.

14. When you feel ready, record your experiences in a Book of Shadows.

Tips

The ritual described above can be modified according to your needs, the number of participants, etc. It is just a basic structure for helping practitioners who need to do many rituals.

Collect several universal symbols and always keep them in a place near the altar. One of the best universal symbols to use contains all four elements, Fire, Air, Water, and Earth.

An easy way to represent the four elements is to use a blue pillar candle on a glass or stoneware pedestal, used for pillar candles (blue is water, the lit candle is air and fire, and the pedestal is the Earth).

Sandalwood incense works very well in most rituals: it provides protection, helps healing, spirituality, and fulfillment of desires.

You may find yourself in a magical group that honors a particular deity. Feel free to propose your model, both on the basis of what has been said previously and on the basis of your inventiveness. Having a model is very useful for busy practitioners, and helps prepare the set up in advance, making you stay focused.

You can also use the Rider-Waite Tarot Wizard card, as all four elements are represented on the card. If you choose a representation of the elements that do not have a candle, put a white one (representing universal energy) next to it.

Altar

The centerpiece of many forms of spirituality and magic, the altar, is present in many traditions. Christians, Buddhists, pagans ... From the simplest to the most elaborate, how can we find our way to know which one to adopt, or how to understand the diagrams of the one we have chosen to use? Here are some answers.

Overall, it is a sacred space where objects and representations linked to a cult or other practice are condensed. Its primary purpose is to pay homage to one or more of the deities. It can also be used for contemplation, but also for putting into action the specific energies which it symbolically condenses.

Each tradition has its own references, but some common traits remain. Essentially, an altar contains at least a spiritual image (usually of the deity (s) of your faith), and offerings.

The most used offering is incense, as well as the flame of a candle or a night light. This flame generally represents the "Divine Light" or "Energy-Source," the manifestation of the deity (s) to which you pay homage. It is also the symbol of the flame of knowledge dissolving the shadows of ignorance, the light repelling darkness, etc.

The place

Where to place your altar?

It is a problem that has caused much ink to spill ... Hopefully, in a sanctuary or other space devoted exclusively to your spiritual practices. Yet since we don't all have the chance to devote a whole room to this stuff there, we need to learn how to adapt!

In general, an altar should be private, and neophytes should not enter (or even see) it. Frequently used furniture which can be locked. Some would even select ephemeral altars, assembled and then dismantled to keep them hidden at any opportunity.

Others, who are less rigid, can accept the concept of their altar being visible. A drawer box, coffee table, sideboard or similar is sometimes used as a foundation. It is up to each to choose the room where to put it.

Some scholars warn against the bedroom because it deviates from the sacred by the respondent who performs there. It's the same, among some! To order to protect the private/sacred nature of the energies to place, some would warn against putting it in the rooms where you receive. Others would feel the need to be ostentatious etc. Anyway, this must be a position in front of which you can work easily, and which obviously varies from a simple decorative item for you. It should, literally, inspire you.

The height of the altar

As for the height options, it depends on how you work. If you practice standing primarily, a tall piece of furniture is fitting. When you practice sitting on the ground instead, a tiny piece of furniture would be a lot more realistic! When you practice standing, you can also position a shelf or small piece of furniture on the wall at face height.

Creating the altar can also be done on the concrete. In this case, the use of at least a small tablecloth or table set as a foundation is advisable, so that sacred items are not mounted on the floor. It is also accepted that the placing of sacred items on the ground is considered respectful. Yet, here again, it is up to each one to see in accordance with his intuition, because even in the more shamanic cultures, many practice the opposite.

The orientation of the altar

Another big mystery ... Each tradition comes with its own edition! But most frequently, turning an altar to the north or to the east is preferred (in the sense that the practitioner faces one of those directions while he stands in front of his altar).

The East is symbolically the place where the sun rises and thus symbolizes birth, development, the new ... The South symbolizes strength, motion, wealth, water ... The West stands for receptiveness, psychology, feelings, fluidity ... The North symbolizes the planet that nourishes but also cold, mystery, anchoring, etc. And those symbolic values can differ from source to source.

There are also a few houses or apartments at the cardinal points, with walls specifically oriented. Others will place their altars in angles; others will not pay attention to them and will put them in the most realistic possible location.

And everyone is free to do their best again, based on their opportunities, their beliefs and their personal feelings.

Some different types of altars

So, you can take inspiration from the suggestions below if you want to own an altar without knowing where to start. I will point out that all are free to adjust to their personal feelings. Even the domestic altar being personal, on the contrary, it is important that it resembles us, that it really inspires the one who uses it. So, draw the ideas that motivate you here (or elsewhere), and adapt them to yourself as best as possible. Your honesty to you will always be the strongest!

- The Simple Altar:

A depiction of the deity or other inspirational image of your preference (sacred statuette, printed image, landscape photographs ...), a candle (of the size, shape and color of your choosing, personalized to your needs) and an incense (there too, but try to select an incense appropriate for what you are looking for. Everyone is free to decorate all the other elements (stones, trees, symbols, etc.) and to inspire or explicitly. Tradition chose.

- The double Altar:

Used to honor two separate, preferably compatible deities (most frequently religious masculine and feminine). There, then every half of the altar is devoted to each of the deities. Most frequently, we offer left the feminine / receptive polarity and right the masculine/active polarity, but some practices do the reverse as well. And do as you wish, even though you sometimes want to change though you feel the need.

Here ideally, two candles are required to reflect each of the deities chosen. You are free to use the same (usually white) paint or choose the opposite. Others associate silver candles in the feminine (lunar goddess) and golden in the male (solar deity), others blue for the deity of the sky and green for the goddess of the earth, or red for the goddess of the mother and green for the wild god, etc. You know! Very frequently, in the symbolism of the mother who begets the son, we light the female candle first and then the male candle, but this concept can also be adapted to the idols you have selected.

Eventually, the inclines are positioned between the two, and usually between the two. The altar may be decorated with certain items reflecting the deities in question. Hollow objects (chalice, cauldron, bowl ...) most often represent the sacred feminine, and blunt/phallic objects (wall, knife ...) represent the sacred man.

- The triple altar:

Conceived as the double altar, it simply adds a third between the two polarities, which some call the great All, or even the One, or simply God. A third candle (sometimes on high to symbolize a higher power) is placed between the two others. We rarely use an image but rather a symbol to represent this entity, which is generally said without name or face since universal. But then again, it's up to everyone to adopt!

- The two-story altar:

This involves creating several levels on your altar, using small shelves, boxes or the like. At the highest will be placed what is most sacred to you, the highest. In our example, we can place the representation of the One on the highest shelf, then below those of the sacred feminine and masculine, then again below the offerings or other tools.

- The elemental altar:

Some do not feel comfortable with deities and do not feel the need to honor anyone. It is then possible to create other types of altars, made to condense the energies of the universe symbolically. For example, an altar with four elements.

Divide (at least mentally) the altar into four parts (or five according to your traditions), preferably in accordance with the correspondences that you attach to the cardinal points, and place in each corner symbols evoking each element. For example, a feather or incense for the air, a candle or a stick for the fire, a shell or a filled chalice for the water, a pebble or sand for the earth... In the center, you can place a symbol which will condense these energies (rock crystal or your pentacle, etc.). Again, this is to adapt to everyone.

Tips to Set Up Wiccan Altar

- ➤ Find a table suitably sized to start from the altar. Let the table be sturdy, in good shape, and clean as it will be used for sacred purposes, of course. Be careful with the positioning when putting the table. It is best to choose the room area which receives moonlight and sunlight.
- ➤ Throw on an altar cloth that is appropriately appropriate for altar table size. Not all colors work for the cloth; select green symbolizing nature, black symbolizing the earth aspect or blue and silver symbolizing goddess.
- ➤ Since Wiccan is all about harmonizing the energies, make sure you don't end up overcrowding the altar, or you will have a chaotic flow of energy. Begin by placing the statue of the god or the goddess in the center of the altar and ensure that there is some kind of offering under the statue as a sign of reverence for Deity.
- ➤ Place candles on each side of your statue, and they can be candles for seven days or daily candles. Using suitable candle holders if possible. You may also use essential oils to dress the candles, which are filled with a different energy.
- ➤ Make sure you choose a spot at the altar with minimal intervention and exploitation. This is your sacred position, and so nothing can be easily abused or exploited by

others. Treat the altar with care and reverence, for it represents the spiritual self directly.

- ➤ Leave some place for divination upon your altar. This could be a crystal ball, tarot, pendulum, or some other form that you personally find suitable. If you want to do divinations somewhere, so that you don't interrupt the flow of Chi from your altar, that's okay.
- ➤ Tend towards the altar on a daily basis to experience results directly throughout your life. For e.g., thoroughly clean it, put on fresh altar cloth, ideally in a bright color, and decorate it using new stuff from Wiccan to decongest or release a stuck kind of life.

The Wicca Altar is a very significant part of Wiccan ism, and that is what many witches do. This is not only a spot for witchy things but also acts as a focal point of mystical powers, a reminder of values, the sanctuary of the sacred and echo of beliefs and wishes.

The Magic Circle

Part of the Wiccan liturgy includes the "construction" of a circle of power that has various functions, although not all the works available on the market on this matter clarify exactly what the circle's functions are in Wicca, how it is carried out, how it is it opens and what it is used for exactly, as well as it is not clarified if it is to be performed in absolutely all the circumstances surrounding a ritual act. For starters, the magic circle can be defined as a spherical-shaped energy construct, although its functions can vary widely.

The circle, as a construct or energy construction

A construct or energetic construction is all that agglomeration of energy to which the practitioner gives a certain form. An energetic construct can, in addition, have a certain intelligence (the case of the egregor), or it can serve a particular purpose.

To make any energy construct, several elements are required:

- ➤ A practitioner who voluntarily shapes it, otherwise it is not an energetic construction but an entity or entity. There are many types of energetic forms, such as vortices, that are not created voluntarily but semi-unconsciously by people, through recurring thought or emotion, until they acquire a certain form at the energetic level, but this cannot be considered a construction because there is no conscious manipulation of energies.
- ➤ An energy source from which the building can «feed.» Since the energy is neither created nor destroyed, what the practitioner does when making the circle is to modify

existing energy, giving it a certain shape. Sometimes it is energy from the environment, other times energy from the magician himself, other times elemental energy, and other times a combination of various sources.

➢ A purpose, an element that normally defines the shape. The circle is not spherical by chance: it is about recreating in miniature a representation of our own world, following several principles of magic: "So above, as below" and "Similarities attract." When the practitioner gives the circle around the shape, it is because he is going to recreate on a small scale what he wants to change on a large scale.

Magic circle functions

There are many opinions about the functions of the circle, and here they go on to collect the most common or known.

In the first place, there is the use of the circle as an element for targeting energies. This is very important because what the practitioner is going to try is to accumulate within the circle the greatest amount of energy according to what he wants to achieve, and then release it and be able to create a "knock-on effect" in reality. Therefore, the circle serves as an "energy battery" for what will manifest after the magic act in the other planes.

Second, there is the use of the circle as a method of protection. There are many people who believe that this is not necessary or that it is not one of the functions of the circle, and there is some controversy in this regard. What is often said is that, if you really believe that someone or something can harm us while doing magic, it is safest to create a circle, although it really is not always necessary if the magic practitioner has good psychic defenses. In this case, the best protection is the one that is carried out during the day to day, maintaining good psychic hygiene.

Third and not least, the circle helps to enter an altered state of consciousness. This is usually achieved through conditioning: if whenever we are in a circle, we enter a trance or reach an altered state of consciousness, with practice it is possible that every time we close a circle, we automatically enter this altered state of consciousness.

Closing and opening the magic circle

Typically, the ritual space is usually cleaned and consecrated prior to creating a circle. This is done to eliminate any previous energy structures or patterns of energy that may be in place, as well as to prepare you for the following ritual. Here we are not going to go into these cleaning techniques, as we would go too far, this is also a separate subject.

The circle is formed after cleaning and consecration, that is to say, closed. There are several ways to put the magic circle to a close. The traditional approach is to use the athame, but you can also use the skillful hand's index and middle fingers (which you compose with), or you can even shape a community of people if they shake hands and create the appropriate picture. Before the creation of the circle itself, however, many practitioners include the sprinkling of water and salt to purify where the circle passes and the passage through a priest's or priestess 's future circle with lit incense to load it with energy. After this, we establish the building itself:

- If the athame or hand is used, the practitioner should face East and point the athame or the tip of his fingers outward. Now, you should visualize a light, usually white, coming from the tip of your athame (or the tip of your fingers), and while always walking in Deosil (clockwise) it goes through the South, West, North, and again This until the circle is completely sealed. Some Wiccans perform an invocation pentacle in the air at the time of sealing.
- If you use a group of people who shake hands, it can be done in a multitude of ways. Some prefer that practitioners stand still and perform a simple visualization whereby, lifting an energy pillar from their heart chakra, they expand their own energy and move it in Deosil at once throughout the circle. The circle can also be made through song and dance, or through a circle.

Opening the circle, that is, undoing it, is usually much easier than creating it. For this, the simplest thing is for the person in charge of creating it to move, starting from the East again, in Widdershins (counterclockwise, called Tuathail in Wicca Correlliana) until returning to the starting point, imagining that the energy of the circle returns to the tip of the athame.

If you have created the circle with several people, imagine that the circle is reversed just the opposite of how it had been created: if a dance or run has been done in Deosil, it is done in Widdershins, and if a group visualization has been done, it is visualized that the energy returns to the bodies of all the participants, specifically to the heart chakra.

Again, both the closing and opening of the circle operations vary from practitioner to practitioner and from tradition to tradition.

To create or not to create a circle for magic work

There are many people who wonder if they have to create a circle for all magical work or every celebration. The answer is no, although it may help. The circle serves as an energy battery, but what is created with magic is only maintained with magic, so it can generate a significant energy expenditure to maintain it for a long time if it is a single person, and the practitioner can end physically and psychologically really tired.

To avoid exhaustion in the case of long rituals, it is advisable to "anchor to the ground" by means of the exercises intended for this. This operation, performed before and after each magical act, not only prepares and purifies us for the rituals but helps us focus on reality once the magical work is done.

How to Create the Magic Circle

The Wicca and other neo-pagans who conduct Magic Rites create a sacred circle with rituals being performed within it. The circle serves as a gateway to the divinity realm, as a shield from evil powers, and more literally as a psychological device for getting you in the right mood. The circle represents security.

Create the Circle

Find a comfortable place to build your circle. It may be outside or indoor, at midnight, or early in the morning. There is no perfect location for the magic circle, and if that makes you physically uncomfortable, there is no need to go to a remote spot. The best place is wherever you feel comfortable and confident, able to communicate in the way you want, and ready to practice in the appropriate manner for any rite or ceremony. That's perfect if this is your office, basement or garage.

For the duration of the ceremony, make sure the place is private and safe. In the middle of a routine, being disrupted is a disturbing and even dangerous experience.

Purify the location you want your circle to be in. Second, it physically purifies the room, arranges items and puts the place in order. When you are outside, remove branches, leaves, and stones from the field. Then spiritually cleanse the place. Meditate, use your hands (or a wand or broom if certain elements are involved in the practice), and chase the negative energy from the spot.

You can also use a witch hazel-based cleaning product to clean up the area, and a few drops should be enough in every corner of the room and around the circle area.

Set the boundaries physically, if you wish. To do this, draw a circle on the concrete, spray it with salt water, or make a loop around the circle (be sure to tie it). The circle is typically larger than your height, in any case.

Alternatively, you can use the elements of nature to build your circle, if you are outdoors. If you find it suitable for your ritual or exercise, build the circle with rocks or other natural resources.

Put all the items within the circle you want to use in your ritual. You should remain in it once you start the practice, and not break the bond until the ritual is done. Once you start the ritual, you cannot take a "break" to go get an important candle or totem. Collect everything you need to get going and get ready.

If you're offering something to a spirit, remember to provide it along with what you need to plan it.

Some specific items are totems, black candles, stones, knives, bells, salt bowls and water bowls to be used in the ceremony. Arrange certain objects to create an altar, whatever they may be. Take a plan to put them on, like a box with a small black tablecloth, or a crate. When you are in the circle, the altar has to face north to complete the ritual.

Complete the circle. Place candles or other objects in each direction. Don't turn them on. Many Wiccans prefer anything that reflects north Earth, east air, south fire, west water. Follow every appropriate protocol for your ceremony.

Salt, stone, or green candle can represent Earth. Census, broken glass or yellow candle can symbolize air. Water in every tub or water lamp. A red candle or cigarette is fire-friendly. If you have a deck, you can use Tarot Aces.

Use the Circle

Bless the circle. How to use the circle once it's created depends largely on you, your practice, and your goals. Eventually, however, you can start blessing the area and liberating it from negative energies by beginning spirit invocation. Some congregations, whereas others are rather formal, ritualize their practice. Do what's normal for you.

Walk outside, light the candles, leave a salt trail around the edges. In every cardinal direction, he recites an invocation like: "Blessing the North's creatures and spirits."

Indicates the circle's function. Walk around three times, claiming, "Three times I take the circle away from bad spirits."

"O Ring of Power, I beg you to be a place of beauty, joy and truth; a shield against all bad and bad, a barrier between men and the realms of the Mighty, a bastion and a defense that must maintain and contain the force that lifts us to you.

Invoke the elements, ghosts, and gods you want to draw. Name them with objects reflecting them. Take each entity representing the elements around the circle, filling them with each one's force.

Meditate a moment. Meditation or astral projection may be the central behavior or shift of consciousness.

Complete your ritual. Remember: "And don't hurt anyone, do what you want." If you have to leave the circle before you're done, cut a door (literally, imagine a door being cut off the edge of the circle. Close the circle once you're back inside).

Close the circle when you are finished: pay homage to all the divinities you have invited, thank the elements before removing the objects that represent them, and finally cancel the circle by making the circle in the opposite direction.

CHAPTER FIVE
Wicca Meditation and Visualization

Meditation is an activity that aims to bring us to a state of equilibrium or a state of consciousness that enables us to detach ourselves from the outer world and thereby to be able to perceive, control, project and obtain energy outer of each day. Such activities concentrate on the awareness of images, objects, and even our own breathing before a meditative state is brought to mind.

For example, by concentrating on the flame of a candle when we are working with the Fire aspect from meditation, we seek to perceive its strength, its heat, its colors, evoking all that fire represents to us. The focus is often so strong that it may seem that we see figures dancing in the flame, and this is precisely one of the results we expect in meditation, particularly with the elements.

Instead of the flames of a candle, we may also meditate to consider the movement of the leaves of a tree or to feel the cool wind that caresses our cheeks, to work with the element Air, or to lie on the root of a tree, to lie on the grass, to focus on the texture of the dirt, and in the color of the earth, as is its depth, to work with the Earth dimension.

If we were to deal with the Water element instead, it would be enough to consider the flow of the water, a fountain, the stream, etc., as is its depth, everything that comes out of it, dealing with the Earth element. If we were to deal with the Water element instead, it would be enough to consider the flow of the water, a fountain, the stream, etc., as is its depth, everything that comes out of it, dealing with the Earth element. Unless we were to deal with the Water aspect instead, it would be enough to consider the wave movement, a fountain, the storm, etc. There is also the possibility of meditating with your eyes closed. We use this technique frequently when we want to carry out the practice of visualization, to see with our inner eye, that is, our imagination. For the exercise of visualization, we need first of all the exercise of meditation, of bringing the mind to a state of calm, relaxing the muscles, leaving the mind free of worries, getting comfortable, concentrating on the breath, and there are even those who like to work with the chakras to propitiate this state.

Visualization is vital to magical practice; in fact, we use it in spells, projecting all our energy into that purpose we wish to be fulfilled. It is an exercise that surely all children once used, but we have lost that ability as we have grown. It is another tool that we can exercise or develop, and that allows us to know our inner self from the symbols and sensations that occur to unexpected messages from our unconscious.

It is important to clarify that once we have reached the end of meditation and visualization, we must reconnect with our reality, for this we can applaud, laugh or touch the ground with the palms of our hands, as well as perform actions that remind us of what every day, such as drinking water, eating, etc.

Visualization exercise

First step: Clean the place where you are going to perform the meditation physically and energetically. You can use rosemary, sage, myrrh incense, etc. You can also take before starting an immersion bath with salts or herbs.

Second step: Put on comfortable clothes, light an incense that you like, you can accompany it with music or in silence. You can light a candle or not. If you light a candle, let it be white and that it be lit in a safe place.

Third step: In this item, you will define what you want to work on to focus on it, it can be a symbol, stealth to attract or repel something, it can be the figure of a Tarot arcana from which you want to exploit its virtues or characteristics, or simply entrust you to the Gods to reveal to you what your power animal is, what your magic name should be or who is the God or Goddess who accompanies you.

Fourth step: You can trace the circle of protection with the athame, with your index finger or simply visualize that you are enclosed in a circle (in reality, it is a sphere) of white light around you. It is also a good option to draw the circle with objects, such as stones, branches, coarse salt, fine salt, black salt, etc.

Fifth step: Focus on your breathing, on leaving worries out of your circle, on loosening up.

Sixth step: In this instance, you would have to be in a meditative state visualizing a temple or simply an open place, and you enter that landscape. As you move forward, consider what elements there are, if there are doors, if it is open to the sky, if there is vegetation, if there is water nearby, if there is fire, if you feel cold or hot, if it is day or night, if there are aromas and at some point, something or someone will get your attention. Pay attention to what or who it is, if it is talking to you if it is offering you something if it is an animal, a person or an object if it is a person or an animal if it has any message to give you. Suppose you can ask him a question if he gives you something.

Seventh step: Now is the time to return. You must say goodbye to your host and slowly return to the place where you arrived. Once you feel ready to return to yourself, focus again on your breathing, count down from 10 to 0 and open your eyes.

Eighth step: In this step, you will write everything you can remember from this experience, from the sensations, colors, objects, symbols, landscapes, animals, people, messages that any of them have transmitted to you, etc. And in the morning on waking, if you had any special dreams or related to your visualization, also write it along with your notes.

Ninth step: Do not forget to drink water, eat and do things that connect you to the underworld.

These exercises can be carried out at any time of the year but are usually more productive during the Full Moon and the Dark Moon.

How to use creative visualization to improve your spells

Training the mind for creative visualization is the key to casting effective magic spells since by clearly visualizing the desired result (creation of a way of thinking), the result is configured as a form of energy in more subtle planes. This form of energy is the first step towards the reality of the desired result, which must be realized in the material world.

How to use creative visualization with spells:

- Creative visualization can be used in any magic spell, following these simple steps:
- Find a quiet place.
- Before beginning the spell, be clear about the exact nature of the desired results.
- Start the spell with simple but clear action, such as lighting a candle or burning some incense.
- Quiet your mind with meditation by concentrating on inhalation and exhalation for a few minutes, then let the breath be natural.
- Start visualizing the desired result, and this visualization should be as real as possible. For some people, the images are easier, while others can use emotions, sounds, smells or actions. Imagine that everything happens now, in the present moment.
- Focus on the desired result of the spell, if you need to rest do it, but then you must return to meditation again.

> When in your mind, you are clear about the desired result, perform the spell with confidence, knowing that the visualization will add energy.

You must believe that the result is possible, and have positive thoughts of support in this regard. Before completing the spell, visualize once again the desired result for a few moments; then, you must end the spell by extinguishing a candle or incense.

Precautions when using creative visualization:

Remember to be careful what you want when using creative visualization in magical work. The thought-forms created are very real and can generate both negative and positive results.

CHAPTER SIX
Wiccan Crystal Magic

In the past few years, alternative therapies have become much more common in our everyday lives. Evidence shows that all of them affect our wellbeing extremely well.

Crystal therapy is an ancient therapeutic method at the levels of energy, physical, emotional and mental. Historical records indicate that, to this day, all cultures have understood and used the power of crystals in the broadest sense-for disease care, for defense, for meditation, for spiritual enlightenment. This approach is thought to date from Atlantean times.

"Crystals have the ability to absorb, store, transfer, transform, preserve and channel energy. They have the property of balancing energy fields. Because of these properties, minerals and crystals are commonly used in the treatment of various diseases, as well as catalysts and enhancers in the development of human consciousness.

And the most stable form of matter in the universe. The essence of each crystal is the atom and its particles rotating around the nucleus. But even if they look calm in appearance, crystals are a fluid molecular weight vibrating at a certain frequency. That's where their energy comes from. "Because each crystal has specific energy - vibration, treatment with minerals and crystals is an energy treatment that affects not only physical symptoms but the whole body as a whole, accelerating and facilitating the process of recovery and healing. It involves working on the chakras (energy centers in the body) and the energy field - the aura of a person and allows healing at all levels - physical, emotional, and mental.

The treatment with minerals and crystals is the focusing and channeling of energy that vibrates at a certain frequency, and that enhances and amplifies all other energies at a lower frequency.

As an example, when a stone is placed on a specific energy center (chakra), it enhances its vibration and helps it function properly, cleansing, balancing and improving the function of the endocrine gland and the organs around it. When the organs have strong enough energy, they are healthy and function normally - and vice versa, if they lack energy, they become ill," said the specialist, adding: "When working with crystals, concentration and intention are essential.

Our thoughts are long electromagnetic waves that transmit into space. Crystals can capture and store thoughts (emotions and feelings) and send them back. This applies only to natural crystals of nature. Synthetic does not have these properties, and they cannot retain human mental energy. If your attention is focused and your intention is to program the crystal, it will save the program and broadcast it until you stop it. "

Crystal Healing

For the purpose of healing, we use crystals or gemstones in crystal healing. These crystals are either used to cure any kind of body pain, or even to purify our body from various impurities. There are many different regions in our body known as "chakras," the healing of crystals is done by keeping the crystals on these body chakras. In all of our bodies, there are seven chakras where the crystals are put for healing purposes. In Hindi, the word "chakra" means spiritual force.

Such seven chakras are known as our body's seven energy centers. The crystal used for healing purposes comes in different colors, and each of these colors has great importance in the process of healing.

These chakras aid in our body's flow of energy and thus make our bodies pure and free from all pain and illness. This process helps to regulate the energy flow within the body of the person. The healer who does the healing process on someone should first undergo the crystal healing procedure to make his body pure and free from any form of negative energy. The energy can then be transferred via the crystals from his body to another human. Thus, the person who suffers from any illness caused by negative energy will be healed.

Crystal healing has gained a lot of attention nowadays, and not only people suffering from the disease are receiving this procedure, but in some cases, nurses and physicians also have a crystal healing session in order to cure their patients. Not only for the purpose of healing the crystals to be put on the chakras, but these crystals can also be held on the bedside where you sleep and can be worn as well. The crystals used differ depending on the type of disease the patient is looking for or the type of treatment.

No-one knew where the cure came from. Humans have used this practice for ages. Earlier people didn't believe much in crystal healing, and many of us thought it was pagan. Yet, people have gradually started to understand the importance of crystal healing nowadays. Although it is not scientifically established that crystal healing really does work, its actual strength is known only to those who have undergone these sessions.

Because of its color and form, the majority of crystal healers use transparent quartz to do their work. But certain stones and crystals can differ depending on which chakra the crystals are put.

Does healing cause harm? Most of us see little benefit in using the crystals for the purpose of healing. But it can be very dangerous for a person who suffers from some illness and stops his medicine only because he is practicing crystal healing. It is believed that if incorrect energy is passed through the cycle of crystal healing, it can take the life of that person. These transferred powers are not god linked and thus can be very dangerous.

Minerals and crystals have wonderful healing properties and help with a wide range of diseases, but the most important condition must always be respected - always work with purified crystals only. Due to their ability to retain information, if it is not properly purified, there is a risk that disease can easily be transmitted from one person to another.

"They can help ease headaches. For example, with amethyst by placing it on the 6th chakra or doing a massage in the temple area. In the case of cardiac disorders, green aventurine, zoos, quartz, rhodonite, etc. are placed, which are placed on the heart chakra or to structure water with them. The bone, the system, is a very suitable massage with labradorite. One unique mineral is the clinoptilolite zeolite, which has a strong detoxifying effect and extracts toxins and toxic substances from the body. It has a beneficial effect on cardiovascular diseases, regulates blood pressure, blood sugar, gastrointestinal disorders, gastritis, ulcer, colitis, as well as on the nervous system, cleanses the kidneys and bile of grit, skin problems - acne, seborrhea, cancer diseases, it increases the overall tone.

The Benefits of Crystal Healing (emerald)

Emerald Stone

While buying the crystals for personal use in healthcare, try to wash them first and rinse them well. It removes any kind of unwanted energy obtained from those people who have worked with this form of crystal. Only after the crystal has been cleaned you need to program it.

One way of programming the crystal is to place it on your side, hold it until your thought is transferred to the crystal. It helps you to begin your healing powers.

The practice of medicating the body with crystals has been around for thousands of years. A lot of people in other countries such as India and Egypt are doing it.

This notion may be peculiar to those who don't know the 'chi' energy and special activity. Nevertheless, our body is composed of carbon. The crystals we use to cure a particular ailment turn the substance into biochemical energy that goes into the body and revives the structures.

One way of programming the crystal is to imagine a person picking up the crystal and see their sad face turn into a happy smile. Then imagine them enjoying life and exceptionally good health.

The same happens when you meet someone who has some sort of disease. Think of them as a safe, happy person, free from any disease. Visualize them when keeping the stone on quartz. Such thoughts are energy, and whatever thoughts you have, whether positive or negative, they will be stored in the crystal and can be passed to the person you are thinking about.

It's also necessary to believe in their strength. Otherwise, your attempt to pass the positive energy won't work. If you believe this, though, then you can use more of the crystals to cure the body, mind and well-being.

Crystals have magical powers, belief in them, and they will heal you!

Motivational crystals:

- amethyst
- carnelian
- citrine
- unakite
- rutile quartz
- fluorite
- tourmaline
- tiger eyes
- apatite

Confidence-building crystals:

- citrine
- ruby
- carnelian
- rhodonite
- tiger's eye
- vanadinite

Crystals that help remove fear:

- aquamarine
- iolite
- amethyst
- pink sapphire
- yellow tourmaline

Good mood crystals:

- pink quartz
- agate lace
- carnelian
- tangerine quartz
- sapphire
- vanadinite

Mental health crystals:

- amazonite
- smoky quartz
- shungite
- unakite
- orange calcite

Crystals that strengthen self-esteem:

- sodalite
- carnelian
- lapis lazuli
- sunstone
- hematite
- lace agate

Beneficial crystals in exhausting moments:

- opal
- pietersite
- lepidolite
- ruby
- rutile quartz
- carnelian

Crystals for healing emotional balance:

- rhodochrosite
- moonstone
- calcite
- pink quartz and smoky quartz
- pink opal
- amazonite
- onyx
- apache tear
- lepidolite

Beneficial crystals in love:

- rhodochrosite
- pink tourmaline
- emerald
- stilbite
- smithsonite
- rhodonite
- pink quartz

Crystals for past life regression:

- lapis lazuli
- amethyst
- hematite
- petrified wood
- carnelian

Crystals and Wicca

Crystals and gemstones all have various mystical and healing qualities, depending on the Wicca culture you operate within. This is a particularly rich area for the solitary practitioner who is free to work with the correspondences of crystals and gems that most strongly speak to them.

Compiling a complete and detailed list of crystals and all their names and associations would be virtually impossible, as is the case with plants, but these are among the most popularly known.

Agate-Associated with the Earth dimension, agate has calming powers for the mind and is used for the treatment of depression and energy gain. Through a mystical connection, agate elicits reality and creates new insights, and is useful in resolving depression and isolation.

Amber-Associated with the element of Fire, and linked to the Light, amber is used to cause eye and throat disorders. It provides transparency, confidence, security and power.

Amethyst-Synonymous with Water dimension, amethyst has astrological links for those born under Aquarius and Pisces signs. This is used for the treatment of tension, anxiety and depression and during ceremonies will sharpen the mind and spiritual forces as well as cleanse and clear the sacred room.

Gemstones and their meanings

- **Agate**-Associated with the Earth dimension, agate has calming powers for the mind and is used for the treatment of depression and energy gain. Through a mystical connection, agate elicits reality and creates new insights, and is useful in resolving depression and isolation.
- **Amber**-Associated with the element of Fire, and linked to the Light, amber is used to cause eye and throat disorders. It provides transparency, confidence, security and power.
- **Amethyst**-Synonymous with Water dimension, amethyst has astrological links for those born under Aquarius and Pisces signs. This is used for the treatment of tension, anxiety and depression and during ceremonies will sharpen the mind and spiritual forces as well as cleanse and clear the sacred room.
- **Bloodstone**-Associated with the fire factor, bloodstone (also known as heliotrope) is linked to all blood and circulatory issues. This is a general healing stone and one that is magically used to work with fertility, abundance, and wealth.
- **A carnelian**-An aspect of stabilization, carnelian has infertility and impotence-related healing properties and is believed to stop excessive bleeding. This is magically used to protect the bearer from a supernatural attack.
- **Diamond**-Linked to Air and Fire elements, diamonds have healing powers linked to sexual dysfunction and reproduction. Diamond is used in magical usage for intuitive research, meditation, astral flight, and scrying.
- **Garnet**-Bound with Fire, it is the stone most bound with the Persephone goddesses. This is used to treat fertility problems and is closely linked to the beauty of the female moon.
- **Hematite** — Associated with Fire and used to cure inflammation, illness, fever, and blood disorders, hematite is a protective stone, especially from home. This also gives trust to the individual, improves the motivation and helps in psychological understanding and problem-solving.
- **Jade**-Connected with the Earth and related to the healing of the inner organs, jade is often used to encourage longevity and is a sign of serenity, true love, truthfulness and innocence.

- **Jasper-**Associated with the Earth, jasper is used in cancer treatments and blood disorders and is a calming and ritualistic centering stone. It also brings good luck to the person holding it or wearing it.
- **Lapis Lazuli-**A stone linked to the Water part, a lapisis used to raise the spirits and treat depression. In mystical works, especially meditation and trance work, lapis alters the consciousness and more explicitly links the wearer to the divine.
- **Moonstone-** A water stone and linked to the Moon, this is a stone of goddess with great healing powers for women. It is used in rituals of Goddess, particularly those pertaining to intuition and wisdom.
- **Obsidian-**A stone of the element Fire, obsidian will remove toxins from the body, especially from the liver, and is often used in energy work. It has defensive properties and is good for intuitive and scrying magic operations.
- **Opal-**In conjunction with all the elements, opals can be replaced by any other crystal and used in emotional and spiritual healing. These are defensive stones that will strengthen the workings of magic and absorb whatever energies they come into contact with, positive or negative.
- **Quartz, Rose-**Rose Quartz is a stone of the heart aligned with the Wind, providing comfort in matters of love and friendship. Their mystical uses involve connections of all sorts, from friendship to romanticism.
- **Quartz, Pure-**White quartz is connected with all the elements and is used as a tool for connecting to the Sacred in healing rituals as well as serving. It is a stone of insight and spiritual growth and development. Sapphire-Associated with water and used to treat respiratory and throat conditions, sapphires are magically used to touch and prophecy spirit guides.
- **Tiger's Eye-**A stone of the element Fire, the tiger's eye, improves overall physical health and energy and is magically used in defensive and brave rituals.
- **Turkey-**A Water-related stone, turquoise treats stomach and eye disorders as well as helping to heal broken bones. This is a stone of spiritual insight, healing, and intuition.
- **Zircon-**Associated with the element of Fire, zircons are useful for rituals of love, beauty, harmony, and relationships in overall healing. Owing to their resemblance to diamonds, in the workings of some customs, zircons can be substituted for diamonds.

Balancing the Mind with Crystals and Gemstones

Crystal healing is an alternative form of healing, using crystals and gems. The theory behind that is that crystals are often said to help stimulate the process of healing. This form of treatment has been used for headaches, depression and cancer, as recovery can be as emotional as it is physical.

The crystals are said to contain energy that can be transmitted as well as provide spiritual guidance to restore health and battle disease. The point some crystal healing supporters make is that while the stones don't actually cure disease, they do help to correct the underlying issues. Each healer has his own opinion, and some use the process along with other methods.

The main premise behind the need for crystal healing is that when there is a person's mismatch of divine energy, sickness arises. Many healers believe that this divine force, or light, is the very basis of universe formation. It is said that the crystals help to fix the disparity between us and our universe.

The gemstones, known as chakras, are added to certain energy centers. They are said to bring light and color into the body's aura, thereby generating a flow of energy. This flow is often thought to promote a sense of healing by re-equilibrating the energies of the body.

It was believed that some of the best crystal therapists had an ability that could sense the exact location in the body where the energy is being trapped. This means they can place the crystals on the parts of the body, which will most effectively promote healing. The stones are of varying sizes and colors, each supporting a distinct quality of healing.

Sapphires are said to improve mental insight, while amethyst stones are thought to cultivate a relaxed mind. Rubies have been known to help inspire bravery and cleanse the blood. The crystals are all selected according to the needs of each person. To others, keeping the crystals in their pockets is not uncommon, and for others, placing them on strings, in the bath with the tub, as well as placing them around the room.

The healing of crystals can be traced back to ancient times when Greeks and Indians believed gemstones brought light to another dimension. Some people believed spirits existed within the crystals. This is well known for its use as an alternative method of treatment for a number of diseases.

CHAPTER SEVEN
Candles Magic

Candles have existed in our culture for thousands of years. They were used not only to illuminate the rooms of houses or while traveling. The candles were and are magical! They illuminate our path not only in reality but can also illuminate the recesses of our mind or contribute to the good fortune sent by gods or other beings from other realities. What is candle magic, and what is it about? Is it worth using it?

What is candle magic?

Candles combine with the element of fire, and the magic of candles takes advantage of it. It is a kind of sacrifice, gift, thanks. It is a kind of ritual - meditation that is performed for something. They could also be used for fortune-telling, or more specifically, candle fire, on the basis of which it was assessed what could happen in the future.

A brief history of candle magic

Candles in spiritual practice have been used all over the world, starting from the East. Indian beliefs and Buddhism not only use the candle as a sacrifice for intention but also in yoga practices (not as physical exercises) to build concentration.

Candles were once very expensive and difficult to access. They were not easy to perform; it was a tedious process. They were a kind of sacrifice. By renouncing some good that could be bought instead of burning a (ritual) candle, there was a change in man.

What is the magic of candles?

The magic of candles consists of using the physical candle as the real plane and the mental plane - transcendental, where the change of reality takes place. By changing ourselves through candle meditation, we are changing the world around us. We use some external object (candle) that changes the subject (us). It would not have to be candles (often they are not), but they carry great universal value. However, burning a candle is not always positive. Say to someone: "I lit a candle for you.", This can be seen as a signal and a signpost for the dead, and then we treat that person as one we want to throw out of our lives.

Completing the rituals depends largely on ourselves. Merely lighting a candle will do nothing, although the intention alone can have an effect.

How does candle magic work?

In fact, candle magic is considered sympathetic magic, which is basically a principle that canalizes the power of attraction, or "like attracts like." Candle burning is essentially a tool for most experts and practitioners in which a person focuses their energy and will to manifest their greatest dreams and desires. While most uninformed audiences relate burning candle rituals and ceremonies to black magic or dark magic, that's not what candle burning practices are made for.

Candle Color and Magical Properties

Witches have used candle flames in dance for decades. Candles help to enhance the strength of the ritual by establishing a suitable environment, or, in particular, to manipulate a specific force. Candles consume personal energy when burned, and release that energy. When you're performing a ritual using a colored candle, you know that each color emits a certain vibration and attracts certain influences.

Ideally, you can make candles from beeswax using natural colors and essential oils. The beeswax, which is sold, is a fast and easy way to make your own home candles. You will clean the candle before using any candle in your rituals, and lubricate it with a small amount of oil during the moon's growing period. This light up the candle and loads it with magical energy. You may also use these energies to carve or paint fitting magic symbols on your candles to strengthen them further. The warm Atame peak will do you a good job. It is better to use a ritual or magic candle and not use a candle previously used for another purpose.

Candle magic is one of the most basic ways of spell casting. This method is considered sympathetic magic and does not require ritual or ceremonial instruments. Basically, the strategy is to agree with the target and envision the end result. Then concentrate your intention or will to manifest this result by lighting the candle.

White candles

Balance of all colors. They symbolize peace, purity, innocence, and the power of the higher nature. Promoting peace, tranquility, purification, truth, spirituality, and sincerity. It is also used for meditation, truth, self-seeking, spiritual enlightenment, summoning spiritual guides, astral travel, and for strengthening psychic abilities. They can be as strong a protective as black and can replace any color candle. Healing properties include treating broken bones, relieving toothache, and increasing milk production in nursing mothers.

Red candles

The fiery, invigorating color of energy and life. Always associated with blood, birth and death, and gender. They are associated with love, passion, fertility, physical energy, and strength. They increase magnetism in rituals and are used in defensive magic. They also express feelings of courage and enthusiasm. They are good at magic for health, strength, and vitality. They are used in the treatment of neuralgia and exhaustion. Red symbolizes the element of fire.

Pink candles

A positive color that symbolizes emotional love, nurturing relationships, and romance. Promoting spiritual awakening, healing of the spirit, femininity, friendships, honor, and morals. Standard colors for rituals, to attract feelings and bring friends, lively conversations at the dinner table. Excellent for treating anxiety and depression as well as heart disease.

Orange candles

Stimulating and toning color. It is associated with attraction, stimulation, control, personal strength, power, and power. Also, encouragement, adaptability, luck, and sudden changes. Attracts features from other instruments, spells, and rituals. Very good for treating coughs, colds, and asthma, as well as arthritis and exhaustion.

Yellow candles

Stimulating and inspiring color, which is the color of creativity, intelligence, confidence, movement, and energy. It is associated with clairvoyance, divination, wisdom, life, imagination, and inspiration, as well as the power of concentration and communication. It is used in the treatment of skin diseases, as well as stomach complaints and menstrual cramps. Yellow symbolizes the element air.

Green candles

The color that is associated with nature, fertility, and rejuvenation. Stimulating work related to financial matters and money; and promoting good luck, well-being, luck, ambition, and success. Carrying love and renewal, green is an emotional pacifier and balancer used to counteract greed and envy. Good color for the treatment of headaches, colds, and nervousness. Green is the color of the Earth element.

Blue candles

A cool color that soothes and relaxes. Blue is the primary spiritual color used in rituals to obtain wisdom, serenity, harmony, peace, inner light, and truth. It is associated with inspiration, occult power, protection, understanding, good health, patience, and loyalty. Help with meditation as it connects with the intellect and mind. Promoting happiness, laughter, and cheerful disposition. It is used in the treatment of insomnia, high blood pressure, and small wounds. Blue symbolizes the element of water.

Indigo candles

Vitalizing the color of inertia; used to cleanse the spirit and remove fear. It is used in rituals that require a deep meditative state to neutralize other magic or counteract negative energy. Treatment applications include dementia, depression, and mental disorders.

Purple or purple candles

A vibrating color that is strong spiritually and traditionally associated with mysticism, inspiration, wisdom, idealism, purification, success, peace, and strength. Help with meditation, sensitivity, and higher psychic talents, as well as associating with idealism, ambition, power, success, and protecting households. Treatment applications include the treatment of allergies, sleep disorders, and stress-related disorders.

Purple candles

A combination of red and purple, very high vibration frequency, which works quickly. It energizes rituals that require immediate action and high levels of energy or spiritual healing, such as rapid change, exorcism, or spiritual healing.

Brown candles

Earthy, balanced color, used to attract money and financial success. Help for emotional stability and balance, eliminate indecision, improve concentration, study, intuition, and telepathy. Also related to finding lost items. Assistance in the protection and healing of pets.

Golden candles

A color that promotes understanding and attracts the forces of cosmic influences, intuition, persuasion, charm, and confidence. Favorable in rituals designed to achieve quick success or financial benefits.

Silver or gray candles

Neutral color. Remove negative energy or influence and enhance stability. It is useful when thinking about complex questions during meditation and magic. Reject or neutralize when necessary. They help to developmental abilities.

Black candles

Burned for positive purposes, they open deeper levels of the subconscious. Black is used in rituals to evoke a state of deep meditation and is good for banishing evil or negativism. It is associated with self-control, quiet strength and endurance, absorbing and destroying negativity. Offer strength and support in spells; protect from retribution and help during the loss.

The colors and days of the week

- ➤ Sunday - Yellow
- ➤ Monday – White
- ➤ Tuesday - Red
- ➤ Wednesday - Purple
- ➤ Thursday - Blue
- ➤ Friday - Green
- ➤ Saturday – Black

how to Preparing the Ritual Candles

Each ritual is an act of magic itself. Carried out according to specific guidelines, it works with the force of the laws of physics, according to which the triggered reactions bring the expected results.

If we are going to perform any ritual, we need a place where we will do it, a place that will also serve concentration and meditation. This place will be our kind of altar.

Preparing the altar is very easy. You just have first to choose the right place in your home, a quiet place where no one will disturb us and which should be a permanent place for rituals. It should always be clean, free from possible negative energies.

Place a table or stool here and cover it with a white napkin. The table should be either round or square. The place for the altar and table should be wiped with water mixed half and half with vinegar.

On the table, in addition to the items needed for a specific ritual, there should always be a glass of water, a small plate with salt or earth, one white candle that should always burn during the ritual, and a stand with incense. These objects symbolize the four elements: Water, Earth, Fire and Air.

You can also put on it a picture with the image of a saint, whom we consider our patron, an angel figure, precious stones, a vase of flowers. You should never put flowers on it, and at all have dried flowers at home because they mean dead energy. Artificial flowers are already better.

Now we can start performing the ritual, remembering that each of them consists of five basic moments:

- **Preparation.** First, we need to choose a ritual that is to help us solve a specific problem, collect all the necessary elements, place them on the table, choose the right day, time of day, phase of the moon. It is also good to take a cleansing bath. It can be rinsed after a basic bath, e.g., with salt water (a handful of salt per liter of water), or washing with coconut soap, which, like salt, removes all negative energies and attracts positive vibrations.
- **Invocation.** This is the moment when we recognize the power and Higher power that we ask for protection and intercession. We use our own words, sincere and flowing from the heart. It is a kind of prayer that should be related to the purpose of the ritual, to our request. You can also say the Our Father or the Hail Mary.
- **Request.** We should write down our request on a piece of paper. Formerly parchment was used for this, but today it is enough that it will be a blank sheet of paper. The card should then be folded in four so that the text of the request is in the middle.
- **Carrying out the ritual.** Here we follow the recommendations of a specific ritual.
- **End of the ritual, and thanks.** When we finish the ritual, we burn the note with our request in the candle flame. Wrap the resulting ash together with the remains of the burnt candles in tissue and either throw it into a bin, or bury it (without a tissue) in the ground, or throw it (also without a tissue) into flowing water. Thank you for listening to the energies summoned during the ritual, for protection during the ritual, and, in advance, for achieving the purpose for which it was carried out.

CHAPTER EIGHT
Witchcraft Symbols and sign

There are hundreds of different symbols of witchcraft, and each of them has its own use and significance. Many of these symbols of witchcraft are now well known and are still used in modern Christianity.

Different witchcraft symbols are meaningful. Even the simplest symbols used by craftsmen can have nuanced, highly suggestive meanings. Simple and complex witchcraft symbols may be used to decorate personal products, magic objects, or they are used in spell functioning; symbols essentially contain strong meanings that come to reflect beliefs, customs, philosophies, activities, feelings, thoughts, or they serve as an emblem that simplifies abstract ideas or concepts.

The Symbols of Witchcraft

Certain symbols have been used since the dawn of time in the practice of witchcraft. Each of them is heavy with meaning and can be used in different types of magic rituals or worn in the form of an amulet, which diffuses its powers. Here are the seven most famous symbols of witchcraft and their meaning.

1. The Triple Moon
Among the symbols of witchcraft, this consists of a full moon surrounded by two crescent moons. It is thus associated with the phases of the moon and, therefore, by extension, with the cycle of life and with perpetual renewal. It promotes unity, especially in Celtic culture.

2. The Triple Circle
This famous symbol, represented by a triskele, has been used by the Druids since the dawn of time. It is associated with nature and the four elements that make it up: air, water, earth, and fire. It is an eminently feminine symbol that evokes a perfect harmony between body and mind. It is often used in the form of a talisman.

3. The Heptagram
The heptagram is a star with seven branches, and it is a particularly powerful symbol. The number seven is endowed with incredible powers and is linked to various elements, such as the seven colors of the rainbow or the seven planetary zones. This symbol represents the harmony of the cosmos on all planes.

4. The Pentagram
The five-pointed star is one of the most important symbols of witchcraft, and one of the oldest as well. It can be used in a wide variety of magical rituals, as it symbolizes the union of the cosmos. It is also very frequently used as a lucky charm, thanks to its famous virtues of good fortune.

5. The Pentacle
One of the most well-known symbols of witchcraft is the pentacle, represented by a star drawn in one stroke and contained in a circle. It symbolizes the unity between nature, with its elements, and the ether, which represents the spirit.

6. The Mother Goddess and Cerunos
This symbol represents the feminine and is well known in the Wicca religion, practiced by witches. Its male equivalent is Cerunos, a horned god who symbolizes male power. These two symbols of witchcraft are not enemies but are related. They are revered and very frequently used in rituals.

7. The Oval Cross
Very well known in ancient Egypt, this symbol is mainly used in protection rituals. It also has benefits on fertility and longevity: it would allow you to live longer, even forever ...

Signs That I Have Considered Identifiers of a Witch

Power of The Earth. A witch is a woman of the moon manifested on earth. Heir to the knowledge and ability to develop her psyche. The transformer of realities, healers, and capable of carrying out rebirths. These are the powers of the woman, one with heaven and with the earth.

Do you find the answers to life through the patterns of mother nature? Is their wisdom your wisdom? Are you, your life, your body aligned with the seasons?

For example, do you find yourself highly sexual and creative in the summer, letting go and cutting what doesn't work in the fall, dying of age in the dark silence of winter, and being reborn in the spring?

Wisdom. People come to you to ask for advice about their life, they ask you about pain, love, life...

In your nature you find that you are a woman or a man who send hope to their hearts, and

what you tell them, that advice that you have given them have changed their perspective of life to improve,

you even find yourself gifted tinctures, aromas, remedies, natural things for your healing?

Nature Do you live near or in a forest, or has it always been your desire to live in a place surrounded by nature? Contact with nature is very important to you, and can it be restorative and healing?

Witches, intertwined with nature, which incorporates the powers of the Great Mother herself, perform their rituals in the water or in the forest since that is where they feel their home is.

The Storms. You are not afraid of storms. In fact, they revel in the power of Mother Nature, sometimes wondering if yourself - your passion and energy - caused the storm?

Animal Nature. Animals are naturally attracted to you, and you feel a deep love for them, a great empathy towards all beings in nature. You naturally know who your

totems are, and you find wisdom and insight in their visits, stray dogs follow you home, birds fly in your windows, horses rush to you in the fields, did you know you can talk to animals?

Witches and animals are so aligned with nature that they speak a similar energetic language and recognize each other.

The Moon. Even without knowing what phase or sign the moon is in, are you significantly affected by its transit? Have you found yourself talking to her, have you been enlightened with her light since you were a child? Is it aligned with its phases?

For example, unconsciously, you find that you are devising new projects or starting them when the moon coincidentally is in its new phase. Or you find yourself completing projects or relationships when the moon is in its waning phase.

On the New Moon, on the darkest nights, do you sit with the mystery, the void and unknown, the potential and the possibility of darkness? Do you dream of new plans in the dark of the new moon?

Power Do you suspect that your wishes are coming true - good or bad, and it turns out that you have become cautious about this as you are afraid of your own power? Have you ever been called an old soul, an indigo child, a crystal, or a rainbow?

Witches are as old as time; her eyes - they are indeed the windows to her soul - hold ancient stories and secrets, myths and mysteries, answers and possibilities.

You can probably find yourself talking about very old truths and wisdom, even - or especially - as if you had lived it yesterday.

Healing. Are you attracted to the healing arts? Do you tend to seek natural or energetic remedies for yourself, and is that what you offer to others? Have you ever laid a hand on someone's back injury, and did it heal the next day? People can also heal just by being around you.

Witches, being so in tune with the earth, are natural healers.

Memories of Past Lives Do you have painful memories of past lives or images of being thrown from somewhere, burned or drowned - just for being savage, wise, and liberal? There are some witches who are currently afraid of confinement, jail, fire, torture, rape, etc. ... images come in dreams. They are hermits.

Most importantly, are you scarred for being different, not satisfied, for loving who you wanted to love, for telling the truth / saying what you had to say- in an old life? This is the karma that is awake to heal. It is time not to be afraid and to be you.

You may not know this, but many witches have returned in this era to heal their memories and to be totally free.

How are you going to heal your karma? Freeing yourself from fear, freeing you from slavery, expressing yourself totally as you are.

Strange Have you always felt a little strange- you have even felt privileged to know or know or see things that others do not even suspect.

You do not fit the norm, and you are different, you know that there is something sacred in you, secret, special - that only others like you can see and above all understand.

You don't like crowds; you are more like a sensitive but powerful lone wolf; you need a lot of time to think, dream, recharge, and live with the Source - Nature / The Universe / The Goddess. It is very difficult for you to adapt to society.

Crystals Attraction / are drawn to beautiful rocks - pieces of the energy of the earth - and have kept stones like clear quartz, turquoise, rose quartz around them for as long as you can remember, even if you didn't know its properties at the moment.

They introduce themselves to you, and you pick them up on the way.

Witches know the properties of earth stones and work - among other things - healing, love, abundance, and protection benefits, and are often using their special stones in jewelry.

They also like to keep candles around - because candles are invitations to spirits and angels, and create a more magical divine atmosphere. And you probably like good, sage or incense to clear energy.

Magic. Do you believe in magic as a child, do you see the magic in the air and in life? Were you drawn to magical things, creatures, fables, stories, even as you got older, despite everyone saying "there was no such thing?"

Your life is even surrounded by magic creating at every moment and manifesting everything you want.

Even though the rest of the world doesn't believe, were

you draw to movies and books about witches, magic, the creepy, the mystical, the unknowable? Have you always thought that there was no such thing as a coincidence, that we were not very alone, and this is not all there was?

More Magic and Divination: Speaking of signs and symbols - you get premonitions like you have an internal crystal ball. When you hear a person speak somewhere about you, the image and connection of that event are being revealed, and you are obtaining more information than what they tell you.

Sometimes you see or feel flashforwards - you have dreams and visions of past lives and the future. You can read other people and their energy and intentions quite well. You have a sixth sense. It is also a reason why they are drawn to the Tarot, Runes, or other divinations.

CHAPTER NINE
What are runes?

Runes are old symbols of a lost Germanic alphabet that was based on a mythology that focused on the idea of a tree that supported all the planets, which had three sources, a sacred one of destiny, the second one had the power to give and regenerate life and the last the force of knowledge, science and wisdom. The origin of the rune's dates from 100 BC and its use was implemented until 1600 AD. The best known of the currently known Rune collections is the Ancient Futhark, also called the Germanic Futhark, consisting of 24 symbols, each representing a letter of the alphabet and also a condition, characteristic, or feeling.

The shamans understood that the runes were a divine revelation, given with love and with the intention that they would bring benefits to humanity through the understanding of how nature worked and how the guidelines that are in it also reside in human beings. The use of Runes today has been focused on the search for wisdom and prediction of the future, Hundreds of seers and people who study the Tarot use these pieces in order to open a gap between the present and the future to study the confines of that mystical mythology.

The ancients knew that all things are full of runic power; all things had their runes. Runes are keys that operate within the causal worlds of the cosmos. They are symbols that come and act on behalf of the forces they represent. The magician who uses them is in charge of directing the forces through a ritual act and thus being able to transform, manipulate, and intensify the forces. These forces manifest themselves according to the laws inscribed on a rune, the Perth rune. In runic magic, there are mainly two forces involved. These are psychic and dynamic.

Dynamic forces are more mechanical and largely devoid of what we might call consciousness or will. Runes, in general, would be part of this force, although they possess a certain degree of animism.

The Magic of Runic Talismans

This is one of the most widely used runic magic systems. Talismanic magic or ties, as it is known in popular terminology, is about using an object that will carry the person it is going to affect. For this, a piece of wood from a tree is usually used. You should choose a tree and please ask to leave one of its branches. To know their response, you must visualize or wait for some stimulating sensation. This may sound picturesque, but the effectiveness will be greater. By this act, we do not consider a tree or an animal to be inferior.

The universal language of all beings in the cosmos is that which is expressed through the Wyrd (synchronicity) with sensations, mental images, intuitions, etc. that one (the magician) knows how to notice, and through which we can communicate with the use of runes.

Once the branch is selected, the magic runes that have that end will be written on it. This is done by imagining what you want to happen by symbolically translating it into runes. For this, it is convenient to have at hand the meaning of each of the runes to be used, at least within the context of the situation to be treated.

Examples of talismans with runes

An example would be that you are going on a long trip and wish you had good luck. For this, you should use (For example), the Fehu, Radio, Wunjo and Sowilo runes. The first two are associated with movement and travel. Wunjo is a bearer of harmony and union. And Sowelu is a rune of luck and victory. If the journey is dangerous and risky, you could add Nauthiz, since this rune helps you cope with the situations that are beyond you.

If you need help to get love, you should use, for example, Kenaz, Gebo, Berkana, and Wunjo. If it is a love that you want to last, you could add Ehwaz. Regarding the moral value of trying to provoke the desired love, the magic of love is more effective when love is true. Otherwise, it gets used to bouncing (it will lead to long-term rejection).

If you want to gain a defense against an enemy, a good choice is the Thurisaz, Teiwaz, Sowilo, Ansuz, or Isa runes. If it is more powerful, one can help with Nauthiz.

How to use the Runes

First of all, it is convenient to understand the magic laws of runic magic. The magician, before doing rune magic, should know the nature of each rune so that his forces are more fruitful and effective. Perth's law directs the rune forces in the sense that it has been imposed. There are two systems of the use of runes, and one would be the Stadhagaldr and the other the talismanic magic.

The first is to adopt the position of the rune as a Yoga posture, pronounce the Galdr of the rune and visualize the rune.

Mythological origin

The manifestation of the runes and their ordering in the Futhark is linked to cosmological and cosmographic processes, similar to astrology. In the division between the Muspellheimr and Niflheim, the runic forces are polarized into bright runes (Heidhrúnar) and dark runes (myrkrúnar). They are the opposite aspects of the runic power of the body, which, at the same time, constitute a duality. And as in all duality, the law of the opposite poles, ying-yang, these runic forces attract each other to unify and create the cosmic seed contained in Ymir.

The runes were obtained by Odin as a shamanic experience. These can be achieved in altered states of consciousness, as narrated by Hávamál. This experience can be done in countless ways according to tradition, but it requires effort and daily training.

Runes and Meanings

1. Fehu rune

Cattle, ram, herd land, movable possession, fertility, wealth, chaos, fire, energy, gold, money.

It is the proto-German word for "Cattle," or it can also be understood as "mobile wealth." It is a word to designate money, quota, money flows, referring more to wealth assets (goods, income, possessions).

It also represents the bovine with its outstanding horns, although the influence of the Latin letter "F" is also evident in the form of this alphabetic character.

The bovine is known to have been a cult animal among English princes, of whom Tacitus says they worshiped Mother Earth, under the name Nerthus, whose processional chariot was drawn with cows. The use in English and Nordic of the rune restricts the meaning of "wealth" and the notion of "cattle," having been lost in later languages; In some passages, Fehu has connotations of "princely treasure," with all the associations of ancient glory and personal honor of the highly valued Germanic peoples.

Meaning like talisman

The Fehu rune, like a talisman or amulet, is appropriate for happiness and well-being. It also provides love, fertility, and abundance. It is also called the rune of wealth (even in the sense of spiritual wealth), hence it is widely used to increase economic wealth and protect things of value.

Magical qualities

Earnings, love, fortune, wealth. Material possessions, cattle.

It also represents the energy of the Big-Bang and the primary fire.

Love. Loving conquests and unexpected emotions will make you discover the most pleasant side of life.

Work and money. Interesting proposals and good opportunities to work. New financial possibilities and a streak of good luck. We must not forget new meetings, projects, and initiatives.

Health. The strong "physical" character inherent in the symbolic meaning of this rune, may also provide a surplus of creativity with the joys or problems of chaos.

2. Uruz rune

Brute strength, vigor, male sexual potency, virility, health, even aggressiveness, but also bravery and courage.

The Uruz rune is the rune of magic power and vitality. Represents retained energy, earth energy, primitive energy, outbreaks, and the result of constancy.

It is useful in healing magic, to maintain good health and promote new situations in life. It gives strength.

The Uruz rune is probably the word of the Uros, a kind of primitive cattle with which the Germanic youths tested their courage and skill with weapons; hence it can have a translation that means "virility, vigor." The horns of the beast were highly prized, and drinking vessels were made from them, by adding elaborate metal accessories.

Meaning like talisman

Help against sadness, illness, and discord. It provides inner strength, constancy, and firmness, iron will.

Uruz represents important achievements but will require effort. Sudden onset of new situations.

Magical qualities

Health, progress, endurance, energy, the strength of spirit, and body.

Love. You can experience moments of rapturing passion, but rather rampant. You have to be careful; it can only be a bet with Eros himself. It is necessary to accept the risks only if there are patience and perseverance.

Work and money. New responsibilities in the professional field. A series of agreements will provide good possibilities for progress in the profession, but doubts about one's abilities can cause little adaptation, so uncertainties can arise when taking on tasks that may be heavy or superior to one's abilities. Good internal discipline can ensure success.

Health. It is mistakenly believed that there are more than enough resources to jump headlong into any physical activity or effort. On the contrary, this rune advises to tone the body and avoid the stress of any kind.

3. Thurisaz rune

Giant, thorn, magic, herculean force, storm, quarrelsome character, protection.

The Thurisaz rune is a powerful but very heavy rune. It has three meanings. The first is the giant def Thurs, being of the oldest generation of the gods. From here comes the strength of this rune. The second meaning: the god Thor. The outlines of the rune present Thor's hammer: Mjolnir. In this sense, it represents the defensive cosmic force, the pure will. It contains the life-death polarity and with-it regeneration.

Its third meaning is that of Door.

In the case of Thurs, it is a kind of evil creature that is often translated as "giant," although perhaps "demon" or "sorcerer" is closer to the original idea. The name of this rune was altered in Anglo-Saxon England from þorn "stinger," because of its shape, and brought to manuscripts to represent the sound "th" (Þ, þ).

Meaning like talisman

The rune shows the negative force behind illness and serves to recognize it and prevent its negative effect. It is used in magic as protection and defense (neutralizing enemies), projection or renewal of personality, and to force results in love magic. It provides inner strength and spiritual authority.

Magical qualities

Notice, transforming force, renewal, protection, defense.

Esoteric meaning

We can say that the Thurisaz rune is the effective, but brutal, triggering of events. There may or may not be a pain, but it announces a new life. In any case, if there were, we could say that they are growing pains that have to happen to go to the next level in your personal or inner growth. This does not mean that a bad change will happen.

Love. The oracle is not one of the happiest since fatality, and the unforeseen is inscribed in the meaning of this rune that, in its divinatory sense, is linked to the deepest impulses of the self, to the most primitive instincts and, as such, destructive. Consequently, rather than having to do with the deceptions devised by others or by someone who is truly an enemy, it is the individual himself who has to safeguard and know how to grasp the true essence of all spiritual manifestation.

Work and money. The advice of this rune is to reflect long before taking any action or dive headlong into any undertaking, which only apparently seems to offer real chances of success.

Health. This rune comes to tell us that prudence should guide all actions and allow us to accept for the moment that phase of decline, which unfortunately is felt in the different areas, especially in the immediate reality, and therefore also affects the physical plane.

4. Uruz rune

Brute strength, vigor, male sexual potency, virility, health, even aggressiveness, but also bravery and courage.

The Uruz rune is the rune of magic power and vitality. Represents retained energy, earth energy, primitive energy, outbreaks, and the result of constancy.

It is useful in healing magic, to maintain good health and promote new situations in life. It gives strength.

The Uruz rune is probably the word of the Uros, a kind of primitive cattle with which the Germanic youths tested their courage and skill with weapons; hence it can have a translation that means "virility, vigor." The horns of the beast were highly prized, and drinking vessels were made from them, by adding elaborate metal accessories.

Meaning like talisman

Help against sadness, illness, and discord. It provides inner strength, constancy, and firmness, iron will.

Uruz represents important achievements but will require effort. Sudden onset of new situations.

Magical qualities

Health, progress, endurance, energy, the strength of spirit, and body.

Love. You can experience moments of rapturing passion, but rather rampant. You have to be careful; it can only be a bet with Eros himself. It is necessary to accept the risks only if there are patience and perseverance.

Work and money. New responsibilities in the professional field. A series of agreements will provide good possibilities for progress in the profession, but doubts about one's abilities can cause little adaptation, so uncertainties can arise when taking on tasks that may be heavy or superior to one's abilities. Good internal discipline can ensure success.

Health. It is mistakenly believed that there are more than enough resources to jump headlong into any physical activity or effort. On the contrary, this rune advises to tone the body and avoid the stress of any kind.

5. Raidho rune

Riding, advice, movement, dance, rhythm, wheel of life, four elements.

The Raidno rune represents the act of "riding" or when this occurs, the "way." The two modern senses have been separated from the only original idea of "road" by which one decides to travel.

Raidho also represents the cosmic law of order and law. It is the mystery of the divine law that is manifested in humanity (spiritual path).

This rune may have been used as a travel amulet, as a modern "Saint Christopher" medallion, or to hasten the dead on the road to Hel. Many Anglo-Saxon funeral urns feature a heavy "chevron" (Insignia or mark in the shape of an inverted V or V) as decoration, where a group of serials "R-runes" can be reflected.

Meaning like talisman

This rune transmits strength, reconciliation, purification (even of oneself). It provides patience and prevents risk-taking too quickly. It helps adapt to the flow of life, letting it run its course. It is very suitable for travel (also spiritual).

Raidho in magic is used as a protector and security in travel and in legal affairs to obtain justice.

Magical qualities

Journey, soul, foreigner, road, journey, justice

Any trip promotes an evolution, which involves an internal change, an open mind, a search for new goals. So, we could say that he may also be talking about internal and external renewal.

Esoteric meaning

The Raidho rune comes to indicate changes in life or displacement. The changes will be at the individual level and will open new paths.

Love. Fantasy and feelings are dominant. Thus, for many, a constant flow of visual images and creations is assured and impalpable in which beauty will prevail over any aspect of practical utility. With this rune, love and sexual incontinence are exalted, which can make life exciting, interesting, and lively.

Work and money. Accumulating experience and in-depth study will undoubtedly be beneficial for those who want to start new professions or conquer important positions in their careers, while those who feel already accomplished will live situations in which order and perfection, perseverance, and method will prevail.

Health. There are no excessive problems. In any case, outdoor walks and breathing exercises are advisable.

6. Kenaz rune

Torch, fire, primitive fire, light, mirror, lighting.

Fire as an element gives the Kenaz rune, also known as Cen, Kennaz, Kaun, Kusma, the property of lighting, vibrating, allowing better vision, purifying. The Teutons believed that fire was one of the basic components that made up the world; the other was ice.

Kano, another name of the rune, means canoe, means of transportation to get to the other shore. Another possible interpretation is desire, a fire that ignites passion. In the Aettir, it symbolizes the encounter with pleasure in the unconscious realm and the use of intelligence in the conscious.

Meaning like talisman

Increase courage and skills; provides inspiration and a will to live. It serves to develop creative skills; helps solve problems.

The Kenaz rune also deals with the demons of disease; It helps to expel them and thus be able to treat the disease.

It is the rune of the magicians (a rune of protection against enchantments), of the artist and of the craftsman, embodies knowledge and wisdom. It is passion, desire; it is the emotional root of man. Communicate with the ancestors. It is seeing, recognizing.

Magical quality

Enthusiasm, dynamism, desire, purifying fire, place of offerings, self-awareness, spontaneity, openness, giving, and offering.

In magic, Kenaz is used to start works with creative nuances, for stability and passion in relationships, for healing and physical well-being, and to protect things of value.

The Kenaz rune is also the rune of lovers, artists, even craftsmen.

Esoteric meaning

The time has come to emerge from the darkness. Kaunaz lights your way. The best conditions for you to advance on your path are emerging or are going to emerge.

Love. The oracle with the Kenaz rune advises assessing very well all the pros and cons of a possible union first, because it may happen that a couple is found who acts calculatively and is too interested. Care must be taken, even if it involves a certain effort, in all situations. The ideal would be to escape the usual routine by studying, for example, the mysterious signs of esoteric languages.

Work and money. Kenaz tells us that it is time to act. When approaching any company, it will be necessary to use the reason that will undoubtedly open the way for the realization and conquest of new spaces. It is important, in any case, not to light up in easy enthusiasm, because unforeseen events can arise that force you to weigh each one of your own acts or elections.

Health. Kenaz indicates that overall health is good, although it is advisable to follow a less stressful lifestyle. Since a desire for exoticism can mentally take you far, it is advisable, when traveling, to explore new and mysterious places.

7. Gebo rune

Gift, gift, exchange, compensation, the balance between giving, and taking.

The Gebo rune is the "act of giving," as well as the thing given. It is a bestowal on a companion or a sacrifice to the gods.

Gift-giving was a central theme in Germanic culture, creating bonds of mutual loyalty and obligation throughout society helped to hold communities together and establish links between distant parts of Germanic Europe.

Warriors were publicly honored at parties where they were presented with presents such as lands, treasures, warfare, and items of personal equipment as a sign of their success, loyalty, and courage. The one who gives, by inference, also increases his prestige by proving himself willing and able to offer magnificent gifts.

In this way, the Gebo rune represents everything that has to do with societies; Union, society, gift, gift, marriage

Meaning like talisman

Protection against disease; Helps to find friends and partner; It is a rune of help in case the counterattack is required in the spells.

It is widely used to help find friends and partners.

Magical qualities

It means gift and represents generosity, gratitude, forgiveness. A friendship, partner, union or partnership may be approaching. It represents the power to integrate the energies of two or more people, to produce a greater force. It is used in the magic of love and sex, to increase magical powers, for the union of couples and societies.

Esoteric meaning

Gebo is the most favorable rune for relationships. Generosity and peace are fostered by sharing.

Love. It is the rune of mutual attraction and elective affinities. Giving and possessing become the only important thing. Chasing dreams and taking advantage of the present moment will become a necessity and a relief at the same time. Therefore, love will automatically enrich itself precisely because of the symbolic influence of this rune. It is also possible to contemplate the possibility of marriage or, in any case, the idea of creating a family, if you are single, it will be advisable to trust in some new experience or friendship.

Work and money. There is no need to over-fatigue, as everything that has been done or is being done is sufficient to ensure proper satisfaction. In any case, you should not stop accepting new offers made for fear of not being up to the task. It will soon be seen that everything is much simpler than it seems. Otherwise, there will be an agenda rich in important commitments.

Health. The Gebo rune indicates that this is the best time to start a healing treatment that, through movement, restores the nervous system as well as muscle agility, attenuating pain, and tension.

8. Wunjo rune

Delight, joy, luck, happiness, flag.

The Wunjo rune is literally translated from English as a conquest. To win out means to succeed, succeed, succeed, and that is the sense that prevails over the other runic interpretations.

Wunjo is the name given to it by the Germans, Winja, and Wynn, it is in Old English, and its remote meaning is a jewel.

The Wunjo rune, like the state of perfection achieved by a diamond when worked by human hands, reminds us of the painstaking spiritual work we have to carry out to fulfill our mission.

Meaning like talisman

Wunjo is a rune of luck; it provides joy, happiness, glory, and friends.

The Wunjo rune is the amulet that stimulates inner growth, the enjoyment of the results obtained, the happiness of having walked the path to success, or an expected result, especially at work and in love.

Magical qualities

Joy, glory, happiness, victory.

In magic, it is used for satisfaction in any field, especially at work and in love, and also on trips. It is used to unite other forces or runes.

It is the result of a long period of work resulting from the use of moderation to achieve.

Wunjo does not indicate something surprising, so the term glory fits him better than that of joy. Glory is conquered; it is molded every day. It has solidity (reached by the stages that forged it). Joy, in turn, can be momentary, external, temporary, the result of a stroke of luck.

Love. Special moments will be lived that will allow the person to be selective in their actions and promises, the most favored being those who precisely like to be the center of attention. Love impulses and feelings will be reaffirmed or renewed.

Work and money. Skill and talent are the ingredients to achieve success, which will be especially for those who have given a new impetus to their profession. In any case, it will be necessary to be measured against adversaries who will show to be rather inconsiderate and disrespectful, becoming somewhat less diplomatic than usual.

Health. Although this is an aspect that does not worry too much, and not without reason, nevertheless, you should take more hours of rest and carry out light physical activity constantly, preferably daily. This will better strengthen the character.

9. Hagalaz rune

Hail, destruction and creation, primitive violence, spiritual force, harmony, fertility, the balance of forces

The Hagalaz rune means "grain." In English, Icelandic and Nordic Rune Poems, everyone refers to it as a kind of "hail"; it is the first of the so-called "winter runes."

Meaning like talisman

With the Hagalaz rune, the internal and external balance is produced again. Helps to face the demands of everyday life bravely. It helps create strength by going through the dark side of consciousness.

It is a slow but safe evolution rune, and due to its fixed nature, it favors security and prevents negative energies from entering your space.

It is a rune of friendship and provides stability and firmness.

Magical qualities

Divine Justice, alert, interruption.

In principle, Hagalaz may seem like a negative rune, since it tells us of a normally unforeseen event that causes us to have a bad time. But we must bear in mind that after the storm comes calm. A beautiful calm that often comes loaded with opportunities.

After the hail storm that represents the Hagalaz rune comes a new day with a beautiful rainbow, a day full of renewed and stronger energies.

In magic, the Hagalaz rune is used to bring about the positive result of a fact, also as a protector against natural obstacles and storms.

Love. Hagalaz Indicates a particularly difficult period to overcome, but it will be above all the desire for freedom and the fear of encountering experiences that are not very gratifying, also from the spiritual point of view, that will restrain any impulse. It is as if one were thrown into a sea of instincts in which sex played a leading and exciting role, being fueled by eccentric fantasies. Care must be taken, however, to avoid excessive fun.

Work and money. Hagalaz indicates that a tiring period is contemplated; therefore, it will be necessary to face all the small or big problems of daily life with a positive spirit, making ideological or political aspirations more incisive and all this linking it to the reality of life.

Health. Despite some problems that are not easily solved, it is necessary to worry more about yourself, and giving more value to the rhythm of life, will combine in the best possible way physical form and inner balance.

10. Nauthiz rune

Need, pressure, destiny, obstacle, imperative, overcoming

The Nauthiz rune means "need, anguish" (and maybe a euphemism for "death"). It is the antithesis of the Wunjo rune.

Old English describes Nýd as 'Wyrda heardost,' "the harshest of events," and its range of meanings seems to cover all kinds of physical deprivation and negative emotion.

It represents a kind of adversity that can act as a test of moral strength. It also comes to represent the cosmic force that forms the "destinies" of humanity and the world, the need and the lack, but also the end of hardship.

Meaning like talisman

It provides protection, defense, creativity, karma, patience, the wealth of ideas, and the achievement of peace; let things work.

Magical qualities

Struggles, obstacles, pain, need, crossroads, separation.

The Nauthiz rune has great power in the magic of love, and it is used to find a lover, it gives strength to overcome suffering and crises and to achieve goals. Using it with force, you can change destiny.

Esoteric meaning

The Nauthiz rune indicates an interior crisis, painful but necessary learning, because it is what hurts from within but can make us react.

Love. In the affective field, a rather difficult relationship is contemplated. Difficulties that have to be faced because of an untrustworthy partner can make life bitter. Anyone who has to legalize a union is advised to wait a bit longer to weigh the pros and cons well.

Work and money. The Nauthiz rune indicates a period of many efforts and new burdens, not all of which is gratifying; For this reason, there will often be deceit and controversy. This is a period in which responsibilities must be assumed.

Health. Nauthiz tells us that calm and caution are the best antidotes to improve the current psychophysical situation, thus also warding off the terror of disease.

11.   rune Isa

Ice, freezing, immobility, coldness, containment

The Isa rune is "ice," a fitting partner for Hagalaz and the last of the "winter runes" before Jera 's "spring." In the Germanic tradition, ice was the primeval solid matter from which it was created or released through the action of its opponent, fire.

Meaning like talisman

The Isa rune gives inner firmness, strength, will, self-awareness, patience, and personality. Strengthens the interior of human beings.

Magical qualities

Cold, distance, strength, firmness, will, inaction, inertia, paralysis, be calm, reflect before acting.

It represents the ego and governs the forces of inertia. Isa in magic is used to develop the will, to stop a situation, to stop unwanted forces, to prevent something unwanted from advancing.

Esoteric meaning

The Isa rune means ice, and therefore it is fundamentally speaking of immobility. He warns that it is time not to act. Rather, it encourages us to stop and reflect before acting.

Love. The appearance of the Isa rune symbolically initiates the period of "thaw," which, after a stage of stagnation, makes a person less available. That's why it's wise to accept new invitations, project new unions, and return to the light, fun, and exciting love climate.

Work and money. Isa indicates that work will be positively influenced by this rune. Profits are assured, and some new projects will return to interest in order to favor, especially the financial field, so there will be some profitable operation in the short term.

Health. Although everyone wants to age less quickly and avoid any disease, the Isa rune warns us that it will be advisable to control your own energy rhythm, especially the circadian, that regulates the sleep-wake cycle.

12. Jera rune

Year, season, spring, life cycle, perfection, beginning, time, the spiral of life.

The Jera rune represents the "year," both the time measurement and the harvest cycle, but excluding the winter months. It comes to refer to the time of flowering, to spring. It has strong associations with the fertility of the land and with fruitful crops.

Jera, therefore, represents the reward for past actions. It is the rune of the harvest and the reward.

Meaning like talisman

This rune protects friends in battle. Promote a good harvest after hard work and exhaustion. Jera is also a help in life-changing moments.

It provides a positive state of mind and high morale, which are powerful weapons for success in life.

Magical qualities

Time, justice, triumph, success, reward.

In magic, it is used as an aid in legal matters. It gives fertility for tangible matters of any kind.

Esoteric meaning

The Jera rune predicts that justice will be done, and they will give us what they deserve, no more and no less. It is long-awaited. What should be, what is fair.

Love. Jera indicates that there is an intense bond with the loved one, and serious ties are emerging; moments of nostalgia and long-range wishes may accentuate the temptations to escape, which is generally inherent as if it were united by a magical fluid. A promising future.

Work and money. Many previously pursued job opportunities will be consolidated, obtaining tangible recognition. In the legal field, some pending problems may create complications of various kinds, which can be overcome in any case by patience and time.

Health. The Jera rune indicates some innovation on an emotional level and certain external impulses that may cause unpleasant disorders that should not be underestimated.

13. Perth rune

Mystery, secret, luck. The hidden, the new. Wizard

Perth is by far the most enigmatic rune, in part because the value of its sound was a rarity in Germanic. The Old English runic poem mentions something that is a pleasure to men in a room, and various suggestions from "dice box" or "chess pieces" to "sexual intercourse," but none have been generally accepted.

An interesting speculation is that its shape represents the primordial good of a past time, which periodically overflows when a world epoch passes, at which time the shaking of the world tree and cataclysmic events take place on earth - the Ragnarok or death of the powerful - as described in the Icelandic poem Voluspá.

It probably adds up to itself the synthesis of all the indicated meanings.

The Perth rune is endowed with special powers. It is dedicated to Idunn, a young woman who cultivates the golden apples from the garden of the Asgard, which, in turn, prevented the aging of the Viking gods.

The status of god was recognized by the abilities of each one (Thor, the strength. Tyr, the fight. Frija, the beauty), but those virtues did not make them immortal. Only with the magic of Iddun's enchanted apples was the phenomenon of eternal youth produced. If they stopped eating, they died, just like life without mystery and love without seduction.

That is the enigma of the rune of the mystery, the halo that surrounds it: the peel of the apples of Idunn that return the lost youth. The secrets of luck, which makes no distinction of race or creed. Seduction as a weapon of conquest and all the fantasies of pleasure are Perth's territories.

In the Aettir, it marks the domain of the five senses and the perfect admission of the others. It represents the hidden world that arrives with all its enigmas.

Meaning like talisman

This rune helps make decisions and direct our own destiny. Unexpected gains and surprises are also due to him. Good luck in the game, secret matters.

Magical qualities

The hidden, the new, the mystery. Initiation, occultism.

It is used to develop magical ideas, to find lost things and for good mental health.

Esoteric meaning

With Perth, things that were hidden may be revealed. Or something that was considered lost returns. Unknown secrets, open paths, but we still do not know of their existence.

Love. Using your own gifts of kindness and kindness, you can venture into a love story. It is a good period to establish emotional ties as long as you are aware of it, without aspiring to great passions that will surely appear over time.

Work and money. Skill and diplomacy play in any case, especially if you know how to use the right friends at the right time.

Health. Dreams must be released because, through relaxation, visualization, and cognitive elaboration techniques, there can be more security and tranquility.

14. Othila rune

Possession, country, family, magic knots.

The Othila rune is the last of the Germanic runes, meaning "inherited wealth, country, farm, family roots," which apparently complements and contrasts with the "movable wealth" of the first rune.

Othel, Ethel, Othal, Othala or Odhal are some of the names of the twenty-fourth rune of the Futhark alphabet, and eighth of the Aettir of the Star.

It's corresponding in the life cycle is old age, and its other meanings are prosperity, family, land, country, noble nature, innate quality. It is the ancestral source from which all Mimir's wisdom springs.

In Teutonic society, the older adults enjoyed a lot of prestige, due to the enormous accumulation of stories and legends that could not be written but transmitted orally from generation to generation.

The hierarchical authority of the old clan sage was central to the group. He was the patriarch responsible for the secrets of the tribe that were not written.

It is known that it was used in magical rites in relation to money, marriage, and friendship and that it is consecrated to the goddess Syn, guardian of borders, so the Othila rune protects the space-place where humans develop their social and private activities.

With the Othila rune, the Futhark alphabet completes the wheel. A wheel that does not stop turning since it is the cycle of life on the physical plane. It starts from the matriarchal beginning with Fehu to the patriarchal with Othila, climbing through each of the stages of human development. Both runes also keep the Earth element as the only access door to this knowledge. Through them, one enters, and through them, one leaves.

Meaning like talisman

This rune helps tie energy and reinforce concentration. It transmits protection and security to a family or a community.

Magical qualities of the Othila rune

Inheritance, the material. Homeland, home, real estate, law benefits, old age, antiquities, wisdom, hierarchical power.

A sign of abundance and wealth, of desire and material possession

Love. In love, Othila is a rune run warns of a true explosion of sensuality. They will have gifts of a special charm that will provide the possibility of making very stimulating choices. Naturally, there will be no shortage of occasions for new and special encounters and the charm and magnetism to inspire or seem irresistible

Work and money. A proposal for consultation will provide the opportunity also to expand the group of faithful collaborators, thus opening a rich and fruitful period of results. It is probable that a reason of a social nature is at the base of this change.

Health. Great energy fed by a state of restlessness and various intolerances or rebellion, will compromise rather stressful searches. A little rest never hurts.

15. Laguz rune

Leek, water, fluid, canvas, let flow, drop, feelings, ability to convince.

Laguz rune means "water." A more specific meaning would be that with a "body of water, the lake." Possibly related to the water landscapes, rituals of Jutland (Norway) where sacrifices were made to the gods. The passage of time among the first Germanic peoples was conceived as a current that periodically overflowed.

The name of the Laguz rune is associated with the sea, the vehicle of great voyages, and curiously, the word leek.

In Scandinavia, a leek was given to adolescents who had passed certain tests as a symbol of virility, perhaps because the leeks were called the same as this rune there because the Laguz rune represents organic growth and perhaps because of the similarity of said vegetable to the male parts.

In runic engravings, Laguz is a magic word that opens the way for the kingdom of the waters, which governs intuition and clairvoyance.

The Moon and the woman, closely related by the circuit of the tides, appear in the Futhark as the number twenty-one, the power of three by seven. Three, the creator, circling the seven energy centers, the seven planets, seven days a week. It is not for nothing that the age of majority was stipulated at the age of twenty-one when all the rules are already known, and the evolutionary manifestation occurs spontaneously.

Meaning like talisman

The Laguz rune attracts love, mutual understanding, finding the partner of your life, fidelity, and wealth of feelings. Help overcome difficult tests. Provides soul balance and harmony with creation. Help flow like water, without fear

Magical qualities

Invisible powers, changes, fluidity.

Laguz is water. The primordial water. It symbolizes intuition, the moon, the tides, urging us to go inside ourselves, the thoughts, the sensations, the subconscious. Observe ourselves through dreams. She talks about sensitivity, intuition, the world of dreams, the true vocation, the hunches. It represents creativity, and also intuition, and some other psychic power.

Love. The Laguz rune indicates that everything will become easier, words will not be necessary to understand each other, because a gesture, a simple allusion will suffice and very romantic moments will be lived, but first of all one will have to face their deepest and most intimate desires. The availability of the loved one and the sensuality that he will know how to provoke will attract a sea of emotions.

Work and money. Avoid comparisons that lead to nothing. If you are not happy with the current situation, this is the optimal period to introduce changes. In any case, there will be an attraction for professions related to the aquatic sector, for the world of dreams, and for inner silence.

Health. Among the many sports, water gymnastics, which should be practiced in the sea or in a swimming pool, is advisable because it is a fun way to carry out a physical activity without that competitive eagerness typical of traditional gymnastics.

CHAPTER TEN
Wicca Spells

Spells are spells made with elements, most of the time natural, to achieve an objective. Spells with words are very important in the Wiccan religion. Words can open channels, cracks, and doors between this world and others. Some are so strong that it is enough to mentalize for the effects to occur. Lyrical, poetic, strong, magic words should be part of the life of any Wiccan practitioner.

Spells with Magic Words

Magic words can be used by any Wiccan practitioner. Most of them are of the Celtic origin or even Orthodox Wicca. They have been used for millennia by sorcerers and magicians and passed through grimoires (medieval collections of spells) and ancient books of magic. The Celts left few records about their magic. The little knowledge about their practices was passed on through testimonies, and if they had magic words, they survived by very rare documents dating from the times before Christ. See some examples of the use of Wiccan magic words below:

- Strong Word

There is a simple spell, which recommends that from the end of the year until January 6, you say goodbye to people with the word "prosperity." This is a simple act, practically a kindness, which can attract good luck and fortune throughout the year.

- Traditional Word - Psalms of David

Known in High Magic as propitiatory prayers, the Psalms of David have been used by wizards and witches for many years and have great power. There is a belief that words must be pronounced in their original language (Hebrew), but Latin is also allowed. The use of Greek, or another language, is not recommended. The instructions for use are faithful to ancient traditions, as is the Psalm itself. Here are some examples of using the Psalm:

To have a good trip

- You must say Psalm XVI nine times and take it under your left armpit.
- I looked up, Domine, they justified meam.

To be articulate

- You must say Psalm XVIII seven times over a glass full of wine, the moment the sun rises on a Wednesday or Friday.
- Coeli, enarrant gloriam Dei.

To ward off temptation and control low instincts

- You must say Psalm XXXII three times, the first in the morning, the second at noon, and the third in the afternoon standing above a bowl of oil.
- Exultate, justi, in Domin

Love Word

Love spells are in great demand, and this is an old charm found in old grimoires. It is a manipulative spell, and the person for whom the enchantment is intended has no idea what you are doing. On a full moon night, do the spell with faith:

"That (name of the person below is intended) be united to (name of the person requesting), in the same way as Fire, Air and Water are united to Earth, and that the spirit of (name of the person to whom intended), be stimulated by (name of the person requesting), as the sunbeam stimulates the light of the world and its virtues, and that it composes (name of the person for whom it is intended), in its works, in order to (name of the person requesting), in the same way, that the sky is composed of stars and a tree for its fruits. And place the spirit, high and sublime of (name of the person for whom it is intended), on the spirit of (name of the person requesting), like water on earth. And make sure that the said (name of the person for whom it is intended) has no power to eat, drink, walk or rejoice without (name of the person who requests it)".

Spell of the four elements

When we think of doing a spell, it's very important to be mindful of the action and reaction we're going to cause, and if we don't mess with the fate of another person and the reaction it will cause in the life of this individual, then whatever we want will always manifest in the other person and in us. So, making a spell will merge with the supernatural and physical terrain, where you need to be aware of what's right and wrong, and be sure what you want to do and how the question will be caused by not being natural, so we'll have to use magic to help or get rid of that spell. Or, when casting a spell and realizing that it is really necessary and how important it is to our lives, it is necessary to think carefully about everything so as not to fall into the karma of return and punishment.

Air element: It is very common for people not to know how to deal with this elemental because it is a small and simple ritual. However, it is necessary to have maximum attention and knowledge. Your portal must be opened with respect and with a pure intention since they are high and touchy spirits.

When asked, you have to have your hand: myrrh incense, honey, milk, good quality seeds, a bowl of the gourd, and seven blue candles. In the night of a crescent moon, a circle is made with sesame seeds and a little consecrated land (church land), all the belongings are placed in this circle, and the elemental directed towards the south is evoked. You are asked aloud to be present and start formulating the request. It is necessary to be very firm, with a clear and direct request and only then after feeling a slight breeze will the request be accepted. Do it with respect and dignity as your request will depend on how you ask and your humility.

Mother Earth line: It is very common to make wizards in this line and end up invoking other entities not being successful because they are primitive spirits, and, in the end, absorbing more negative charge and ending up destroying the objective in question.

First of all, mother earth should be evoked, and then a portal can be opened where you can ask for what you want, that is, you will first make a circle, then a pentagram, place pots with earth from different places and consecrate at each end. Them and put white candles on each end and in the center by roots of verbena and then put the order on paper.

To evoke mother Earth in a sense, that is, directed where the Sun rises, then treat the request with honey and milk and light a brown candle and start offering and then ask. This request must be made thirteen times without stopping.

Now begin to evoke Mother Earth so that she will listen and involve you and return your request very strongly, that is, that it will spring up and be reborn and so it will be fulfilled. After seven days, offer flowers, roots, and seeds to the elemental mother earth.

Fire Element: To obtain a spell using this element it is necessary to be careful because it is a very powerful force, in which we must first have a cauldron proper for this purpose if it is for love, we have to bear in mind hands seven types of roots, three types of fohlas, three types of waters, and finally, good paraffin.

The elements have their order to be able to function and also their moons. For the elemental fire, the order is placed on the crescent moon. Then place the cauldron in the middle of a circle crossed out with red chalk, another circle in parallel. Then the salamander is evoked, and the seven candles around it are lit. Put the person's name inside the cauldron, use the person's name together with yours, and add the roots and let it taste. The next day, put everything together and put it in a clay pot and bury it in an open field. Ginger, sunflower, mangerone, marigold, pansy, red rose, and dandelion roots are used. The leaves are of laurel, mugwort, and verbena and the waters of the essence of absinthe and star anise.

Water Element: In order to obtain a spell with this, which is one of the most important elements, water, one must first obtain the blessing of an Ondine, that is, place a glass of water blessed with stone in a gourd. Of amethyst crystal, let it sit overnight in the serene and remove before sunrise, as you should not bathe in the sun's rays.

Put a circle of sea salt and wound the water three times with a dagger, and after having raised a dark red candle, grease the candle with olive oil and powdered cinnamon and sprinkle the whole candle. Twenty-one scales of freshwater fish. These must be clean and dry so that they can put the name of the person you want for you to repeat the name twenty-one times. Now summon the freshwater mermaid three times and repeat three times, light the candle and call the person's guardian angel three times.

This water must then be mixed with absinthe essence and must rest for seven days in a dark place and out of sight of any person and animal. Thus, it will be ready to be used and bring the person to you, being able to be used on the body and also in roses that would be offered to a water entity.

Wiccan Spells for Protection and Prosperity

Wicca is a Neopagan religion that exalts nature, celebrates the cycles of life, hosts seasonal festivals, and defends the existence of supernatural forces. Wiccan magic rituals are used to achieve the goals of their practitioners, but always in favor of good. The worship of God and Goddess must be done in a wise and cautious way, always emitting positive energies. Meet amulets and Wiccan magic for protection and prosperity.

The Key to Protection

Select an old key, which is no longer used, and wash it with water and salt to purify it. Then, bury it overnight and, the next day, wash it again. The next step is to pass the key in the door of places that have great power such as police station, court, fire department, medical clinic, store, and, finally, a cemetery. You must carry this key around your neck. Thus, you will gain authority, respect, and dignity.

The Oil of Prosperity

In a glass bottle pour a part of frankincense, two parts of lavender essence, a part of lemon essence, an eighth of part of citronella essence, some powdered allspice powder, complete saffron and eight parts of mineral lightweight, which will serve as a base. This oil can be used to anoint your Wicca charms.

The Dust of Plenty

Inside a glass jar, place a part of powdered mint, a part of powdered basil, a part of allspice powder, half a part of powdered nutmeg, an eighth of part of citronella and five parts of talc. Whenever it is necessary to change your luck, spread this powder around your house and sprinkle a little on your head before going out into the street.

Wiccan Magic for Self-Protection

Preferably on a full moon night, place a clove in a previously consecrated bowl. Fill a cup of basil and place it in front of a white candle. Light the candle and breathe slowly and deeply. When you are focused, think of your inner powers and visualize a strong shield around you. Then, recite the verses with faith:

- "I invite the guardians and in the power of the Lord and the Lady
- I get involved with fire protection
- I am supported by the strength and grace of the land
- The winds bring me gentle changes and the flow of water facilitates energy at this time
- I believe in this protection, and I release my fears so that I can keep in touch with the pulse of life
- Let this be done within a greater good
- So be it, so it should be!"

Casting Love Spell

Casting love spells don't have to be a complicated task. Below you will find three simple spells that will help you organize your love life. Just remember that magic cannot be used to force someone to love it!

Discover what that someone thinks about you

It's simple Wiccan magic. On a piece of paper, write the name of the person you are interested in. Fold the card in half and again. Draw an eye on top. Put the folded piece of paper under the pillow, mentally repeating the spell: "I close my eyes to see what I mean to this person. Let it be good. Let it be bad. I want to know it and let it be so." Then lie on the bed, close your eyes and imagine that the person whose opinion you want to know is in a crowded room where everyone is gossiping about you. Begin to approach this man while trying to fall asleep. When you wake up, write down everything you "heard."

Attraction of love

It's best to cast a spell on a full moon. Prepare a piece of paper, an envelope, your favorite perfume, red lipstick and a few fresh red or pink petals of any flower. Write on the card the characteristics of the person you want to meet and love (beware, you cannot describe a specific person you already know. Then the spell will not work). When you're done, fold the card and use your right hand to sprinkle the card with perfume and put it in the envelope. Take flower petals in your right hand, squeeze them and imagine yourself as a person happily in love. Put the petals in the envelope, seal it and seal it with a kiss (your lips must be painted with lipstick). Hide the envelope in an inaccessible place and do not open it, or you will break the spell.

New Moon, new love

This is a spell that must be cast during the New Moon. You need a card, a pen and a pink candle. Sit in a place where nobody will disturb you. Light a candle and write down what you want on a piece of paper. It can be the simplest of sentences like "I want to fall in love with reciprocity" or a more precise one: "I want to love with reciprocity someone who will be honest and kind to me." Look at the candle flame for a moment, then close your eyes and imagine that your dream is really coming true. Then burn a piece of paper using a candle flame. Repeat the spell for 12 nights.

CHAPTER ELEVEN
Herbs and Essential Oils

Understanding the magic herbs is the first step in how to make spells. Each herb has a magical meaning, linked to a particular item. Once you've learned what each herb can do, they can be mixed and matched to give each spell strength.

All plants, herbs, and trees have the ability and powers to heal. In the same way, they can also offer their powers and benefits to the Warlock so that their magical strength can be used in rituals to bring about desired changes. Some ways of using them:

- **Infusion:** it is the original form of a potion. An infusion is similar to a tea. After the water boils, a handful of the chosen herb is placed in the liquid. Let it rest for approximately 15 minutes. After that, it can be used for its purpose.
- **Oil:** the best oils to use are almond, grape, olive oil or sunflower oil. Macerate the herb chosen in a cup of oil and heat it over low heat. Another way of preparation is to place a portion of the herbs wrapped in cotton fabric. To soak and simmer without boiling. Continue the cooking process until the herbs have lost their original color.
- **Ointment:** you can mix a little essential oil or tea made with the chosen herbs in a neutral ointment or glycerin just read. The ointments are ideal for applying on the wrists and chakras, promoting harmonization and purification.
- **Tincture:** mix herbs related to your intentions in cereal alcohol and let it rest in a dark place for 1 to 2 weeks. Use it to light the cauldron to burn orders or light the ritual place, always remembering to take the necessary precautions to that accidents do not occur.

Wizards have always recognized that plants and herbs have magical properties, and that is why all the remedies, ointments, flitros and oils commonly called sorceries use them as a starting point of nature 's composition and representation. Herbs and their efficacy are founded on the idea that anything that happens to something depends on what happens to something else, or on an entity in which a mystical relation has been created.

Witchcraft has its underlying assumption that all animals and plants are divine embodiments and therefore have innate forces. When we do a spell in which plants are used, we assume that we are coming into contact with her inner Divinity and that it is through this that her powers, along with our psychic energies, that the change, of course, takes place for our benefit. Large herbarium below.

Herbs and their magical functions:

- **Agrimony** - Protection, banishes negative energy, sleep (air)
- **Jamaica pepper** - Prosperity, courage, energy, strength (fire)
- **Almond** - Money, wisdom (air)
- **Angelica** - Protection, exorcism, health, meditation, divination (fire)
- **Assafetida** - Exorcism, banishing (fire)
- **Basil** - sympathy, happiness (fire)
- **Belladonna** - Astral travel, flying ointments (water)
- **Benzoin resin** - Prosperity, astral projection, purification (air)
- **Betonica** - Protects from nightmares and despair (fire)
- **Thistle** - Protection, cleaning, removal of hexagons (fire)
- **Borage** - Psychic abilities, financial gain
- **Saggina** - to bless weddings (air)
- **Burdock** - Cleaning, Protection (Water)
- **Carnation** - Female energy, healing, strength (water)
- **Cedar** - Home purification, good luck (fire)
- **Chamomile** - Love, meditation, peace (water)
- **Cinnamon** - Energy, creativity, passion (fire)
- **Cloves** - love (fire)
- **Copal resin** - Purification, cleaning (fire)
- **Damiana** - Love, lust (fire)
- **Dill** - Money, luck, protection (fire)
- **Fennel** - Protection, healing (fire)
- **Incense resin** - Exorcism, purification, spirituality (fire)
- **Gardenia** - Love, peace, healing (water)
- **Ginger** - Success, courage, strength (fire)
- **Hazelnut** - Divination, psychic abilities, dreams (air)
- **Erica** - Peace, beginnings, magic (water)
- **Hemlock** - Purification, cooling emotions (water)
- **Holly** - Protection, luck (fire)
- **Honeysuckle** - Healing, love, creativity (earth)
- **Horehound** - Protection, exorcism, mental clarity (air)

- **Hyssop** - Purification reject negativity (fire)
- **Jasmine** - Dreams, sexuality (water)
- **Lavender** - Love, sleep, dreams, meditation, protection (air)
- **Viola** - love, divination of love, desires, luck, healing, peace, memory, study
- **Lemon** - Friendship, love (water)
- **Lemongrass** - Psychic abilities (air)
- **Lilac** - Protection, divination (water)
- **Calendula** - Legal issues, dreams, divination (fire)
- **Mandragora** - Protection, love, health (fire)
- **Mint** - Healing, prosperity, creativity (air)
- **Mistletoe** - Protection, fertility, exorcism (fire)
- **Artemisi a** - Psychic abilities, divination, protection (earth)
- **Myrrh resin** - Purification, healing, spirituality (water)
- **Nettle** - Protection, passion (fire)
- **Orange** - Happiness, joy, purity (fire)
- **Iris root** - Love (water)
- **Patchouli** - Money, lust, fertility (earth)
- **Pine** - Prosperity, Fertility, Healing (Air)
- **Rosa** - Love, healing, friendship (water)
- **Ruta** - the protection (fire)
- **Sandalwood** - Spirituality, exorcism, healing (water)
- **Star anise** - Protection, psychic awareness, rejects evil spirits (air)
- **Thyme** - Sleep, protection, courage (water)
- **Valerian** - Love, sleep, protection (water)
- **Vanilla** - Lust, love, courage (water)
- **Verbena** - Love, prosperity, sleep, healing, creativity (earth)
- **Absinthe** - divination, (fire)

Fantasy Garden: Learn How to Make A Magical Garden

Every witch who can afford it should have an herb garden. Although simple in its design, the garden of the witches contains a large amount of magical material necessary for the witch, which with her knowledge, can be used at the time of performing her spells and rituals, incenses, aromatic oils, and amulets.

To get a good garden, the witch must be alert for destructive pests and pests and have some general gardening knowledge. We will develop some points below that will be necessary for the creation of the garden, and perhaps those who cannot afford a large garden are encouraged to grow a special herb or flower.

Whether a witch or a witch, anyone can grow their herbs according to the ancient magic methods.

Of course, the first thing we should do is select the plants, and it is necessary to carefully choose the herbs we want to plant in our garden. We will have to think that herbs or flowers will serve us more often in our rituals or if we wish to engage in all herbal activity. Also, to take into account this space we have and of course time, this activity takes a lot of time, we cannot forget our plants.

There are many sorcerers and witches who are dedicated to having one in their house, either in the back garden of their home, on the balcony, or in the patio, to change those spices in powder without taste and often false for aromatic herbs and fresh medicines. Here I give you some tips to keep in mind when setting up your own magical garden:

First, if you are going to do it on your balcony or in your backyard, choose pots that are deep (at least you have each pot between 30 and 40 centimeters), to give you a good space for the development of the roots of the grass that you decide to cultivate. You should always keep in mind that all the pots you use for this garden have good water drainage, for this check if the pot has it before placing the soil and the plant if it does not have it, take a few minutes to drill the base before placing the earth so that the water flows later when you water it.

Before planting, if you can, place a 2-centimeter layer of leca (some clay pebbles) or broken stones in the pot and complete with a good mix half of fertile soil of good quality if it is possible to buy it, a quarter of a fertilizer or earthworm humus and another quarter of coarse sand. Fill the pot or container you are going to use up to one centimeter from the edge of the pot. You can sow with seeds or directly buy the seedlings to transplant from some nursery.

How to Make a Magical Garden

- It is architecture that is the first thing to worry about. Much will depend on your garden size, but the key aspects will be:
- Fairy-friendly flowers, such as wild blossoms
- A natural layout rather than a formal template, ideally part-wild
- Homes and provisions for animals, birds and insects
- Compost heaps, butts for rainwater, and other environmentally friendly garden areas
- Statues of a Fairy
- Trees and hedgehogs
- Sensory enhancement-fragrant trees, twinkling bells, fairy lights, running water, edible fruit
- Small houses and hidden hiding places for fairies
- A hidden area of the garden where the fairies will dance!

How to Use Magic Herbs?

Herbs in magic can be used in various ways. For therapeutic purposes: through "popular healing" or by using cloth dolls and filling them with herbs. They can be burned on incense, to give smell or power to the rite. Finally, they can be used in bags.

For therapeutic purposes

To heal a person with herbs, folk medicine is used, that is, what was once used when they could not be called doctors. It is carried out with the use of certain herbs based on their therapeutic properties (not recommended without the help of a doctor, as it is quite dangerous for those who do not know how to treat herbs), which are usually found in the topics on herbs in this section.

In addition, there is the magic method that you find here, under "Curative use."

During the rituals, burned as incense

During the rituals, to purify the area or expand the power, it is possible to burn the herbs. Usually, there are recipes for the "incansi" indicating the "parts" (unit corresponding to about half a teaspoon) to be inserted on the charcoal. The herb or incense that is created is chosen on the basis of its magical properties.

Bags with magical herbs Herbal

- bags are special amulets.
- They are usually made by hand.

To create a bag with herbs yourself you need:

A rectangular piece of white fabric (or of a color that can be connected to magical use, here you will find a list of useful colors.)

Herbs based on use in magic (e.g., to purify: bay leaf)

Method:

Fold the piece of rectangular fabric in half, sew the edges, remaining an opening from which to insert the herbs.

Insert the herbs

Now you can close the bag with a ribbon or sew even the side left open.

As you can see, the preparation is simple. Usually, they are carried in the pocket, in the wallet ... Or they are arranged in the house: under the kitchens, in the corners, at the door. Also, to enhance the bag, stones can be inserted, which have a similar purpose. Now I will list some simple bags.

Herbal bag for personal protection

- 1 hot pepper
- 1 new nail
- rosemary leaves

Bag of herbs to find love

- 1 piece of rose quartz
- 3 rosebuds

Herbal bag for prosperity in general

- 3 copper coins
- 1 rock crystal
- Chamomile flower heads

Magic oil

In traditional magic, the history of essential oils is full of symbols, mysteries, and rituals connected to their perfumes, to the magic potions they potentiated that promised supernatural powers.

Preparing a magic oil today as then is easy, but knowing the significance of the plants that will be used to make it is nice.

Even candles, crystals, amulets, talismans, and other pendants can be useful in being anointed with one or more magic oils that you want to purify.

For magical purposes, it is better to use authentic oils prepared by us, to ensure their authenticity if this is not possible.

➢ Dragon Blood Oil Very

A strong oily magic compound whose strength interferes with any sign of negative influence. Indispensable for neutralizing Black Magic 's effect on any entity. This can be used for the house, spaces, people and anything else it is deemed appropriate for. DRAGON oil is also very useful to increase courage, passion or the power of magic formulas.

➢ Turmeric Oil

Oil to increase the charm and beauty. In India, turmeric is considered a real beauty secret. In fact, women use it to prepare a precious mask to be applied to the skin to keep it young and healthy! 500 ml of extra virgin olive oil, three full spoons of turmeric powder (not fresh root) are needed. Pour the oil into a jar with an airtight lid and mix the Turmeric. Close and leave to macerate for a week, shaking the jar once a day.

On the eighth day, do not shake the jar and pour the oil into a dark glass bottle, pouring carefully so as not to shake the turmeric that will have deposited on the bottom of the jar and separate the oil.

➢ Hypericum Oil

Very ancient procedure for an oil that is used against sunburn or erythema but also to invoke San Giovanni or for protection.

In massages, it is used against the pains of sciatica and joints.

Put the freshly picked and dried flowers in a glass jar (preferably collected on June 24th) and cover to the brim with sunflower oil or better, olive oil. Leave to macerate for one whole month by shaking it once a week. When the oil changes from yellow to red, it will be ready.

It should not be exposed to the sun. Store in a dark jar.

➢ Lavender Oil

This oil is suitable for attracting the divine spirit, for coming into contact with ancestors and heavenly spirits. Attract love and luck Add a handful of lavender flowers to extra virgin olive oil.

➢ Divination Oil

Oil suitable for amplifying mediumistic potential by greasing tarot cards and forehead during sessions. Macerate a small handful of berries and bay leaves in seed or olive oil, exposing the influences of the full moon for one month.

> ## Acacia Oil

Used in rituals to increase spiritual vibrations, to encourage spirituality, inner elevation, clairvoyance, and is useful for removing negativity. A handful of dried acacia flowers in a jar of seed or olive oil is sufficient. Store in the dark.

> ## Anise Oil

It removes nightmares and gives lost serenity; it is used to reduce anxiety and stress and to restore calmness. It combines with sweet orange, lavender, and rose.

> ## Artemisia Oil

Also known as the "devil hunt" herb, it was seized on the summer solstice, and various uses and popular traditions also give the plant anti-epileptic properties. Use this oil to enhance the prophetic qualities, and it gives the power of visions. Strong exorcising it removes the evil eye and misfortunes. A little lavender and mugwort oil in the home or car is useful for creating a protective shield for ourselves or the people we love.

> ## Basil Oil

Helps against spiritual and emotional poverty is also indicated for spells aimed at increasing love and respect for oneself and for one's neighbor.

> ## Hawthorn Oil

Hawthorn leaves and berries are used in the rituals of prosperity and fertility, and it helps to find a solution in couple's problems, it removes depression, if placed on the eyelids, it shows the fairies.

> ## Garofano Oil

Use this oil to increase sexual strength in love spells and to attract your loved one.

> ## Summoning OIL

It is used to summon an entity, spirit, or fairy. And very powerful it, therefore, does not abuse it. This very powerful oil is used by macerating (in equal parts) of the dried flowers of Jasmine, lavender, and Artemisia in balsamic Eucalyptus oil, exposing everything to the influences of the new (black) moon.

> ## Love Oil

This oil is used to attract love, by macerating red rose petals, jasmine, and verbena from the influences of the full moon, it is used to grease talisman candles, hands, and body before a love meeting.

➤ **Money Oil**

The word says it, and it is an oil used to increase revenue and money Macerate clover leaves, lemon, and cinnamon in equal parts in olive oil. Candles are joined, or portfolios are polished to attract luck and money.

CHAPTER TWELVE
Shamanism and Wicca

Shamanism was described as being the first religion. Before our ancestors took the first steps on the long road to the present, it existed before the earliest civilizations.

During this period, healers, children, and women were the shamans who exercised power. They practiced magic and interacted with nature's spirits.

The Shamans were the first intelligent human beings. They built and nurtured it, and they used it. Knowledge is power; in those days, the men and women who possessed it were shamans or sorcerers.

How did they get the power, or discover it? By trance-altered states of consciousness in which they were interacting with universe powers. In practice, the first shamans accomplished this state through the use of "devices," such as fasting, hunger, pain self-imposition, hallucinogenic drug absorption, concentration, etc. Those techniques, once learned, allowed them to be aware of other non-physical worlds.

All supernatural intelligence was gained by these "changes in consciousness." Communication with spirits and deities, plants and animals, has opened up new opportunities for learning. Shamans also shared with their own people some of this information but kept secrets for personal use. Shamanic rituals were not meant for common use.

They later progressed in the use of tools to facilitate consciousness shifts, marking the emergence of the magic ritual. Shamans worldwide still use sticks, rattles, reflective artifacts, poetry, songs, and dances. In reality, the most powerful shamanic rites are those that use natural and artificial instruments-a gentle wind, a steady drumming, the roaring ocean, the light waving from the flames, the hiss of a rattle-. Such devices, coupled with darkness and chants, gradually overpower the senses, pushing the real-world consciousness into a greater domain of energies. These are the shamanic rituals that still exist today.

Each magic and religion originated from those primitive origins, including Wicca. Given the current debate surrounding Wicca's "antiquity," the sacred substance stems from these rituals. And though our culture has developed and modified it, Wicca still reaches the spirit, triggering an ecstasy-shift of consciousness-that unites us with God. Some of the religion's techniques are of shamanic descent.

Wicca may also be defined as a Shamanic religion. Only a handful, as in shamanism, feel compelled to join their circle of light.

Wicca has currently suppressed painful experiences and the use of hallucinogens, favoring songs, meditation, concentration, visualization, music, dance, invocation, and ritual dramas. Using these spiritual devices, Wicca maintains a state of ceremonial consciousness through the most intense and comprehensive shamanic practices that have been accomplished.

I deliberately used the term "altered consciousness states." Such changed consciousness states are natural, a deviation from "normal" waking consciousness. Wicca teaches that nature encompasses a wide range of mental and spiritual states that most of us are ignorant of. An effective Wiccan ritual allows us to enter those states, facilitating communication and communion with higher entities - the Goddess and the God.

Unlike some religions, Wicca does not consider the Divinity to be remote. The Goddess and God are within us and manifest themselves in all nature. It is universality: it is not of the gods.

The research of shamanism essentially exposes the core of the magical and religious experience in general, and particularly of Wicca. The shaman or Wicca continually increases his experience of ritual as a way to reach the ritual consciousness, which, in effect, is power. Wicca helps to understand the universe and our place in it.

Wicca is a religion characterized by many variations. Because it's such a personally structured system, I can only present generalities about its creed and form here, filtered through my experience and knowledge, to create a sketch of Wicca 's nature. It considers the Divinity as dual power, in accordance with other religions. We venerate Goddess and God. We are real, moist and caring, not remote and resident in the "heaven," but everywhere in the universe.

Wicca also states that one of its truths resides in the physical universe. The physical manifestation is not supreme and absolute, nor is the spiritual "purer" than the foundation. The only difference between the metaphysical and the physical is the denser existence of the latter plane.

As in the Eastern religions, Wicca also contains the reincarnation theory, the often-misunderstood issue. Like some of the Western religions, however, Wicca does not teach that our soul can reincarnate into anything other than a human body upon physical death. Furthermore, few of this religion's adherents believe that we begin our life as rocks, plants, snails or birds until we grow to the point that we can incarnate as humans. While these beings and substances do possess a soul, they are not the kind that humans have.

Millions of people in the East and the West embrace reincarnation as a reality. Answer many questions: After death, what happens? How do we continue to recall things we never made in this lifetime? Why are we attracted to places and people we've never seen before, sometimes?

Reincarnation cannot answer those questions, but for those who wish to study it, it is there. This is not something to believe in. By reflection, meditation, and self-analysis, many reach a stage where reincarnation is recognized as a reality.

Wicca ethics and morals

Certainly, the issue of ethics and morality predominates in all religions. Therefore it is common to find in Christianity and other important world religions, a series of dogmas and traditions that are executed in order to apply all the principles and precepts stipulated

In the same way, Wicca is not exempt from having this type of precepts, since being a religion and a lifestyle it contains certain norms of general use that must be applied. In this book, I decided to do a little research in which I will describe the usual behaviors in Wicca proper, avoiding the degeneration of concepts through subjective opinions of my own and others.

The Basic Wicca Standard

The first rule that any Wiccan must know in a mandatory way is one that says, "Do what you want, as long as you don't harm anyone"; This law is mentioned in the Rede Wiccan, a poem from which most of this Neopagan tradition is derived. Thus, a set of rules is implied within it, such as:

Avoid at all costs any work of witchcraft in which a second or third person is involved.

Avoid black magic, love ties and any other type of magical work in which the mind, body or consciousness of another person other than the one who does the ritual is controlled.

Only more people should be involved in magical works of healing, prosperity, and bliss ... with due consent. If it lacks; The person involved is being controlled and hurting.

Among other rules that, in a nutshell, turn the magical work of Wicca into a kind of selfish witchcraft (in the good sense of the word) where each job is preferable to do it for one's own benefit avoiding relations with third parties.

In this order of ideas, in the daily environment of a Wiccan, he must avoid doing bad actions (with or without magic works) towards other people; then, kill, steal, rape, etc. These are activities banned in the current Wicca. In the same way, any action was taken against himself ... is vetoed, since the self is also someone who must be respected in all aspects.

This is where traditional paganism disagrees.

Differences between current Wicca and Ancient Paganism

Unfortunately, this is where it is said: "Traditional values have been lost," and it is thanks to the changes suffered by the current Wicca against the old Paganism.

Recall that Wicca is a religion called Neopagana in which it is intended to recreate part of the ancient Celtic and Shamanic traditions in the European regions, but when recognized as a neo-pagan, Buddhist and Hindu precepts come into play.

Doing a previous investigation, it can be demonstrated that the old Celts and Nordics, like other non-Christians, used practical practices such as murder and rape in their daily lives ... for fun; they even traveled to other lands in order to steal the wealth of those strange territories.

The Nordic and Celtic rituals of which one has the knowledge involved human and animal sacrifices, which served as an offering to appease the wrath of the Gods; Sexual promiscuity was extremely normal and well-seen practice for the ancients ... not Christians. The rituals corresponding to the Solstices had in their specific canon the sacrifice of animals or humans in which their blood penetrated the earth while running through wooden canals and plowed holes on the same earth.

All this is completely different from the current Wiccan traditions because, in the celebrations of the Solstices or the Sabbats and Esbats, the maximum offering for the Gods is plants, dances, and fire ... but the life of another living being is never involved. In my humble opinion, that makes Wicca a wonderful lifestyle.

Preparation for a Wiccan ritual

A ritual is a moment of fraternal union with the Gods, through it, the magician or sorcerer has a special connection with all the energies that surround him and also allows himself to transform himself into a part of those energies.

Before starting any type of magical work, a small preparation is necessary that allows the mind to be controlled during it and thus be able to direct the energies towards a clear and specific objective correctly.

Imagine that we are going to a battle, if there is no previous preparation in the art of war, we could clearly die in the process or end up very injured, however with the proper preparation, once we enter the battlefield, we can perform better, and we will not be so prone to suffer the consequences.

The same happens with magic, if there is no preparation prior to a ritual, spell or spell, it is possible that spirits with bad intentions want to intervene in our work, which would cause us to fall into terrible diseases or mental conditions and harmful to our spirit.

Also, in all spiritual work, this type of preparation is necessary. Now, there are several methods to prepare that will be stated below:

1. Meditation: Meditation is one of the fundamental practices in the art of witchcraft and magic, because, from this, the mind prepares and enters an intermediate state between the complete trance and the lucidity of the moment.

To start a meditation, first, if you want to light a stick of incense, sit on the floor or in a chair and put your hands with your palms up lying on your lap.

Now, you can close your eyes or not close them, you can meditate by visualizing a series of situations in the depths of your mind, or you can also look at a specific image of the Gods at best.

Stay in focus for at least five minutes, and you will see a noticeable difference in your mind.

2. Ritual Bath: Another of the methods that can be used to prepare before a magical work is a ritual bath, the bath you can do either as you would normally bathe but with a different consciousness or with herbs and incenses that allow a greater concentration and direction of energies.

3. Dance: One of the fastest methods to enter a mental trance is dance; through it, you can reach very high states of consciousness that allow you to increase the power of energies during a ritual. However, this method must be used cautiously because well done can lead to very high states and take the soul out of the body.

Clearly, with dance, I mean a special dance aimed at the art of magic, not the dance that people would normally do in a mundane way.

There are also many other methods to raise energy before a ritual and thus prepare the spirit for it, yoga, for example, is quite useful, singing is also, the important thing is that anything you do before a ritual is specifically directed to prepare your spirit before the ritual.

Do not do a ritual without prior preparation, and during the ritual, always keep your mind focused solely on the Gods.

How to do a Wiccan (Physical) ritual

Previously we were talking about how to prepare for a Wiccan ritual, and now we will delve into the practice of the Wiccan Ritual proper.

A Wiccan ritual is a special moment that the practitioner of magic has with the Gods; it is a space of rapprochement with them where they enter into perfect spiritual communion with them. Through the ritual, the Wiccan can communicate with the Gods and expose their needs or simply glorify them.

Before any ritual, as explained above, there must be prepared and also take into account the following points to enter a magic circle.

To have a lot of respect and love for the Gods, it must not be done during the ritual, obscenities or anything like it, and there must be solemnity.

The ritual can be with a robe to allow solemnity, or it can be naked, the naked rituals are especially powerful because energy can easily come out and be transmuted; However, nude rituals should not be practiced by people prone to lust because a magic circle should not be desecrated by any bad energy.

The minimum elements must be kept on the altar, a cauldron, a pentagram, the book of shadows, statuettes or something that reminds the Gods, a chalice, water, salt, candles, and incenses.

A specific and physical space should be dedicated to the ritual, it is not good to perform rituals in small or enclosed spaces, especially by the use of candles and incenses and also because the influence of bad energies is less dispersed in closed places so there is less protection.

Always during the ritual, the thought must be directed to the Gods, before making any request to the Gods it must be asked Is it something worth asking for? Is it something that I really need and benefits other sentient beings? Do I deserve that the Gods care about this need? Among other questions.

Moments of the ritual:

Once all the above considerations have been taken into account, you can proceed with the ritual. It consists of several moments or phases that should not be ignored or changed in order because changing it will lose the solemnity so important that we need it.

Close the circle:

As we all know, in ritual energy of spirits intervene that see that something strange is happening there, then we will need a circle of protection so that they cannot interfere in some kind of magical work.

To close a circle, it is first necessary to have water, salt, incense, a wand and an athame, which can be replaced by the right arm and hand, respectively.

Invocation of the Divine:

At this point the spirits of the Watchtowers of the Elements are invoked to protect the circle and charge it with their powers, it is also here that the call is made to the Gods and they are invited to fill the circle with their presence.

Ideally, when invoking all these members of our magical work, do not lose solemnity and also respect and love prevail.

Stabilization of purpose:

Stabilizing the purpose is like somehow explaining to the Gods what has been the reason why they have been invoked there, and they are asked for permission to have them as participants in the magical work. It is here that the Wiccan practitioner justifies himself before the Gods to do what he has to do.

If the justification is not good enough for the Gods, they will surely leave and leave the circle only with the protection of the guardians of the elements, and the ritual may be unsuccessful even if all the steps of the magical work are followed.

Magic Work:

The magical work is the set of actions to be carried out to fulfill the purpose of the ritual, such as purification baths, the recitation of spells and spells, songs, dances, among other things that, according to magic could make the objective I can meet.

As we said before, even if everything is followed to the letter, if the Gods do not give permission, even if the practitioner draws his own blood and offers it as a sacrifice, it will not help.

Thanks to the divine:

At this point, thanks are given to the Gods for their power and for their presence, and all the magical works that are being done during the ritual are finished. The spirits of the Elements are also thanked for their presence and power.

Opening of the circle:

Opening of the circle means that the ritual is over, and protection can be opened so that other spirits can be there if they need it, but they will no longer have interfered with the sacred ritual.

CONCLUSION

Wiccans have a deep and systematic belief in the "Rule of Three," which essentially means that everything we submit to our planet must return to us "3 times 3," both good and evil. With this in mind, a "Real Wiccan" should take care to use magic to injure or control another, because the boomerang we launch will eventually return to us much longer and stronger than we launched it.

In all this, though, we don't mean that Wiccans are flawless because we're just like anyone else and we make mistakes. Just as parents love and nurture their children, parents neglect their children. Just as there are those who devote their lives to helping and doing good, there are others who commit their lives to exploit or using others for their own gain. Unfortunately, the same human flaws apply to Wiccans.

All of us do our utmost to consider the potential implications of our thoughts and acts as we do gradually before performing any spells, rituals or rites. It is when we follow the path with the love of Goddess in our hearts and stick to our only commandment that our works are fruitful and we find peace and balance with all.

The heart of the Wiccan Faith is not something that can be represented with a few basic terms, such as these, and much of the time Wicca can have different meanings for different people because God and Goddess affect us in various ways. Therefore, in order to gain a better understanding of this direction and art, I encourage you to continue visiting and reading this site's pages and others, such as those suggested in the Links section. By reading other people's words and experiences, and gradually through your own practice and experience, you will be increasingly able to understand the foundation of our values and how they can be implemented best throughout your life. Recall reading with your hands.

Book 2

Tarot for Beginners

INTRODUCTION

Starting Out Your Journey to Tarot Reading

We all start our journey to tarot in different ways; different circumstances lead different people to tarot reading. Inevitably, people are going to view the very practice of tarot reading from different individual perspectives. The most difficult fact to accept about tarot reading, however, is the fact there is no absolute right or wrong way to carry out specific actions, or to make certain deductions from tarot cards.

Unlike other more accurate scientific fields, tarot reading is an art that has thrived over the ages on generating controversies in interpretations; bringing people together using differences in their reasoning. So, the way you are going to understand how the reading of a particular card or spread appears to your peculiar situation might differ slightly from how even your reader would see it.

They key to being a great tarot reader in the long run, therefore, is for you first to find yourself, and come to terms with who you are. You need to realize exactly who you are, underneath the cloak of educational backgrounds, social class and all those cloaks we use to mask our real selves in the modern society. You are not your occupation or job description, you are not your position in your family, you are not the role that the society has foisted on you.

You must go back to the very basics of your consciousness and discover who you are and the ideals you hold dear. Discovering yourself will help you to have an independent voice and a self-reliant thought pattern that will be able to help your intuition bloom. Once you as a person are in perfect harmony with your intuition, then reading the cards and relating them to your personal life becomes easier.

Discovering yourself will also let you find out you are intrinsically different from everybody else. Who you are fundamentally as a person differs from what people think you are, and it sure differs from who other people are? Therefore, since we all different on a very primal, basal level, it is not expected for our intuitions to work the same way. What your intuition regards the interpretation of a card to mean in your situation is likely to be slightly different from what someone else would think if they got that particular reading in your same situation. So, self-discovery will let you understand who you are, and will let you come to terms with the differences that exist between yourself and others.

Now that you have understood that the basic requirement is knowing who you are to enable your intuition to bloom unrestricted, the next step is for you to learn the basics of Tarot. For a tarot reading to be carried out, five basic pre-requisites must be in place. First and most importantly. There should be a reader. If there is no reader, then exactly how is the interpretation of the card going to be determined? So, a reader has to be in place to examine the cards drawn and the spread created, and to guide the person who asks the question on the core meaning of the reading produced.

This leads to our second most important factor, the querent. In Tarot literature, a querent is simply the person who asks the question (or who makes the query). In circumstances of personal divination therefore, the reader and the querent are going to be the same person. So, the querent is the one who is seeking an answer to a burning problem.

The third pre-requisite is the question itself. This is the most important thing the querent has to possess for a tarot reading to be successful – a concise, clear-cut question that has been decided on in advance or on the spot. For a querent to be able to relate a tarot reading to his circumstances, the question asked has to be as concise and unambiguous as possible.

The next most important pre-requisite is the deck of cards. There are different types of tarot cards in existence currently, but the most common and most widely accepted tarot deck is the Rider-Waite-Smith tarot deck. The original version of this deck was first created in 1909, and its simplicity and conciseness has endeared it to the hearts of many tarot readers over the years. This has made it the deck of choice for both avid tarot enthusiasts and beginners who are just starting in the game of tarot reading.

The whole tarot deck can be divided into two major sections, the major arcana, or the major mysteries, and the minor arcana, or the minor mysteries. The cards in both sections of the deck will be explained in detail as we move on.

Finally, a spread is the last important pre-requisite for a reading to be completed. A spread may be an arrangement of cards picked out in a particular fashion based on the direction of the reader's or querent's intuition. In other types of readings, the spread may be a single card pulled randomly from a deck or a random pile of cards. Whatever form it takes, the most important thing to note is that the spread is the card, or sequence of cards that is interpreted to answer the question asked by the querent.

Even though a lot of tarot readers practice personal divination in the modern dispensation, back in ancient Europe, there were huge concerns about the ability of readers to be objective when seeking answers to their questions from the cards. So, when carrying out a personal divination through a tarot reading, as both the reader and the querent, you need to strive consciously during the tarot reading to remain as objective as possible when carrying out the reading.

Of course, as stated earlier, there is no specific way to interpret a spread. People examine core meanings, and then relate them to their specific situations based on their convictions. So, whether you like it or not, your convictions about that question you asked will come into play as you seek answers from the cards. It is now up to you as a reader to look deeply at the core meanings of the cards in your spread, and make an objective deduction based on your intuition, and not a deduction that aligns with your wishes.

Since the heyday of Tarot reading, the practice has never been seen as a form of inquiry from an absolute supernatural source. Tarot reading have always been regarded as a way of providing a mirror for us to gaze back unto ourselves, our unique predicaments, circumstances and situations and reflect deeply to come up with intuitive deductions and solutions. Tarot aims to help you reach into the deepest recesses of your mind, and relate the tarot reading you have done by yourself, or the one an expert reader has just done for you to your unique circumstances.

It's that simple. Having to distill the path to the solution of your problems to just one image or a few sequential images allows you to think deeply from a unique perspective. See how the core meanings of the card relate to you, and begin to work out a simple, basic solution to your problems. Tarot helps to eliminate complexities by forcing you to come down to a basal level when attempting to solve a problem. Instead of engaging your analytical mind and trying to find various complex solutions to mostly simple problems, tarot brings your intuitive mind into the picture. It allows you build your solutions from the simple to the complex phases, which is the most efficient mechanism of problem solving.

Contrary to popular opinion, you don't need to have studied the entire tarot deck to be able to perform a simple reading. The key to a successful tarot reading is your intuition; the limitless power of your mind. So, as a total novice with no prior knowledge of tarot, you can still carry out an effective tarot reading using the power of your intuition. All you have to do is get your deck of cards (you can do that right now if you have your deck with you), think of a particular question, pull out a single card (we don't want any complications yet), and then think of how the image on the card relates to the question you asked.

You can just write down the first couple of things that comes to your mind. It might take a while for you to be able to effectively establish a connection between the question you asked and the image on the card you pulled. That's where the power of your intuitive mind comes in. The more you ponder intuitively on the image, the clearer the path between your tarot reading and the question you asked becomes to you. It's so simple, yet so unbelievably powerful.

Finally, we'll be looking at how to read a spread appropriately. The spread, is the layout of the cards that allows the reader to provide an answer to the querent's question using his interpretation of the core meanings of the cards and the sequence in which the cards appear. Sometimes, the sequence of the cards may not be put into consideration, it all eventually boils down to your intuition.

Most tarot readers like to use a three-card spread. The first card represents the events of the past, the second represents the events of the present, while the third represents how the past and present will lead to a particular future occurrence. For some readings, only once card is used, and in some readings, more than three cards are used. No hard and fast rules apply.

Tarot Through the History

Leaving the tarots card invariably evokes the illusion that old gypsy people pose before their crystal ball in a nebular room full of strange artifacts. The word "Tarot" has an aura of mystery too, for no one understands when Tarot is operating or when. While scholars are aware that the majority of recorded tarot card history comes from Italy.

Many people believe that the Knights Templars carried the Tarot into Europe after the cruises. In contrast, others say that it is the Gypsies who would enjoy reading the Tarot as they visited the continent in the Middle Ages.

Historians also found evidence that the Tarot decks of 78 cards were used during the Renaissance to reveal fortunes in Italy and France. Researchers believe that these early tarot decks can be a by-product of current playing cards.

Because of the various interpretations, one thing is certain. For seven hundred years, the reading of tarot cards saw the daylight as one of the most important sources of the western world's spiritual knowledge.

Some tarot historians believe that the tarot cards were developed as a game called Triumph, which today was equivalent to the game of "Bridge." The game was called "Tarocchi" (later Tarot), which spread rapidly across all parts of Europe.

The markings on the cards were quickly recognized in France and England by the practitioners of the mystic. They were often used as a divination device, and eventually became a component of the occult theory.

The tarot readings were, however, still quite easy at that period.

By the eighteenth century, the tarot readers had begun to give specific meanings to each card, and in 1781 the French freemason published a complex analysis of the tarot. The hypothesis was that the images in the Tarot were drawn from Egyptian priests ' ancient mysteries and linked to the stories of Isis, Osiris, and other Egyptian gods.

In 1791 Jean-Baptiste Alliette published the first Tarot box, and curiosity in occult research quickly gained momentum as it was a popular pastime among dull high-class families.

A British occultist, Arthur Waite, and artist Pamela Colman Smith published the most famous tarot card set, the Rider-Waite deck, for the first time in 1909.

Today, reading tarot cards is very common, and more and more people depend on a tarot reading to lead them through their daily lives. Tarot readings help seekers think about themselves and others and see what their future holds. These cards can also be used for reflection and meditation. The cards are now distributed in almost infinite styles. Any deck with which the user is confident can be used.

The 78 Tarot deck cards consist of the Major Arcana and the Minor Arcana, which essentially translations into "grand secrets" and "little secrets." Once upon a time, the origin of the Tarot could be traced back to ancient Egypt, perhaps the cards representing the lost Egyptian Dead Book. This is the idea that has mostly been uncovered, but the appeal and attraction of the concept remain, and many occultists still retain it.

He also found clues to the Egyptian symbols in contemporary tarot cards. In his view, the Star card was the Dog-star of Sirius, who rises with the Nile flood at the start of a new year, and the Lady below, whom he perceived as Isis, Queen of Heaven who strewed water out of her vases (the tears of Isis which each year flooded the Nile). He identified the Devil card as Set, the god of darkness and chaos.

But many scholars challenged the findings of De Gébelin. Thoth's now completely interpreted book contains two charms, one of which ostensibly helps the reader to comprehend the animals ' words, and the other encourages the reader to interpret the gods. The legend of Thoth, the god of writing and knowledge, includes the book itself, which is said to be first buried near Coptos at the bottom of the Nile, and was locked into a serpent-protected shell.

There are many other hypotheses, including the suggestion that Tarot originated from magical numbered cart decks that existed in India and the Far East in ancient times and could be transported by the Templar Knights to Europe during and after the Holy Land cruises. This hypothesis is pure conjecture, like the others. If there were these games, how should we learn that they created the Tarot?

The fact is, nobody understands from whence came the Tarot box. Its true roots are covered in mystery. Even the word's etymology is uncertain. Whereas de Gébelin suggested an Egyptian word, other historians believe that the word "Torah" is corrupt and that others interpret the Hebrew Law Book as "wheel" and "rota" as the anagram of the Latin word "rota."

So, what can we say for sure about Tarot's origin?

Sometimes in Milan, Ferrara, and Bologna in Northern Italy between 1430 and 1450, the first known Tarot cards were created, perhaps when a famed four-suit player card set was developed to include additional cards trumps with allegorical diagrams. Such modern decks were originally called cartes da trionfi, trump cards, and other cards became simply known as trionfi. A written statement in Ferrara's court record, 1442, is the first textual evidence of the existence of the carte da trionfi. The earliest surviving Tarot cards are fifteen splinter decks created for Milan's kings, Visconti-Sforza, during the middle of the 15th century.

This secondary use of the cards gradually became their main function. Eliphas Levi Zahid from the 19th century (1810-1875), who studied for priesthood like De Gébelin, then switched to sorcery, mysticism, and occultism. Convinced that the root of the Tarot dates back far beyond the 14th century, he noticed connections between the Tarot and the Jewish spiritual method, known as the Kabbalah. Levi noted that the Tarot 22 trumps match the Hebrew alphabet's 22 letters. His research found many other similarities, including the similarity between the Tarot and the Tree of Life. He became convinced that the Tarot was a compass, a way of traveling around the Tree of Life, being divine and wise, and eventually finding the heavens.

A contemporary of Levi (Jean Baptiste Pitois, 1811-1877), the French occultist Paul Christian wrote a book called The History of Magic (1870) that defined the ritual of Egyptian initiation, related to the Tarot. The Giza Sphinx also acted as the gateway to the holy vaults, according to Christian, where the Magi performed their initiation. Corridors led to the Great Pyramid's subterranean portions. A candidate was faced with life-threatening ordeals to test his courage and intelligence. Once these tests had survived, the initiate descended into a bottomless pit on the ladder of 78 rungs and found an overshadowed opening in a long gallery, lined with 22 statues on each side and faced by pairs of mysterious bodies and symbols. At that stage, a magus called Pastophore ("guardian of the holy symbols"), according to Christian, seemed to unlock the postulant's grating. "Son of earth," he smiled, he said, "welcome. You have escaped from the pit by discovering the road to wisdom; a few Mystery aspirants have triumphed in this test; all the others have been destroyed. As your protector is the great Isis, she will lead you, I hope, safe to the sanctuary where virtue is crowned.

The Tarot has developed over the years. In the 1940s, in collaboration with Lady Frieda Harris, famous British occultist Aleister Crowley crafted a Thoth deck that incorporated several different elements, including the Jewish, Roman, Christian, and Islamic icons. Initially a member of the Golden Dawn Order, Crowley gradually split from that group and founded his order, the Silver Star, to represent his special (and erotic) occult brand.

Hundreds (if not thousands) of various Tarot decks have been constructed over the years. The Tarot continues to evolve while its origins remain unclear. And the root of the Tarot is perhaps less relevant than what it is. After all, the past is the past. If the Tarot will allow you to grasp your existence more fully, whether you consider universal truth in the cards, all items before this realization become meaningless, including the past of the cards themselves, of course.

The Modern Tarot Deck

Art makes the Tarot. There are thousands of professionally published Tarot decks on the market. The standard-bearers are, of course, the Tarot of Marseilles variations, the Thoth Deck (by Uncle Al and Lady Frieda Harris), and the progenitor of the modern Tarot: any deck with line art hand drawn by Pamela Colman Smith (e.g., the "Rider-Waite" deck and all its derivations).

The Tarot of Marseilles is not one deck. Still, a style of decks popularized in Marseilles after the French invaded Milan, Italy, in 1499 (roughly 60–80 years after the invention of the Tarot). Marseilles was a hotspot of artistry and mass production of Tarot cards, so this style of deck was distributed throughout Europe and eventually became the basis of new designs all over Europe by the 19th century. The specifics we are interested in here are the lack of illustrated pip cards. The so-called "minor" Arcana is populated with images of swords, cups, batons, and coins; but there are no people—just the number of swords, cups, batons, and coins of that card. This is a difficult deck to learn for divination, but when playing the game of Tarot, it is quite easy and addictive.

When Pam illustrated the "public deck" for Art in 1909, she did so over a few months. Art (Waite) was almost exclusively interested in the "major" Arcana, court cards, and aces, so she had almost complete discretion over what scenes were portrayed on the pip cards (now called the "minor" Arcana). Her choice of scenes cemented the meanings of the Tarot for generations to come. Even Crowley (whose real name was "Ed") used her art as a basis to work from, or rebel against, as he was disappointed with Art's take on the Tarot. Art was super-Catholic, and Crowley—not so much it turns out, even though he was the son of a wealthy brewer and preacher in England. It is through Pam that we get the core of modern Tarot philosophy (what people think the Tarot means and how they interpret it). Over time, thousands of authors, scholars, and endless uninformed individuals have written on the Tarot or designed their own version of the Tarot sourced from or based on Pam's imagery.

Many modern decks are pretty to look at but nigh-impossible to read without memorizing keywords and phrases or stamping one belief or another onto the Tarot to create an artificial system of interpreting "what the cards really mean." This is why so many Tarot books disagree completely and why, for the most part, the Tarot is notoriously unreliable and difficult to read. The cards are not "wrong," it is a two-fold problem of quality of design among some decks and bad Tarot teaching. By absorbing the art of our favorite deck, we can draw meaning from the images presented to us. The image must conform to the meaning of the card or we get a dichotomy of instruction where the image says one thing to you but the author (or deck designer) tells you the card means something else. Each card must, by the nature of the Tarot, have thousands of interpretations or the Tarot cannot accurately and precisely reveal the future, locate hidden or missing items (and people), or unveil secrets.

You need to hold in your hands a deck that speaks to you. The art must do its part by conveying to you the exact visual stimulus that sparks your intuition to feed your conscious mind the details you are looking for. Therefore, you must be able to notice the large and small details of each card image. Various parts of the image will be prominent in different readings. In the 9 of Coins, the snail is hardly a "main character," but depending on the question, it could take on the role as garden pest, unwelcomed visitor, or Nature bringing blessings from even the smallest of sources. How do we know when the snail is at all important? It comes down to our questions. If you were doing a reading on the problems your client was having with her prize tomatoes and the 9 of Coins popped up, it might be the cards handing you a tongue-in-cheek message about pest control. You will see this level of subtle humor from the cards quite often as you develop your mastery of the Tarot. Being able to pull tiny details from vague images and delivering great accuracy in a reading is the mark of a Tarot master. To get there, we need to understand the art of our cards and use a well-designed deck that is rich in symbolism.

How to Begin

When you first become interested in the Tarot, it can seem incredibly overwhelming to try and remember all of the Major and Minor Arcana cards, their numbers, and their meanings. Lucky for you, many have gone on this journey before you, and they have come up with a few helpful tips to make the job a bit easier. Learning and working with Tarot cards should be fun, so all of these tips are designed in a way to ease your stress and make the experience an enjoyable one.

Tips on Learning the Tarot Cards

The most important beginning step is to determine what the Tarot means for you. Since Tarot is such a personal art, everyone's answer is different. Knowing what it means to you, though, will allow you to utilize this tool in the most effective way. Once you have determined what it means to you, it is important that you recognize that even though Tarot has "rules," they should be used more as guidelines. If you find that something does not sit right with you or that after you have tried a certain method or spread, and it did not work for you, it is 100 percent okay to drop it. Your gut feeling will not lead you astray, so even if you have read 10 books that claim that this one, specific way is the correct way, if it does not work for you, then it was not meant to.

Next, it is time to pick a Tarot deck that resonates with you. Many people recommend using the Rider Waite Smith Tarot Deck, to begin with, and there is some value to that, but if you find a deck that really speaks to you, go with it! Connecting with the deck you choose is one of the best things you can do for yourself to ensure accurate readings. If you are working with a deck that does not resonate with you, it is still possible to get accurate readings, but you may have more difficulty with it, especially since you're just starting out.

Once you have an understanding of that and have chosen your Tarot deck, it is time to move on to learning the cards. There are quite a few helpful tips so that we will cover a few of them here. Many Tarot readers recommend keeping a journal, where you can keep track of notes that you make over the cards, as well as readings that you do for yourself and others, along with any other Tarot-related information you would like to look back on.

Divide Your Journal into Sections

- Tarot card meanings – personal insights, stories, and card meanings
- Tarot reading techniques – asking the right questions, how to shuffle, and how to select cards
- Personal tarot readings – write down the name of question, date of the reading, cards you drew, and key message
- Look back at these after a few months, and reflect on what happened since then.
- Tarot spreads – keep your favorite spreads that you find here or ones that you come up with yourself.
- Personal reflection – work with particular energy (inviting abundance), so pick the card that exemplifies that energy and journal about what that Tarot means to you, along with how you can access deeper lessons in that card.

The first step is to take a card from your deck. Many recommend working with Major Arcana first because there are fewer of them. When you pick up a card, study its image. Spend about 2 to 4 minutes looking at the card. What are some things that immediately pop out to you? Do you feel anything particular? Can you see the story the card is portraying? Remember that all of these things are subjective and to be intuited by you. There are no wrong answers when it comes to what you are feeling. You can take note of those in your journal or not. This exercise is just to familiarize yourself with the Tarot and begin building a connection.

When it comes to learning the meanings of the cards, it is not the best idea just to try and memorize them. It is unlikely you will remember all 78 meanings this way, as you have no personal connection with them, and it will become overwhelming incredibly quickly. Instead, choosing to draw one card a day is a wonderful way to take it slow, give yourself ample time to familiarize yourself with each card, and even see them in action. Here is how:

1. Before you draw a card, think about a question you would like an answer, or maybe you would just like to know about a type of energy that you should focus on for the day. Whatever it is, keep that in mind as you draw your card.
2. Once you have your card, study the image, and take a few notes on what you feel when looking at it and the general definition that the card has, but do not take it too seriously. If you connect to a meaning that differs from what certain books say, that is okay. You are connecting to your intuition and your reading of the card.

3. Now, it is time to go about your day, but keep the card in mind.

4. At the end of the day, grab your journal and reflect on what happened and how it could relate to the Tarot you drew. Doing it this way will allow you to forge a personal connection to the cards, as you will have experience with them from your everyday life.

5. Repeat this each day for all the Tarot cards.

Another simple way to form connections to your cards is to relate them to people in your life. Which card best depicts how you felt today? Which card represents your mother? Your best friend? Learning about the cards this way, alongside drawing a card a day, can speed up the learning process simply because you can connect them to a person in your life.

Method for Discovering Card Meanings

One of the most important things to know and spend some time thinking about when first deciphering the Tarot is that the Tarot was devised under a culture of Feudalism. Everyone had their fixed place in society. Kings and queens, dukes, knights, and peasants all existed in their own worlds of experience. A cobbler, farmer, or blacksmith could not begin to fathom the world his or her emperor lived in. The very notion of endless days without manual labor, and dirt from it that got under your skin and never truly went away, was as foreign as any invading army.

The "common man" spent his days from sunup to sundown working his trade for his family and community. The luxuries of court were completely unknown and unimagined to most peasants, lest they rebel or go insane at the injustice of it all. This very schism of society naturally found its way into the Tarot and continues to this day. Looking at the cards, we are looking back in history, where ownership of land and animals or standing armies meant power of life and death over others as far as one's eye could see. These cards record history and its societal beliefs in picture form, and the stories they tell reveal humanity, often in a very dark light. This is why we have an overclass of cards (the "major" Arcana) as well as a permanent underclass (the "minor" Arcana—which include the court, or ruling cards of the underclass). For beyond the command of the kings and queens of every country were the gods themselves, the very forces of nature. The Tarot is at once both polytheistic and monotheistic, being born of that time of Christian domination of Europe, but when old beliefs still held tightly among the majority of its citizens. "God" above all was the mantra, but peasants and nobles alike still hung horseshoes above their doors, warded off vampires with garlic, and left honey cakes out for the fey.

Poverty, abuse of all kinds, death, and disease were far more commonplace than we can begin to imagine today, and generally thought of as evil spirits, thus necessitating good luck charms and various protections to keep them at bay. The Tarot reveals these beliefs in images, but so many beliefs of the Middle Ages and even the Renaissance are so laughable today that it is hard to fathom people taking them seriously. Because the Tarot is so steeped in these beliefs and opinions of how the world functioned, it remains a mystery to most people inaccessible through its saturation with the mindset of times long abandoned. So, when we look at the images of the Tarot, most especially those of the oldest surviving decks, we see concepts that appear almost fairy tale-like, and often alien to common sense. We have to look at their symbolism rather than seeing cards as concrete ideals of nature and science. Ultimately, we realize that the world is hardly flat, but the creators of the Tarot did not. Thus, we must translate a vision of the world around us that has long since been displaced into our own "modern" views (for certainly future humanity will laugh at us as well) and apply the inherent wisdom left behind in the cards to our own existence to create healthier and happier lives "here and now."

In the end, it all comes down to this: "historical meaning" versus what the cards say to you overall, and what they say "right now." Who is "right"? Why, you are, of course! You learn to listen to your intuition which will tell you whether the scholarly interpretation is applicable or not. The Tarot is notoriously capricious at times. Practice makes you an expert. Knowing the "traditional meaning" is as essential as knowing how to read cards at face value, and knowing when to trust your instincts, even in the face of obstacles or "obvious" meanings.

Meaning of The Cards and Cards Interpretation
Part 1

The Major Arcana

The Fool

This card can be the start or end of the deck as its number is 0 and therefore doesn't have a permanent place from either of the two options. It's a card with unlimited potential as it signifies a clean slate. As the whole deck is sometimes interpreted as "a fool's journey through life", this card signifies new beginnings of a journey.

The card features a man staring out from the edge of a cliff. He seems to be without a care and looks set to embark on an adventure. In his right hand is a small bag tied to a stick and it is slung over his shoulder and it contains all he needs. He is gazing at the universe (skywards) and looks unaware that he is about to fall off the cliff's edge into the unknown. His left hand clasps a white rose which represents his innocence and purity and a small dog at his feet which signifies loyalty and protection. The mountain in the background signifies future challenges but the Fool's attitude shows he's not concerned with the right that moment and is rather focused on the new adventure that awaits.

Upright
When the card is upright, it signifies new beginnings, opportunities, and potential. It is a sign that you are starting a journey into the unknown and trusting the universe to take you on an adventure that you are committed to even though it might seem crazy. The Fool encourages you to be curious, open-minded and adventurous on this new journey. Forgo the anxiety and worries of what may be or not and sink yourself into the experience and excitement coming your way. The card is a sign to take action on a new endeavor even if you feel you don't have all you need. Be creative with what you have and let spontaneity guide you on this adventure.

Go with the flow, have fun and relax. Embrace your carefree spirit and unlimited potential and don't let the doubt of details hold you back. Take a chance and trust the universe to catch you as you fall off the precipice into this new adventure.

Reversed

The reversed Fool card can signify that you are moving too fast too soon. In an attempt to be free and trust the universe, you are committing to too many risks and thoughtless actions without considering the consequences on yourself and others. The card calls you to slow down and take stock of yourself and your adventure. As you trust the universe, let your actions also show that the universe can trust you. The reversed Fool can also signify indecision and hesitation. You are letting too many thoughts cloud your free-spirited nature and are holding back from embarking on your adventure. While forethought and caution are okay, don't use it as an excuse to hold onto the past rather than explore the unknown of the future. The reversed Fool urges you not to be "a Fool"

The Magician

The Magician is numbered 1 in the deck and that is a number that represents new beginnings and opportunities. This signifies his connection to both the cosmic and physical realm. He uses this connection to tap into energy from the cosmic realm to create matter in the earthly realm. His white robe signifies purity while his red cloak signifies knowledge and experience of the world.

On the table are objects symbolizing each suit of the Tarot with each representing an element (Wands for Fire, Coins for Earth, Cup for Water and Sword for Air). This signifies that he has the resources needed to manifest his thoughts into action. Above him is an infinity symbol and around his waist is a snake swallowing its tails and this both signify unlimited potential. The foreground contains an array of blossoming flowers that symbolize the fruition and blossoming of his ideas.

Upright

As a master of making his thoughts a reality along with having all the tools, energy and potential, The Magician signifies that you have all the resources to realize your dreams into reality. You have spiritual energy (Fire), physical energy (earth), mental energy (air) and emotional energy (water). It signifies that it is a perfect time to go ahead a make a dream into a reality. You have everything you need to make your dreams become a reality and you are ready. Tap into the unlimited potential and energy at your disposal, establish a clear image of your goals and take the necessary steps towards achieving it. Remember, it is not only about having the energy, resources, and potential. You also have to take action and seize control. Focus and commit to the task at hand and take steps to manifest your dreams into reality. You are the master of your fate.

Reversed

On one hand, the reverse Magician can signify that you are exploring an idea to make into reality but are yet to take action to pursue it. You are being limited by your doubts in your ability to make it work with the resources at your disposal. Trust yourself and stay awake to the signs around you for the opportunities they can bring. On another hand, the reversed magician can signify a struggle to accomplish a current goal. You either don't know where to begin or what the next step to take is. You have failed to create a clear mental image of what your goals are and you are suffering from poor planning. Or you have lost touch with why the goal is important and no longer feel joy in following that path, therefore the universe is telling you to look back before you continue forward. At its worst, the reversed Magician signifies greed and manipulation. You are achieving your dreams to the detriment of others and doing it solely for your gain. This can either be intentional or unintentional. It can also mean untapped potential in hat you have all the resources and are the one holding yourself back from achieving your dreams.

The High Priestess

This card may also be called the Papess or Popess, as the term "High Priestess" would be anachronistic in historically accurate decks designed before the late 1700s. It represents intuition, mystery, and the divine feminine. In an upright position, this card signifies the need to trust in one's gut instincts, keep faith in spiritual wisdom, or to trust in the mystical knowledge of a feminine sage or diviner. It encourages stillness, passivity, and introspection, urging the querent towards a level of inner balance that will allow them to hear their own intuitive voice. Her message is: look within you, not without.

The High Priestess also indicates an enigma: things disguised or hidden, mysteries that have yet to unfold, people, objects, or institutions that are not what they appear to be. This is hinted at in the card's illustration; the High Priestess sits before a temple but the building itself is hidden behind a patterned veil. When you find this card upright in any spread, it is advisable to trust in your gut and stay wary of anything that seems particularly tempting, seductive, or too good to be true.

Reversed

When the High Priestess is reversed, it may signify cognitive dissonance, secretiveness, self-doubt, or other intuitive challenges that could be preventing the querent from trusting in their own judgment. It can also represent a duplicitous female or dishonest feminine energy in the querent's life, distorting their perception of reality. In the context of health issues, a reversed High Priestess may indicate a hormonal imbalance or underlying health issue that impacts the querent's mood, capacity for impulse control, and judgment.

No matter the context or question, a reversed High Priestess is most often an urgent call for self-care. The querent needs to focus on reconnecting to the self and getting in touch with their inner voice and core desires.

In earlier decks, the High Priestess or Papess might be depicted in a more traditionally religious light, wearing a Papal tiara with modest vestments and a Holy Bible in hand. In many modern decks, the High Priestess is renamed as "the Seer" and may be depicted as an androgynous or gender fluid being. No matter the era, this card always references inner knowledge and some form of divine wisdom.

The Empress

The twelve stars, however, signify the months of the year and planets. She dons a white robe patterned with pomegranates which symbolize innocence and fertility and she sits on a luxurious arrangement of flowing red velvet and cushions. One cushion has a symbol of Venus which symbolizes love and it is symbolic of fertility, beauty, grace – all these which are attributes of The Empress.

A vibrant forest and winding stream surround her to signify her connection to the Earth, nature, and life. Golden wheat in the foreground reflects abundance for harvest.

Upright

It is a sign of a powerful connection to femininity which translates to elegance, sensuality, fertility, nurturing, etc. all of which are necessary to create a balance between man and woman. You are urged to synchronize with your femininity. Connect with beauty. Tap into your senses and experience pleasure and fulfillment from your environment. Express yourself and be creative through art forms. Apply yourself to a new hobby that will tap into and improve your creativity.

The Empress also signifies abundance. Reflect on the beauty of abundance around you and take pleasures in the luxuries that life is offering. As an archetype of Mother Earth, The

Empress also encourages you to involve yourself in nature and sync with its energy. When this happens, you'll take in Mother Nature's caring nature and feel love, compassion and the urge to care for others.

This can also suggest pregnancy, birth or stepping into a mothering role. Birth and pregnancy can be literal or metaphorical in the sense of coming up with a new goal or even a sense of self.

Reversed

The reversed Empress encourages you to prioritize yourself. Love and care for yourself and focus on caring for your needs. It can also suggest a creative block in birthing a new idea or in creative expression. Don't bother with what people think and express yourself in ways that make you happy. The card may also make you aware of your body image. It asks you to love yourself and recognize your beauty inside and out. Don't depend on other people's perception of how you see the beauty in yourself and others.

Meaning of The Cards and Cards Interpretation Part 2

The Emperor

Sovereignty, leadership, strong masculine energy, structure, achievement, responsibility, safety, protection. The power available through discipline and self-control.

As the fourth Major Arcana archetype, the Emperor is associated with construction, formation, and solidity. If the Empress teaches that we are the creators of our reality, the Emperor shows us how to create with intention and discipline. This card often points to the need to build lasting support structures. Structure provides safety and protection, and creates a framework for achieving goals. Overall, the energy of this card is benevolent, representing the universal forces that wish to see you succeed.

As a side meaning, this card may relate to the positive influence of a male leader or father figure, from whom you may wish to seek guidance.

Upright
Power, leadership, achievement, stability, protection. Use your personal power, logic, and capacity for self-discipline to bring your goals into being. Energies are favorable for a stable path of progress.

Reversed
Domination, inflexibility, excessive control, rigidity. You or someone else may be taking the energy of discipline to an unhealthy or imbalanced extreme. Remember that flexibility is the necessary counterpart to solid structure. You may need to be protective of what you have created.

The Hierophant

Tradition. Wise mentor or leader. Religious or spiritual activity or community. Moral judgement. Conformity to practical approaches or beliefs.

If the High Priestess points to the inner mystery of our experience, the Hierophant (which means "High Priest" in Greek) points to its outward expression, where we have the opportunity to embody our ethical beliefs. This card reminds us that our journey can be assisted by tradition as we search for truth and understanding. There are benefits to aligning with the wisdom of those who have gone before us.

However, the Hierophant can also point to the need to re-evaluate traditions and communal beliefs in light of new information or experiences. As humanity evolves, so does its collective wisdom and sense of morality. Draw upon your inner wise leader when deciding whether to choose tradition or departure from it. This card often appears when you are on the brink of new spiritual growth.

Upright
Practical wisdom, guidance, spiritual progress, ethics. Take advice from someone you trust. You may find, or be, a mentor who can help resolve a challenge.

Reversed
Rigid attitudes, dictatorship, manipulation. Someone may be pressuring you to do things their way. You may need to challenge the status quo, at least in your personal belief system.

The Lovers

Choices, decisions, relationships, love, friendship, passion, partnership, growth, loyalty. Balancing desires with the needs and wishes of another.

As the sixth archetype of the Major Arcana, this card carries the energy of adjustment to new circumstances. As such, card might involve sudden changes, or the more gradually dawning understanding that one has outgrown a relationship or an environment.

Upright
Love, choices, unions, relationships. Positive alignment between one's beliefs and actions. You are capable of making the right choice. A favorable card in a love or relationship reading.

Reversed
Disharmony, fear of commitment, relationship issues. An inability to commit to one choice over another. Disharmony related to relationships or misaligned values. If a breakup is indicated, know that it will ultimately be for the good, even if it doesn't feel that way now.

The Chariot

Victory, achievement, journey, destiny, willpower, determination, self-discipline, control. Harnessing energy to accomplish a goal.

The Chariot archetype speaks to the elements of our life journey that involve determination, forward movement, willpower, and self-control. As the seventh card of the Major Arcana, the Chariot represents the potential to move closer to perfection through spiritual exploration and tempering the ego. Travel in the literal sense may be indicated, but typically this card has more to do with setting out on the road to self-mastery. We are no longer stepping blindly into new adventure, but setting a more determined course.

However, the Chariot also offers a warning, particularly if appearing during times of swift-moving events and high-intensity energy. In the Greek story of Phaeton and the Chariot, young Phaeton's impetuous, over-confident nature causes him to lose control of the chariot that pulls the sun across the sky, ending in global disaster. This card advises us to respect the power of our own will and use it wisely.

Upright
Determination, assertion, a drive for adventure. Often a favorable card with regard to journeys or long-term endeavors. Can also point to public recognition for a specific achievement or general success.

Reversed
Halted progress, lack of control, impatience. Heading in the wrong direction, the pitfalls of aggression, ego, and arrogance. As a side meaning, can point to travel delays or difficulties.

Justice

Right action, truth, law, fair decisions, objectivity, discernment, honoring your conscience.

As the eighth card of the Major Arcana, Justice brings the energy of stability and cosmic order. It represents truth, right judgment, resolution, and dealings with the law. Doing what we know is right can be challenging when we are opposed by others. This card may appear when you need to stand up for yourself (provided you are in the right) and for your beliefs.

Justice also teaches us about cause and effect, and the balancing role of karma as a universal principle. It reminds us that actions have consequences. We are impacted by the decisions of others as much as we are by our own. You are advised to pay attention to details in order to come to a balanced and fair conclusion.

At times, this card may appear when you're being too harsh on yourself or others. Remember that Justice isn't about shame or anger—only balance.

Upright

Virtue, balance, fair evaluation, right judgement. It's important to remain objective and stay out of ego as you evaluate the situation. Favorable with regard to legal or other decisions not in your control.

Reversed

Dishonesty, unfairness, lack of accountability, a moral dilemma. Someone in the situation is behaving dishonorably. The present situation may need to evolve further before a clear understanding of the circumstances can emerge.

The Hermit

Retreat, spiritual quest, needing a break from social activity. Following one's own path through inner guidance.

As the ninth archetype of the Major Arcana, the Hermit carries the energies of the mystical three and points to a successful integration of spiritual wisdom. He is a wise figure not only because he has studied and contemplated the mysteries of life, but also because he never stops seeking. As the ninth archetype of the Major Arcana, the Hermit carries the energies of the mystical three and points to a successful integration of spiritual wisdom.

Associated with inner knowledge and self-discovery, this card reminds us that as we seek intellectual and spiritual growth, we have to spend some time in seclusion. You may need to retreat to your inner thoughts to work out how to adapt to new circumstances, or take time and space to process recent developments (whether positive or unwanted).

The Hermit can also indicate a wise mentor, whether you or someone else in your life.

Upright

Solitude, inner wisdom, contemplation, going within. A state of solitude and searching, whether in academic study or spiritual pursuits. As a side meaning, the need for recovery after an illness or a harrowing event.

Reversed

Loneliness, excessive withdrawal, isolation, confusion. Unpleasant bouts of isolation and loneliness should be tempered with some positive social time with supportive people. You may be ignoring or resisting solid advice from a wise source.

The Wheel of Fortune

Cycles, turning of events, changing seasons, positive forward motion, the need to stay centered.

The Wheel of Fortune is all about the one constant that we can count on in life—change. As the tenth and final card of the decad within the Major Arcana, it highlights the cyclical energy of the Universe. As events and circumstances come to a close, the stage is set for new developments.

This card often appears in a reading concerning unexpected or unforeseen developments that change your plans or alter your course, for better or worse. Whether you're in advantageous circumstances or in the midst of struggle, know that the Wheel is always turning—the most stable place to be is actually in the center, rather than on top or bottom. In that sense, this card may be advising you not to get attached to particular outcomes at this time. No matter how well we plan or prepare, no one is ever completely in control of events. But this card reminds us that everything—the good and the bad—is temporary.

Upright
Positive change, end of delays, a lucky break. A positive turn of events, whether happening presently or somewhere on the horizon. May manifest as a new career opportunity or a financial windfall.

Reversed
Instability, unexpected disturbance, short-term success. A temporary downturn in luck due to external forces beyond your control. Be prepared for contingencies. Success that can't last or is built on shaky ground.

Strength

Fortitude, perseverance, inner strength, grace under fire, forgiveness.

Composure and tranquility in adverse situations. The Strength card often appears when we are facing challenges that seem insurmountable, reassuring us that we have what it takes to persevere.

Strength can often be confused with the ability to exert brute force, but as a virtue, strength harnesses the powers of patience and love and actually tames the energies of anger and ferocity. You are being encouraged to exert control over your life through love and confidence rather than force.

This card also acknowledges that we struggle, as imperfect beings, with desires and instincts that may not always be best to pursue. Here, will-power and determination are required to in order to follow the path of our highest good. Powerful spiritual forces may be at work in your life at this time.

Upright
Compassion, endurance, patience, courage, self-confidence. You have all you need inside you to weather any present storm. As a side meaning, can also indicate good health.

Reversed
Self-doubt, lack of self-discipline, weakness. Resist the urge to act out of anger, frustration, or fear. Avoiding conflicts or confrontations will only make a problem worse in the long run. It may be time to face an unhealthy or addictive behavior.

Meaning of The Cards and Cards Interpretation Part 3

The Hanged Man

"I can't fight or force the things that I cannot control. For this reason, I surrender."

Love

The Hanged Man indicates that you are in a state of limbo; there is no movement forward or backward—you're just hanging around, waiting in suspension and suspense. You may need to abandon any expectations for the relationship temporarily at this time—pause and not force or rush anything. If you are ready to move forward with a relationship, The Hanged Man could indicate that your partner may not have the same idea or that you are fearful of speaking the truth from your heart. For singles, it may seem like there is no progress in your dating life—or at least not the kind you may have been hoping for. This card reminds you to trust that the universe is holding you in good hands and doesn't want you to move forward for a reason. Let go of your need to control.

Career/Work

The Hanged Man symbolizes feelings of powerlessness regarding your work situation. You may find yourself waiting for a message or for something to materialize. This card can also suggest letting go of your need to control, instead being more open to taking direction from others and hearing different points of view.

Personal/Spiritual

The Hanged Man in personal readings is incredibly powerful because it shows that learning to let go and trust in something bigger than yourself will lead to your highest and greatest good. This card reminds you to have faith in yourself and the universe. Believe it or not, it is possible to enjoy this limbo phase if you relax into it and know that this will make the progress that much faster!

Reversed

When reversed, The Hanged Man shows that you are struggling to maintain control, refusing to let go to the point where it has become a detriment to your well-being. You may be fighting the inevitable or refusing to see things for what they are out of fear or a resistance to moving forward into the future. On the other hand, this card can signify that you may be staying in a space of helplessness and making yourself a victim.

Death

"I'm experiencing a period of incredible transformation!"

DEATH.

Death is the card of total and complete transformation. It is one of my favorites within the Major Arcana because when this card appears, it reveals that the circumstances around you have entered into a cycle of purging, cleansing, and releasing. Something around you now is coming to completion to make room for new growth. Wherever there is an ending, there is always a beginning, and the Death card is a symbolic representation of that process occurring in your life now. With any kind of "death," that energy is born anew in some other form. You may be releasing toxic people, thoughts, or things; moving from one place to the next; or saying goodbye to someone or something for now.

Love

The Death card symbolizes the end of some aspect of the relationship. Your love life is totally changing and revamping itself. It's possible that this can bring feelings of sadness, but at the same time, I have seen this card (very often!) show up for people who were moving from one phase of love to another or saying goodbye to singledom and welcoming love into their lives.

Career/Work

Your career and work life are under a spell of transformation when the Death card shows up. Something is coming to an end and the universe is preparing you for a new beginning. This card is a wonderful sign if you have been setting intentions to create a major change in your life, but if you are to be laid off from your job, it can definitely bring disappointment, too. Either way, you are reaching an end, experiencing a cut of some sort and being asked to be flexible as this transformation takes place.

Personal/Spiritual

You are laying to rest aspects of your life that no longer serve you, as indicated by the Death card. You may be forced out of a situation or find yourself in the midst of a total transformation as parts of your life melt away and take on a new form. With Death, it's important to remain open to these changes, even if they seem to your detriment initially.

Reversed

When reversed, the Death card can signify that you are avoiding necessary change. You may be holding on to something or grieving to the point where you have stopped experiencing the magick of your own life. Remember, every ending is the beginning of a new journey that will bring gifts all of its own. Resisting change doesn't stop it from happening, but it can and will prolong suffering.

Temperance

"I am working to bring opposite energies together to create something new."

Temperance signifies that this is a major moment to bring balance, moderation, and alchemy into your life. This card represents taking two very separate and different things and bringing them together to create some new form. This requires trial and error, which is why this card also symbolizes patience. Balance is needed, but in the eyes of the Temperance card, balance doesn't have to be a 50/50 split. It means finding the right mix of elements that works for you or helps you meet your goal. These two elements can be two people from different backgrounds or with different lifestyles. Either way, the appearance of the Temperance card means they are now working to come together in a magical new form in a way that's best for them.

Love

Temperance is about two people trying to figure out how to merge together. It represents patience but also respect for each other's differences, including finding out what works best for you both. You may be experimenting with different ways of communicating or working your schedules to make time for each other. If you are single, it may signify that you need to be patient with the universe as it works to find your "better half" for you. Take your time, the Temperance card says—don't try to rush to work things out. Patience is needed now more than ever, as well as understanding and an open mind.

Career/Work

When Temperance appears, you are trying to find balance or a system that works for you at your workplace. You may be trying out ideas, trying on new roles, or working with totally different groups of people to bring a project or goal to completion. Because there are so many different variables involved, you want to make room for some trial and error and not expect perfection right out of the gate. If you learn more about the project or the people involved with it, you will find you have a better shot at moving forward and creating something special and unique. Remember, patience is always needed with the Temperance card, no matter the question asked.

Personal/Spiritual

The Temperance card signals a need for moderation and balance. Where in your life does there seem to be too much or too little? Now is the time to rework this chemistry in a way that makes you feel better and supports your ability to thrive, not just survive. This card gives you permission to slow down, forgive yourself and others, and take it easy. You can also find yourself working out a balance within yourself—between your shadow side and light side—or trying to find where you fit in the world and who or what belongs beside you.

Reversed

When reversed, the Temperance card is symbolic of some kind of extreme. Balance is lost—there is either too much or not enough of something. We see this card when we are overindulging, worn down and not resting, or forcing an issue. Also, sometimes two different things are not destined to come together or to work, at least not now. Reversed, this card suggests that the differences are just too great to blend successfully. Find something else or pause to restore order once more.

Meaning of The Cards and Cards Interpretation Part 4

The Devil

Astrological Association: Capricorn

Kabbalah Path: Ayin, the Eye

The Devil shows a carelessness of results. In a way, he shows the ecstasy in all material things, but also how far they can drag us down.

There is a simple joy in indulging the desires, of cutting loose and letting wild. On its surface, there is nothing wrong with that. The problem with the Devil is that he is indiscriminate in what he indulges in. He revels in it all, be it healthy or poison, and does not suffer from a moral dilemma. He does not care what is right or wrong, only what makes him feel good. The Devil tempts with his simple joy, and when you're not looking, binds you to worldly pleasures he offers. He shows the short-sighted view of pursuing what you want without regarding the consequences. He also shows the abandonment of the spiritual. One does not need to be an ascetic to fulfill their spirit, but the Devil's trap is an easy one to fall into, and if not careful, the worldly can replace the spiritual very quickly.

The Devil comes and offers you a drink. "It's a long Journey, you should take a break and have fun for a while," he says. You join him, and one drink turns into another, then another, then another, for many days. It feels so good and easy at the time. But one night you pass out, and when you wake up, you find a chained shackle around your ankle. The Devil stands over you, chain in hand. "You've done so much already. Do you really need to keep struggling? You should just stay here," he says, offers you another drink.

Meanings

Instant gratification is the Devil's mantra. This is you giving over to your shadow side and allowing bad decisions to rule your life. You are stuck in the rut of the patterns of your behavior. At his worst, he often shows addiction or abuse, even violence. His appearance in a reading shows the chains that bind you from living as your best self. However, in seeing the chains, you are that much closer to freeing yourself of them.

Shadow Aspect
The Devil has fully blinded you. Under his influence, you have grown weak and allowed your petty desires to own you fully. As a result, you suffer the consequences.

The Tower

Astrological Association: Mars

Kabbalah Path: Peh, the Mouth

More than the Death card, this is the sign that makes a tarot reader sweat. The Tower is a swift catastrophe. In this card, everything is annihilated.

The Tower is that which shakes your fundamental understanding of the universe. All the rules you have lived by thus far are shown to be lies and you are left without a leg to stand on. More than at any other time, you are left disoriented. How can you be sure of what to rely on when everything can come crashing down at a moment's notice? As painful as if may be, this is the quintessential core of spiritual awakening. It is similar to concepts from Eastern philosophy, in which Nothingness is perfection, and so all manifestations of this world, for good or evil, are blights upon Nothingness. The Tower, then, becomes the vehicle of emancipation from the existence that traps us. Its destruction shows you how foolish it was to cling to it in the first place. Life is all an illusion. Not even your ego means anything. The Tower strips you of everything so that you may see nothing within everything.

The Devil has you imprisoned in a Tower. He binds you there by placating you with an easy life and tells you how wise you are. So, you stay. Every once in a while, you think about your Journey and see the path of it from your window, but always you turn back to the comfort of the Tower. The Journey was difficult, and you learned enough. Life here is good. Then, lightning strikes. In a rain of fire, it comes crumbling down, and the only way to save yourself is to leap from the window. You land on your Journey's path and watch as everything in which you found solace is destroyed. At that moment, you realize that all that matters is being present in the moment.

Meanings
This card heralds' imminent calamity. Utter ruin is foreseen, and the misery of having to pick up the pieces. The confusion will destabilize everything you've ever known.

Shadow Aspect

This card is one in which the shadow aspect actually brings out the good in it. In this case, this means spiritual enlightenment. You've seen the chaos around you and used it as a means of personal growth. You now see the facade and become aware of the true value in things.

The Star

Astrological Association: Aquarius

Kabbalah Path: Tzaddi, the Fish Hook

After the apocalypse of the Tower, in the light of the Star, we see the Truth revealed in its full light. She is the gifts of the Spirit flowing freely.

The Star brings immortality in that there is no separation between the core of the Self and the Divine Spirit. She embodies the personal growth that happens after the Tower. This is the soul who withstood the worst and came out its best. This is because, with the Star, all things are fully understood and appreciated for what they are, be they good or evil. Everything has a purpose in this world. In her light, blessings flow forth, and the farthest Star is within reach.

Through the razing of the Tower, your Journey has stripped of all that kept you from what you are at the center of your being. The ego has been dissolved and you exist in your purest sense. The Star shines down on you and pours the Divine down onto you like water. Faith is your power.

Meanings
Its most basic interpretation is hope in the sense that the Star shows bright prospects. That's only a surface reading, though. The Star represents much more. The Divine is everywhere, and you are connected to it. One does not need hope when united fully and totally to Spirit. Remain open to the gifts pouring down on you.

Shadow Aspect
There's an arrogance here, an attitude of being higher-than-thou. This is not true spiritual inspiration. If your faith is tested, you may find it to be shaken easily until the Star can shine through for real.

The Moon

Astrological Association: Pisces

Kabbalah Path: Koph, the Mind

This is the dark night of the soul. After the enlightenment found in the Star, after that blissful, perfect fulfillment, the soul swings back into doubt and fear. This is the power of the Moon.

This is a time when it will feel like you're feeling your way through the dark. The Moon is the unknown. This kind of pressure raises the animal instinct in all of us and so the natural response of fear. This is all subconscious activity of the deep processes that drive us. In defense of the intensity of the previous two cards, the subconscious draws up veils again and makes us see bogeymen where there are only shadows. Now, more than ever, our intuition is our only guide.

The brightness of the Star fades, and you are only left with the light of the Moon on your Journey. You stumble and fall, and freeze in fear. Everywhere around you, danger lurks and wolves howl. You don't know how you will ever make it through. But deep within you, something pushes you along, makes you look twice at the shadows. You begin to see they are just branches moving in the wind, and that the wolves are just dogs alert to your presence. Uneasily, you move through your fear and push forward through the night.

Meanings
This card serves to show you that there may be many things hidden deep within your psyche that are rearing their head. You may not know what they are exactly, but they are affecting you, and you feel their presence. This card embodies uncertainty and fear. Things are never what they seem under the light of the Moon.

Shadow Aspect
This is the silence when you know there should be sound. There is still an element of fear, but this silence only brings out what is unknown. You know there are intuitive messages coming your way, but you can't hear them. And yet, you're still afraid, because you know there's something out there you need to be aware of. Be still and listen harder.

Meaning of The Cards and Cards Interpretation Part 5

The Sun

Astrological Association: The Sun

Kabbalah Path: Resh, the Head

The Sun exposes all visions for what they are and detangles all mysteries. It is the most positive card in the deck and shines its light on everything around it.

Rather than the subconscious rising up, this is complete consciousness. This is the soul in full realization of itself. There is a certain simplicity in this card, of just being what it is, the warmth and joy and energy of all happiness made manifest. The subconscious and the conscious are joined as one. The soul goes forth as a whole being.

After the night comes the dawn. The Sun rises over the horizon, chasing away all shadows and leaving the Journey clear for you ahead. You bask in its light, allow the warmth to charge you, and with a deep breath, continue on your path in its light.

Meanings
This is a time when you can share the absolute best of yourself. This card has a lot of energy in it and may indicate a period where you will be so full to brim you won't know what to do with yourself. Life is good with this card. If you're looking for a 'yes' in your reading, this is a 'yes' shouted from the mountaintops.

Shadow Aspect
Everything is exposed in the light of the Sun. Some things may come to light that may not be pleasant to look at. However, the Sun is a uniformly positive card, even in negative contexts, so this exposure is always a good thing, like hanging something out in the sun to air out. Nothing can ruin this beautiful day.

Judgment

The judgment card is a call to stop and stare long and hard at your life and how it has been going. When it comes up in a reading, this card reminds us that we are working towards a future and what the future is can change at any moment. If you want to work in movies but ended up in TV because you thought it was your way in, it is more than okay to change your goal to something related to this new circumstance. You can aim for whatever kind of future you want; it is entirely up to you at any moment. You are the emperor of your own life; you get to decide. Because of this, you also know that you can change and leave your past self behind. That doesn't need to continue existing and holding you down. These are powerful reminders that will help greatly. When you see the judgment card, you should take some time to reflect on where you have come from and where you are now. Then consider where you want to be. How far have you come, and what do you need to do to get there? Is it still something you want, or is it time to set a new future? All of these are under your control, and the judgment card reminds us to recalibrate these values so we can get a better understanding of who we are and live more fully in line with our values.

The World

The world represents everything, and this means the end of the fool's journey; every desire has been achieved. Each part of the tarot deck so far has either been about a part of you or the way that events are going to play out. The world represents you as each of these parts combined into a single whole. You are every other card and the lessons they hold, now in a single card. When the world is drawn, you know that you are doing well and that the road you are walking is leading you directly to your unique destiny as a complete individual. However, as wonderful as this is, it needs to be remembered that this is referring to the question being asked of the tarot cards and not just life as a whole. So, the world points towards the answer, the positive outcome, the resolution of an issue. Whether it ends poorly or well, it ended the way it needed to end for you to continue on the path you are on. The world is a treasured card because it comes at the end of the deck. The deck doesn't end on a downer. Life is an extraordinary thing according to the fool's journey, and there are hard lessons to be learned, but they're what gives us greater power over our lives, and this is a truly excellent way to end the major arcana.

Meaning of The Cards and Cards Interpretation Part 6

Suit of Cups

The suit of cups deals with emotional energy. When these cards appear, it's time to examine your relationships, feelings, and whether your amount of emotional expression is appropriate. When trying to make a decision, cups tell you to let your heart and your "gut" guide you.

Ace of Cups

Ylang-Ylang EO

When this card appears in a reading, you are channeling loving energy from a higher power. Look around, because the Universe is trying to give you a gift. Receive this loving energy and let that love flow through you into the world around you. The energy of all Aces is the energy of new beginnings. The Ace of Cups can indicate a new relationship, a new creative opportunity, or a call to show your compassionate side. Know that if you say "yes" to these new endeavors you will experience great emotional fulfillment. This card is a call to open your heart and allow love to flow to you and through you.

Two of Cups

This card is a symbol of partnership, but because all cups cards deal with emotions, this is a very loving union. Whether a romantic partner, a business partner or a best friend, you are on the same energetic frequency with another person. Right now, you're in the early stages of your relationship, but this is likely going to be a long-term connection. Your similarities are in deep alignment and your differences complement each other well. Keep your eyes open for this potential new relationship and if you have found it - nurture it.

Three of Cups

Loyalty EO blend

When the Three of Cups appears in a tarot reading, it's a sign that you need to connect with your tribe. So much can be gained from time spent with good friends: from filling each other up with love and support to providing inspiration or collaborating on a project. It is often around your closest friends that you can let go of inhibitions and temporarily step away from your day-to-day stresses. This is not a time to take turns complaining, but instead it's a time to truly lift each other up and celebrate with joy and optimism. If it's hard to identify the group of people who make you feel this way, this card may be a sign to seek out a group of like-minded people or start a group of your own.

Four of Cups

Grounding EO blend

When the Four of Cups appears in a reading, it's a sign that you may need to say "No" to certain invitations and opportunities. By declining an offer now, you'll be in a better place to say "Yes" to new experiences later. You may be eager to take any opportunity that comes along because you're feeling bored and unfulfilled, but this card is telling you to wait for a better option. You may just have too much on your plate right now and you need to say "No" to avoid overwhelm. Give yourself permission to sit this one out. This is the time to examine your deeper purpose and passions so that you can focus your energy in the right direction. One caution - make sure you're not saying "No" out of fear or because your expectations are unrealistic. While you don't want to accept something that you know isn't a good fit, you also don't want to turn away every opportunity because you can find a minor flaw.

Five of Cups

Acceptance EO blend

The Five of Cups is a sign of disappointment. A situation didn't turn out as you expected and now you can't stop thinking about how you could have changed the outcome. You may also be focused on the unfairness of the situation and where others let you down or did you wrong. It's ok to feel disappointed, but when this card appears, it's a sign to start wrapping up the pity party and moving forward. Forgive yourself and others. Learn from mistakes that were made and if others showed their true colors, learn from that too. Often when things go wrong it's easy to focus on just the negative, but were there some positives too? Look for

the people who stepped up during this situation and the new opportunities that became available because of the change of direction.

Six of Cups

Inner Child EO blend

When this card appears in a reading, it often symbolizes a connection with people and places from your past. It's a call to reconnect with the energy of happier and less complicated times. Consider brightening someone's day with a random act of kindness. If there was an activity you loved to do years ago - painting, dancing, singing - try it again now. Make yourself and others smile today. This is a fantastic time to be playful and creative with no concern about how you'll be judged by others. Approach projects and relationships without expectation or prejudice. If your childhood was an unpleasant time, use this as an opportunity to nurture your inner child. Use affirmations to speak love to the younger version of yourself who lives within you. Say the words you longed to hear and give yourself the love you never received.

Seven of Cups

When the Seven of Cups appears in a Tarot reading, it's a sign that you are facing multiple choices or opportunities. When you're presented with too many options, it can actually be more confusing than beneficial. Take a close look at each of the choices in front of you. If something seems too good to be true, it probably is. Beware of abandoning your current project in favor of something else just because it's new and shiny. Instead of focusing on the promised outcome, make a plan for how you will achieve this success and decide whether that plan is something you can really commit to. This card is also a reminder that sooner rather than later you DO need to make a choice. Time will be wasted if you wait for the answer to become clear instead of actively exploring your options.

Citronella EO can be beneficial in improving focus when you're feeling "wishy washy." Apply to the corresponding alarm point: at the junction between the base of the skull and the top of the spine at the back of the neck.

Eight of Cups

When the Eight of Cups appears in a tarot reading you are walking away from something that no longer serves you. This will be difficult because it means letting go of something you once loved. Unfortunately, you've realized that this situation, opportunity, or relationship isn't truly in line with your desires and ultimate goals, and it likely never will be. You are not experiencing the spiritual or emotional fulfillment you were hoping to achieve, so it's no longer worth staying. Use this to card as a sign to seek out what brings true happiness into your life, even if that means a tough goodbye. The only caution is to be sure that you aren't running away simply to avoid addressing a difficult situation. If it doesn't serve you, move on. If you leave solely to dodge an uncomfortable issue, you will likely encounter that same predicament repeatedly until you finally deal with it.

Nine of Cups

The Nine of Cups calls you to express gratitude for all the blessings in your life. When this card appears, the results you've been working and praying for in your work, relationships, and within yourself are coming to fruition. Enjoy this time and appreciate all that you have.

Remember that you will attract more blessings when your grateful energy is sensed by the universe. Consider seeking out ways to share your abundance with others, as your generosity will be similarly rewarded. If you're experiencing financial success, reward yourself with a purchase that makes you happy. If you've found love, let yourself be swept away for the weekend. Good times will come and go. Fully experiencing this time of abundance will refresh your soul and make the difficult times easier.

Ten of Cups

It symbolizes genuine happiness within your family and relationships. You share love, joy and deep connections. When this card appears in a reading, look for opportunities to spend more time, emotions, and experiences with your loved ones.

Page of Cups

The Page of Cups signals a spark of inspiration the messages might not make sense at first but as you remain open to new information the pieces will begin to come together.

Knight of Cups

Upright - A youth who is flirty, romantic, sensitive, kind, loving, poetic, idealistic, an invitation, the hero or knight in shining armor, possibly fickle, love offering or engagement.

Reversed - Love interest moving away, sight is on another or another thing, emotional distraction, chasing dreams or fantasies, idealism, hopeless romantic who can never find

perfection and therefore is not reliable or committed.

Queen of Cups

Upright - A woman who is sensitive, kind, loving, romantic, idealistic, maternal, intuitive, psychic, deep, spiritual, nurturing, emotional, could be a psychic reader.

Reversed - Self-effacing, too shy, gifted but too timid or weak to trust in yourself, needs not being met, needs emotional support and nourishment, very psychic but not speaking it, no

one is listening.

King of Cups

Upright - A man who is kind, sensitive, loving, romantic, likes water, intuitive, psychic, nurturing, emotional, sometimes unstable, generally good natured, needs to be able to relax and integrate his experiences and feelings.

Reversed - Needs some time out for self-reflection, retreat near water, be careful near water, solo is best for a while, wise counselor, deep feeling and kind, genuinely concerned for the welfare of

others, may seem aloof.

CUPS people usually have blonde hair and blue or green or green eyes.

Their astrological signs most often are Pisces, Cancer and Scorpio.

Meaning of The Cards and Cards Interpretation
The Swords

Ace of Swords

Upright - Onrush of swift and powerful energy, bringing clarity or courage or causing someone to act in a quick and decisive way for good or ill, cutting through, force, double-edged sword, use force wisely.

Reversed - Death to a person or situation, 'no' is the answer, inability to decide, conflict is ruining clarity of choice, put down the sword and call a truce, don't use force or aggression unwisely,

peace is a two-edged sword, be graceful and gentle, but firm, time to give

something or someone a rest.

2 of Swords

Upright - Caught between two choices, perceptions or opinions, unable to decide, temporary truce, stalemate, neutrality, having blinders on, poise, unsure of the outcome, other forces at work in the situation, pointing the finger at someone, not wanting to be involved.

Reversed - Staying balanced and firm in a difficult situation, holding 2 points of view of equal value, waiting for something to blow over, time will tell what will be decided, waiting patiently for the outcome.

3 of Swords

Upright - Heartbreak involving two or more people, love triangle, sorrow, loss, separation, breakup, abortion or miscarriage, grief, sometimes in the past rather than the present or future, the ending of a relationship, past, present or future, suffering from others affecting you, need to withdraw from a situation or from circumstance which does not involve you, need for self-recovery.

Reversed - Let the past go, healing from emotional trauma or wounds, good health, having much love to give, heart operations successful, forgive others, bad weather for travel, beware of accident potentials, don't let other's drive your car.

Upright - Retreat, rest from strife, recuperation,

hospitalization, meditation, solace, needed healing, peace and tranquility, things on hold, timing not right for action, reviewing religious beliefs and doctrines.

Reversed - Prayers helping, lie low and concentrate, your inner self heals all your ills and troubles, you have your own power within, need a new bed, nurture and nourish yourself now, you

have more strength than you think but need to take time for renewal, read

and record your experiences.

5 of Swords

Upright - Arguments, power struggles, envy, jealousy, competition, blame, anger directed towards others or oneself, accusations, punishments, revengeful thinking or actions, strife, shame, defeat, going to war, victory in war, resentment, false pride, hidden enemies, gossip, humiliation.

Reversed - Damaging or hurting others by aggression and force, no conscience or remorse, conversely could mean someone who comes to the aid of another - picks up the pieces and repairs and helps heal wounds or trauma.

6 of Swords

Upright - Moving away from strife or difficulties, moving to a new location, period of positive movement, leaving the past behind, learning from experiences, positive move.

Reversed - Going backwards, unable to move, outer influences causing delay or return to old places or circumstances, feeling of temporary defeat, have to wait until

things shift.

7 of Swords

Upright - Walking away from something before it is finished, sneakiness, cleverness, escapism or avoidance, getting out while the getting is good, stealth, lying or deceiving, cowardice, folly, gossip.

Reversed - Thievery, cheating, abandoning a bad situation, not giving notice, and letting others finish the job.

Upright - Feeling held back, confined or trapped by past or current circumstances, imprisonment, being tied down, being held captive by one's own beliefs or fears or by the opinions of others, need to get out on one's own, possessiveness, soda masochism, outside interferences.

Reversed - Freeing yourself from bondage, walking out or away from a bad or imprisoning situation, saying 'no' to abuse, standing up for oneself, time to take your power back, stop self-pity, decide to be strong, you can do it, stop listening to others who are negative or self-defeating, take blinders off and look ahead. Go forward - take the first steps. Just do it! Get the help you need.

9 of Swords

Upright - Despair, worry, depression, illness, loneliness, mental illness, suicidal tendencies, need for comfort, nightmares, hopelessness, pessimism, could be of one's own distorted thinking, insomnia, all of the above leaving one's life.

Reversed - Headaches, despair increased, eye or back problems, hormone imbalances, poor health, need to stop dwelling on the past or on current anxieties, get help, use protection techniques.

10 of Swords

Upright - Hitting bottom, psychic attacks, ruin, feeling defeated, death, accident, negative cycle that will soon pass, the worst is over.

Reversed - Loss of valuable energy or reserves, others can no longer hurt you, you will soon be renewed, take time to heal, surrender your losses and start over - misfortune could be the

beginning of a new and better life.

Page of Swords

Upright - Messages through thought or email, a young person who is astute, mental, observant, intelligent, aware, perceptive, witty, intellectual, analytical, ready to make a move or physically move, good with horses, eloquent speaker, fair-minded.

Reversed - Foolish or rash behavior, decide carefully, be patient and wait, gifted artist or poet, clairvoyant, good teacher.

Knight of Swords

Upright - A youth who is aggressive, forceful, quick to act, compulsive, ready, courageous, sometimes acts without thinking, wants things in a hurry, impatient, progressive, and powerful.

Reversed - Need to take control of a situation, fight for what is right but be fair and just, use caution and then proceed, powerful leadership abilities, use influence wisely.

Queen of Swords

Upright - A woman who is analytical, highly perceptive and intelligent, observant and fair-minded, compassionate, could be a widow or a woman separated or divorced, clear in insight and of a higher mind when positive, decisive, right, knowing, sees through others.

Reversed - Critical or domineering, quick to judge, unfair, opinionated but still highly intelligent, has a soft spot for those in need, expects others to do their best and won't settle for less, strong when challenged, has great endurance.

King of Swords

Upright - A man who is more intellectual and opinionated rather than emotional or sensitive, could be a judge or someone in a position to decide matters, fair and highly reasonable in the positive, can be calm and easy, quiet and observant.

Reversed - Critical and cold in the negative, unfeeling, and judging with limited knowledge and foresight, weak internally, doesn't want the responsibility of leadership or decision-making, silent when he should be speaking up or acting.

SWORD people are usually fair-haired, with any color eyes.

Their astrological signs most often are Gemini, Libra & Aquarius.

Meaning of The Cards and Cards Interpretation
The Pentacles

Ace of Pentacles

Upright - A new business opportunity or money-making proposition, an increase in self-awareness leading to an increased sense of well-being, start of a new abundant cycle, self-definition, rising above limitations into something more productive, being offered a gift of money.

Reversed - Obstacles to achieving the money you need or desire, being held back by others, self-esteem needs to be boosted, may not be feeling well, misuse of money which is causing lack, repressed energies.

2 of Pentacles

Upright - Financial instability, two or more jobs at once, indecision about financial or work matters, in-between jobs, imbalance or fluctuation in emotions due to financial instability, roller-coaster, being at opposite ends with someone or something, things up in the air.

Reversed - Considering the possibilities, making a decision about the best choice, clarity and strength returning allowing for positive action, may move to a new location, feeling capable once again and in control of one's life and circumstances.

3 of Pentacles

Upright - A new project coming together or finishing the initial stages of a project, apprenticeship, submitting plans for approval, artistry, some expertise gained in some area but there is more to learn, arts and crafts, flea markets or craft fairs, the coming together of a project, work being accepted, take constructive criticism as a positive thing.

Reversed - Delays on the finishing of a project but all will turn out well, take the advice of others who are more experienced, be patient, spiritual guidance will come, keep records and plans on paper, more education may be needed.

Upright - Security gained, status quo, can be a hoarder, limitations in going further, fear to move out of current comfort zone, insecurity on a personal level, inhibited, fear of success, grounded or not grounded, inability to let go, self-defamation, treading on thin ice, rigid behaviors or viewpoints.

Reversed - Throwing caution to the wind, health returning, letting go of a stagnant lifestyle or way of doing things, having the confidence to go further, going back to school or taking a new job or position, may move to a new location, letting go of old fears and restrictions, opening up to new ideas and possibilities.

5 of Pentacles

Upright - Unemployment or job loss, financial hardship or instability, changes in finances, need to reevaluate current lifestyle or conditions, illness possible, seeking guidance, wanting to succeed but having a hard time, needing change, need to bring spirituality back into your life, prepare for cold climate.

Reversed - Spirituality regained, things getting better and moving forward, release of victim consciousness, making a decision for wellness, bring children into your life or do something to help others, to give is to receive.

6 of Pentacles

Upright - Promotions or loans granted, help financially or giving help to someone, generosity, benefactors, gifts, financial balance, gain, rewards, winning something, receiving what is due to you, paying off debts, gratitude is the key to prosperity, balance giving with receiving.

Reversed - Money given but not enough, not feeling deserving, have been put down by others, homeless person or situation, do what you can to find work, any amount of pay will increase your self-esteem, bank loan denied or for a lesser amount than needed, don't lose confidence - you can get back on your feet.

7 of Pentacles

Upright - Material accomplishments, resting period after earned successes or hard work, evaluation before proceeding further, gardening, fruition, vacation, strength and maturity gained, a level of satisfaction and peace achieved.

Reversed - Not satisfied with progress to date, re-evaluating a situation or outcome, a perfectionist who wants to do better, a good crop this year, fertilize soil for fruits and vegetables, working with the earth or environment is a good choice, natural healer - use your talents and abilities to achieve greater success, gifted with your hands.

8 of Pentacles

The eighth card in the Suit of Pentacles shows a man sitting on a bench, hanging the eight coins on a tree, far away from the distractions he would find at home, i.e. the village in the background. You can see that he is fully immersed in his task and he does not want to make any mistake whatsoever.

Upright Meaning: Dedication, Development of Skills and Focus

When it turns up in an upright position, the Eight of Pentacles can indicate that you are in a learning phase of a new skill or in the next level of a skill you already had. You are fully dedicated to it, and willing to do the same tasks over and over again just so that you can get as close to perfection as you possibly can. You are completely focused on your end goal, and consequently, on the tasks you have at hands. Remember that learning new skills takes time and a few setbacks along the way and keep up the commitment and hard work.

And if you see this card but you are not invested in any new skill or task, it might be time to do just that!

Reversed Meaning: Boredom, Mediocrity and Self-Growth

The Eight of Pentacles reversed might be a sign that you are bored with the repetitive tasks you have to take on in order to achieve greatness. Try to make your tasks harder or to find others on the same level that will teach you the same lessons.

It can also mean that you are not reaching the outcomes you wished for, either because you are not working hard or because the hard work you are putting in is not showing to be effective. Either put in a little bit more effort or change your approach.

Nine of Pentacles

A card full of bright colors, the Nine of Pentacles shows a woman in a long yellow dress and her whole outfit suggests that she is a wealthy woman, as does the big house you can see from afar. She has a falcon calmly sitting on her hand, representative of her intellectual side. Behind her, the coins and grapes grow, representing her achievements, and she is lightly touching them, showing that she has a healthy connection to what she has gained with her successes.

Upright Meaning: Independence, Rewards and Affluence

The Nine of Pentacles upright means that your efforts and all the rewards you have gotten from it have allowed you to be independent, to support yourself without the aid of others, and that can mean financially and/or as an individual, with your spiritual growth. More than anything, this card turns up as a reminder that you should celebrate, do what makes you the happiest and enjoy everything you have worked so hard for to the fullest!

Reversed Meaning: Working Too Hard, Spending Too Much and Self-Care

The Nine of Pentacles reversed can mean that you are working too much and you're harming your wellbeing. This is starting to become a pattern in this suit, but this card can show up as a reminder to take care of yourself. You are the most productive when you are healthier and happier, so don't slack off on those things.

It can also be a sign that you got so comfortable with the abundance that you may have started to spend a little bit too much. Remember that the money you worked so hard for can disappear in the blink of an eye. There is a fine line between spending it on things that you enjoy and splurging. At the very least, make sure to have a savings account that you do not touch unless it is an emergency.

Ten of Pentacles

There is a lot going on in the Ten of Pentacles card. It shows an older man sitting, with his two white dogs in front of him. It also depicts a young couple and their child, who is petting the dog. When we see all these people together, they seem to be three generations of the same family, and the older man is the wise patriarch who has achieved a lot during his younger years and is now able to provide comfort and security to his family.

Upright Meaning: Support, Family and Stable Foundation

The Ten of Pentacles upright is a great family card. Not only do you have each other's backs financially, but if there is something that is not lacking, it is love and affection between everyone.

All the hard work you have been putting into your career has paid off, and you are able to establish a safe foundation for yourself, as well as share it with your loved ones. Seeing them living comfortably makes you extremely happy, especially because you know first-hand what it took to get to where you are now.

As you get to such a stable phase of your life, this card also reminds you to think long term, so that you and your family don't end up losing everything you have now.

Reversed Meaning: Broken Family due to Inheritance-related Conflicts, Financial Loss and Instability

Wealth does not always bring up the best side in people and you might be going through a situation where that is clear. If you are going through disputes with family members because of an inheritance, understand how far you are willing to go for that money and remember that some things are not worth losing, not for any amount of dollars.

This can also suggest that you are going through some difficulties regarding your finances after you had just achieved a good level of comfort, which might be hard to adapt to. However, what you cannot do is keep living the same lifestyle. In order to get back on your feet, reduce your spending and work to go back to the stability.

Page of Pentacles

On the Page of Pentacles card, we can see one single man looking at the coin he is holding, representative of his wealth, comfort and aspiration, he is trying to understand how he can get even more benefits of that kind. In the back, the green scenery suggests affluence and the mountains stand for the setbacks he will come across.

Upright Meaning: New Opportunities, Development of Skills and Manifestation

The Page of Pentacles upright tends to show up when you are looking for new financial opportunities that will allow you to get where you wish to in terms of money and material possessions. It reminds you that in order for you to find them, not only do you have to keep your eyes open, but you have to be determined and willing to put in effort and time into your professional journey.

One way to do that is by learning new skills and/or learning even more surrounding an area you are already familiar with, so that is what this card encourages you to do.

Reversed Meaning: Laziness, Stagnation and Missed Opportunities

The Page of Pentacles reversed comes as a warning sign that you are letting procrastination get in the way of you achieving your objectives, either by not working on your project as much as you should or by not grabbing new opportunities. It invites you to understand why you are being lazy and how you can change that.

It can also mean that you have reached a point of stagnation when it comes to your project, so this might be a good time to either change the approach or distance yourself from it, so that when you come back to it your brain has had time to refresh and hopefully, you will see possible ideas that you did not see before.

Knight of Pentacles

The Knight of Pentacles shows a knight on his black horse, holding a coin while carefully looking at it. This indicates that he is really thinking and planning before he takes any action, which is very different from the other knight cards we have seen before. This knight thinks long term, while others only consider their short-term objectives and possible victories.

Once again, there is a reference to repetitive tasks needed to do in order to succeed, with the fields in the background, but the knight is willing to do them.

Upright Meaning: Planning, Routine and Long-Term Goals

The Knight of Pentacles upright means that you have been applying a more thought-out, rational approach to the way you work, which might delay the moment you take action, but also allows you to make informed decisions. You don't let yourself rush because of your short-term goals; rather, you consider the long-term ones, as you know that those are the ones that will give you a stable foundation in the future. This might mean starting a daily routine that is not the most exciting one, but when you see this card, you can rest assured that you are on the right track.

Reversed Meaning: Irresponsibility, Monotony and Inflexibility

Firstly, the Knight of Pentacles can be a sign that you are not being mature and responsible enough for the work you have to do. Avoid doing things like leaving certain thing for tomorrow when you can do them today and doing things just so they are done, instead of doing them well.

It can also mean that you have gotten bored with the monotony of routine. If so, change it up to make it more exciting, while achieving the same outcomes.

Lastly, it can be a sign that you want everything to be so perfect, that you are lost the ability to be flexible with yourself and with others. This card encourages you to relax and accept the fact that everybody makes mistakes.

Queen of Pentacles

The scene depicted in the Queen of Pentacles happens in nature: The Queen sits on her throne and observes and nurtures the coin she has on her lap (i.e. her wealth). Look closely and you will see a little rabbit at the bottom of the card, representative of her energy and fertility.

Upright Meaning: Success, Nurture and Practicality

The Queen is a very compassionate and nurturing figure, and this card in an upright position represents just that. With the energy, practical thought and calm attitude, you have been treating those around you, you make everyone feel good and loved. And still, you find time to dedicate yourself to your professional life and be continuously successful. You have found the perfect balance.

Reversed Meaning: Unbalance, Inner Conflicts and Self-Care

The Queen of Pentacles in reverse can signify that you are having a hard time balancing your professional life and your personal life, and that is making you feel guilty. Remember that there is time for everything and some adjustments in your time management will make you feel a lot better.

It can also signify that you are taking care of yourself. This is very important in able to achieve success, so even if now you are doing it with bigger gestures - maybe you treated yourself with an expensive massage or you bought a ticket to a country you have always wanted to visit - you should find small ways of treating yourself every single day.

King of Pentacles

- Upright: discipline, self-control, self-mastery, personal power

- Reversed: controlling, abusive, domination

Meaning of The Cards and Cards Interpretation Wands

Ace of Wands

It is a sign of expanding consciousness and knowledge. There is a creative process ahead, and new things will be born. This may also state the birth of a new baby as well as a new project or a new idea. In either case, the process is a healthy and productive one. If you put enough effort into it, the progress is inevitable. Reversed, this card symbolizes problems. Because the person is not yet equipped enough to solve them and they might make decisions that are not well thought. Usually, it might mean that the timing is not right for the things that are planned or the person is not mature enough.

Keywords: Activity. Initiative.

Concise direct/positive meaning: Great start! Be as active as you can.

Concise reversed/negative meaning: Premature start. Excessive self-confidence, impulsivity, and adventurism.

Two of Wands

It tells you to listen to your intuition if you are facing a problem. You have the potential of being creative and the potential to be original too. You have all the knowledge for that. The card also means that someone is strong minded and they know how to get ahead of the game. This might sometimes look as over-ambitious, but actually, it is strong willed. It also shows balance and fairness.

Reversed, this card means Indecisiveness which in turn causes to put things on hold for long periods of time. It also symbolizes the lack of originality and not having enough inspiration. Instead of being strong willed, this person can easily be manipulated because they feel weak and they do not have enough self-confidence to make a decision. Usually, they are afraid of doing the wrong thing and being criticized for it.

Keywords: Equal rights. Business partnership.

Concise direct/positive meaning: Successful negotiations. Constructive cooperation.

Concise reversed/negative meaning: Do not compromise. Unsuccessful business partnership. Different interests and points of view.

Three of Wands

This signifies being rewarded for hard work. This is the card of a good outcome when it comes to work. When it comes to a relationship, it indicates someone being picky. But they will be rewarded for it too. For people who are single, it can mean a new romance with someone who will feel like a soulmate, for ongoing relationships, it means that the relationship will move on to a deeper level.

Reversed, this card symbolizes that the person is experiencing delays for the outcome. There are obstacles and blocks in the way. The person might be dealing with something they are not capable of handling because they do not have enough experience. It shows disappointment.

Keywords: News awaiting.

Concise direct/positive meaning: Wait a little more, and you'll get a result.

Concise reversed/negative meaning: Long and pointless waiting.

Four of Wands

This signals a happy event is about to occur. It could be a wedding, engagement. It might also mean the purchase of a new property. It shows an increase in wealth. For people who already have a house, this might mean a second one to use as a vacation home or life in the countryside.

Reversed Four of Wands means the cancellation of plans and change of plans. If there was a plan for a wedding or engagement, there might be problems. The conditions might not yet be ready so you should avoid making important decisions.

Keywords: Celebration, Holiday, crowd.

Concise direct/positive meaning: A deserved success. Rest after a hard day.

Concise reversed/negative meaning: Premature jubilation.

Five of Wands

This signals irritation, opposition, and argument. Especially in teamwork, the need to stand out individually. But it also shows a personality that defends what is right, even if there are people who oppose and disagree. For relationships, it can be an argument. Personality wise it shows problems with authority, self-doubt, and insecurity.

Reversed, this card means not having enough faith for a favorable outcome, thus, not giving enough effort towards it. There is a lack of self-confidence, fear of success and fear of conflict.

Keywords: Chaos.

Concise direct/positive meaning: Don't be afraid of mess and clutter, that is all not for long and won't harm.

Concise reversed/negative meaning: The intrigues, quarrels.

Six of Wands

This symbolizes recognition, feeling good about yourself and feeling achieved. It also symbolizes success and victory. If you have been working on something, this signals a good outcome. You will be pleased with the result. The person for whom this card appears is someone who is popular in his/her circle.

People find this person friendly and approachable. In relationships, it means admiration by their partners. At work, it symbolizes successful projects.

Keywords: Triumph.

Concise direct/positive meaning: Success and confidence.

Concise reversed/negative meaning: Overconfidence, pride. Premature jubilation.

Seven of Wands

This symbolizes a person who is capable of adapting to different situations easily. However, this also indicates a personality that puts up barriers. It is because they prefer to protect themselves and their personal space. This might make other people think that the person is not approachable. In a relationship, it means the person is putting up walls because they are afraid of being hurt.

Reversed, this card means lack of self-defense, inability to take action. When this card is reversed it might also show that something the querent has been working for is falling apart. Or simply not going anywhere.

Keywords: Fight with invisible and obscured enemies.

Concise direct/positive meaning: Skillful protection of one's point of view.

Concise reversed/negative meaning: A person takes a defensive position. He stubbornly defends his point of view though no one tries to persuade him otherwise or attack him.

Eight of Wands

This signals a quick turn of events. This card usually appears when someone is expecting visitors or is planning to go on a trip. It also means that the person is planning to visit someone. For those who are in a relationship, especially a new relationship, this card symbolizes falling in love. If single it might show that the querent will meet someone with whom they will fall in love rather quickly. Career wise it signals a change ahead, in a good way. Reversed, this card means physical exhaustion. Certain things are not going in the right direction at work or in a relationship. Beware of unnecessary arguments.

Keywords: Speed.

Concise direct/positive meaning: Fast and confident actions.

Concise reversed/negative meaning: Slow down. Don't rush headlong.

Nine of Wands

This is about finally finding the courage to do something. Maybe you have wanted to do something but were hesitant to do so. If this is the case, you will feel braver to take the next step. You discover a side of you that is stronger. However, this card also shows you currently do not have enough trust in others. You strongly defend what you believe in, and you are a family-oriented person. You protect your family. In a relationship, this might signal stressful times.

Reversed, this card means you are feeling weak, and you are stubborn. You have thoughts and beliefs, but you do not stand by them, you rather let things be, instead of making an effort to progress.

Keywords: Conclusions the complicated fight. Weariness.

Concise direct/positive meaning: You need to rest and to think.

Concise reversed/negative meaning: Fatigue, apathy. Delay, procrastination in all affairs. Difficulty. Hardships. You should stop waiting and start acting!

Ten of Wands

This symbolizes having more responsibilities than one can handle. It might cause someone to get overwhelmed by it and lose track. You need to remember to focus on the result instead of worrying too much about the little details. If a person is in a relationship, then it means this relationship requires too much effort to keep. If the person is single, then they are more focused on what others will think of them, instead of trying to show their real personality. Reversed, this card symbolizes fear of taking on responsibilities. It could be due to lack of motivation or lack of self-esteem. They do want the experience, but they are at the same time ready to call it quits and walk away.

Keywords: Reload. Powerful tension. The last effort in finalizing of important business.

Concise direct/positive meaning: hard work and diligence will help you overcome any troubles.

Concise reversed/negative meaning: A person took more than one can carry (physical and mental strain). Responsibilities that you cannot manage.

Page of Wands

This means the querent is curious and willing to learn new things and experience different things. There are also new ideas that will come to the surface, but the cards before and after will determine better how the situation will progress. There is an overload of communication. Because this card is about "news" of any kind. It could mean the person is receiving news or they are delivering the news. In a relationship, it means there could be ups and downs as each party is learning to grow.

Usually, people like this attract others who will challenge them both spiritually and intellectually because they love learning. Reversed, this card means lack of enthusiasm and not having enough motivation to learn and experience new things. Instead, the person wants others to pay them attention. If they are in a competitive situation, this is most likely an unhealthy process due to unnecessary drama.

Keywords: Good news. Delight.

Knight of Wands

This denotes a person who loves being the center of attention. But they are the center of attention, whether they try it or not because they have a charming, fun and loving personality. The card also symbolizes high energy, passion, and love. In a love reading, this card shows a relationship that is working well. There are fun and romance and love and passion. The couple might be planning to travel together. Professionally, it means new and exciting job opportunities. But depending on the person's position, it could also mean that this job requires a lot of interaction with people and requires problem-solving skills without being carried away in other people's drama. Reversed, this card means a highly competitive person in a destructive way because they will stop at nothing to get what they want. Revenge, bad temper and bad thoughts should be kept under control.

Keywords: Activity, courage.

Concise direct/positive meaning: Courage and resolution. Active steps.

Queen of Wands

This indicates a warm, likable, passionate personality. Usually, this card appears for people who are interested in metaphysics, supernatural and spiritual things. It also symbolizes an inner journey towards self-discovery. Career wise it can symbolize learning new things to advance. Reversed, this card symbolizes a dominating and intimidating personality. Usually, these people complain about not having real friends. They think everyone around them is superficial and fake, but in fact, they are the ones who push people away with their dramatic personalities.

Keywords: Energy. Generosity.

Concise direct/positive meaning: Success in all affairs. Joy and happiness.

Concise reversed/negative meaning: A self-confident, scandalous, ambitious person. An obtrusive and excessive care. Redundant generosity, extravagance, and the desire to splurge.

King of Wands

- Upright: leadership, valor, honor, successful business ventures
- Reversed: unsatisfied, hasty, expecting too much, ruthlessness, ego

Reading for Yourself and For Others

Tarot cards are visual tools to help the subconscious mind perceive messages. Tickets can be used as a mediator between your conscious awareness and the source of information ("God," "Gods," religious leaders, hobbies, angels, ancestors or whatever);

Tarot cards work because they are not magical, and they are well crafted. Magic "you." "You." "You." You're the intangible being who knows more than what you can see, taste, hear, feel, and sense every day. The problem is that you are so aware that your brain can't work, and most of it stops. Peens when you are overwhelmed, and too many people talk at once or when the boss shouts and the radio play while the TV is on (extra loud to compensate for the yells). Your brain tries to shut off a great deal of excess noise to focus on what you decide. If it's too much, the brain tries to shut everything out, so that you can regain the center.

Your overall performance is similar but on a much larger scale. Life calls for survival (sleep and food that do not require experience over time). All of this is a mental disturbance that must make you feel like dreaming, producing "tunnel vision." Its trance-like state is no different from the trance in which all the others are. Therefore, enlightened people "above all," the object of wealth and luxury is the elimination of the psychic psychobabble of everyday life and the enhancement of your consciousness. Ironically, it often leads to people who have a higher level of insanity (untrained in the theory of knowledge), but this time to a deeper level of self-gratification.

You're already psychic. Some don't get a special gift, and some don't. Training is needed, but you can become more conscious of your own destiny and power. Tarot cards are an insight escape when you are able to get rid of all conversation and stress, and they also take you in the right direction to solve problems and answer questions. You can do it with a bunch of players, but it's a lot harder. This is why even centuries after they reject the idea that "rich people are closer to God" rather than the poor (the principle of God's activeness, "Nobility," and aristocracy is mainly rich people who abuse poor people, and poor people who somehow accept it as' right and faithful').

Tarot card images can seem outdated or absurdly obsolete, but they symbolize major human events, motives, and behavior. See the pictures and see with your eyes what is there. The trick is not to memorize a bunch of (non-useful) keywords and words or try to force astrology into cards that do not match. This maintains the urge of dogs and cats to mate. It's not right! It's not right!

However, what works is throwing away all the superstitions and the myth of reading cards and sitting down and looking at the cards. Get to know them. Get to know them. Get to know them. Get to know them. Hello, everybody, see what the images are telling you. Please reply (It's always best to ask a question, so you know what your cards respond to) and look at the cards.

1) When you are comfortable and open to all texts, it is easier to read tarot cards.

Often said, but not as often clarified. The reason this is so critical is that you are very tempted to test your cards when you hope for results. Sadly, this will only impede your comprehension of the cards, and you will lack their knowledge. I am afraid it does not count as a reading of wishful thinking. If you are worried or worried about a problem, but it is tempting, try to wait for you to remain calmer.

2) The Major Arcana or the Divisions of Minor Arcana have tarot cards.

If you're a novice, you might have a book to hand to help you with your ticket definitions. This is a great idea, but don't lose out on the implications of a set of cards. Major Arcana, for instance, has a stronger message often and can mean that you really have to sit and consider that if one of these cards appears. The cups usually apply to emotional problems in the Minor Arcana. Know these general rules and concentrate on individual interpretations because they can subtly change your message.

3. You may find it useful to try various spreads for a particular purpose when reading tarot cards, such as love reading.

A tarot spread means that the cards are placed and positioned in accordance with the spread rules selected. The position of the map represents something like the past or present, etc., and yes, it is another way of subtly changing the meaning of the card! The Celtic Cross is a popular tarot spread, but variants can be searched for.

4) Not everybody has a mighty intellectual talent.

Nonetheless, everyone can rely on the latent abilities they all have. This skill will be significantly improved by daily or at least a persistent reading of tarot cards. Each time you ask a specific question, you can notice some pictures or symbols or cards often appear in specific fields. Learn how to accept this new voice— it's yours, and you're different. The first and most reliable response to a question is often psychic intuition, so learn to trust your associations and to be on the right course.

5) Pick your tarot deck carefully.

The Rider-Waite deck is the most popular and reliable and precise, so it is an excellent base for beginners. The Tarot of Marseilles is another famous one. The main factor is that you have to talk to the symbolism. Have you always been attracted to holidays? Maybe a fairy deck depicting the cards is perfect for you? The same is true if you are still aligned with ancient goddesses. Recall that it is personal to read tarot cards, so move on and understand what you like. Feel free to have several packs to choose a mood-based rack.

6) Tarot can be used to ask questions quickly or to obtain a situation snapshot, but keep your question straight and just select one card. It is perfect, for example, for "how will my day be? For a quick morning read.

7) Did you know you can also use cards in a simple spell while tarot cards are used primarily for divination? Spell candles derive their color power, for example, emitting energy that overcomes specific difficulties? Orange is excellent for creativity.

Techniques for Reading Tarot

When you are ready to start practicing spreads, find a few that you are most comfortable with. You only need simple spreads that use a few cards when first starting out. Even the most advanced Tarot readers still find benefit from a three-card spread.

Begin by clearing your cards of energy and shuffling them thoroughly. With any spreads, you'll want to meditate on your question while shuffling. Continue shuffling the cards as you repeat your question until you feel ready to lay them down.

Feel free to cut the deck as many times as you want or have the person you are reading for shuffle and cut them. Find a ritual that gets you in the best head space to analyze and interpret the images you are about to see. You may feel the need to use a "clarifying card." This is when you pull an additional card to provide more context to a spread. You don't want to use this as a crutch, but it can be used when more information is needed.

If you have a friend that's able to help you, try doing this exercise to improve your contrast and comparison abilities. You can use this method of practicing for focusing on the entire deck, the Major Arcana by itself, or the Minor Arcana independently. In any case, you'll start by shuffling the deck. Once shuffled, take the top card and put it in front of you to the right. This is the card for your friend. Then take the next card and place it slightly to the left of the first, as the card that represents what happens to yourself. Perform a mini-reading. Do this again with the next two cards and work your way through the entire deck. This will increase your familiarity with the cards and get you used to look at all the cards equally. We need to remember that these cards are all equal and that we should have any reservations with drawing certain cards. Also, try to come up with different impressions and meanings instead on one rigid definition of each card. Don't spend too much time on any card or pair of cards. You can ask a simple question before each draw, or you can simply perform this exercise to create your own stories for the cards simply.

For even further insight into the relationship of the cards in a spread, pay attention to if they are facing one another or if they are facing away from each other. What type of indications comes up when we take note of the way the figures in the cards are facing? Look through your cards and find figures in each card that are looking towards or away from each other.

Ask yourself the following questions:

- What's the purpose of this interaction?
- Is the subject matter positive or negative?
- Why might they be facing away from each other, or facing each other regarding this scenario or question?
- What are these cards communicating?
- Are they ignoring each other?

Spreads

One Card

As mentioned before, you can simply pull one card a day. Set your intention before you pull the card by asking what energy you need to focus on, or what you might experience in your day. Make a note about what card you drew and what stood out to you about it. At the end of the day, journal any correlations you found.

Three Card Spreads

- Past-Present-Future

Many Three Card spreads relate to the Past, Present, and Future. Place the cards left to right and they will represent the past, present, and future positions. You can find the things that shaped who you are and what's happening in your life now as well as receive an indication of where the energy in your life is leading. Keep in mind that your current actions have the power to change everything.

- Blessings- Challenges- Action

Another Three Card Spread is the Blessings, Challenges, Action spread. If you are seeking clarity regarding the next step, then this spread can be beneficial. Laid the same way as the Past, Present, and Future spread, this shows where you will find help in this situation in the Blessings position. For Challenges, you see what problem you need to solve, or what you're up against. With the Action position, it signifies what you should or should not do to address the challenge.

- Situation- Action- Outcome

In unclear situations, this three-card spread can be particularly helpful. The left card, the Situation, is the thing you've asked about. This may look different than you expected but it will give insight into what's going on. The middle card, the Action card, is a recommendation of the action needed to get to the card on the right, the Outcome card.

Five Card Spread

1. The far-left position, or the bottom, represents the reasons leading to the situation at hand.

2. The left of center position reveals those things in our past that still affect us currently.

3. The center position represents our present situation.

4. This position signifies our future outcomes.

5. The top card is possible outcomes if the course of action is followed.

Celtic Cross Spread

One of the most popular spreads, the Celtic Cross uses 10 cards in a circle/line layout. There are many variations regarding how the cards are laid but they will typically consist of five cards (one in the middle and four cards surrounding it – one on each side of the middle card and one card laid sideways on the center card.). Then a line to the right of those five for cards seven through ten.

1. Center card on the bottom. The first card you lay. It represents the current condition.

2. Center card laid on top of Card #1. Represents your Current Obstacles and Troubles.

3. Above the center card, representing the best outcome possible.

4. To the Right of the center card, representing the cause for the current situation.

5. Below the center card, representing your near past.

6. To the Left of the center card, representing you in the near future.

7. On the Bottom of the Line to the right of the circle. This card represents in general, who you are right now and your relation to the theme of the question.

8. Directly above the preceding card, this position represents your current surroundings as it relates to your question. (environment, family, friends)

9. Directly above the preceding card, representing fears and hopes regarding the situation or your life in general if there is no specific question.

10. The final and top card of the line, this card represents the outcome, or how this phase is turning out.

Horseshoe Spread

A seven-card spread where there is one main card placed in the center and has three cards laid on either side of it forming a staggered version of a horseshoe. This spread is read from left to right.

1. The Past (The first card on the bottom left working towards the Center and down the right side)

2. The Present

3. Hidden Influences

4. You, or the Querent

5. Attitudes of others

6. What you should do

7. The Outcome

There are so many spreads for you to learn, and multiple variations on each one that you should have plenty to practice with. Find which spreads you are comfortable with. You can use certain spreads for certain types of questions, or for deeper understanding in the card's relationships.

You may decide to include reverse cards in your readings, or not. Don't feel pressured to do anything you're not ready to commit to!

Choosing Your Cards or Letting the Cards Choose You

At one point in time, there really weren't very many options when it came to choices in tarot decks. There were a few well respected, well-illustrated standard decks available. In fact, if wanted a deck that was really unique, you would be called upon to illustrate it yourself. Times have changed and those days belong in the past. Today, there are so many choices of tarot decks that the process of choosing the right deck for you, especially if it is your first one can feel overwhelming to say the least.

The process of choosing your deck is a highly personal one. Some people find the deck the resonate with right away and that is the only deck they use for years until the images have become so worn and the cards so frayed that the deck is barely recognizable anymore. Others, have a collection of decks, each appealing to them for different reasons and they alternate between all of them. Unfortunately, there is another group that has a collection of tarot decks, but most of them sit around unused because they were purchased, only to realize after working with the cards for a bit that something about the energy didn't feel right. The cards just didn't resonate with the reader. This is not only discouraging, but also costly since some tarot decks can be a little pricey. Therefore, I would like to present you with some advice on choosing your first deck before we even get started talking about the actual cards. I want your experience with tarot to be as positive as possible.

To begin, let's talk about the difference between a tarot deck and an oracle deck. The traditional tarot deck is standardized in many ways. There is a structure that remains in place regardless of the theme or the artwork. A tarot deck contains seventy-eight cards, including twenty-two major arcana cards and fifty-six minor arcana cards. There is an order in which the cards appear, and there is standard symbolism associated with each card regardless of the deck. With tarot cards, the real difference from deck to deck is the artwork and the energy that it puts off. If you love renaissance art, you might not easily relate to a deck that features simple lines and clean modern art. Even though each card has some standard symbolism, the artwork adds new elements to the card. This is why you might get a feeling about, say the World card, in one deck but feel you are getting a very different message from the same card of another deck. You may also find that some decks are easier for you to interpret while others require you actually to study them intuitively. Tarot cards were originally structured to be a game and resemble the suits that you would find in a traditional deck of playing cards today.

Oracle cards are cards that were designed with divination purposes in mind, but their theme and structure is not in any way regulated. There might be twenty cards in an oracle deck, or there might be one-hundred cards. The cards might contain imagery similar to that of the tarot or they might not. Oracle cards are often beautiful and valuable tools for connecting to your inner voice, however you must learn to read each deck independently. There will be no similarity in meanings from one deck to the next. Most oracle decks come with a guide that will help you discover and connect to the symbolism of the cards. A typical tarot guide might be useful for spreads, but it will not offer you much insight into oracle cards in terms of the individual card meanings.

Whichever type of deck feels most comfortable to you is the one that you should use. It is just important that you know the difference because many a novice has wandered in to pick up a tarot only to end up confused and frustrated with trying to use it according to tarot descriptions. The purpose is to discover tarot, so those are the cards that we will focus on, however everything in here, except for the actual card descriptions themselves can be applied to any tarot or oracle deck.

The most important tool you have for choosing your tarot deck is your intuition. Some might say that you should start out with a well-recognized deck, like the Waite deck, which has been studied and used for generations. This isn't bad advice, but personally I feel that you are only going to develop your intuitive powers, which are necessary for reading the tarot, if you feel connected to the imagery of the cards on a deeper level. If a well-known deck does that for you, then great. However, if you feel no connection to that deck, it is best to pass it by and choose one that really resonates with you. Don't be surprised if you end up with a deck that you never would have thought you would choose. Tarot speaks to us on a level that we don't always understand. This is ok, go with what feels right.

If you have a metaphysical store or a bookstore that carries a variety of tarot cards, take a stop in there and look around. Most retail establishments that sell tarot cards have a sample deck of each style set out for you to examine. Take your time and look over each card. Even feeling negatively about one card can affect your overall relationship with the deck. Go through each deck and choose the one that feels most personal. If you are in a position where you are buying your cards online, do a little research and find images of each card before making your decision.

Don't neglect the guide that comes with each deck. In each box of tarot cards is a little booklet that should explain the history of the deck, the philosophy behind it and a brief explanation of card imagery and symbolism.

Take your purpose into consideration. There is a tarot deck out there that fits just about every area of spiritual and metaphysical interest. You might come to tarot because you want more connection with spirit guides or angels. If this is the case, you should choose a deck with imagery that is relevant. The same goes for other interests such as fairies, nature, goddesses, meditation, etc.

Practical matters are important too. The size of the cards and how they feel in your hands are two very important factors to consider when choosing your deck. You don't want the cards to be uncomfortably large in your hands, and likewise you don't want them to be so small that they are awkward to handle. They should be printed on sturdy, high quality card stock. Some decks have a sheen or lamination to them that is meant to serve a serve a protectant, but also make the decks easier to clean. Decide if you want this feature or if you prefer the more traditional, coarser feel of a matte deck.

Not only does the imagery need to resonate with you, but you also must be able to see and use it. If you have poor eyesight or know that you will be doing readings in a dimly lit environment, choose a deck that is not heavily or ornately illustrated, but has clear pictures and clean lines instead.

Sometimes the deck needs to find you. There is folklore floating around out there that you should never buy your own tarot deck, that instead your cards should be gifted to you. I disagree with this philosophy; however, I do not deny that sometimes the deck will find a way to you, and when it does you should not refuse it.

Finally, if after choosing your deck and working with it for a bit, you aren't feeling a connection to it, please don't get discouraged. Everyone who desires a relationship with tarot can have one, it is just a matter of exploring different decks until you find the ones that opens the door for you.

The Most Effective Method to Read Tarot Cards – Your Step-By-Step Guide

1) Align Yourself with the Tarot

Understanding imagery is an incredible begin to figure out how to read tarot cards however the most ideal approach to acclimate yourself with the energies of the cards is to concentrate on them individually.

Inundate yourself in the story by reading the understandings – using a decent source book just as confiding in your own instincts.

Set aside the effort to assimilate the energies of each card, by concentrating on the symbolism, hues, numbers and images.

Keep a Tarot diary and record your impressions of each card.

A few people like to put a card under their pad before resting, then recording their impressions and dreams toward the beginning of the day.

2) Meditate on the Tarot

Seeing as the Tarot is a story, you should utilize your very own account while investigating the cards.

Locate a calm spot where you won't be upset. Beginning with the Major Arcana and working through the Minor Arcana and Court cards, place each card – individually on a table before you.

Reflect on the card and once you've retained the symbolism, close your eyes and consider what that card intends to you.

Give it a chance to happen normally – regardless of whether you feel that your brain is meandering – watch where it proceeds to record your impressions.

Rehearse this with each card and return to this reflection once in a while.

Another reflection is to convey the card with all of you day – particularly if the imagery matches what sort of a day you believe you will have.

You can likewise pick a card that speaks to what you need to occur.

Look out for anything identified with the card and record your encounters once you return home.

3) Use Memorization Tricks

There are 78 cards in the Tarot and incalculable mixes including the large number of various inquiries you may pose, so retaining the entirety of the cards can be an overwhelming one.

Understanding that it will require some investment to get familiar with the numerous aspects of every one of the 78 cards is the initial step.

Split it up into segments to make it progressively serviceable for you, for example, starting with the suits in the minor arcana.

Or then again you may get a kick out of the chance to deal with the Court cards in the first place, then proceed onward to the suits, then to the major arcana.

Anyway, you choose to do it, focus on each segment and once you feel that now is the right time, proceed onward through the deck.

Observe repeating subjects, pictures and mixes that feed significance to one another.

Using watchwords is another valuable strategy for remembering the implications and translations. Think of them in your Tarot diary and submit them to memory.

Imaginative perception is an incredible method to recall that anything, so if you return to reading the Tarot as a story, you'll recollect each card in accordance with the account of the Tarot.

For instance: think about each card as a part – nourishing from the past card and streaming onto the following.

4) Create a Sacred Space

Having a holy space where you can direct your exploration and Tarot readings – deferentially and undisturbed – implies that you will have a superior possibility for adjusting yourself to your cards.

Dispreads a zone where you're more averse to be occupied by other individuals, clamor from the road, TV and so on.

Enrich the region as indicated by how you feel about your hallowed space, the Tarot, otherworldliness and so on.

For some it may be precious stones, plants and silk scarves; for other people, it could be New Age pictures on the divider and incense.

Whatever your decisions, ensure your region is a genuine impression of who you are profoundly.

5) Explore the Tarot Spreads

There are such a significant number of various kinds of Tarot spreads, so it's a smart thought to investigate what works for you.

You will find that it relies upon the kind of reading you will do, regardless of whether it's a short – one inquiry reading or a mind boggling, year spread or Celtic Cross.

If you intend to bargain Tarot cards for other people, get them to rearrange and hand the deck back to you.

Do whatever it takes not to translate the cards as indicated by what you think they need to know and exhort them that you will just be uncovered what the cards state.

Let them know not to tell you what they're asking, which is an incredible method to test the reading and your aptitudes.

In your consecrated space, take your cards and cautiously mix them in the wake of ruminating over the question and explanation behind the reading (except if reading for another person.)

When you feel that you've rearranged well, either fan them out (face down – from left to right) or cut the deck with your correct hand from left to right in case you're just doing a one card spread.

Celtic Cross Spread

Pick (as quick as possible) ten cards from your fanned deck. Beginning from straightforwardly before you, lay the cards as pursues:

Each position spreads an alternate subject or viewpoint in your life, as pursues:

- First Card: Your present position and perspective.
- Second Card: Your test; what crosses you.
- Third Card: Your past, what acquired you to this point time.
- Fourth Card: The not so distant future.
- Fifth Card: Current objectives and desires.

- Sixth Card: The subliminal considerations behind your inquiry; shrouded mysteries.
- Seventh Card: Recommendations and guidance for going ahead.
- Eighth Card: Events or potentially individuals influencing your inquiry; outside your ability to control.
- Ninth Card: Your expectations and fears.
- Tenth Card: Outcome (contemplating your present direction.)

In case you're doing a 6-card spread, you won't have to spread the staying four cards on the correct side of the cross.

In this occasion, the initial 5 cards have indistinguishable implications from above, with the 6th card being your result.

3 Card Spread

As in the past, mix the cards while you think about your inquiry.

You may ask "What is wanting me throughout the following month?" or "Educate me concerning such and such circumstance, individual, occasion and so forth."

Fan the cards out and pick three cards rapidly. Spread them out in a line from left to right.

- First Card: Recent Past.
- Second Card: Where you are presently.
- Third Card: The Outcome.

One Card Reading

In the wake of rearranging the cards and thinking about your inquiry (make it straightforward and immediate, for example, "Will I land the position?" or "Should I confide in my beau/sweetheart?") – slice them from left to right and lift the main card up from the highest point of the uncovered stack.

Translate the appropriate response and mix again and repeat if you need explanation.

12 Month Spread

Rearrange and fan the cards, then pick twelve from left to right (which demonstrates going from the past to the future) and beginning from straightforwardly before you – going clockwise – place the cards face down around.

You'll have to neaten it up once you're finished. Beginning from the main card, turn them over.

The main card speaks to the present month and from the second card onwards, the next months will be spoken to by a card each.

Decipher the reading and record your impressions in your diary.

This is helpful to recollect your reading just as to twofold check when the year is finished.

Here are some more spreads you should play with, from fundamental two card spreads up to five card spreads.

Blend it up to make your own, when you feel great enough to do as such.

6) Interpret the Tarot Reading

Inquiries to pose

Obviously, this all relies upon what's happening in your life at some random time and what you need to think about.

It's imperative to get directly to the point with yourself.

If you as of now have a notion that the relationship you just began will end in tears, a Tarot reading won't offer you interchange responses.

More often than not, us people have a skill for having the option to anticipate what will occur, in light of our chronicles and motivation.

Using the Tarot to approach questions ought to be kept for the occasions when greater issues are close by, instead of for unrealistic reasoning, negligible things like tattle and other unessential subjects.

Keep your inquiries straightforward, for example, "What's desiring me throughout the following year?" or "Is it a smart thought for me to go after this position?"

The most ideal approach to test yourself is to pose extremely fundamental inquiries, so you can guarantee that you don't infuse the cards with a previously modified and wanted result.

Attempt to clear your mind and state unmistakably, "You let me know?"

It's astonishing what can come up when you don't drive the issue or confound the reading to go for whatever you might prefer.

Astonishments and privileged insights can be uncovered when you don't color your inquiries with tangled objectives and ulterior thought processes.

Mixes and Correspondences

As referenced already, it's critical to look at encompassing cards to improve thought about what the message is.

In many cases, readings bode well when every one of the cards are translated – like looking at the woods instead of the trees.

How would they all identify with one another?

Is there a consistent idea?

Now and then you'll see themes, for example, cards being overwhelmingly pentacles or Queens.

If there are a great deal of Major Arcana cards, then the reading means a significant arrangement of occasions coming up.

The mixes are what makes the Tarot a captivating technique for divination, because of the profundity of importance.

Correspondences are the additional components to be remembered for the translations, for example, Astrology and Numerology.

The components of earth, air, fire and water are likewise used.

Visionary affiliations are additionally significant when looking at the Court cards.

Here's a short breakdown of the relating affiliations:

- Pentacles: Taurus, Virgo, and Capricorn
- Swords: Aries, Leo, and Sagittarius
- Wands: Gemini, Libra, and Aquarius
- Cups: Cancer, Scorpio, and Pisces

There are numerous minor departures from the prophetic affiliations and different correspondences, contingent upon the various styles and customs used by Tarot followers – just as the various ways of thinking, where interchange thoughts regarding what component or sign relates to what Tarot card are shifted.

- Pentacles: Element – Earth; matters managing cash, down to earth concerns, security, insurance.

- Wands: Element – Air; matters managing the astuteness, thought, thoughts, insight.

- Swords: Element – Fire; matters managing power, energy, activity, change, sanitization.

- Cups: Element – Water; matters managing feelings, the psyche, imagination, dreams.

Note: a few people say that Wands are the component of fire and that Swords are the component of air.

This is available to translation, however observing as Wands for the most part originate from wood = trees, it's reasonable that the branches waving noticeable all around are ascribed to that component, alongside Swords produced in fire.

Selecting A Tarot Deck

You will find a number of variants of card divination methods in addition to real tarot cards available nowadays. It's vital to realize that several card divination methods aren't the tarot per se. To get most on your own you will be encouraged working with one of the most commonly accepted types of the tarot deck comprising of a seventy-eight-card deck.

There are lots of decks available on the market which will differ in fashion off artwork and in written interpretation to which of the conventional deck. This has frequently been done creating a themed deck and may well integrate the tarot with a few other causes of cultural knowledge or esoteric belief. Contemporary artwork has come quite a distance after 1910 when the initial deck was published. You will see numerous fantastic decks that incorporate artwork and information from some other subjects of esoteric interest like astrology, mythology, runes, different countries and herbalism to mention only a couple of. While these decks are excellent, they'll only delight you in case you have a genuine interest or maybe feel a strong link for the extra subject or perspective of approach.

The seventy-eight cards of your deck should be split into 2 primary sections: the greater, or maybe key arcana as well as the lower arcana. The higher, or perhaps major arcana must contain twenty-two cards numbered sometimes one to twenty-two or zero to twenty-one. The lower arcana must have the other fifty-six cards that are ordinarily split up into 4 suits, each one of which comprises fourteen cards.

To arrive at grips with the origins as well as an understanding of tarot, a conventional deck will aid you establish a straighter program around the Royal road you try to walk without becoming distracted by a theme. Consequently a good conventional deck could serve you best to start with and also function as the equivalent of the learners driver's license, for in case you figure out how to look at signs as well as indicators of tarot healthy you are going to get to your destination and reach your aims without obtaining mixed up as well as lost.

Mastering the Tarot is usually a lifelong pleasure and quite possibly will see you purchasing multiple decks in your lifetime. By realizing a deck including the conventional ones, or those really much like it, you will have the ability to make a simple move to the themed deck of your choosing afterward.

Tarot Reading - Choosing A Deck That Works for You

The best goal in picking a deck is discovering the deck you resonate with. In case which was the case, I likely in no way would've embarked on the Tarot journey. No rules or even rituals are needed. You can just choose any deck that individually speaks for you.

To begin with, there's no wrong or right approach to selecting a deck. You can just begin your process by exploring what is available. I constantly encourage individuals to begin this particular undertaking with a bit of research. The very first strategy will consist of looking up different tarot decks on the web. This is a terrific way to enjoy the different symbols as well as iconography depicted in the Tarot. Every artist has a tendency to have their own interpretation. Several artists decide to stay dedicated to standard symbolism while others will improve their own unique interpretation for the Tarot cards. Either way, it is essential to learn what moves you. When I find myself drawn to a specific deck's imagery, I generally question myself what's it relating to this deck which makes me should find out more. Can it be the layout, color, symbolism or perhaps general feel? Do I determine with the images? Will I connect with them? What can they make me think?

Learning to identify your own feelings about particular decks may help you limit your options. You might in addition, nonetheless, have to see the cards very first hand. The most effective places to purchase Tarot decks locally are at metaphysical bookstores and stores. Metaphysical retailers tend to have a lot more decks and also have samples you are able to deal with. Bookstores have a tendency to have a smaller amount of Tarot decks and usually don't enable you to open them. It is usually good to go through a deck's imagery, but in case you're restricted, you are able to definitely get a "feel" for a tarot deck by managing it inside the packaging of its. You will be attracted to the weight or the size of a specific deck and also, in several cases; you could get the best perception about a specific deck whenever you notice it or manage it in person.

It is additionally really important to be aware of what deck type you're drawn too. In case it's a divinatory deck that isn't associated with Tarot including oracle cards or maybe angel cards, it's actually all right to select this as your deck. Nevertheless, the interpretations of theirs won't be just like anyone in the Tarot. Generally, these decks come with an accompanying book or maybe pamphlet which covers the card's significance as well as meanings. Conventional Tarot decks have a total of seventy-eight cards. Based on the kind of Tarot deck it's, the visuals of theirs might differ, but their general objective is definitely the same. Probably the most unique feature to Tarot cards is the ability of theirs to direct you through your life challenges by assisting you to realize who you're.

As you go to understand the cards and feel far more at ease with the meanings of theirs, you are able to add to your collection of Tarot decks. Sooner or later, you might want to explore a deck which is much more meditative and abstract in nature. The most crucial thing to keep in mind would be that the Tarot allows you to take advantage of your intuition. In the long run, allow your own intuition to be your guide.

How Tarot Cards Connects to Astrology and A Zodiac Signs

Tarot and astrology combined are ideally matched like two peas in a pod.

Such connections belong to the major arcana. The astrological definition is extended and then disintegrated by an abstract division of the little arcana. Every astrological sign has an affiliation with tarot cards.

The elemental groups are as follows:

- Water—Cancer, Scorpio, and Pisces—The Tarot Cups
- Earth—Taurus, Virgo, and Capricorn—The Tarot Pentacles
- Fire—Aries, Leo, and Sagittarius—The Tarot Wands
- Air—Gemini, Libra, and Aquarius—The Tarot Swords

Looking at the cards aligned with the astrological signs, we see that the bond between the two is something very spiritual in nature.

There are two Tarot cards for each astrological sign complementing the energies already existing in the zodiac signs. It offers them the opportunity to say a far broader tale than they ever do.

TAURUS (April 20-May 20) The Hierophant and the King of Pentacles

The hierophant is given the Zodiac sign Taurus as the hierophant transmits love so that the same characteristics can be seen in the Taurus symbol. The King of Pentacles is the earth's first fundamental party symbol of tarot and Taurus is the largest of the earth's astrological signals.

GEMINI (May 21-June 20) The God of Weapons and Lovers

The Lovers tarot deck shows Gemini as a metaphor for the duality between the symbol and the token. Gemini as a zodiac symbol of the twins paired with the lovers' card displaying the dualities of the male-female partners.

The Sword King is the main air party's first card. This card simply places Gemini, as it represents the Air Signs, as the first astrological emblem.

CANCER (June 21- July 22) The Chariot and the Cup Monarch

The Zodiac sign Cancer correlates to The Chariot Tarot card signaling movement as development; the transition is provided by this card, and the Chariot represents the sign of cancer, the signs of insight that can shift through a higher emotional perspective. For the location of the sign as the first sign of the elemental tarot community, a tarot card The King of Cups is added to cancer.

LEO (July 23-August 22) Power and the Queen of Walls

The Leo zodiac sign has the Strength Tarot card for its symbolic strength; the tarot card often represents the lion.

This accuracy is attributed to the star of Leo. This is the second card on the fundamental fire group, and Leo is the second fire sign in the position of mirror astrology.

VIRGO (August 23-September 22) The Pentacles Hermit and Queen

When tarot and astrology are mixed, the Ermit is identified with Virgo, which is curious because Virgo is connected with the idea of innocence and is a metaphorical situation through a more symbolic image of purity contained in alone, time to examine the lessons of the search for perfection.

The Queen of Pentacles is the second basic party of Tarot and Virgo fits the second earth sign as an astrological symbol.

LIBRA (September 23-October 22) The Princess with the Swords

Libra and the tarot-card Justice have a conceptual link with fairness, evaluating choices and decision-making.

The Queen of Swords is the corresponding Libra card to show the air elemental group's mutual link.

SCORPIO (October 23-November 21) Death and The Queen of Cups

The "Death Card" is a wonderful card to discover in a lesson, which reflects the ideas of death, conception and regeneration.

Scorpio with the zodiac is the gift with human life with these abstract attributes.

SAGITTARIUS (November 22-December 21) Temperance and The Page of Wands

The Tarot card Temperance is an equilibrium deck that aims to light a metaphysical temper. Sagittarius' astrological form is indicative of the same concepts. Temperance and Sagittarius are the incarnations who scan the world in order to improve what was already known.

CAPRICORN (December 22-January 19) The Devil and The Page of Pentacles

The tarot deck indicative of Capricorn's astrological position is the Devil token. This card has certain complicated misunderstandings; it appears to build fear when read. The Devil card symbolizes expectations and seeks to fulfill the needs of all kinds.

Naturally, not everyone's cravings are good, particularly if you concentrate on them with one head, for example with alcohol or smoking.

Capricorn is synonymous with the Devil symbol, since the coin and the sign aim to fulfill their desires, whether it's commodities or company conquests, and this association reflects certain issues which may eventually take over one's existence and not the general gain.

As a symbol of the third world signs for astrology and the basic Tarot group, the Page of Pentacles is linked to Capricorn

AQUARIUS (January 20-February 18) The Star

The Aquarius and the Sun in their conceptual manifestations are also the "wind bearers".

Both the Aquarius sign and the Star are linked to the same concepts, demonstrating in one sense that sticking apart and being unique and floating together can be completely combined.

The Swords website is a tarot card connected with the Aquarius for the third air sign role they hold.

PISCES (February 19-March 20) The Moon and The Page of Cups

The Moon tarot symbol is aligned with the astrological sign Pisces. All the Moon and the Pisces reflect visions and delusions symbolically. The complexities of the ocean's waters and the passage of tides as in feelings and relational cycles are the subjects for both.

The Tarot card on the Cup Page is linked to the fish symbol, which is the third position for the elementary water community.

The Energy of The Cards

The Playing Card Numbers

ACE - New beginning; decision

TWO - Union; partnership; division

THREE - Working together; conflict

FOUR - Foundation; death

FIVE - Change

SIX - Relationships

SEVEN - Cycle of return; spirit, burden

EIGHT - Abundance; money; health

NINE - Final actions

TEN - Completion; success; journey

(11) JACK - new situation; new person

(12) QUEEN - relationships among people; global perspective

(13) KING - getting things done; taking charge; focused energy

We will examine the energies of each number in much greater detail as we work our way through each of the 54 playing cards.

The Playing Card Suits

HEARTS ENERGY

- Love

- Happiness

- Emotions

- Relationships

- Bonding

- Desire

- Connection

- Matters of the heart

- Honesty

- Good intentions

- Creativity

- Healing

- Blood

- Life

- Faith

- Hope

- Spirit

Hearts are represented by the element of water. They are the most flexible and changeable of the four suits. The energy they represent is very fleeting and temporary and all by themselves will not maintain their resonance through the trials of life. In other words, love not backed up by concrete actions will fade; good intentions and compassion without the follow through of putting "your money where your mouth is" will not make a material difference in the world or in another person's life. At their worst, Hearts on their own, unsupported by the more substantial energies represented in the other suits can be nothing more than wishes, good intentions or the proverbial "bleeding heart" of all talk and no action.

More positively, hearts represent the purest energy of all the suits. A marriage without love is a chore or worse. Sex without desire can become twisted into something very different than love. Hearts represent the ideals for which we strive as humans. Hearts represent prayer, angels, the Holy Spirit and the workings of God. Hearts represent bodily healing, the life sustaining blood in our veins and the literal heart that pumps blood through our body.

Diamonds Energy

- Money

- Investments

- Physical comforts

- Food

- Shelter

- Transportation

- Material success

- Manifestation on the material plane

- Technology

- Communication

- Contracts

- Legal judgments

Diamonds represent a combination of earth and fire energy. As the energy progresses through the suits from hearts to diamonds to clubs to spades, the energy represented by each suit slows until it reaches the spades where the energy of the spades is a road block, stagnant or even destructive. Here in the diamonds suit, the energy is still very fast but also very solid and material.

Diamonds represent money, physical goods of material value which can be as literal as diamonds and the finer things in life. A car, a job, a home, a bank account and stock investments may all be represented here. Fine dining, extravagant vacations, success and the material abundance of life are also here. Diamonds manifest the pure desires of the hearts suit into this material reality.

Clubs Energy

- Growth

- Hard work

- Mundane details of life

- Progress through effort

- Structure

- Nurture

- Earth

- Stable

- Grounded

- Yin

Clubs energy is very stable, rooted and foundational. Clubs energy reflects earth energy in its purest expression. This is life on the physical plane. Clubs energy is grounded and immensely practical. It gets the job done and moves forward on to the next task on the "to do" list. Clubs energy is yin energy which is very passive and unmoving. All progress that is made grows out of the solid structure and foundation of what already exists and is relatively unchanging from day to day. Clubs energy is like a farmer sowing his field with corn.

Spades Energy

- Conflict

- Pain

- Loss

- Illness

- Endings

- Negativity

- Destruction

- Death

- Deception

- Judgment

- Decisions

- Reasoning

- Logic

- Saturn

- Restriction

- Addiction

- Anxiety

- Confinement

- Unclean spirits

Spades are the polar opposite energetically of the hearts suit. Spades are ruled by the element air and roughly correspond to the swords in tarot. By the time the energy reaches the spades suit it has reversed its natural positive flow and works restriction, chaos, destruction and pain wherever it goes. When something ends, something new begins; when something dies, something else is born. The vacuum left by the person, thing or activity that dies is naturally filled by something different, something better, and often something stronger. We cannot have what is superior until we let go of what is inferior.

Spades clear out the dead things in our lives. They are the vultures, undertakers and reapers. Death is painful. Loss is never an enjoyable undertaking.

Spades represent the natural cycle of decay, pruning and death that is essential to the life cycle of any healthy organism, microcosm and macrocosm.

Tarot Spreads: Three Simple Spreads for Starting Out and Strengthening Your Intuitive Power

There is an endless possibility of ways the cards of the tarot can be spread out and read. With this, you will find that through time, certain arrangements, or spreads have become gold standards of tarot reading. Some are very simple, others quite in depth. To start out with, I would like to give you an overview of three simplest and most popular tarot card spreads. These three spreads are simply suggestions for initiating yourself into tarot reading. Explore and practice each one before moving on to more complex and complicated arrangements.

Three Card Spread

The three-card spread is arguably the best spread for beginners and experienced readers alike. The process is simple and it can be used for a variety of situations and questions. The three-card spread is exactly as it sounds. Three cards are placed in a row, to gain insight into the question at hand. Each card represents one element of the question. The cards are read from left to right, just as you would read a book. You can use this spread to gain insight into any situation and you will likely find that you adapt the spread to suit a limitless number of needs.

- Past/Present/Future
- Mind/Body/Spirit
- Problem/Action to Be Taken/Outcome if Advice is Followed
- Situation/Obstacle/Advice for Overcoming the Obstacle
- Thoughts/Feelings/Actions
- What is fluid and changeable/ What is concrete and fixed/ How can I gain more insight
- Choice #1/Choice #2/Guidance for a decision
- Your place in a relationship/the other person's place in the relationship/ What needs to happen in the relationship
- What is the uniting factor/What is the dividing factor/ what needs to be focused on

- Thoughts and behaviors to stop/Thoughts and behaviors to start/ Thoughts and Behaviors to continue

Celtic Cross Spread

The reasons for this are that the layout is simple and memorable, however the energy is strong and the results reliable. This spread involves two components, the center cross figure and a row of cards to the right that represents a wand or staff. The cross, which has a bit of a circular patter to it represents female energy, while the wand next to it represents male energy.

There are ten cards used in the Celtic Cross Spread. There are spread out and read in a certain formation. You might choose to spread the cards in the order illustrated in this diagram, however some people prefer to lay out cards three through six in a circular pattern rather than across from each other. It really is up to you and which way feels most comfortable and intuitive. Regardless of how you spread the cards, the placement and the meaning remain the same. Meaning, that you should follow this diagram for reading the cards, regardless of the order in which they were placed.

Card 1:

This card is the foundation, a representation of the present

Card 2:

This card represents the question or challenge at hand. Be prepared for a card that represents some sort of struggle or conflict to appear here. If by chance a card appears that is more general or positive in nature, look deeper into the imagery to discover how this card best conveys the message of question presented.

Card 3:

This card represents the best possible outcome. If the card the turns up in this position is one of negativity, it is worth thinking about if the best option is to let go and release yourself of the issue at hand rather than put more of your energy and resources into it.

Card 4:

This card represents the recent past. This does not tell so much of the origins of the problem or conflict, but rather a recent event that has affected it.

Card 5:

This card represents the immediate future and foretells of what to expect in the short-term over the next few days

Card 6:

This card represents the distance past and helps to recognize the root of the problem.

Card 7:

This card represents the internal factors, such as thoughts and emotions that are affecting the situation.

Card 8:

This card represents the external factors such as people or events that are affecting the situation.

Card 9:

This card represents a combination of hopes and fears centered around the situation. This card often requires careful contemplation as hope and fear are normally thought of as opposites, but, are actually closely related and intertwined.

Card 10:

This is the final outcome. This card should never read as a stand-alone card, but rather as a conclusion and solution to the entire puzzle presented. If upon turning over this card you feel that there is need for more clarification, it is advised to continue to draw cards from the remaining tarot deck and read in them in relation to the card that is present in the number ten position.

Twelve Month Circle Spread

This is a simple spread that is used to for insight into the coming year. This is a good spread to use for general tarot readings, and it can be used to illustrate how a problem or question will play itself out over the next twelve months. You can also place a card in the center if you wish, however it is not required. The center card would be used as a general overview for the next twelve months combined.

There are multiple ways that you can use this spread depending upon your experience, how in depth the question and how detailed you want to be in this reading.

The simplest method of using this spread is to place 12 cards, counterclockwise, in a circular pattern, starting at the 9:00 position and working your way around, with one in the center, if desired.

You can read the spread as is, using only one card in each position, or you can go around the circle again and add an additional card to each location. With each new addition, you place the card on the outside of the previously placed card so that the circle eventually forms a pattern that resembles the sun. If you were to use a complete tarot deck, you could place up to six cards in each position.

When reading this spread, you will look at all the cards that for each individual position and read them together, in relationship to one another. The first set of cards placed, in the 9:00 position represents the current month that you are in, with the following month represented by the card, or set of cards, that is next, going in the counterclockwise direction.

Types of Tarot Decks

A lot of them are similar, but there are those that have a lot of striking differences in theme and imagery. With that said, we are only going to list down the top most famous and essential tarot decks.

Aleister Crowley Thoth Tarot

This deck has fantastic artwork and is also considered as a classic tarot deck. Thoth Tarot deck contains 80 cards with three different versions of the card Magus. Also known as Crowley Thoth Tarot and Toth Tarot. A beautiful and classic deck indeed, but it is one of the darkest and most controversial card decks.

Shadowscapes Tarot

This tarot deck is a must for all those fantasy lovers out there. Each card is endowed with stunning images and the watercolors added more to the mythical sight. Shadowscape follows the Rider-Waite theme, it even comes with a book.

The designs are inspired by folklore, fantasy and nature. Fans and enthusiasts waited six long years before this tarot card deck made its debut. The most noticeable and appreciated in this tarot deck's design is the fact that everything is painted in a way that gives it the illusion of fluid motion. Hands down to the artists Stephanie Pui-Mun Law on her card designs.

Deviant Moon Tarot

What makes Deviant Moon Tarot is its design. Each card is surreal, unique and sometimes quite disturbing. A borderless edition is available and a white booklet comes with the deck. You see, the theme is all about cemeteries and mental asylums, it's kind of gives the users a sneak peek into the deepest and darkest part of their subconsciousness. Patrick Valenza, the creator, really put the dark and mystery into the twisted forms of nightmares and the elements of death. All the figures in the deck are nonhuman, the colors are gloomy and a lot of small details has something to do with the creator's childhood and imagination.

Druidcraft Tarot

From the name of the tarot deck itself, it's evident that the drawings are based on Druidry and nature spritualties. Also, as you guessed, it has a lot of natural elements in it. Just by looking at the tarot deck, you might even see the movement of the characters alongside their calm background. Keep in mind that there is a little nudity involved in both male and female, but that doesn't mean that they look any less attractive. It's incredible to think how brilliant Stephanie Carr-Gomm, Philip Carr-Gomm and Will Worthington were when they created DruidCraft Tarot and another tarot deck called Druid Animal Oracle.

Legacy of the Divine Tarot

You can't go wrong with the name, everything about this deck is simply divine and amazing. Not only are the designs rich, but also the color and ideas. Don't be afraid to own this deck if you're not a tarot expert, because it won't matter. Looking at each magical scene, all the details really to pop up since each one has a highly realistic and digital design.

Though he has minimal experience and background when it comes to tarot cards, he still managed to design a deck that didn't deviate too much from the original ideas.

Wild Unknown Tarot

A tarot deck that focused on nature, wild animals, symbolism and a lot of black and white. If it was possible, the lack of color gave it even more charm. Each line in every card can speak for themselves.

This kind of theme and design is so unique that it would be a crime not to have in your collection, it's also one of the reasons why it's popular. The creator, Kim Krans, really put a lot of thought into each stroke and small details.

Victorian Romantic Tarot

This tarot deck is based on the engravings from the artists of the 19th century. Historical and the Victorian era are the main themes of this deck. When you look at the 78 cards on this tarot deck, you will be transported back in time. It's filled with everything concerning the Victorian passions and medieval styles.

The creators Alex Ukolov and Karen Mahony sought to put various women from different levels in society; from the queen to the poor. Not only that, but there are intricate images and engravings scattered all over the cards.

Gaian Tarot

Gaian Tarot is solely dedicated to the earth, nature and Gaia herself. Before, this deck was only available as majors-only set until the minors were completed. This tarot deck is very traditional, from the number of cards to most of the titles and more. All the designs are so down-to-earth, they show communities interacting with nature and with each other.

Not to mention tons of compilation of intricate designs and interpretative work. It's a fresh break from all the kings and queens of most of the tarot decks, better thank creator Joanna Powell Colbert for that.

Rider-Waite Tarot

This is a classic among all the classics in tarot decks, also the most famous. This widely circulated deck is also known as Rider Tarot, Waite Tarot and Waite-Smith Tarot. It doesn't matter if you're a beginner or an expert in tarot reading, this deck should be added to your collection. This deck is available in multiple formats like miniature, pocket, standard and giant. The cards in this deck may not have the most colorful and extravagant designs, but that doesn't make them any less enjoyable.

Taking the Next Steps

You will need to stay aware of what you feel throughout this new adventure and to make it fun for yourself. At first, this will require you to stay motivated and fight procrastination, but eventually, you will find your perfect learning rhythm and techniques.

Something you can do to try and make learning tarot more exciting is meet up with people from the community. Nowadays with all the social media platforms, it has become easier than ever to find people who have the same interests as us. Use that to your advantage, by joining groups with other tarot readers and finding real-life events related to tarot.

Tricks for Rote Memorization

Rote memorization is the process of learning something based on repetition. When you learned the alphabet in school, for instance, you did it using this kind of learning. Although it isn't the best technique for every discipline, the reason why it works for some is that it is very time-efficient.

The downside to rote memorization is that it can get a bit repetitive and end up being boring, so it is important that you find ways for yourself to keep it fun.

- Turn your learning sessions into games. Look for ways that you can gamify your learning process, or even make up your own games.
- Use mnemonics and rhymes. If a sentence is catchy, it becomes simpler for you to memorize some concepts and meanings.
- Use visuals. The human brain is able of processing images 60.000 times faster than text (Business2Community, 2015), so having a visual learning approach can be very helpful.
- Write it down, instead of typing it in your laptop. Using a pen and paper activates your reticular activating system, which causes you to pay more attention to what you are noting down.
- Talk about what you are learning. If you have someone in your family or friends who is interested in tarot, try to explain concepts to them when you are trying to memorize. When you are by yourself, you can verbalize these concepts. Having someone on the other side can be more interesting though because they might ask you questions that had not crossed your mind before, which is always good in any learning journey.

Motivation Tips to Learn Tarot

Nobody learns anything new without having some bumps on the road, and those always affect one's motivation. But giving up is not an option! When you find yourself feeling blocked and not knowing what to do to get back on track, what you should do is adapt existing learning habits and/or adopt new ones.

- Define small goals. If you want to be amazing at every single thing the art of tarot entails from the get-go, it is more likely that you end up being disappointed and, therefore, unmotivated. Baby steps are easier to achieve and they will give you the satisfaction of victory more often, making it even more exciting to reach the next milestone! You should increase the level of difficulty as you get more familiar with tarot, otherwise it gets boring and stops being challenging.

- Define a schedule or routine built around the hours of the day when you tend to be more productive (when you are free, of course). For instance, start your day off with a meditation session using your daily tarot card, and finish it off with 30-60 minutes of studying tarot and making exercises of the rote memorization games. This way you will make a commitment to yourself, which should serve as motivation.

- Rest! If you are studying and you see that the session is not only not being productive, but it is making you even more tired, stop. Put your materials aside, go to sleep or do something that doesn't require any effort from you. Get back to it after a few hours or even the day after and you will see that you'll get a lot more out of it. Sometimes our brain just isn't in the right place for you to try and push more new information in, and that is okay!

Other Uses for Tarot

A Powerful Set of Tools for Everyday Life

If you have always thought of the tarot deck as a mysterious object, meant to be tucked away in a secret drawer and only pulled out for deep-rooted, soul-searching questions, you might be half correct.

The tarot cards are indeed mysterious, but they can be used every day for any question at all, mundane or life-changing—or even if you don't have a question to ask of them.

Tarot for Self-Reflection

One wonderful way to make daily use of your tarot deck is to pull a card for each day. Consider this the day's "theme"—things you should be aware of that this day may reveal, shed light upon, be concerned with, or bring towards you, as well as things that might be moving away from you and no longer influencing your life.

A tarot journal is essential here, as you will want to look back at previous days' readings to see if you can discern a pattern in how things have been going.

It's not what the cards are telling you, it's what you see in the cards. Some people have trouble with the fact that a single tarot card could mean "anything", depending on how you interpret it. And that's exactly the point of this exercise. Tarot cards are based on archetypes—universal imagery that usually means the same thing to the viewer, regardless of culture, nationality, or background. What catches your eye as well as your imagination when you look at a card is a message to yourself, from yourself. The subconscious mind knows a lot more about what's going on than most of us give it credit for—but it doesn't speak in words, it speaks using images. That's why our dreams are often so colorful and quirky. Tarot cards give the subconscious mind a language it can relate to, so that it may impart wisdom and important lessons for us to use in our daily lives.

Tarot for Daily Focus

One way is to simply shuffle your entire deck, and pull a card either each morning, or each night before you go to sleep (the card you draw being indicative of what the next day will bring). A second approach is to separate your deck into two decks: The major arcana and the minor arcana. You can choose to pull your daily card from the major arcana deck, and pull a second card for clarification or details from the minor arcana deck if you need more information.

Your daily card can be looked upon for any of these ideas or themes:

- What you should focus on that day

- What you need to be aware of

- Something that needs your attention

- The day's strategy for success

- The best way to navigate this day happily and peacefully

Before you draw a card, if one of these topics resonates with you, say it out loud before you shuffle, cut the deck one time, and pick your card, and as always, write down your impressions when you see which card you've drawn.

The benefit of daily focus cards is that the cards you draw can guide your attention towards something you may not have realized. If you have been having a challenging week, for instance, in which you thought you lacked the courage or initiative to deal with a particular problem, drawing say, The Chariot, or the King of Swords may give you the nudge to think otherwise, and further believe in your abilities.

Tarot for Meditation

This way of utilizing the tarot doesn't involve randomly selecting a card. Instead, choose a card that represents what you want to enhance or draw closer in your life. You might spread the cards out, face up, and choose one that resonates with you for this exercise.

Meditation is not a complicated task, but its benefits have been scientifically proven study after study. Meditation has the power to shape the brain—a phenomenon called neuroplasticity. This means the brain is capable of changing its structure, depending on our thoughts, our practices, and our lifestyle. Meditating on a regular basis has been proven to cause greater production of serotonin and other positive, mood-enhancing hormones in the brain, as well as reducing the areas of the brain that release stress hormones.

To meditate, all you really need is a place to sit, some time to sit there, and a commitment to focus on breathing and good posture. Ten minutes of your lunch break is perfectly acceptable for a beginner to meditate. You may choose a comfortable chair to sit in as long as your spine can be straight while sitting. Always remember to keep your spine straight, and your breathing deep and even—and from the belly. Your shoulders should never move when breathing properly.

If you want to focus on a specific thing, choose the card that best represents that to you. Alternatively, you can shuffle the deck while you focus on your thought, then cut the deck once and choose the top card as your focal tool. Set the card where you can easily see it in detail, then begin to meditate—perfect posture, deep, controlled breathing.

Tarot for Creativity

You might be beginning to notice that the tarot deck is a fast-track hotline directly to your subconscious. This resource can be invaluable to your creative work. When navigating a rough spot in a creative project, you can pull a card to ask yourself:

- What do I want to convey at this point in the story?

- Which emotions am I investing in this piece?

- What should I create next?

- What aspects of my skill am I neglecting?

- What should I work on improving?

Add them to your journal with a description of what you're working on at the time, or what you hope to be working on in the near future.

Tarot cards can help writers get to know their own characters better. Knowing the reasons why certain characters make the choices they do can help writers craft richer, more believable stories. Remember that tarot cards are based on archetypes, and every character has an archetype that they closely resonate with. Additionally, as tarot cards already tell a story—in the major arcana and throughout each minor arcana suite—several cards can be pulled to give the writer an idea of which direction to take their own story.

Tarot for Manifestation

Tarot cards are not only used for the receiving of information. They can also be utilized to send our desires for manifestation out into the universe. By using a tarot card to work towards your goal or dream, you are also programming your own mind to reach for that goal.

A powerful exercise that can be done to manifest goals and dreams is to build your own tarot card.

Start by choosing a card that best represents your goal or dream. Then, on a piece of poster board, paper, or fabric board, assemble images cut from magazines that best convey your interpretation of that tarot card. Make sure to include images that coincide with your goal. Set this personalized tarot card in a place where you'll be able to see it every day.

You can use this method to reach such goals as:

- Buying a house
- Landing a dream job
- Getting a promotion
- Doing well in school
- Attaining a new level of health or fitness
- Traveling to a place you've always longed to go

A Tarot Spread for Self-Realization

Here's a spread you can do when you want to look inward and check in with yourself. After you shuffle and cut the deck, choose seven cards:

1. Which motivations am I hiding from myself?
2. Which qualities are my most positive ones?
3. Which qualities are my most negative ones?
4. In which ways am I being deceitful to myself?

5. What do I need to be more accepting of?

6. What do I need to let go of?

7. What is my next life lesson?

The answers may require some courage on your part, but practicing this spread now and again can help you keep on track for emotional health and better life choices.

Tarot for Special Events

When planning a dinner party, wedding, or any other special event, building the theme of that event around a tarot card can be a fun, imaginative way to go about things. Many of the tarot cards go well with themes of food, drink, and celebration, such as: The Empress, the Moon, the three of cups, and the four of wands.

A Tarot Adventure

A fun way to use the tarot when you have a day to yourself, is to draw one card in the morning to give you a clue as to where to head out to. Perhaps you draw a card with a forest in the background—take a trip to your local nature reserve or arboretum. Take your deck with you, and pull a second card to tell you where you'll next be going. Carry your journal along to make notes of your impressions.

Sometimes, doing this can reveal much more about what's going on in one's life than a mere reading can convey. This game can be especially useful if you've found yourself lacking energy, stuck in a rut, or unable to make an important decision.

Tarot for Magic

Whether you dabble in a little moon magic or are a seasoned practitioner of Wicca, tarot cards can add a potent emphasis on your altar or magic workspace. To add a heady dose of good fortune and luck, add "The World", "The Sun", or "The Magician" to your spells, taking cues from the card itself to help you add components, colors, and ingredients to them.

Using one of the court cards of the minor arcana can help you feel as if you have a mentor present to make your spells truly successful. You can ask these masters for guidance, drawing additional cards after your work is complete to receive personalized messages from them.

Developing Your Intuition

Not everything in life appears in plain sight for us—some things are hidden, either by design, or by someone else's deception. Using tarot cards regularly can assist us in empowering our own intuition, as well as provide clues for us to tune into places in our lives that need the most attention.

Consider your senses: Sight, hearing, touch, taste, smell. Insight is a sixth sense; it is what enables us to make uncanny decisions or save ourselves from making mistakes. A powerful sense of insight can be the single advantage that gets you the job from among 100 applicants.

What to Do When You Get A "Bad" Card

Points to Remember

• There is no completely bad card. Every card has a range of meanings from clear warnings to a hopeful message.

• Different people view different cards as difficult.

• Remember the cards are there as a guidance, if you spot a problem you can work on changing or adapting to it.

• Often the hardest cards happen when change is needed, you know it, but continue fighting to maintain the status quo.

What to Do

• If the card is from the Minor Arcana pay attention to suit, this will suggest where the problem lies, and how to address it.

• Look at the other cards around, or pull another card for clarity about the issue.

• Don't keep re-reading for the same issues; spend time contemplating the reading you have.

• If you find your mind settling on the negative card, instead of how to get through/through/around the problem, you can add an appropriate "positive" card to the reading to help your unconscious through the block.

Good choices would be

• Ace of wands: energy needed, focus, determination.

• Ace of cups: positive emotional help, love and supportive relationships.

• Ace of swords: positive thought, clarity, strength of will.

• Ace of pentacles: abundance (issues with job, home, money, health).

• The sun: joy, hope, happiness.

You can place this card as a part of your reading to let the symbols integrate with the reading, or place the positive card somewhere you will see it often as a subtle nudge not to worry.

The Tarot is a tool; it is your responsibility to use it for empowerment, hope and happiness. It is of no help if it is causing you to worry.

Throughout the course you will learn various Tarot spreads, several of which focus on support and guidance not outcome. If life is difficult these are very useful spreads!

What is the question?

An important (and often overlooked) part of the Tarot reading is the question?

• Don't ask the same question each night (or every hour). If you've done a reading and you don't understand/feel comfortable with the answer it is better to add a clarity card (at most three) or to choose a positive card to add a psychic smile to your reading. It also helps to leave your reading out, go away and clear your mind (ideally overnight) and then come back to the same reading.

• It helps to write down your question before you start. It's important to consider how the answer is going to help you. "Am I going to get the Job" is better re-written as "what should I do to give me the best chances of getting the job?" or even "is this a good job for me right now?"

• It might help to consider your opinions on fate and destiny, and what the Tarot actually tells you. I believe the Tarot illustrates how your life is unfolding from that moment forth, but the future illustrated in the cards can be changed if you alter your actions and assumptions. This is why I often ask the cards for advice from the cards, rather than what will happen.

• You don't need a question! Asking for inspiration, guidance or advice (about a day/week/job/relationship) is a simple yet very powerful way to use the cards.

• Keep a Tarot journal. It is a useful practice to note down your question, cards and initial thoughts – and to go back through your journal adding notes as to how the day/job/relationship developed. This turns the Tarot into a dynamic tool for self-development and reflection – Tarot at its best.

Is It Possible to Make Your Own Tarot Cards?

And you have agreed that you enjoy reading Tarot, however you can't consider a deck that resonates with you entirely. Or maybe you've found some that are all right, but you just want to channel your artistic spirit and make your own unique set. Will you? Will you? Absolutely!

Have you known?

Creating your own Tarot cards is a perfect platform for artistic interpretations of your passions and desires.

Using pictures that uniquely connect with you, but be aware of copyright concerns.

You can purchase and pre-cut blank cards and make your own designs on them if you like.

Why Buy Your Own Cards?

You find a way to get or create something if you don't have anything, so why not think outside the box? People have been creating their own Tarot cards for years, after all, and all those widely produced decks had to come from somebody's thoughts, right?

Over the course of the years, several men have produced Tarot cards. You can buy blank one's for you in a package, already cut and measured, and make your own artwork for them to go with. Or you can print them on photographic paper or card stock and break them down yourself. The very process of formation is a powerful one, which can be seen as a medium for spiritual transformation, which grows. Whether you have a particular passion or a talent you love, you might quickly integrate it into your artwork.

A significant thing to note is that photographs are still protected on the Web, and if you choose to use them for personal use, you may be permitted to do so, but you will not be able to use or reuse them for commercial use. When you have some questions as to how an image may be lawfully copied for personal use, you can speak with the website creator. There is a range of platforms where people have made their own Tarot templates accessible to anybody who wishes to use them at no price.

For example, if you're a knitter, you might find a way to draw a deck using sword knitting needles, pentacle yarn balls, etc. Anyone with an affinity for crystals may use various gemstone symbols to build a table. You may want to design a collection of cards with school sketches for your kids or consider planning out a deck of picture stills from your favorite TV show.

Ideally, what you want to use our images that resonate personally with you. For starters, if you really don't feel a bond with a wand's conventional picture, choose something different to reflect the suit— and do it in a way that makes it interesting to you. It's also crucial to note that in order to make a Tarot card set, you don't have to be a skilled artist— use pictures and thoughts that appeal to you individually, and you'll notice that you like the end product.

NOTE: A custom deck will be something you can customize to your own needs, your desires, and your creativity. When you tie your own symbols into the magic of the Tarot, the sky is the limit. If you're someone who can't connect with Tarot altogether, don't worry— you can always create an Oracle deck based on your own divination system.

How to Clean Tarot Decks?

There is a tradition of purifying and clearing new or old, tarot cards in the tarot culture.

Here's the good news: It's both optional and straightforward.

Many readers may not wipe their tarot decks – which is utterly perfect. I know those who don't clean their cards, and the readers are great. But many people do believe their tarot cards are capable of having energetic gunk stuck on them. And why would you like to clean your tarot cards, or bless them?

If they are used- Who knows who owned the deck. Is there an obsessive, nervous or derogatory energy surrounding their use? As the new owner, it's best to freshen them up and get them tuned to you.

When they were struck by someone else – this is a piece of polarizing tarot legend. Some practitioners of tarot will not let anyone touch their cards.

Given what your tarot mentor insisted, or what you read in a manuscript, it's optional to stick to that belief.

When you find that your cards read differently when someone else touches them, then don't let the folks contact them. It's a personal preference otherwise – not a hard-fast statute. Do good tarot etiquette practice: inquire first, before touching the tarot deck of another person.

When your readings are regularly negative or ambiguous – there could be odd electrical gunk attached to your cards that will muck the reading. Reading on a negative situation will yield negative card results. But occasionally you get a weird, inexplicably unpleasant vibe that needs explanation.

Too much reading on a subject will cause the readings to become confused. The common practice then is to let the deck "rest" or restart by sweeping it up.

You feel the need to reconnect with a deck – cleaning or clearing them is a perfect way to reconnect if your cards have been put away for a while. The same applies to an older deck you plan to use again.

1. Incense/Smudging

One of the most common methods by which tarot cards are cleaned is by incense.

In rites of purification, many religious practices burn incense. Throughout the West, white sage, sweet grass, or Palo Santo are the most common incenses used for cleansing. Palo Santo is my favorite with a woody and light flavor.

Many readers clean every card, one at a time, in their deck. So, if you want the entire deck to have a go at it, do that.

Cleaning yourself or your reading room is also a good idea to flush out any tension around you. Smudging yourself with tarot readers before and after readings (especially when reading for someone else) is a common practice.

Whether you like incense but have awful allergies and smoke addiction, use sprays made from essential oils instead—spray to clean up work thoroughly.

Sprays can be used in several base oils. Be careful not to spray your cards deliberately, or risk damaging them. Smudging is a collective term for the cleaning of incense.

2. Under the Full Moon

Put your tarot decks in a window sill, or on a table where they are struck by full moonlight. Each 29-ish days the Moon is full. You can get applications that alert you to the full Moon a few days before. When the moon switches phase it passes even around the zodiac wheel's twelve locations. If you want the energy to be intensified, you can also use the full moon zodiac sign to fill your deck with purpose.

Capricorn, for example, has an attraction to industry, profession and authority. Let's assume in Capricorn; for instance, it is a full moon. Under that Moon, you could clean and charge your deck to imbue it with business- and career-related assets. That night, or the next day, you might read for yourself or clients on business or career-related matters. Your deck will have a little extra oomph on Capricorn-ruled subject matters. But if that's too difficult, then plain old moonlight is still working fine!

3. A Sun Bath

Unlike a moon bath, on a rainy day, or at a spot where they will obtain enough sunshine, you should leave your cards off. I wouldn't suggest this if you're living in a humid climate-unless you're bothered by twisted or bent cards. I had cards warping from late-afternoon sun exposure, even on my reading table indoors. Granted, I'm living in a dry, humid area. Your mileage could change! Also, this is a perfect system to use if you want to charge good, radiant energy on your cards.

4. Singing Bowl

If you've got one, then try. Many folks claim the bowls' sound will cleanse people or artifacts and attune them. Place your deck in the bowl as you ring it, or in the presence of the bowl.

5. Reiki

Reiki is a calming energy device using energy channeled through the hands. Practitioners are usually accredited by an instructor or organization within the program. Try this as a way to clean your cards, if you know Reiki. If in Reiki, you are not trained, try meditating with intent while holding the cards in your hands.

6. Salt

Most readers swear by the process of salting. Wrap your cards in plastic and cover the deck within a salt jar. If the idea resonates with you, then try. Personally, it looks too messy, along with risking card loss (can you tell me how picky I am with my cards yet?). But, again, the approach is valued by many tarot practitioners.

Here's a less messy suggestion: put your cards on top of a salt slab of the Himalayas. These can be found in most major grocery stores.

7. Crystals

One of the most common forms of cleaning and cleansing a Tarot deck is through crystal potent strength. By selecting one or more crystals which absorb negative energy, you can easily clean and recharge your Tarot Deck.

8. Knocking on the Deck

That's Okay. Knock on your tarot deck three times, just as you'd do a door.

I had it clarified to me that the cards are both transparent and "wakes up" my inner animist is fond of that notion. It is probably the best and purest form to use in pinch clearing.

9. Blowing on the Cards

Some readers clear their cards by fanning and blowing the deck out. Cleaning up your breath is an exciting process. I don't know the origin of this practice, but it reminds me of folklore gambling. There's a tradition in the Baccarat card game where players blow to the cards to take away bad luck. Perhaps this is a continuing tradition from the early history of tarot as a game of cards. For a lot of people, it works anyway!

10. Visualization or Meditation

The methods of visualization or meditation work well for cleaning tarot cards. Imagine a ball of light that cleans the cards or wind that sweeps away the leftover energy. That can be done as you shuffle or keep the deck in your hands. Similarly, some writers recite prayers to cleanse their cards and charge them. Tell yourself what you want your deck to support you with while creating a meditation or prayer for your cards. Some examples include encouragement from your spirit or higher self, helping your clients, assisting with healing or shadow work, etc.

11. Reordering the Deck and Shuffling

It is one of my favorite ways of getting acquainted with a deck that has been in storage for some time or finding a new deck. To do this, first reorder a shuffled deck with Arcana Major, followed by Arcana Minor. So, for me, I start at 0 with the Fool and last at 22 with the World. Instead, I stack the Ace-10 suits with the court cards in order from Title, Knight, Queen to King. I put all of them back in a stack (no choice what suit comes first with). It is similar to pressing the reset button on a tarot deck for me. It even refreshes my memory on deck images I haven't seen in a while. Occasionally new insights into a card's 0imagery can pop up in this process. Each of the above strategies can be mixed and combined. Test one out and see if the readings work. Hopefully, you have found a form of cleaning that is resonating with you. If not, make no worries! There are also brilliant, talented writers who don't use any of these forms of washing.

Putting It All Together

You'll learn some more techniques on how to prepare yourself and also your cards before making a reading. It's very important that you are prepared not just mentally but also intuitively. All the tips, methods and techniques given will only serve as your literal guide in interpreting the tarot cards but your intuition will ultimately become your "inner guide" to help you learn the true message of the cards that will help improve your clients' lives.

Now if you're going to do a Celtic – Cross layout for the cards wherein you have to layout 10 cards and the positions as well as the connections of the cards matter, you can organize your deck by arranging the major arcana cards (0 – 21), followed by the minor cards (ace cards to King) with wands coming first, followed by cups, swords and last is pentacles. This kind of arrangement is only a suggestion; of course, you can arrange your deck in which you see fit but that order is based on how the energies come down in the tree of life. Again, it's totally up to you, if you feel that the deck must be arrange in this way or that way for a particular reading or whatnot then it's your call. What's important is you arrange them in a certain way and not just randomly shuffle them since the Celtic – Cross layout is quite a complicated method of reading tarot.

A Step-By-Step Guide in Basic Tarot Reading

Step #1: Set the mood - do a tarot reading where you feel comfortable in and as much as possible avoid places with distractions.

Step #2: Relax your mind and your client – if it helps you can talk to your subject about his/her current feelings, if he/she is comfortable or just simply try to connect with him/her.

Step #3: Ask or Read the Question – remember though that when it comes to questions, it should not be like a yes/no type of query, it should be more about what to do in a certain situation/the best advice. Tarot readings will help a person deal with particular things not necessarily answer a direct question.

Step #4: Shuffle the cards – shuffle the cards or let your subject shuffle it

Step #5: Cut and pile the cards - you can also let your subject cut the cards until you think or feel that it's enough, then pile it up or stack it up in a manner you see fit.

Step #6: Layout the cards – you can make your subject pick out the card (depending on the type of layout you will use) and let him/her feel the energy within those cards. Once the cards are drawn, you can now place it in the appropriate position in a spread, make sure that the cards are still faced down.

Step #7: Reveal the cards – depending on the type of spread or your reading method, you can reveal each card one by one or simultaneously for you to see a connection.

Step #8: Interpret the Card – note the interpretation of each card as well as the pattern or position in which a card is placed and start analyzing or relating it to your subject's question/life. Consider the techniques mentioned about the relationships of the card as well as the card placements.

Step #9: Create the story – once you have analyzed or interpret the card and have considered all the other factors, you can now create a story based on the theme of the session or the query being asked

Step #10: Finish it Up – once you have interpreted the cards and perhaps send the message to your clients as well as clarify their follow – up questions. You can then conclude the session and clear the deck. You can also express gratitude to your inner guide as well as your tarot cards and pack it up on its container.

The Art of Storytelling

There are an overabundance of books and articles about reading Tarot cards and many of them oppose each other. When you are just starting out learning to read, this can be very perplexing. You can get caught up in wondering which interpretation is the "correct one."

Honestly, there is no correct one.

The images on Tarot cards tell a story making them a great way to connect with your higher self, because images are the first method of learning and can make a direct connection with your unconscious mind. Because the Tarot is individual to everybody, this is why you get very diverse viewpoints on each card.

As you practice, each card will mean something specific to you. Notwithstanding that, you can still unexpectedly get an instinctual flash as you look at a card, and it might mean something that it has not meant before.

It is important to build your own relationship with your cards and develop your own explanations.

When you have selected a deck of Tarot cards, remove a card from the deck.

You can begin with the Fool card, the first card of the Major Arcana. Or you can pick a card randomly. It does not matter.

Notice the colors and symbols, as well as any direct feelings that you get when you look at the card.

Does it remind you of somebody?

Do you find yourself thinking of a specific situation?

Do you relate to the circumstances in the image?

Now, take another card and take a good look at it. Observe. Lay it next to the other card and notice how the story changes.

As you look at the 2 cards together, build up a story of what is happening. How have things changed from one card to the other?

Just envision that you are telling a story to a child, and use the images to arouse your intuition.

It's not imagination, and you are not just making things up, so never let anyone tell you that. The Tarot is a powerful way for your intuition to connect with you or the person you are reading.

When reading for somebody else, simply describe to them what you see going on in the images, and you will be astonished at how precise the reading is.

Then add another card and continue the story. A reading based on 3 cards is one of the easiest spreads. It is frequently used as a Past/Present/Future situation, while it doesn't need to be.

Learn How to Read Tarot Cards by Looking at the Colors and Pictures

Color plays a substantial role in your deck of cards, especially in the Rider Waite Tarot deck.

The main colors of each card have an instant effect on your senses, how you feel about that particular card and any messages that your awareness may be trying to provide to you.

When you draw a card, take a minute and have a look at it. Take note of the colors and notice how the card makes you feel. The very first response you get will be the correct one, so it is vital that you don't dismiss it.

Really look at the images. What is essentially happening in the card?

Does anything jump out at you?

Do you get any specific emotional state when you look at certain cards?

Do some cards give you an immediate good feeling or an immediate feeling of anxiety?

Take note of any observations that you make in your Tarot Journal.

Yellow as a dominant color largely gives a positive, cheerful, sunshine feel to the card. This will regularly be related to your feelings and tour outward expression of things.

Red as the strongest color will frequently point to material things and matters having to do with the outside world.

There are some cards which are very dark in color or have a predominance of Black in them. Sometimes, these cards can cause a momentary brief fear. The color black can have different meanings in diverse cultures. In some, it is sign of death. In others, it is a sign of rebirth and new beginnings. In others, it is a sign of power.

Grey is customarily linked with wisdom and old age.

Colors also relate to the energy centers or chakra points in our bodies. Each of the colors and chakra points have a different meaning and are related to our interpretations of the Tarot cards.

Prior to doing a reading, shuffle your deck of cards to make sure that any energies from earlier readings have been cleared, and then give the cards to your client to shuffle.

The reason for doing this is so you can make a connection with the cards so that your energy is in them.

While shuffling, think about what you want the cards to help you with. And ask your client to do the same. The better you phrase the question, the clearer the answer will be.

Be sure that your cards are all the right way up prior to beginning the reading. That way if any end up reversed, it will be significant for that particular reading and not just a leftover reversed card from a former reading.

There are a couple of ways you can shuffle your cards:

1. Hold then upright and shuffle them like playing cards.

2. Put them on the surface in front of you facing down, and mix them up however feels the most comfortable to you.

Shuffle for as long as feels right for you.

If a card is to fly out while shuffling or you drop a couple of cards, it is because they are expected to be significant to the reading. Take a look, and note what they are. If you are reading for somebody else and they are shuffling, ask them to see what the card is, and make note of it. It might appear in a prominent place in the reading. If not, then it was simply a matter of slippery cards.

Put the card back, and continue shuffling.

If you drop all of the cards, pick them up without looking and carry on.

Put them all back together in 1 pile, with the pictures facing down.

With your left hand, cut the deck into 3 piles. Customarily, you will use the hand that you don't write with. So, if you are left-handed, you would use your right hand and vice versa. This is so you have less control over that hand, and you will be more likely to allow in the inspiration of your unconscious mind.

Cut the cards 2X so that you have 3 piles, and then put them back together as 1 pile.

Then take the cards off of the top of the pile and use for the reading.

Prepare Yourself and Your Tarot Cards Before Every Reading

There are several steps you can do this:

- Light a candle in the space you are going to use.

- Spray some cleansing essences around the room.

- Envision the Blue Flame of St Germain, which is used a lot for clearing. This is a blue flame that consumes everything negative and turns it into positive.

Before beginning any reading, it is also imperative to make sure you are ready and in the most open frame of mind.

If you can't fully let go of your own troubles, it might be advantageous to visualize that you are putting them in a wooden box and closing the lid firmly. Your worries can stay there until after the reading.

You can cleanse your own energies in the same way that you cleanse your cards. Also, deep breathing works very well. As you breathe out, release all negativity, and as you breathe in, fill yourself up with light and peace.

Ground yourself by imagining roots coming out of your feet and going deep down into the Earth. Then connect yourself up to the Universe so that you are drawing in light and energy.

You can also ask your angels and guides to bring you the info you need from a place of the highest love, truth and rightfulness and that what is coming through is for the highest good of all concerned. Trust in that

And, always remember to thank your angels, guides and helpers when you have finished the reading.

The more peaceful you are when you are doing a Tarot card reading, the clearer and more useful the answers will be that you are receiving.

Reversals

Some individuals use reversals. Others don't.

Some folks totally disregard reversed cards and look at them like they are simply upright. Some make it so there are always reversed cards in the reading. The choice is yours, and you will know better as you go along.

I have a tendency to make sure that all of the cards are in the upright position. If a reversed card appears, then it is most likely because it is what is meant to happen, and there is a significant message coming from it.

Sometimes a client will shuffle the cards by mixing them up through some elaborate card-splitting. That being the case, there might be many reversed cards, and sometimes it can be tough to know which way should be upright. Then it becomes a matter of instinct to know which cards look to be relevant.

Notice what feels right or not to you.

Work with the reversed cards the same way that you would an upright card. Take note of how the picture is now different. Ask what is now happening? Is there anything that is more prominent in the reversed position? Look at the colors, shapes, symbols and how things now relate to each other in the reversed position. Does something stand out more than it did earlier?

See how the card makes you feel and any visions that come to mind. You might get an entirely different sensation from the card. Look at the reversed card with regard to the other cards around it. Take note of how it changes the image with those cards as well.

When a reversed card is important, it will have an effect on the other cards surrounding it. See the entire spread as a complete picture.

In the Rider Waite Smith Deck of Tarot Cards, the cards are very graphic with clear images which can be a very valuable trigger to your intuition when the cards are in the reversed positions.

If reversals do not happen very often in your readings, it is perhaps more effective to use your intuition to decide the meaning in the situation that it has shown up instead of trying to refer to a book for meanings.

How to Make Your Cards Cranky?

There's a lot of mystery around the cards, and it's hard to know the true origin of Tarot, but the first cards discovered using the signs that later became the Major Arcana were in a 500-year-old card game called 'Trumps' (ahem). Seeing the future of someone in cards, tea leaves or entrails is a long-standing human tradition.

And, while there is no real agreement as to How it All Got Started, it is presumably satisfyingly plain and logical, like all human origins, and then wrapped in many slips of romantic embellishment over time, because that is one of the things human beings do best: we make things interesting by all agreeing to accept that they are important, and then add a dose of time for gravitas. This often works and that's amazing part about it. This important thing of the imagination is true, and it works. That's a kind of real magic.

Now that we are on the topic of divination, it is important to note that Tarot is not at all telling about the future in a manner that is "set in stone." Is your reading a bummer? Okay, that's fine, because what Tarot does is that it gives you a snapshot of your current state, and then say that there's a possibility of the following happening, given the current circumstances, and only if you don't do anything to alter them. The future is very dynamic, so Tarot predicting anything entirely out of your control to alter is extremely rare. Exceptions do exist. When the Tower shows up... there's something coming down, and in that experience, you're going to be a spectator, and soon, but it's rare.

It is one's own power and control, apart from your own subconscious, and the cards, with their archetypal ideas (archetypes are fundamental human concepts present throughout all cultures: light, moon, wife, husband, life, death, rebirth, hope, etc.)... tap into that energy and convey it by telling you where you're going in the Big Blue Life Experience on Earth.

Or, if that's too woo, you can think of the cards as a fancy way to make you think; it's a symbolic kick in the pants to unstuck you or look at things from a different perspective.

Either way it works. In reality, they are so uncannily accurate most of the time that it is completely unnecessary to trust in them to be able to work with them.

Ultimately, it's important to realize that the cards are simply a useful tool that can keep you conscious, focused and creative about issues, but you never need to feel helpless about their outcome. Here you have all the energy, and this is just a mirror that will help you see clearly.

And that's an important point! You don't have to think about the same issue again and again and again. Use the examples and spreads below to see options, and then let go until a new development happens. Then you can read again, so to speak, with the cards blessing.

When you read compulsively, like when you're angry or very close to someone and want to know what's going to happen next, the reaction will get muddier because muddier, and there's no consolation in it. After a while, the cards can even become tricksters, giving you utter gobbledygook or hilariously horrific, impossible poor readings.

Shuffling Your Cards

Since you have begun to get comfortable with your cards, the subsequent stage is to rearrange them up and to have a go at some straightforward spreads.

There are two or three different ways you can rearrange your cards. You can hold then upstanding and blend them up.

Or on the other hand simply put on the table before confronting downwards and blend them up anyway feels generally great for you. Mix for as long or as short a timeframe as feels directly for you.

If I am reading for another person, I would rearrange the cards first to ensure that every one of the energies of past readings have been cleared and afterward give the deck to my customer to rearrange.

Set up them all back together as one heap, still with the photos confronting downwards.

Then with your left hand cut the deck into 3 heaps. Generally, this is using the hand you don't compose with, so if you are left-given you would utilize your correct hand. The thought behind this is you have less power over that hand, so you are bound to permit in the impact of your oblivious personality.

That is the hypothesis in any case.

Likewise, if you utilize your left hand, it associates with the correct side of your mind which is do with the innovativeness and instinct.

Cut the cards twice, so you have three heaps and afterward set up them back together as one heap.

I would then take the cards off the highest point of the heap to use for the reading.

Any way you can likewise spread them out, blend them up and essentially pick anyway numerous cards you are going to use from anyplace in the deck.

I will in general ensure that the cards are all the correct far up before I start, so that if any end up switched, that is probably going to be huge for that reading and not only a left-over turned around card from a previous reading.

What occurs if a card drops out while rearranging or you drop them?

If a card flies out or you drop a few cards, they are probably going to be critical to the reader. Investigate and them and note what they are. If you are reading for another person and they are rearranging the cards, request to perceive what that card is and make a note of it. It might come up in a noticeable spot in the reading. If it doesn't, then, it was simply a question of slippery cards.

Set the card back in the deck and keep rearranging.

If you drop the cards, lift them up, without looking at the photos and continue.

The general purpose of rearranging is for you to make an association with your cards, so your energy is in them.

While you are rearranging, it is a smart thought to consider what you need the cards to assist you with. The more clearly you can express an inquiry in your psyche, regarding "what do I have to know at this moment?" the clearer the appropriate response will be for you when you put your cards down.

Blending cards on a table

If you or the customer put every one of the cards on the table and essentially blend them all up in an erratic manner, you can be sure that the cards are stirred up and you will wind up with a decent number of cards that are switched. The main test with this technique is that you don't realize what direction up your deck ought to be and run your danger of giving a totally false reading.

Turned around Cards and rearranging

I have seen tarot readers and instructors express that you should ensure that a portion of the cards are as of now switched before you offer them to another person to rearrange. I would differ with that in light of the fact that right off the bat, who chooses which cards are turned around and furthermore how would you know whether the switched cards are really important to the individual you are reading for or whether that was really material to a past reading.

As an individual inclination I generally ensure that every one of the cards are in the upstanding situation before rearranging them and doing a reading, regardless of whether for myself or for another person. Assuming then, cards end up switched through rearranging or through the cards being dropped or flying out of the deck. If there are, then any turned around cards in the reading, then they are significant to the reading and can be translated in that capacity.

The Tarot and Secret Tradition

The Tarot encompasses symbolic presentations of universal ideas, which have the whole implications of the human mind. In that sense, they contain a secret doctrine which, however, has not been explicitly acknowledged in ordinary people by the few truths imbued with the conscious. The hypothesis is that this ideology has always been present— that is, that it has been engrossed in the mind of a chosen minority; that it has been perpetuated from one human to the next in the underground, such as Alchemy and Kabalist literature; that it is also found in those established mysteries of which Rosicrucianism has set an example in the past, close to our ears. To solidify claims, it is very evident that there is an experience or practice behind the secret doctrine by which the doctrine is justified. It is evident that I can do little more than state the arguments in a textbook such as the present one, which, however, have been thoroughly addressed in several other documents, while it is designed to treat two of its most important processes in the books on the Hidden Religion of Freemasonry and Hermetic Literature.

This combination may, for example, lie in the numerical sequence of its series, or its fortuitous assembly by shuffling, cutting, and handling, as in the ordinary luck games played with cards. Two scholars have taken the first opinion without bias to the second, and I may do well to determine what they mean at once. Mr. MacGregor Mathers, who once wrote a book about the Tarot, which was primarily dedicated to fortune-telling, stated that according to their numerical order, the twenty-two Trump Major could be formed as a' linked sequence.' It was indeed the chiefs of the philosophical theory on human will, the liberation by reason, which the magician embodied, its manifestation. He always spoke about prudence, determination, commitment, hope, and eventual satisfaction in the usual way. But if this were the message from the coins, there is no need at all to publish them today or take pains to explain them for some time. A work written with passion and zeal wasted no effort to think or to study in its specific directions— but unfortunately without any true insight — Dr. Papus gave the Trump Major a singularly elaborate scheme. Like Mr. Mathers, it depends on their numeric sequence but shows their interrelationship in the Divine World, the Macrocosm and the Microcosm. In this way, we see, as it were, the metaphysical part of the man or of the soul coming out of the Divine, going back to the darkness of the material body. I believe that the author is in a measurable distance from the right track here, and his views are in this way informational, but in some ways, his method confuses the issues and modes and planes of being.

Trump Major was handled in the alternative way I described. In Grand Orient's Manual Of cartomancy, the product of certain illustrative readings of cards was actually organized as a result of a fortuitous combination by mixing and sorting under the assumption of a style of intuitive divination. The use of divinatory techniques, for any reason or intention, holds two ideas. It can be assumed that the deeper significance is not real, but that certain cards, such as the Magician, the High Priestess, the Wheel of Fortune, the Hanged Man, the Tower or House God, and many others, that do not correspond to life conditions, arts, sciences, virtues or the other subjects in Baldini's denarius, are not real. These are also positive evidence that the series cannot be explained by simple and normal values. These cards testify to themselves in another manner, and, although the condition in which I left the Tarot is so much more difficult as it is so much more open, they indicate the real subject matter we deal with. The methods also show that the Trump Major has at least been adapted instead of belonging to fortune-telling.

Both the two meaning classes that are attached to the Tarot in the higher and lower worlds and the fact that no occult or other writer has sought to attribute anything but a divinatory meaning to Minor Arcana justify the hypothesis that the two series are not one to the other. It is possible that their marriage was first carried out by the Prince of Pisa in the Tarot of Bologna, whom I mentioned in the first part. It is said that his device has been given the public recognition and reward of his city of adoption for producing a tarot which has missed just a few cards in these fantastic days, but since we are dealing with a matter of fact that has to be taken into account somehow, it is conceivable that a sensation may have been created through It would have been more applied to the other chance game, known as fortune-telling. It should be understood here that I do not deny the option of divination, but as mystical of the dedications that bring people in these paths, I take exception as if they were linked with the mystical quest.

Risks of Tarot

Tarot cards are a form of Divination. They are the tools or instruments you use to complete a reading.

Tarot cards when read for someone should be used for entertainment purpose. Tarot cards cannot predict the future. Tarot are not intended to replace physicians, psychiatrists, lawyers or financial experts. Tarot readers or Astrologers are not a regulated field, although many take courses and study a great many of them have no formal training.

Anyone can offer Tarot readings whether online or in person. There is no well to tell how experienced they are or their true intentions.

There is a big risk if the Tarot reader is not familiar enough to interpret the cards in a reading. Although a reader may preface a reading by saying this is just her/his opinion of the cards drawn often the client will believe every word and suggestion given to them. If it is way off base, they may act on the advice and put their present and maybe future in jeopardy.

Divination and Tarot are impossible without learning private things that client's share. People overshare and the danger is someone who is unscrupulous can use the information for personal gains. Or they may share what they have learned with others and this can harm the client.

Asking the wrong questions may cause more harm than good. If the client receiving the reading has an idea for a new business and asked, "Will my business be successful? "and the answer in the reading is No, then the person might decide not to waste his time starting it. However, if the Tarot reader was new, inexperienced and did not know how to interpret the cards maybe they were wrong and changed the client's life forever. Tarot cannot foretell the future. Ask open-ended questions. Most one-word answers will not work for you.

Using Divination or Tarot to make every decision in your life is wrong. It is not a substitute for free choice. It is an instrument that can help make clear your thoughts and issues. The pressure to take ownership of our actions and decisions changes when we consult the Tarot for everything. It is easy to blame the cards then rather than take ownership for our mistakes. In reverse we give up all our power and wins to the cards as well. We did not get the new job because of our skills and abilities but rather because the cards foretold it.

The belief that a set of cards can lock in our future is harmful in our lives. Clearing up an issue or opening up possibilities to us can be helpful. If the vision of your future does not appeal to you, if you are not happy with your path then work on and change it.

Used judiciously and with restraint, divination instruments can be a benefit to us, and help us with the challenges we face in life. You should not be controlled by or governed by the cards. You always have free will.

Insight and the Tarot

We all have a certain degree of what is called insight or intuition. This may or may not comprise of being psychic as well. Intuition/insight is our inborn capabilities to sense things in the world everywhere around us. It is our innate or unconscious perception that has nothing to do with our cognitive aptitudes of reason. Insight or intuition warns us when there is danger around. It is the inborn inner sense we have that turns on for specific situations when logic isn't the way to deal with it. For instance, you may meet a person who seems to be very nice, but your intuition instinctively tells you otherwise. That being the case, just be sure to keep your guard up until that individual proves themselves. It usually just feels like something isn't quite right, and our gut instinct tells us that something is wrong. That is intuition.

Life as a psychic is the outward understanding to things outside of what is recognized as the typical range of awareness. It can take many forms. The media always makes it seem like some extraordinary capability to bend objects or move tangible material with our minds. While these marvels do occur and individuals are skilled with that capability; not every psychic can do that. Some individuals possess the gift to hear things, some see things, some are able to channel in the spiritual realm. Not all psychics implement their psychic skills the same way. For example, some have such skills as clairvoyance (hearing things spiritually) and others might be telepathic (able to read or hear what a person is thinking or saying nonverbally). Others might have paranormal gifts or supernatural predispositions (see and feel beyond the ordinary range of reason by interacting with spirits). A person can possess intuition and not be psychic, and a person can be both psychic and intuitive.

To read tarot cards, it isn't required that you be psychic, but it is significant to tune in to our insights. However, the more we use our perceptions the more we open up our senses and have psychic flashes as the result. Every tarot card has a standard connotation, but the variance between a good tarot card reader and an average one is how advanced their insights are. An intuitive reader uses their senses and gut feelings together with the precise explanation of each card in order to obtain the complete crux of the cards meaning. As with everything else in life, the more we use our perception the sharper it will become. And, the more solid our intuitions grow, the more precise our readings become. Tarot cards are tools which helps emphasize the intuition for those with innate skills. Some individuals possess intuition as a gift, and others might have to work harder to open that part of themselves in order to have a slight intuition. Many times, individuals with robust instincts to the point of being psychic may have had it in their families, and it was passed along from generation to generation.

Many individuals who aren't open to the idea of tarot cards and intuition dismiss the idea of reading them as a cheap shop hoax. The reality is, though, that most individuals have a misunderstanding of what a reading actually is. It is the intuitive gift that the reader possesses and how he/she applies them to the tarot cards which makes the reading real. Most folks who read tarot cards are already intuitive to some degree when they take it on early in their lives, which is what made them gravitate to the tarot to begin with.

The tarot cards are not magic when you remove them from the box. It is actually the individual's energy that is used to create that magical interaction between themselves and the cards.

Another thing that is significant for that magic linking to the cards is the life force energy in our bodies. Life force is the energy in our body that circulates through our existence and links us to our spiritual core. It is what gives us will, vitality and a spiritual connection to things outside of ourselves. This energy is set free when we touch the tarot cards. In other words, our energy is conveyed into the cards by simply placing our hands on them. When we use the cards during a reading, our energy streams into the cards from our hands since we willfully direct our attention to the cards.

Readers use this energy in different ways. Some will basically permit their client to touch the cards so that they can feel the person's energy, and other readers will not due to the fact that they don't want to blend their energy with the individual's they are reading. In fact, it is totally up to how every individual reader chooses to work with the energy we have as well as the energy of the individual who is being read.

When we select the cards (and this is true predominantly for veteran readers), the cards transpose an energy through our hands and tell us when to stop shuffling and/or when to throw a card down on the table. There are readers who will use the other individual's energy and ask them to shuffle and pick the cards for their reading. In either case, it is that energy that motivates the individual to select and shuffle the deck for the message they are going to obtain.

The symbolic meaning of tarot cards also varies between readers. It rests on how their perceptions construe and relate to a specific card. For instance, the death card for a particular reader might literally mean someone is going to pass away; and for others it might mean the end of a certain period for a person in life. Therefore, if a person goes to a reader and sees the death card, it does not necessarily mean someone is going to die. It might mean the end of a relationship or routine, or that that person needs to change their life totally. It's really all about how the reader attaches to the imageries in the tarot cards and senses how that relays to the individual being read.

When a person initially begins to read the tarot, there might be misperception about the interpretation of a tarot card. This is when the person's intuition truly is asked to work. When this occurs, it is best to focus all of your care and energy on that card and ask your intuition to inform you as to what that card is saying.

In addition, it is a great means to grow your insight in relation to reading your tarot cards. You begin by receiving the traditional standardized meaning of the card, and then question your inner self, your intuition, as to what it means. Then, you will begin to assume the energy of the cards and connect it with your intuition. This serves two distinct purposes - it aids in memorizing each card by a standard meaning and then aids in developing your intuition as to what that card means to your senses. Take note of the sensation you get when you do this with each card because the feeling you get is the energy that that card draws on. This is what will make the difference between just anyone reading cards and a good reader. A good reader will be in tune with their energy, the joining they have with the cards and their intuition. These two elements – energy and intuition - are what goes into the cards from the reader to give a vibrant and precise reading.

There are readers who are also channelers. They use spiritual guides to help them with the readings. They are basically individuals who possess intuition and also possess a spiritual element to some degree and their psychic aptitude is able to work in the spiritual realm. They are the tarot readers who invite their spirit guides to come in and assist them when they do readings. A guide is a spiritual entity who helps them. They might speak to them, they might guide their hands, or they might, in fact, enter the reader's body. It is not essential for reading the tarot. What is vital is that you are open enough to permit your intuition to work for and with you when you interpret the cards and their meanings

Whatever works for you is what is best. Take the basics and run with them and then read the cards to the best of your ability!

Teaching Yourself Tarot Mastery

There are as many ways as there are people who do to read the Tarot. Tarot doesn't have to be a parlor game, and it doesn't have to be the sophomoric one-card-to - a-time routine, it doesn't have to be New Age fluff. It will take a lot of work to master tarot by introducing it to yourself, but it has the same advantage as teaching yourself how to cook: the recipes are unique to you.

The main genuine one is the Rider-Waite deck. The books are put together by fools who offer you implications. Eden Gray's "The Tarot" is valuable in the event that you need a book to' surrender you a leg,' particularly the part where she has passages on the implications of the cards dependent on the photos on Rider-Waite deck. The page-via card composing is a precious alternate way to take cognizance of each major arcana. Keep your cards upstanding, disregard all the turned around implications. This authority of tarot by training it to yourself undertaking will be a long stretch, something' not for everybody. The Middle Ages do - it-in reverse put-it-upside thing was a counter-response to the authoritarian intensity of the Roman Catholic Church at the time. ' Remember variable based math: in the event that you need to fathom it, there can be just a single obscure in a condition. That is the reason posing inquiries will reveal to you the significance of the cards you know the appropriate responses.

You're simply going to pose inquiries to which you know the appropriate responses. For every one of these inquiries, you will utilize the whole deck since you need to comprehend what the cards mean, and utilizing the entire deck includes every one of the cards in the subject. You need to find how various mixes of cards are utilized to express a similar thought. There is a picture of a circumstance on every Rider-Waite ticket, from which its implications arise. Keep in mind consistently that in a given spread, your sense for a given card may include any part of the card picture's story. (You may be outmaneuvering or defeat.) Look at the remainder of the format to perceive what the parallels are, apply for that one card.

These are cards with the theme: very important. They set the dominant purpose, and for the rest of the cards in your layout, and you choose goals that agree with them. You will be able to identify a recurring pattern in your response when you see them as you become professional. That repetition shows precision. First, you'll learn to search for these theme cards to identify your answer faster.

Some things that can happen when you delve into tarot:

(1) Three-dimensional cards will appear. Don't let that disturb you; it's your subconscious saying that for this message, this card is essential.

(2) The pictures appear to be making a film once in a while. This is the stage where you start putting things together and getting an overview.

(3) You begin reading card combinations as they glomerate together changing each other: this is the skill of the tarot; you are on your way.

Some parts of the pair of cards layout. The center cover/cross (the second and third cards you put down) is closely related to each other and maybe the microcosm reading. The cards side of those commonly called' Before' and ' Behind' are paired, with left representing the past and the one to the right representing the future. The card below is known as ' Foundation,' and the one above paired with it is called' Future.' You'll gradually get the hang of that. The first sentence of your three-sentence layout is these seven cards, and the penalties are accurate to the degree they repeat and support each other! It's a search.

Due to the Celtic background of this layout-style, the next sentence is three cards going up, popularly called' A Tower.' The second Self card is the bottom card. (The first self-card is the first card that you put down before the combination Cover / Cross) The second card that goes up is called' Others,' which is self-explaining. The last up is the turning point or the point of confrontation commonly referred to as' Hopes and Fears.' Add two cards and make three across the deck to use the whole deck evenly. All of these combines to be the result together.' And the result is the third sentence.

You're not going to find the idea of the three sentences anywhere but here. And it is also unusual the concept that the theme cards are correct as they appear in each of the spread's three sentences. As a beginner, you might prefer to answer the question with just three or four cards at a time. This is working. Try not to use the entire deck like this; only some of the spreads would be clear answers.

The distinction just read the cards between and a tarot master is the ability to combine card combinations (not only card pairs) into a single sense. Variations of the same cards will connect together and appear in spread after spreading standing for a concept introduced earlier in the session when the knowledgeable and are no asking anymore only questions you know the answers to. They're going to do this regardless of how you shuffle. It's just a shorthand. Many or even all of the cards in the entire layout occasionally blend into meaning. You've come when you can see that.

Let me note here that in your Tarot Mastery Endeavor, like all you do, there will be good days and cussed days! And let me also remember that the uncertainty is mirrored in your spread when you tap into a confused person or situation with Tarot: it explains something contradictory accurately! Allow this to happen!

You have the truth when you have control, and you have the facts. Now you can ask more personal questions about your own life than you would like to share with anybody else. At your own pace, you will discover your own motives. You can psychoanalyze yourself, and something will tell you not to do by any good psychologist. (But they don't see!)

Starting Out Your Journey To Tarot Reading

We all start our journey to tarot in different ways; different circumstances lead different people to tarot reading. Inevitably, people are going to view the very practice of tarot reading from different individual perspectives. The most difficult fact to accept about tarot reading, however, is the fact there is no absolute right or wrong way to carry out specific actions, or to make certain deductions from tarot cards.

Unlike other more accurate scientific fields, tarot reading is an art that has thrived over the ages on generating controversies in interpretations; bringing people together using differences in their reasoning. So, the way you are going to understand how the reading of a particular card or spread appears to your own peculiar situation might differ slightly from how even your reader would see it.

They key to being a great tarot reader in the long run, therefore, is for you first to find yourself, and come to terms with who you are. You need to realize exactly who you are, underneath the cloak of educational backgrounds, social class and all those cloaks we use to mask our real selves in the modern society. You are not your occupation or job description, you are not your position in your family, you are not the role that the society has foisted on you.

You must go back to the very basics of your consciousness and discover who you really are and the ideals you hold dear. Discovering yourself will help you to have an independent voice and a self-reliant thought pattern that will be able to help your intuition bloom. Once you as a person are in perfect harmony with your intuition, then reading the cards and relating them to your personal life becomes easier.

Discovering yourself will also let you find out you are intrinsically different from everybody else. Who you are fundamentally as a person differs from what people think you are, and it sure differs from who other people are. Therefore, since we all different on a very primal, basal level, it is not expected for our intuitions to work the same way. What your intuition regards the interpretation of a card to mean in your personal situation is likely to be slightly different from what someone else would think if they got that particular reading in your same exact situation. So, self-discovery will let you understand who you are, and will let you come to terms with the differences that exist between yourself and others.

Now that you have understood that the basic requirement is knowing who you are to enable your intuition to bloom unrestricted, the next step is for you to learn the basics of Tarot. For a tarot reading to be carried out, five basic pre-requisites must be in place. First and most importantly. There should be a reader. If there is no reader, then exactly how is the interpretation of the card going to be determined? So, a reader has to be in place to examine the cards drawn and the spread created, and to guide the person who asks the question on the core meaning of the reading produced.

This leads to our second most important factor, the querent. In Tarot literature, a querent is simply the person who asks the question (or who makes the query). In circumstances of personal divination therefore, the reader and the querent are going to be the same person. So, the querent is the one who is seeking an answer to a burning problem.

The third pre-requisite is the question itself. This is the most important thing the querent has to possess for a tarot reading to be successful – a concise, clear-cut question that has been decided on in advance or on the spot. For a querent to be able to relate a tarot reading to his own personal circumstances, the question asked has to be as concise and unambiguous as possible.

The next most important pre-requisite is the deck of cards. There are different types of tarot cards in existence currently, but the most common and most widely accepted tarot deck is the Rider-Waite-Smith tarot deck. The original version of this deck was first created in 1909, and its simplicity and conciseness has endeared it to the hearts of many tarot readers over the years. This has made it the deck of choice for both avid tarot enthusiasts and beginners who are just starting out in the game of tarot reading.

The average tarot deck consists of 78 cards. The whole tarot deck can be divided into two major sections, the major arcana, or the major mysteries, and the minor arcana, or the minor mysteries. The cards in both sections of the deck will be explained in detail as we move on.

Finally, a spread is the last important pre-requisite for a reading to be completed. A spread may be an arrangement of cards picked out in a particular fashion based on the direction of the reader's or querent's intuition. In other types of readings, the spread may be a single card pulled randomly from a deck or from a random pile of cards. Whatever form it takes, the most important thing to note is that the spread is the card, or sequence of cards that is interpreted to give an answer to the question asked by the querent.

Even though a lot of tarot readers practice personal divination in the modern dispensation, back in ancient Europe, there were huge concerns about the ability of readers to be objective when seeking answers to their own questions from the cards. So, when carrying out a personal divination through a tarot reading, as both the reader and the querent, you need to strive consciously during the course of the tarot reading to remain as objective as possible when carrying out the reading.

Of course, as stated earlier, there is no specific way to interpret a spread. People examine core meanings, and then relate them to their own specific situations based on their individual convictions. So, whether you like it or not, your personal convictions about that question you asked will come into play as you seek answers from the cards. It is now up to you as a reader to look deeply at the core meanings of the cards in your spread, and make an objective deduction based on your intuition, and not a deduction that aligns with your wishes.

Since the heyday of Tarot reading, the practice has never been seen as a form of inquiry from an absolute supernatural source. Tarot reading have always been regarded as a way of providing a mirror for us to gaze back unto ourselves, our unique predicaments, circumstances and situations and reflect deeply to come up with intuitive deductions and solutions. The aim of tarot is to help you reach into the deepest recesses of your mind, and relate the tarot reading you have done by yourself, or the one an expert reader has just done for you to your unique circumstances.

It's actually that simple. Having to distill the path to the solution of your problems to just one image or a few sequential images allows you to think deeply from a unique perspective. See how the core meanings of the card relate to you, and begin to work out a simple, basic solution to your problems. Tarot helps to eliminate complexities by forcing you to come down to a basal level when attempting to solve a problem. Instead of engaging your analytical mind and trying to find various complex solutions to mostly simple problems, tarot brings your intuitive mind into the picture and allows you build your solutions from the simple to the complex phases, which is the most efficient mechanism of problem solving.

Contrary to popular opinion, you don't need to have studied the entire tarot deck to be able to perform a simple reading. The key to a successful tarot reading is your intuition; the limitless power of your mind. So, as a total novice with no prior knowledge of tarot, you can still carry out an effective tarot reading using the power of your intuition. All you have to do is get your deck of cards (you can do that right now if you have your deck with you), think of a particular question, pull out a single card (we don't want any complications yet), and then think of how the image on the card relates to the question you asked.

You can just write down the first couple of things that comes to your mind. It might take a while for you to be able to effectively establish a connection between the question you asked and the image on the card you pulled. That's where the power of your intuitive mind comes in. The more you ponder intuitively on the image, the clearer the path between your tarot reading and the question you asked becomes to you. It's so simple, yet so unbelievably powerful.

Finally, to conclude this section, we'll be looking at how to read a spread appropriately. The spread is the layout of the cards that allows the reader to provide an answer to the querent's question using his interpretation of the core meanings of the cards and the sequence in which the cards appear. Sometimes, the sequence of the cards may not be put into consideration, it all eventually boils down to your intuition.

Most tarot readers like to use a three-card spread. The first card represents the events of the past, the second represents the events of the present, while the third represents how the past and present will lead to a particular future occurrence. For some readings, only once card is used, and in some readings, more than three cards are used. No hard and fast rules apply.

Conclusion

If you have bought and read this, I am hoping that it has been, and will continue to be, helpful to you in your tarot learning journey. I have written it based on what I would have loved having access to when I was learning because, at the time, it seemed such an insurmountable task.

I have tried to limit the amount of text within knowing that pages and pages of words, when you are starting out, can make the process daunting and also be difficult to retain. If at first, you only use the key meaning references along with some of the exercises, numerology and color, you will then be more well equipped to absorb further information, use your intuition to discover deeper messages, and set out on your own quest for the many vast and varied elements of the tarot that may interest you. Tarot can be used in so many facets of our lives from finding missing objects to communicating with loved ones who have passed on, and much more.

The vast majority of us who are passionate about tarot and devote an enormous amount of time and energy mastering the practice, do so out of a desire to help others.

There is so much satisfaction in knowing that the person you have guided through difficult times, given hope to, or even just listened to, lets you know how pivotal the advice of the cards was to them and to their sense of security.

My own journey of having tarot cards read for me started nearly thirty years ago when I discovered a remarkable tarot reader who managed to give me genuine and constructive advice for all that was happening in my life at the time. I would travel a great distance to see her yearly, and sometimes every six months or so. Eventually over the years as times changed, she would travel to see me, doing readings in my own home. Her husband would drive her, and it wasn't long before relationships with my whole family were formed. She has recently retired, and her wonderful husband has passed away and will be missed by us all. She has been a brilliant mentor for me and her encouragement of my tarot reading journey has inspired and motivated me to overcome many fears and self-doubt.

Tarot can bring so many wonderful and interesting people into your life and broaden your knowledge on innumerable topics and subjects. This in turn, can offer you the expertise and the means to give guidance to others.

It is also a great guiding tool for your own life, often confirming what your intuition tells you.

I encourage you, as I've said earlier, to join any social media groups as they can offer an invaluable source of free knowledge extended by many experienced tarot experts, and also provide you with support should you have any questions of your own. I've also known people to have gained some long-lasting friendships as an additional bonus to their tarot learning experience.

My last words of advice are to follow your heart if tarot is something you are passionate about, as I was. Don't be disillusioned if you are not supported by friends or family members in your decision to study tarot. My immediate family and some friends were extremely supportive of me, but there are always those few who will disappoint you with their lack of understanding or uneasiness with tarot in general. If you are determined and committed to learning, you will remain focused and enthusiastic and become the incredible tarot reader you were always meant to be. It won't happen overnight, but it will happen.

While this beginner's guide may help you to begin your passion with the Tarot, and in some cases other areas of interest such as numerology or Kabbala, always remember that experience is the best teacher.

It is only through practice that you should trust the insights from the cards, and you can easily perform readings

Lastly, I want you to keep the cycle of learning this ancient wisdom. You can choose to pass this along to your friends so they can also develop their intuition.

With these, we can all together appreciate our human existence and our world with more intimate perspective.

Thank you for taking the time to read the book.

Book 3

Astrology for Beginners

INTRODUCTION

Our Universe came into existence with the help of Sun, Moon, Stars and other Celestial bodies. Astrology is a science that studies about the association between the positions of the sun, moon, stars and other celestial bodies and human beings. Astrology, in its broadest sense, is the search for human meaning in the sky. Human beings living on planet Earth looked upwards at the sky to know directions and answers for their life occurrences. Over 25,000 years ago people realized that the moon influenced the tides, oceans and seas. As time passed people realized that the change in night sky did have an influence over humans and they started to look at celestial bodies to seek answers. The cosmic dance that is happening always in the sky is looked upon to get answers for our lives on earth and that study of metaphysics is known as astrology. It is a study that is beyond physical that involves intuition and psychic powers. Astrology is also known as the 'mother of all sciences'.

Before the advent of electricity, people used sunrise and moonlight to calculate days and time. The impact of stars, planets and the moon on plant and animal behavior on earth has been well documented. The indents appearing on animals were taken as symbols and messages from God. The Gods also presented themselves in images and stars with whom they were associated. Even evil stars were associated with a particular planet indicating dissatisfaction or disturbance or adverse events. Such indications were dealt with by appeasing the Gods and found ways to please the Gods so that nothing negative begot the king or ruler. Omens and magic were believed by the rulers of that era.

Ancient temples and architecture were built with sophisticated awareness of celestial cycles. Astrological predictions have been accepted as a science and increasingly further studies and research is being conducted to distil and fine tune the methods and processes. Critics are of the opinion that how can you categorize the entire world population into 12 signs? Well, broadly it is done and that is how astrology can help to determine a person's nature and foretell his future. We all believe that there are energies present within us as well as in the universe. If both are in tune with each other that is when the universe showers us with abundance. This is the fundamental secret of the 'Law of Attraction'. Using this base the time when a person is born is recorded on the celestial clock along with the position of the stars and planets at that point of time in the vast sky. With the position of the Sun, Moon and other planets at the time of birth an individual's birth chart or horoscope is devised and looked into. A professional astrologer, who has learnt the science along with loads of intuition, combines his powers to predict what sort of a person the individual is and how his life on this planet will be.

Numerology, astrology, and tarot all connect together. Each of these divinity reading styles have their own unique way that they fit together with the other two, yet they all come together to develop a persuasive reading format for all. If you have ever been drawn to astrology or tarot, chances are you will be surprised to learn that numerology is not too different from these two reading styles. Read on to learn more about how they all connect together.

Astrology Throughout the Ages (History)

Ancient Astrology

Many great men like Copernicus Galileo, Ptolemy, and Aristotle were some of the early astrologers who stirred in the minds of many other thinkers what the stars and planets may hold and what they tell us. These celestial shifts and movements fascinated others after them to ask more questions about what is beyond our planet so much so that astronomy was once a subject of science. The many suppositions of these great thinkers would eventually pave the way for people to use their imaginings in a way that would allow us to contradict, answer, give solutions and reveal information.

They were not the only ones who had great ideas about the universe and the planets and stars it holds but It was them and others like them who stirred the minds of many other intellectuals throughout time, time and again, to challenge or solidify their initial ideas. Astrology, in a grand gesture of providing knowledge of what is seen in the heavens, allowed the expansion of the study of the universe, man, and his being, as well as other disciplines of science that give us the luxuries and technologies we enjoy today. Many of what were once imagined and fathomed only in the recesses of the mind of man, are now realities in our lives. What once was thought to be only possible in fantasy has become a reality because of the initial work and documentation of sky observers of the past.

But it was also because of those advancements that gave way to more critical questions about the reality and accuracy of what astrology claims to bring to the table. And because it has been so widely misunderstood for what it stands and what it imparts, it had lost its luster and dulled the interests of many when claims relating to and about astrology were made. However, there was always a small minority of individuals who continued to study astrology and adjusted their perceptions to open up a broader more expansive knowledge of it.

The mathematical aspect of this science was dug into more profound and secretly studied by many when others were persecuted, imprisoned and others even put to death because of the information they shared - sometimes a complete false, other times accurate, while there are theories earlier refuted but later (much later) was proven to be true.

Astrology is a set of principles that if followed, practiced, conveyed and understood correctly, tells us of our place under the sun and essentially helps us explain situations and events in our lives. It does not take away free will from us nor does invoke to have an individual believe that they have no choice and "it is written in the stars". Astrology aims to further the knowledge of oneself with one's own using the knowledge man has gained according to the planets and stars pull on our inner being. It aims to shed light on you, as an individual A guide, if you may, to assist you at any given time of your life.

Modern Astrology

The fast movement of scientific knowledge recently has seen significant advancement in terms of machinery and tools that allows us the modern conveniences we have that many of us take for granted. Many of these inventions and tools of the many branches of the sciences are much owed to many individuals of long bygone history whose imaginings went far beyond their space and realm of time. Because of all these we are now able to enjoy many perks and advantages not available to those who came before us.

Astrology may have waned in the interest and curiosity of people by the 17th century but had picked up interest anew when the 1970's rolled around. There are presently a few schools around the world that teach Astrology to students curious about the craft and discipline of the study. To further the institution of astrology, schools have not only streamlined the practice, but have also gone so far as to certify individuals who have passed the standards founded on the study. The advent of these formal schools and eventual certification gives credence to the fact that astrology is and will be a system of looking at their circumstances, events and situations from a higher perspective, if you must.

Today's technology has contributed to the clarity of what astronomy is and has given astrologers a better perception of the relation of planets and stars to the daily events and circumstances of individuals. Because of the significant advancement of our knowledge about the universe, the discovery of "new" planets has allowed astrology to compartmentalize and able to generalize readings, i.e. when is the best date and times to officially open that coffee and pastry shop you've always wanted.

Back then an astrologer's job was a tedious one of creating a chart - and you shall have a good idea of the time spent on this as we shall go over making one later. A chart takes precision and mathematical calculations in order to get all the quantifiers in alignment. It took a lot of sheets of paper, elbow grease, and careful thought to measurements to come up with an accurate chart. Nowadays, technological modernity has allowed

Computers, and computer software has allowed astrologers the convenience of having a software create a chart based on information given by an individual, but it would still take a practicing or seasoned astrologer to read those charts and interpret them using the methods and applying the principles of the discipline they have learnt. This is where the human touch remains. Here is when the astrologer is present for any questions an individual may have. Here is where the astrologer can tell you what you can't decipher for yourself.

Astrology and the Planet

The astrology is focused on stars, signs, aspects, and buildings. For the purpose of predicting or concentrating on a specific branch of astrology, many more rates and interpretation resources can be added. The set stars and constellations form an ancient branch of astrology and come back promptly now. Many stars and constellations appear behind the planets on the map, and can also be interpreted as a rich context that helps to identify specific life problems more accurately.

Karmic and mystical astrology focuses on the person's soul and his rebirth in this particular life and looks at the past karmas and lessons to be learned.

Astrology is prevalent for relationships, and this approach is called synastry. The diagrams and interactions of two or more individuals are collected, providing a rich insight into the way they communicate, whether they be friends, partners, family members, or colleagues. It can be helpful in identifying potential barriers and communication problems and supporting each other. It can demonstrate how far a relationship is going to go and if there is more to it than sex.

The forecasting is a tool that can be used with high precision in astrology because we know potential celestial motions. This can show us today's and future forces in our lives and help us with things such as: Is this a good time for me to find a new job? Should I sustain my relationship, or is it time to pursue my own path? Why is life currently so complicated, throwing obstacles after obstacles? Would my health improve or deteriorate, and what remedies are possible? Will I travel around the world or stay at home? It is important to remember that a reading of astrology will never govern. Your own choice is what you do. It also does not predict things such as death, since the astrologer is ethical and cannot be explicitly defined. What it can do is give you good times to pursue new ideas or relax and find inspiration. It can show you possibilities-it is up to you how you want to use them. This can illustrate to you why and what the object of the complexity is to be measured and how it can best be transformed.

Once a good astrologer first reads his diagram, he is usually surprised and intrigued by how detailed it is. It's not necessary to understand why it works, although fascinating, because it seems to help people anyway. Astrology is an extremely useful method for guidance and transformation, the course of the soul, and the fundamental questions as to why we are here for all aspects of life and personality.

Uranus is a kind of Saturn's nemesis. The structure breaks down often abruptly or unconventionally. At this point, such variables never need again to be studied, but Uranus is once again opposed (creating conflict and breakdown) to Saturn's systems. A bit of an explosive impact will occur-literally or figuratively. An excellent example is a disaster in the Gulf of Mexico. Fossil fuel dependency is part of an old system that absolutely MUST die. Uranus came in explosively to show this fact to anyone who just didn't. Relationships also experience massive change during the transits of Uranus. The laws (which come from the power of Saturn) shift-often because of sudden death (literally or metaphorically), accident, or because someone broke it without warning! Uranus last opposed Saturn before 2008 in 1965-66-the early years of the Civil Rights movement! Think of social change, social change, and personal systems... Although some of the changes may take us away from the guard, the destruction Uranus still liberates us!

Jupiter expresses our ideals, values, self-worth perception, and capacity to expand on the basis of what we believe is our Supreme truth (physical, financial, spiritual, creative, professional...). Many astrologers name Jupiter, because of its vast existence, the planet of good fortune. Spiritual teachers, teachers, and gurus of healing are an excellent example of Jupiter's higher vibration. Nevertheless, when running in a lower capacity, Jupiter can be just. Religious fanatics are manifestations of Jupiter's lower vibration. In line with Jupiter, Uranus is currently cultivating a new foundation of values and ideals, a lot of religious fanatism, a conflict in the Middle East, a greater interest in new forms of non-denominational spirituality and unorthodox business practices, both of which are evolving and carrying a different level. Consider expanding unorthodox ideologies. This strength is somewhat inappropriate because the two planets are in Aries ' feisty position!

Pluto... I love to talk about Pluto because I feel it's more fascinating than any other planet. Most astrologers do not comprehend Pluto, but it's interesting, I believe! While Pluto ' downgraded' several years ago to asteroid status, its energy remains one of the most concentrated as it retains its potential for death, rebirth, and full transformation. Simple: like a tidal wave, Pluto experiences disasters, and the consequences are dramatic. The psychological action of the surfaces as we navigate the Pluto process gives us our weakest attributes because we can fall into fear and survival... Obsessively, we can go on to exploit, control, or distort our world (including others), trying to cover the hidden truths below the tapestry. The energy can be cumbersome, dark, possessive, sexual, and dependent. What was ground and our true intentions have already hit latent (collectively or individually) are visible the explanation for this? Deep beneath the surface of the psyche are obsessive secrets and attributes which have to be purged and transformed for real evolution. Anything but shallow! Anything less!

Examples of the Plutonian role in our Grand Cross include government and corporate corruption, the mortgage crisis, our addiction to oil and materialism, the abuse of money, natural disasters and the surface disrepute, efforts to manipulate, harass and dominate other people, while lying about real reasons for doing this, many of the tough things that happen in our lives have become difficult to do. Phew! Phew! The Moon is our ego. It includes emotions, self-identity, mechanisms for defense, intuition, projection, physical and psychological sense, as well as our homes, personal relationships, and comfort.

I will only talk briefly to Venus and Mars as they will be part of our Grand Cross for a short time, but their role must be taken into account.

Venus: material ideals, representations of the public, connections with commodities, and how we describe ourselves in our material world.

Mars: rage, expression of oneself, imagination, fighter, male power, ability to act.

Saturn, Uranus, and Pluto will continue to conflict cycling through 2012. Jupiter is going to cycle in and out by March 2011. The Grand Cross would be triggered at a number of times when Moon (or other planets) transits Cancer's sign: 10-11 July 2010 7 August 2010, 3 September 2010 1 October 2010 (slightly less intensive) 30 June-11 July 2011 7-15 July 2011 (with Venus in a Mix and not Earth) 17-18 July 2012 (with Mars in a Mix instead of the Saturn) Remove many planets to the mix and add friction and difficulty. We have to incorporate the following features into this particular series of planetary transits: to yield to the fact that an old paradigm simply does not work and allows us to move with waves of change, rather than to fight against them or try to preserve what does not work, modesty, thinking outside the box. All this refers to the ways in which we perform our relationships, expenses, and medical treatment (I think it right now is useful to explore alternative therapies and incorporate them into West medicine), living arrangements, preferences, assumptions about beliefs, jobs, and everyday decisions. It is equally essential that the nuances of the plot are not lost. Take notice, then, of what is awry and take action. Repeating the misery tale does nothing to change it. Taking action as described above and connecting with your inner guidance helps to change the ball!

You can't move in, out, left, or right without bumping your head against the wall with situations or logistics, but IMAGINE yourself fills your heart with passion, light, and transcending-free from a commitment to specific results-knowing that it's better to stay up and out! Right now, your job is not to confine yourself to practical risks. Instead, it is your time to heal yourself, transform your own energy (experience), and believe in endless expansion opportunities. The duty of Spirit is to look after the data.

Horoscopes

Horoscope is a guide of zodiacal hover with Earth at the middle. The highest point of the circle speaks to the Sun at its most elevated point during the day and left and right of that are the eastern and western skylines.

Your horoscope outlines the overall places of the Sun, moon, planets, and stars at a particular time and spot based on your personal preferences. Celestial prophets don't utilize 'clock time'. Instead, they measure it as "sidereal" time, as estimated from the sun's situation at the spring equinox.

When the date and time are chosen and determined ass sidereal time and the area known and plotted, the soothsayer counsels a galactic ephemeris (a table posting the areas of the Sun, Moon, planets, and groups of the stars at some random time) to develop the graph.

While this used to be repetitive and demanding, P.C. programming have made it very simple. The study of building a graph is just the initial step. Legitimate understanding of the diagram is both a craftsman and a science. Appropriately done, it uncovers characters that have bits of knowledge and current patterns, and should just be endowed to a profoundly prepared and licensed celestial prophet.

Many people may consult astrologers about sorting out a relationship issue, changing jobs or changing careers, opening a new business and becoming self-employed.

People usually make changes to improve their earning potential.

We will look at areas of income that relate to other people's resources — for example, bank loans, business partnerships, inheritance, and gifted money.

We will study the indicators in the natal horoscope. I will be using an example that I have imaginary come up with to illustrate well how Horoscope can change your life even financially. By studying one horoscope, we will clearly see the natal configurations sensitive to career and financial changes.

Let's start with the indicators of financial improvement in the horoscope. We want to see solar arc or transit activity from Jupiter, Uranus or Pluto in 8th harmonic hard aspect -- conjunction, semi square (45 degrees), square, (135 degrees) and opposition - to the ruler of the 2nd house (money) and planets located in the 2nd house. We want to focus as well on the ruler of the 8th house or planets in the 8th house since this area concerns other people's resources.

Jupiter is a beneficial planet. It augments and expands whatever it touches. Uranus represents sudden changes, upsetting the status quo, bringing in new and exciting developments.

And Pluto signifies empowerment and transformation.

We are not interested in transiting Neptune. If for example transiting Neptune is in hard aspect to the planet ruling the 2nd house, it can suggest confusion, doubt, insecurity even deception with finances.

Neptune generally is not going to be a positive influence, as well with Saturn in hard aspect to a planet ruling the 2nd or 8th house. Saturn tends to be controlling and restrictive. So, we want to focus on Jupiter, Uranus and Pluto.

We want to look for solar arcs or transits from Jupiter, Uranus or Pluto in hard aspect to the angles of the horoscope. The Midheaven (MC) reflects a change of status, career developments and recognition. As well, in hard aspect to the planet ruling the 10th house or located in the 10th house. Same for the 11th house as well, since it represents income and recognition from the profession.

Another essential combination in solar arc (SA) or transit activity is Pluto or Uranus to Jupiter, and vice-versa such as Jupiter in hard aspect to Pluto or Uranus, or Pluto in hard aspect to Jupiter, or Uranus in hard aspect to Jupiter.

Jupiter to Uranus or Uranus to Jupiter suggests exciting opportunities, success, becoming independent, and heading to where the grass is greener. It is optimism and intensifies (Uranus) reward (Jupiter). Likewise, Jupiter to Pluto or Pluto to Jupiter symbolizes success, wealth, establishing new perspectives of opportunity, leadership, influence, and resourcefulness.

The reward cycle of transiting Jupiter conjunct the Sun, occurs every twelve years. When you test someone's past through this cycle, you should see a theme reoccurring every twelve years of success or reward.

For example, that I had started a business venture every twelve years.

If transiting Jupiter conjunct the Sun does not manifest as reward, there are usually other mitigating measurements or factors that trump or negate Jupiter. For example, transiting

Pluto to Saturn, or transiting Neptune to the Sun or angle of the horoscope can be challenging.

Usually however, transiting Jupiter conjunct the Sun marks a time of promotion, reward and recognition.

We also want to look for solar arc or transiting Uranus to Saturn. This suggests a wake-up call of ambition. Imagine cheerleaders on the sidelines at a football game, jumping up and down. It's time to get things going, to pick up the pace.

It intensifies ambition, bringing in exciting new developments. It can also suggest making changes that will afford the person more freedom or individuality. Sometimes it can be about freedom in relationships leading to a separation, but at the same time, career developments can coincide. Check your horoscope when solar arc or transiting Uranus was in hard aspect with natal Saturn and see what manifested then.

Perhaps the reason people have a fascination with the skies is because they provide a way to learn about ourselves. There is an ancient saying, "As above – so below." One interpretation of that saying is "Know the universe – know you." It could be said that as human beings are part of nature and inhabitants of the universe, they work by the same laws as the stars. From that perspective, we can learn more about ourselves by studying the larger domain we live in. But still, studying the stars ONLY to get a better grasp about our lives, or ONLY to calculate the best timing for doing one thing or another, misses a higher point. Astrology is far more than that.

In ancient times, the knowledge of the more enormous potential of astrology, beyond just personal decision making, was held by only a few trained individuals. For the people who worked with esoteric astrology, the stars in the sky were not only bright lights or a tool for prediction. For them, astrology was inseparable from their way of life. It was part of their cosmic perception, belief system, and religion.

For example, in ancient Greece (and Rome, which adopted a great deal from Greek culture), stars and gods were one. Therefore, not only did the Greek predict the movement of the planets/gods in the sky, they also tried to influence the planets/gods by building beautiful temples for them, by praying, and by conducting rituals and ceremonies. This might seem to us today as superstitious. But it is based on a profound insight, acknowledging that not only do the planets affect us, but we also can affect the planets and the stars. For the Greeks it was known that a simple prayer or heroic act could make the gods change their decisions and hence change the way a planet will influence one's life. Later on in history we will see practitioners like Culpeper using different herbs to change a particular astrological influence upon a person. But the notion of the reciprocity between the stars and human beings goes much further than that, and touches excellent spiritual truths. There is mutuality between humans and the celestial bodies and the connection does not go one way only.

In many ancient cultures there are references to Astrology – the state of the heavenly bodies. Traveling, or just sitting outside without bright lights, people were exposed to the stars night after night, year after year. They would have watched their journey across the sky. They would have known their names and their orbits.

Native Americans believed that when one of the tribe elders died they turned into a bright star in the sky. They identified some of the stars as essential figures from their past. This demonstrates their belief that humans can develop to be stars, shining forth, and leading the way with their light for others, and also changing the celestial scenery forever.

The 12 Zodiac Signs and their Meanings

Aries

Aries is symbolized by the ram which represents the male fertility as well as courage and aggression. The ram's horn is considered as part of the cornucopia thus it is dubbed as the horn of plenty. People who are born under this sign have the affinity towards abundance.

Sun in Aries people are born as natural athletes. They are active, energetic, straightforward and not complicated. They are people who know what they want and how they can achieve them. On the other hand, the moon can also play a vital role in affecting their behavior. For instance, Moon in Aries people are somewhat impatient thus they live for the moment and hardly has the patience to wait for things to happen. This is the reason why they are proactive in solving their problems because they need to see the results immediately. In general, people who are born under this sign are competitive, quick and direct.

Taurus

Taurus has always been the symbol of strength and power. Taureans are believed to be healthy individuals but although they are dependable because they have the habit of being outright helpful. They are also naturally sensual people in all pleasure areas, and they take delight on just about anything like food, a comfortable blanket and even flowers. Since they revel in things that give them comfort, they also have the tendency to revel in material things. Since they are strong-willed individuals, it is unwise to push people born under this star to do things that they are not committed. However, once they are committed to doing things, they put all their time, energy and effort to doing things. This is the reason why people born under this star are very passionate about love and romance.

Gemini

Gemini are perceived to have dual nature as this sign is symbolized by twins. Gemini love to move around freely and mingle with people to get answers to their questions.

Cancer

Being symbolized by the crab, people who are born under this star always move in indirect manner. They direct their lives towards where they can gain a lot of advantages in their lives.

This is the reason why they have strong survival instincts. They are also very protective particularly in sharing their inner selves to many people.

Cancers also have the reputation to be moody. This is evident to those who are born when the Moon is in Cancer. Although withdrawn, people who are born under this zodiac sign are thoughtful by nature. They are also sensitive to love, and they can give a lot of things to their loved ones like security, comfort and care. Overall, Cancers often move about with their business without making a lot of noise. They are gentle people that invest in their inner selves more than anything else.

Leo

The zodiac sign Leo is symbolized by the might lion which represents ruling, courage and sovereignty. In fact, there is an unmistakable regal air to people who are born under this star. They are dignified but they also have the reputation for being conceited.

On the other hand, Leo people also love being the center of attention. Whether they are inside their homes or out with their friends, Leo people want to be always in the spotlight. They also have the incessant need to be in control of things and their all-controlling behavior can be difficult to bear with.

Virgo

Virgo people are, in general, respectable people. The symbol, the virgin, is interpreted as having pure in spirit and also being self-contained. Virgos are reticent especially when they face something new. Virgos find contentment, security and comfort in little things. Having said this, many people under this sign are accused to be underachievers. The satisfaction that they get from simple things prevents them from pursuing great things in life. Although this may be the case, this is the quality of Virgo people that makes them endear.

Libra

The danger for the people with this sign – Financial success is not a priority to Libras, and they will have many ups and downs when it comes to their careers because of this. Libras place more value on peace and justice in their lives.

Scorpio

Scorpios are intense people and they are very determined when it comes to achieving the things that they want to do.

Sagittarius

Sagittarius is people who are outgoing and friendly. The love freedom and they abhor doing routine works. Their love for making friends also puts them at risk because they often have blind faith in people. Their optimism is infectious, but this can also lead them to trouble from time to time. Since Sagittarians are under the fire sign, they also have quick tempers but, fortunately, they quickly forget the source of their anger.

Sagittarians have the need for constant activity and their outgoing personality makes them irresponsible. They quickly forget appointments and they find it challenging to complete tasks that they don't like. Although this may be the case, they can also become good teachers as they are right in storytelling.

Capricorn

People born under this sign are grounded and realistic. Being useful as well as productive is essential for Capricorns because they want to keep their emotions under check.

Aquarius

Aquarius is under the sun sign and people under this zodiac revere the old and traditional ways of doing things. They have strong idealism thus they are likely to have fixed opinions on everything. Unfortunately, this is the reason why most Aquarians are branded as standoffish individuals, but this is just a façade. In reality, they are observant and tolerant in a broad sense. They are also very witty and intellectual people.

Pisces

Pisces contains all experiences of all the zodiac signs. Thus, they have the ability to communicate and identify with people from all backgrounds. They are not only adaptable, but they also have broad minds. Even if they are not sure of their purpose early on, when they find it, they rise to the challenge in a way only a Pisces can.

The Birth Chart

The birth chart or the natal chart is a cosmic blueprint of the soul's incarnation in this lifetime. It shows traits, possibilities, soul lessons, the soul's evolutionary purpose, and more. Contained within that blueprint is you, as reflected in the cosmos. We'll take a look at the individual parts of the chart and what they each mean. If you are familiar with astrology, then it will give you the basics to begin understanding your own chart.

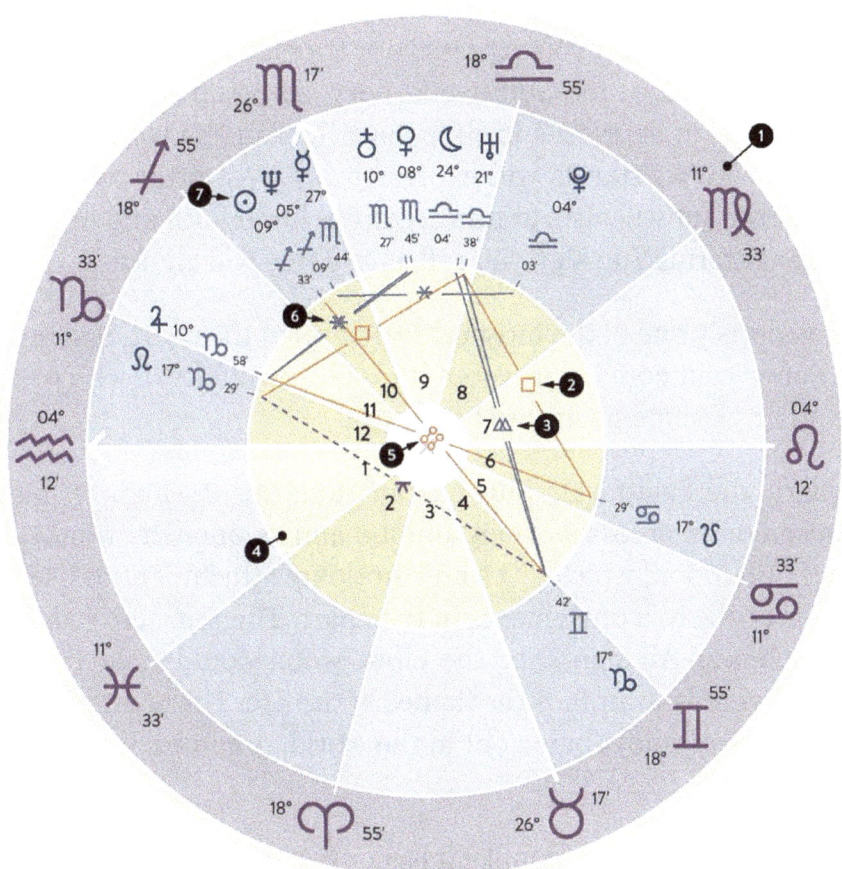

LEGEND: 1. Signs; 2. Square Aspect; 3. Trine Aspect; 4. Houses by number, counterclockwise; 5. Opposition Aspect; 6. Sextile Aspect; 7. Planets

Sample Birth Chart. The chart is a wheel, or mandala, divided into 12 segments, or houses. Each house is ruled by a zodiac sign and represents a specific area of life. The chart shows the placement of planets and other celestial bodies within the zodiac based on the date, time, and location of a person's birth. The connecting lines in the middle are the aspects.

THE SUN

The Sun is our very core or ego; it is both the central organizing principle of the galaxy and our self. Much of our personality is predicated on our Sun sign, which is why the horoscopes you might read online or in periodicals are generally based on Sun signs. It's also the easiest to identify because it is based only on your birthdate. The Sun is how we most often identify as the Self. It is often seen as the "male" or "father" energy in the chart. It's our being and our becoming, what our innate character is, and who we are learning to be in this lifetime. The Sun in your chart represents life, heart, vitality, essence, and consciousness.

The sign that your Sun is in is how you express your core identity—the part of you that shines in the world and acts. Think of the Sun itself—fiery, sometimes explosive, life-giving, and golden. How your Sun sign expresses itself is your light in the world. For example, in the sample chart, the Sun in Sagittarius will express itself most often as the freedom-seeking wanderer and wonderer but will also, at times, exhibit blind faith and moralistic tendencies. The aspects of the Sagittarius Sun sign you reflect is a free will choice.

While the Sun is obviously one of the most critical parts of the chart, it should not be viewed in isolation. The Sun is your core identity, but it is not the totality of who you are. It is always tempered by the other placements in the chart.

In the sample chart, the Sagittarius Sun has an Aquarius Ascendant, meaning that this freedom seeker also comes across as being unique and as one who thinks differently. This person also has a Libra Moon, which gives an emotional attachment to harmony and peace. You would also look at the mix of elements in the chart. The Sun sign (which is a Fire sign), the Ascendant (which is an Air sign), and the Libra Moon would make this person a thinker and always on the move, as the air fans the flames of the fire. The Sagittarius Sun in the tenth house suggests this person enjoys being out in the world. A natural leader, they are also very career-oriented.

Awareness of these placements might make it easier for the person to understand their need for freedom and intellectual stimulation, and this would lead to acceptance that they are not suited to any work or experiences that are repetitive and without mental stimulation.

A deep understanding and acceptance of your Sun sign helps you understand how your ego shows up in the world. It is, however, through this understanding of the sign and house that your Sun is in that you begin to have a greater awareness of your choices. There might be times that it is appropriate to your needs to embody one quality slightly more than the other. The constructs of positive and negative are not always set in stone, so try not to consider those black-and-white terms as you deepen your knowledge.

THE MOON

In the chart, the Moon is your emotional body. It's a reflective and receptive energy that responds and reacts. The Moon is your instinctive and intuitive self and how you unconsciously respond to the world around you. Whereas the Sun is your ego and the part of you that shines in the world and acts, the Moon is your soul, your most private yet most connected, reactive self.

The Moon is very much a feminine energy that acts in all of us. She is the Mother, your female ancestors, your home, and how you see all these things. She represents where you are coming from, your upbringing, and how you felt and feel about the world around you. Her silvery glow corresponds to the reflective, mirror like energy that is within you, and the face known as the "man in the moon" shows her very human side, the side that is the most immediately felt energy in the cosmos.

As children we are emotional beings; it is only as we develop that society teaches us that being "too emotional" or "too reactive" are undesirable qualities. Yet we are emotional beings at the core of our soul. What would it be like to allow more of that? To allow ourselves to feel to the full extent of our being. This, in part, is what this article aims to teach—how you can reach a point of deep acceptance in the way you operate emotionally, spiritually, and physically while learning to take the higher road in all aspects of your chart. A deep understanding and acceptance of the sign and house placement and aspects of your Moon help you understand how you respond and react to external stimuli in the world.

When you reach that point of deep acceptance and understanding, you can choose which path you take with awareness. For example, the Moon rules Cancer. Is your Moon in Cancer? If so, you would understand that this placement makes you more emotionally sensitive than some other signs and more receptive to other people's feelings. Moon in Cancer folk are also more inclined to be deeply nurturing and family oriented. None of these traits are good or bad; they just are. But once you accept that they just are, your awareness helps you deal with the deep sensitivity rather than perceiving it as "wrong." Viewing astrology in this way is all about making choices with awareness based on the embodiment of your energies. In this specific example, you can choose whether to have a good cry under the bedcovers or whether to treat yourself to a gentle healing massage if you are feeling emotionally hurt. Neither choice is wrong, but one might feel like the healthier response to you.

In the sample chart, the Moon is in Libra, which suggests this person likes a beautiful, harmonious, and airy home. This person is a diplomat; they can see two sides in every story and can compromise in almost every situation. This can, however, also lead to smoothing things over when it might be better off to discuss them, as Libra Moons dislike.

The Ascendant

Ascendant in Aries or Aries Rising

You probably have a sturdy, muscular frame with a lively, energetic face. You make intense and direct eye contact with others and may well have been told off for staring at people as a child because of this. You are probably of medium height and can show amazing feats of strength when necessary. Red hair is familiar with those with Aries on the Ascendant.

Always in a hurry, this can lead to your being accident-prone, especially with injuries to the head or face. A hasty temper turned inwards produces headaches or even migraines. Sporting activities or any form of physical exercise is an excellent release for this.

You meet life straightforwardly and energetically. You want to have control over your life, and a feeling of lack of control will manifest itself as illness. You often express yourself through dramatic outbursts, many times in anger or even other forms of self-destructive behavior.

Ascendant in Taurus or Taurus Rising

Taurus is the sign of the bull, and this may reflect in your body shape. Your well-shaped body displays a warm attractiveness and ripeness. In your later years, you may need to watch the tendency to gain weight too quickly. Your strong broad shoulders support either a long slender neck, or else you have an enormous neck size. Your most outstanding feature is your eyes and your gentle smile and voice. You may be bigboned. You enjoy dressing well, preferring soft colors.

You need to have your feet planted firmly on the ground while you aim for the stars, because you like to be able to see concrete results for your efforts. However high you aim, you like to remain in contact with the earthy and material side of life. This can have its drawbacks in as much as you have a tendency to hang on to people, things and experiences out of habit and a feeling of security, when there is no longer any need to. You need to learn to distinguish between when it is necessary to hang on, and when you should let go. When you head towards your goals you like to have plans and a structure to systematically work around.

You may need to consciously develop better habits with looking after your body and its requirements.

Ascendant in Gemini or Gemini Rising

You are the most youthful-looking of the zodiac with veritable Peter Pan looks. You may have neat, sharp facial features and a wiry frame. You can wear bright colors, mix patterns and fabrics and may love bizarre jewelry. You are lithe and agile with slender hands. Some people may think that you can look like two different people at different times.

Your ability to communicate, in fact your need to communicate, contributes to your sense of identity. You are extremely observant and can follow two or more conversations at once. You are a fast talker and may use your hands a lot. In any case, you always seem to have a lot to say. You are an excellent mimic and may also have a flair for languages.

You love to find out how people and things work and are quite clever at taking things apart and putting them back together again. Your curiosity makes you versatile and adaptable, but you may suffer from an over-abundance of diverse interests. In any case, you dislike being committed to only one thing, because you hate to lose alternatives.

Your abundance of nervous energy means that you are always on the move. You may appear highly strung. You are often in two minds about the situations that you are involved in.

Ascendant in Cancer or Cancer Rising

Your face is rounded with beautiful round, sensitive eyes that show concern and innocence. Your whole appearance speaks of softness and tenderness. You may not be that energetic, and you need to watch weight gain later in life. Fluid retention can also be a problem. As a female, you may be quite big-breasted. As a male, you may have quite a broad and fleshy chest in comparison with the rest of your body, especially your hips. You don't dress for glamour or to impress, instead you tend to prefer your old comfortable clothes rather than following uncomfortable fashion styles.

Growth in self-awareness comes to you through fully acknowledging, experiencing and respecting your true feelings, and developing the nurturing and caring side to your personality. You may feel overwhelmed at times by the depth of emotion that you feel. It is difficult for you to simply let go of a strongly felt emotion, unless you have another feeling just as powerful to take its place.

It is very healthy for you to play the mothering role, whether to a group of people, in the context of a business, or by nurturing a strongly felt cause. On the other hand, if you shun the role of nurturer, you will aim to find someone else to mother you. You will constantly be looking for the ideal mother type. There is also the possibility that you over-identify with your mother and find it hard to break away from the family unit.

You tend to approach issues and situations from a sideways angle and in a non-confrontational manner rather than head-on.

Ascendant in Leo or Leo Rising

You have great presence with a strong-featured face and a sunny glow of inner self-confidence. You display a regal quality in your posture and carriage, holding your head proudly, back straight, walking slowly and deliberately. You are probably well-built and taller than average. You have an eye for design and glamour. You are comfortable wearing strong colors and patterns. You may be quite vain about your hair.

You tend to feel that anything is better than being ordinary. You are preoccupied with emerging as an individual in your own right, and to do this you need to develop your sense of power and authority and exercise your creative expression.

Ascendant in Virgo or Virgo Rising

With Virgo on the Ascendant your body is probably neat and wiry, and you tend to use neat and economical movements. Your well-groomed appearance is mirrored in your cool and classic way of dressing, good posture, fine bone structure and animated expression. Physically, you possess good stamina. You tend to look younger than you are, all the way through into your later years.

In creating and defining yourself, you use self-criticism, mental analysis and discrimination, focusing on very specific points of your personality. You need to settle the practical management of the everyday necessities of daily life before you embarks on your grander aims in life.

You are very conscious of making sure that your body functions smoothly and well. You are very good at analyzing yourself and life in general. Still, you need to develop the ability to eject anything destructive to yourself. The danger exists that too much analysis can box you in to an existence that is overly rigid and tight. If you over-emphasize and become obsessive about order, correctness and precision, you may lose touch with your spontaneity and natural sense of flow.

Ascendant in Libra or Libra Rising

You are extremely attractive and have a warm and charming nature. Your features are usually refined, your bones delicate and your skin fair. Your movements are very graceful. You are aware of your attractiveness, but be careful that you don't fall into the trap of being vain and judging others by how beautiful they may look.

You are indecisive and tend to always sit on the fence. This is because you can always see the other's viewpoint. You are able see the viewpoint of everybody else around you. You must learn to force yourself to make choices and be prepared to take the consequences. Don't take the easy option of letting others decide for you. You can objectively and fairly assess any situation.

Ascendant in Scorpio or Scorpio Rising

You most likely have dark, brooding looks with thick, abundant hair and strongly marked eyebrows that frame the most important feature of your face, your eyes. Your eyes have a piercing, penetrating quality, so much so that many people are unable to meet the directness of your gaze. Overall, you give the impression of quietly contained power. Your movements are controlled, and your clothes are chosen for their dramatic value. With your commanding personality, you can instill fear and apprehension if you wish. There is an air of mystery about you, as well as veiled but potent sexuality.

Ascendant in Sagittarius or Sagittarius Rising

The Ascendant reveals how you present yourself to the outside world and the style in which you meet new experiences and life in general. When people first meet you, they meet your Ascendant rather than your Sun sign. The Ascendant may also indicate your physical characteristics.

Although you may not be tall, your legs are probably long and rangy. As a child, you may have been quite clumsy. Your long legs give you a bold way of walking, which you exercise, restlessly pacing up and down when you need to think. Your most outstanding feature is your wide brilliant smile, shining out of your open face. Although you prefer dressing casually most times, when you do dress up, you can look stunning.

Ascendant in Capricorn or Capricorn Rising

Your bone structure is distinctive, and you probably have good teeth. Your shoulders may be rounded, and physically you tend towards a wiry and lean frame. There may even be a certain devilish look to your face. Just as your life improves after the age of roughly forty, so do your looks lighten up, and you seem younger and more frivolous than years earlier. As a child, you looked serious and old for your years, but as you grow older, you seem to grow younger and better looking. You feel better and happier with every passing year.

Ascendant in Aquarius or Aquarius Rising

You are most likely tall and slim with good bone structure and clear, open and refined features. Your eyes are extraordinary, helping to give you an electric or magnetic aura. Your distinguishing feature is your hair, or if you are male, your beard perhaps. Your dress sense can add to your sometimes bizarre appearance, but even more conservatively dressed, you are always arresting. You tend to prefer bright electric colors over the more conservative and quiet shades.

Ascendant in Pisces or Pisces Rising

Your beautiful eyes are one of your most attractive features. Your complexion has a translucent quality, very pale if you are fair-skinned, or ripe and lush if you are dark-skinned. The clothes that you choose don't call attention to you, and they are soft and comfortable rather than fashionably gimmicky. Your feet tend to be large and your hair hard to manage.

Tarot the History

As a beginner in the art of tarot reading, for you to fully appreciate the beauty of Tarot, and for you to properly understand its global cultural significance, you need to be at least slightly familiar with its history.

The origin of the tarot deck and the art of tarot reading is shrouded in mystery and not fully understood. Since tarot reading is such an old art which has been in existence for at least half a millennium, it's easy to see why there would be different accounts about its actual place of birth, and its original inventor.

While the fact that a unanimous agreement on the origin of tarot may never be reached may be a tad frustrating for some tarot enthusiasts, the fact that its origin is mysterious, to say the least adds to the intrigue of the art, making it even more breathtaking and scintillating to learn. So, as you go through the pages and learn about the ancient art of Tarot reading, have it at the back of your mind that you are undergoing a process millions of people have been undergoing for over 500 years. Now, how is that for being a part of history?

According to records from European museums, tarot decks have been in existence since the 15th century, as evidenced in the tarot decks available in the museums' collections. These decks are nothing like modern tarot cards; they are sophisticated and highly elaborate – they are simply miniature works of art dripping with gold, probably made for the pleasure of royalties at the time.

According to some accounts from Egyptian mythology, tarot cards were created by the Egyptian god, Thoth. Thoth was said to have gifted the art of tarot reading to man from the great Egyptian pyramids to serve as a source of guidance and light for his subjects, and to enable them to find direction when they felt lost. It is speculated that somehow, the culture of reading Tarot cards may have died down among the Egyptian population, only for it to surface in Europe in the 18th century, courtesy of the Gypsies in their fancy caravans. They were an exotic sight to behold in ancient Europe.

When the Gypsies came to Europe with their simple yet fancy cultural inclinations, they quickly infiltrated the very fabric of the European society. Soon they were found in a lot of major European cities, especially in France. These Gypsies did Tarot readings for people in a similar fashion to the astrologers who read people's palms at carnivals and quaint little roadside shops today. In return for their services, the Gypsies collected silver pieces they used for day-to-day living, The Gypsies were extremely simple. Yet, incredibly profound people who discovered the secret to happiness was not accumulating wealth and rooting yourself to a point, it was in putting smiles on people's faces, while moving from city to city to find more faces to put smiles on. They didn't have a lot, but they had enough to leave an indelible imprint in the history.

Since Tarot reading encompassed the use of cards in divination and fortune-telling, several religious factions soon came out to condemn the practice of Tarot reading among the Gypsies, calling the Tarot cards 'the Devil's picture.' This notion is one that has been effectively passed down through several generations over the centuries, and one still held by some religious groups to date.

While everyone has the absolute prerogative to determine their own religious beliefs, it still feels pretty absurd that an art that has helped to define the way of life of a people (the Gypsies), and has helped to bring so many smiles to so many faces, create so many bonds, and even helped, in its little way to shape history as we know it is seen to be something evil.

If there is anything evil about Tarot, it would be its dangerous power to addict; once you start, there's no going back. You'll keep craving to know more, and the more you unleash your intuition, the more capable you will be of understanding the intricacies of life from different profound perspectives.

In all, it is important to note the aim of Tarot is not to corrupt your religious beliefs or make you practice voodoo. Not all. Tarot aims to help you find inner peace as you progress on your journey of life. Tarot aims to help you find a channel through which you can unleash your powerful intuition that the modern world has effectively helped you cage through the instilment of rigid rules and regulations right from your childhood. Tarot enlightens you and helps you to think outside the box. Tarot is all about harmony and flowing in sync with the universe – its basic principles are freedom and imagination.

The most reliable account of Tarot's history is it made its first appearance in Europe in the 15th century where the Tarot cards were used in a game called Tarrochi, an ancient form of the card game of bridge. This account is believable because the images used in the cards that made up the decks found in 15th century Europe are similar to the images etched onto the stained glass windows of European cathedrals and public buildings built around that period.

Even though Tarot cards were only played for fun at first, the possibility to use them in conjunction with a sharp intuition, an open mind, and perhaps some supernatural powers in fortunetelling soon led people to start using Tarot cards for divination purposes. Antione Court de Gebelin was one of the first public critics of Tarot reading – calling it an occultist practice only fit for heathens, despite the fact he also believed that some of the cards portrayed principles that formed the core of Christianity.

The first Tarot deck made specifically for divination was first made by a Parisian seed salesman known as Jean-Baptiste Alliete, who wrote under the pen name, Eteilla, which is simply his last name spelt backwards.

The beginning of the 20th century was a remarkable period in Tarot history. In 1909, Arthur E. Waite, a member of the Golden Dawn, a secret English magical society, published the first standardized deck of Tarot cards, and called it the R.W.S Tarot deck. The paintings on the cards were made by Pamela Colman Smith, and that Tarot deck is the most widely accepted and soled Tarot deck in the world till date.

Over the years, slight modifications have been made to improve user experiences. Still, the original Rider-Waite-Smith deck remains the foundation upon which all these developments have been made. In 1943, Aleister Crowley collaborated with the talented artist Frieda Harris to create the Thoth Tarot deck, the second most common Tarot deck model in the world.

In the earlier parts of the 20th century, fortune-telling Gypsies still used Tarot cards for divination. Even though the Gypsies have faded away with time, the practice of reading Tarot cards remains highly appreciated and widely practiced.

In the 1960s, important articles that helped the average man with no contact with Tarot to have comprehensive knowledge about the art were published, further exposing Tarot to different parts of the world. Eden Gray published 'The Tarot Revealed' and 'Mastering the Tarot', both in the 60s. Gray's teachings of tarot reading encompassed the interpretations used by fortune tellers to read the cards, and the practices of secret societies in ancient Europe in using the cards for divination. Other important Tarot articles that helped to lay the foundation for Tarot literature were '78 Degrees of Wisdom' by Rachel Pollock and 'Tarot for Yourself' by Mary. K. Greer.

Over the years, since its introduction, the basis upon which Tarot reading is built has shifted gradually from fortunetelling to psychology. In the first centuries of Tarot reading up till the beginning of the 20th century, the principle of Tarot reading existed on the most people's general belief in fortunetelling. Back in those days, people were open to idea of a supernatural force helping to reveal hidden information through the card readings. However, with time, has come the evolution of the society, and people no longer hold the kinds of beliefs in the supernatural that they used to. Therefore, for Tarot reading to survive as an art, its foundation; its basis had to undergo a paradigm shift from fortunetelling to psychology.

Currently, the principle of Tarot reading is based on a delicate psychological understanding by card readers and querents alike. People in the modern day understand that they have their freewill, no matter what the card readings are. However, they still believe that considering the results of a card reading with an open, intuitive mind would allow them to be able to find solutions to their problems from perspectives that could not be reached by mere analytical thinking. That notion is the current bedrock of Tarot reading among most modern adherents.

However, for any entity to truly thrive and survive through the ages, it must continue to evolve. The truth, however, is people have come to accept psychology FULLY as the basis for the existence of Tarot reading in the modern dispensation, thereby effectively blocking all routes through which tarot reading could further evolve in the future. The basis of tarot reading has evolved from being a type of fortunetelling to being a function of psychological beliefs – it has to keep evolving to keep growing.

Therefore, instead of just accepting psychology as the supreme basis for the functioning of Tarot reading, it would make a lot more sense instead, if we were more open-minded as adherents of this ancient art, to allow different thought patterns to run. People should be allowed to believe whatever they want, so that when the society evolves, tarot reading can evolve along with it.

Tarot Cards and their Meanings

The Major Arcana

Traditionally, the cards are numbered in Roman numerals from I to XXI (1 to 21), with the remaining card, The Fool, either left unnumbered or given a "0." The ordering of the cards is consistent across decks, except for the Justice and Strength cards (which will be explained below), and the position of the Fool, which is typically at the start of the sequence but can also be found at the end.

Various schools of interpretation for these cards have developed over time, with one approach often influencing another. However, the concept of the Major Arcana as representing a "journey" or "path" of some kind has been a recurring theme over the centuries.

In this framework, the cards may reflect the major events we encounter as we move through our physical lives, or they may represent our psychological or spiritual journey, as we experience the lessons our souls chose to learn during this present incarnation. In practice, the Major Arcana tends to address both physical and intangible aspects of our life experience.

There is no standard, universally accepted set of interpretations for the Major Arcana in the context of the Fool's Journey, but many guides and seasoned Tarot experts offer sufficiently similar meanings to create a consensus. As you familiarize yourself with the cards over time, you will no doubt come to your understanding of each one, and how it relates to you on your journey.

The Minor Arcana

While the cards in the Minor Arcana may seem less significant than the "trump" cards, they represent the essential ingredients that make up our lives, without which, the lessons of the Major Arcana would have no context.

Each suit of the Minor Arcana is centered on a particular realm of experience: ideas, feelings, action, and manifestation. As these cards make up the bulk of the deck, they tend to be more prevalent in a reading than the Major Arcana cards.

In modern decks, the suits are most often known as wands, cups, swords, and pentacles. Still, some decks keep to the more traditional medieval names and symbols, while others have adapted different names and symbols altogether. The more widely used alternate suit names are listed beneath each suit description.

Wands

The suit of Wands represents the realm of inspiration, intention, and ambition. When we are feeling creative, inspired, spurred to action, and envisioning outcomes we are utilizing Wand energy.

There is a distinction to be made here between thought and action, however. Action is not yet dominant at the Wands stage, and sometimes this suit can remind us that enthusiastic beginnings still require follow-through. Wands also represent risk-taking and initiative, as we desire to grow, create, and expand our horizons. Because we are essentially motivated by desire—either to manifest a positive outcome or avoid a negative one—feelings of both apprehension and excited anticipation are connected to the cards of this suit.

On the whole, Wands are considered positive cards, and often show up in a reading as a sign of encouragement.

Cups

The suit of Cups is the realm of emotion, creativity, psychic insights, love, empathy, and matters of the heart in general. The Cups tend to represent the feelings that accompany, or arise out of, the thoughts we are having about a given situation. These feelings tend to influence our behavior, whether or not we're consciously aware of them.

A full range of emotions—both pleasant and unpleasant—is present within this suit, so some cards may appear to be negative, depending on the reading. Yet any cards that assist with getting clarity on a situation should be appreciated.

Cups can also speak to the benefits and potential pitfalls of psychic gifts and empathy. While an open and conscious mind is generally an advantage, taking on other people's energy or getting overwhelmed by psychic impressions is not.

Swords

The suit of Swords represents the realm of action, movement, and struggle, as well as logic, reason, and intellect. The effort involved in pursuing a goal, which can often be perceived as struggle, is the realm of Sword energy. It can require much effort to turn our ideas into reality, but this is also where the most learning tends to occur.

Action is the result of the combining of ideas (Wands) with emotions (Cups). Yet, the Swords advise rationality and detachment from expectations of specific outcomes. Because of this, the cards of this suit can be perceived as cold or harsh with their messages, as they cut straight through any illusions we may be clinging to. In some cases, Swords may signify strength, authority, and power, as well as the more unfortunate elements of human nature that lead to violence and suffering.

The suit is not overwhelmingly unfavorable, but the Swords do tend to bring up the trickier aspects of a situation.

Pentacles

The suit of Pentacles is all about manifestation, results, groundedness, and material well-being. These cards often appear to issues of finances, abundance, business pursuits, and the home and family, as well as the physical body.

Pentacles represent the results of the initial inspiration (Wands), which is then responded to in the feeling realm (Cups), and consequently acted upon (Swords). While the other three suits predominantly inhabit the invisible realms of non-physical energy, Pentacles are concerned with the material, physical plane. However, they can also represent the feelings of security we all seek on the material plane, and the sense of being grounded in one's sovereignty as a person.

The cards of this suit are generally considered favorable, as they speak to the rewards of our efforts. Still, they can also reflect fear around not having (or being) enough.

The Significance of Numbers

As with many other forms of divination, numbers are highly significant in the Tarot. From the time of the modern deck's development in Marseilles, the number assigned to each card has been considered to be important to its meaning. In decks with non-illustrated pip cards, numerological correspondences are especially important to interpreting meaning. Each of these cards bears a number between 1 and 10—the number set at the core of numerology, also referred to as "the decade."

While different Tarot traditions may draw from one or more numerological systems (such as Pythagorean, Chaldean, or Kabbalistic numerology) when it comes to interpretation, the number descriptions below are representative of common themes and associations for each number in the decade. These core characteristics can help you get a clearer sense of how each numbered pip card is distinct from the others in its suit.

One is the beginning of that which is about to form or take shape. Represented by the Ace of each suit, it is considered to hold the "seed" or absolute potential of a situation. This potential may be dormant, and may even be unknown to you, just as a seed can be either intentionally planted or arrive unexpectedly on the wind. Either way, this potential needs further action and development for manifestation to take place, just as a single point in geometry needs another for a shape to take form.

Two is the necessary "next step" that allows the potential of the one to become something more. In geometry, where one point has nowhere to "go," two points make a line possible. In the Minor Arcana, these cards often depict two people. Still, this number can symbolize aspects of duality, polarity, balance, and choices as well as relationships.

Three represents the first fruition of the balanced union of the two. It is the synthesis of inspiration, cooperation and growth. Three points are the minimum required for the first closed shape—the triangle—to form. Three is also found three times (3, 6, 9) within the decade. It represents expression, creativity, manifestation, and integration. Three moves beyond partnership into group collaboration—beyond the balanced polarity of two into something more that requires a new, more complex balance—a pattern that will now begin to repeat through the rest of the numbers.

Four is some stability and completion. Added to the triangle of the three, it creates the first three-dimensional shape, the tetrahedron. In this sense the four is the manifestation of the initial idea of the one into material form. It represents balance, as seen in the four legs of a table, and secure foundations. Four is also associated with justice and fair dealings (as in the expression "fair and square"). Its metaphysical significance is seen in the four elements, the four cardinal directions, and the four seasons.

Five, like the three, is some outward expansion, coming along to disrupt the perfect symmetry of the four so that new manifestation can occur. The cycle of creation requires change, which is often disruptive and can cause uncertainty, difficulty and even chaos for periods. However, this imbalance spurs new movement, which opens up opportunities for new developments that could not arise otherwise.

Six brings order to the chaos of the five. Like the four, it is some balance and harmony, but since it integrates every stage of the one's manifestation thus far, its structure is more complex. As the first product of an odd and even number, it reconciles differences and restores equilibrium. Six represents successful adjustments to past challenges, and can often signify a victory. It represents the qualities of compassion and cooperation, responsibility, and service to others.

Seven is some strong mystical significance in spiritual traditions around the world. It is found in nature in the visible light spectrum, the planets visible from Earth, and the musical tones of the scale. We live in the rhythm of the seven through the days of the week. Seven creates a new dynamic out of the six by adding the one, creating new changes and opportunities. It represents choices, mystery, uncertainty, spirituality, wisdom, and the potential for perfection.

Eight brings back the energy of balance and symmetry, now as a double of the four. The continuous line of the eight resembles the symbol for infinity. There is stability on both the material and spiritual planes as circumstances harmonize with the cosmic order of the Universe. This brings new energy and power for accomplishing goals, organizing and integrating what has manifested so far, and bringing things nearer to completion. Eight represents progress, capability, regeneration, success, and personal power.

Nine is the final single digit, and as such symbolizes the end of a cycle, but in the numerological system of the decade, the completion is still to come. Nine appears in every multiple of itself in the form of adding the digits in the multiple, representing the patterns of perfection found throughout the Universe. It is the triple of the three, a mystical and powerful configuration. It represents affirmation, culmination, and the surety of success, as well as boundaries, limits, and strength.

Ten contains the properties of the one, but now on a new level. As the final number of the decade, it completes whatever was left unfinished or unresolved in the nine. It sets the stage for the next cycle of manifestation to occur. Ten represents wholeness, fulfillment, and reaping the benefits of persistent effort. It is some resolution, consolidation, and readiness for new beginnings.

Having a sense of the esoteric meanings of individual numbers can add enormous depth to your understanding of the cards, especially when it comes to non-illustrated pips. But if you don't have experience with numerology, don't worry—you can still access interpretations for all of the cards, either through this guide, your personal deck's guide, or other sources on the Tarot.

If you find that a certain number or pair of numbers keeps showing up in your readings, however, it's worth looking up their esoteric meanings, as this signifies that the Universe is trying to tell you something.

Numerology, what is it?

Known as the science of numbers, its etymological meaning came from the Latin word numerous, which means number and the Greek word logos that means a thought, idea, expression, or word. Numerology links numbers with events in one's life and surroundings. It is associated with astrology and other mystical and divine entities. It foretells a person's future by digging into one's potentiality and nature and other life's projections. It gives you a look into what your destiny is by considering the planets' movements in the sky, attributes, and methodology, as well as deities. This idea has not been recorded in any artifact until 1907. Its origin cannot be accurately determined but the earliest recorded history points to Egypt and Babylon approximately 10,000 years ago. It became popular among scholars in Greece who too are not certain as to this concept's origin.

In Philosophy

Along with other philosophers, Pythagoras, the Greek philosopher who postulated the famous Pythagorean theorem ( ), which states that the area of the square of the hypotenuse is equal to the sum of the squares of the two sides, believed in the greater certainty of numbers because of its practicality and ease in classifying or regulating them. He was known for his famous line, 'The world is built upon the power of numbers'. And numerology was based on this principle. According to the famous Christian theologian and writer, St. Augustine of Hippo, numbers serve as a confirmation of the truth that deities offer to humans. It has become their way of communication or better yet a universal language. He further explained the existence of numerical relationships with basically everything and it is just up to you to know these secrets or have them revealed by divine grace.

In Religion

As this was considered as one that deals with the paranormal side, magic, and other forms of divinations, which were also classified as among the civil violations in the Roman Empire during the reign of Constantine I, numerology was not approved by the Christian authority (council of Christian bishops) and was set aside during their convention. This happened in 325 AD.

Notwithstanding the abolition of the belief, it cannot be denied that its religious significance remained alive. As analyzed by Dorotheus of Gaza, the Jesus number was still used especially among conservative Greek Orthodox circles. Religious architecture and the Bible admit of numerology. In the bible, the number 3 and 7 are among the favorites. The number 7 was usually the number for which a famine would last. More often, 7 is followed by 8, which signified change. To cite an example, Ahab was sent 7 times by his Master Elijah to Mt. Carmel to look for a certain cloud, which he was able to find only on the 8th time. Here is another example: 7 days was required of Miriam to spend in the wilderness after they (Miriam and Aaron) spoke ill of Moses' marriage with an Ethiopian woman. She then joined Exodus on the 8th day.

In religious architecture, the evidence of numerological influences can be seen in Chartres Cathedral that is the number 306.

In Alchemy

Related to numerology are some alchemical theories. Jabir ibn Hayyan, a Persian alchemist had his experiments founded on the names of substances found in the Arabic language.

In Literature

The Garden of Cyrus which is a literary discourse written by Sir Thomas Browne in 1658 embodied the concept of numerology throughout art designs and nature with the use of the quincunx pattern, a 5-point geometric pattern with 4 of its points forming a rectangle or square and the 5th is found at the center.

As an ancient system of learning information about your life and future with numbers, numerology is a useful tool that will help a person gain knowledge and wisdom about one's life story. It is practically one of the oldest self-help tools available to us since it originated back to the years of ancient civilizations.

You may ask, is numerology pure mathematics? No. It is a science of numbers and the math involved is very basic and simple. Even elementary graders would not have any problems calculating for the core numbers that will be mentioned in this article! How wicked is that? And even as we mention math when we talk about numerology, at the end of the day, it is all about characteristics and personality traits that make up a person and how these elements combine to define who we are right now and who we will be in the future. It talks about the way we are characterized and it reveals our most probable goals in life.

Before we get started, let us first look into a couple of things that would deepen your understanding about numerology.

1. Numerology can help you uncover your life's path and purpose. Those reading this article may be doing so for various reasons. However, I bet that they all have something to do with your life. Are you having trouble with your career? Are you searching for love? Do you wish to have good health? Are you uncertain about what to do with your life? Those questions are probably just some of what is lurking in your thoughts and you wondered if numerology could help you answer them. Fortunately, for you, numerology can!

2. Numerology is not a new fad. Even though some of you may just have heard of numerology, its roots can be traced back allegedly to the time of Pythagoras, a Greek mathematician and mystic, around 2, 500 years ago. However, rumor has it that even though Pythagoras may be deemed as the father of modern numerology, the Chaldeans of ancient Babylon can be credited with developing a system of numerology even before Pythagoras' time.

3. There are various systems of numerology. Aside from the Western system of numerology that we are going to utilize, there exists other forms of numerology including Chaldean, Chinese, Indian, and Kabbalistic.

4. It rests on the premise that the whole universe and our lives is a system and there is order to this system. Numerologists claim that the whole universe and its elements are part of a system and systems can be broken down to the basest elements, which are numbers. Basing from the argument that the universe – and with it, the stars, galaxies, constellations, etc. – can be understood, it must also be assumed that life and people's personalities can be figured out as well since we are a part of the whole universe.

5. In numerology, numbers mean the same thing wherever it may appear. It does not matter which system of numerology you use, once you get the grasp of the meaning of each number, gaining wisdom from it is very easy.

6. Lessons and challenges are just some of the facets of wisdom that you will procure from numerology. Since numerology rests on the premise that we are on the eternal search for growth and self-mastery, numbers will present us lessons that we can mature from and obstacles that we would need to overcome. Also, these same numbers will help us break through these obstacles to fulfill our destinies, as there are certain sets of suggested life lessons that we need to acknowledge and embrace.

7. Numbers represent both positives and negatives. Since life does not offer us just good things or just bad things, numbers will hold both sources of happiness and display challenges. Not only that, they will also reveal your strengths and weaknesses. So get ready to be slapped in the face with your faults. Nevertheless, these revelations are not something you should

veer away from because it will make you more self-aware and it can be the platform that you can use to improve yourself.

8. Names and birthdates are vital to numerology. Numerology believes that our names and birthdates can show a comprehensive amount of who we are. This is because both of them reflect our depth and discloses our internal traits and thoughts. How is this so? Numerologists claim that naming a child is so intuitive. There is a reason why a couple named their child Anna even though they may not be privy to the exact reason. There is no randomness when it neither comes to naming a child nor is there in the date of her birth.

How to Calculate your Numerology and What it Means?

Pythagoras developed Pythagorean numerology before the time of Christ in ancient Greece. Pythagoras believed that numbers could be used to explain all things in the universe. He used mathematics for spiritual matters. This method of numerology is often referred to as modern numerology because it is the most recently developed method, and it has come to be the method most widely used in modern times, particularly in the Western world. Popular legend states that Pythagoras used the practice of numerology to use name-changing as a way to alter the destiny of an individual, predict what events would take place at certain locations, and determine the future fates of individuals. In this system, the letters of the alphabet are assigned a corresponding number based on their position in the alphabet. Both the date of birth and the name are used in Pythagorean Numerology, and the relationships between the two are studied.

This method uses the full name that is given at birth because that is the name that will determine an individual's numerical makeup. The birth name will tell what impression a person is most likely to make on other people, what the person naturally expresses the best, and what motivates a person, mentally and psychologically. The other most important number in Pythagorean numerology is the actual date of birth, which is used to determine the number of the life path of the individual.

Those who subscribed to the Pythagorean method of numerology were not simply interested in applying the science of numbers to determining the individual strengths and weaknesses of people. They believed that numbers were present in vast quantities in the natural world and that most things in life were ruled by a series of numbers. They firmly believed that numbers possessed mystical abilities and properties and the "all is number" meaning that anything in the world can be described in terms of proportions and numbers and everything in the world can be measured. This belief is the basic foundation of the practice of numerology.

Every letter in the alphabet has a numeric value, and every number has its related cosmic vibration. When the letters in a person's name and the date on which the person was born are combined in a particular formula, this will give an insight into how the vibrations are related to each other. This formula will give information to the person's purpose in life as a part of the overall plan of the cosmos. It will also reveal details of a person's motivations, natural talents, weaknesses, strengths, and character tendencies. Numerology is one of the best tools in use today that will help an individual develop a better insight into their overall physiological and cosmic makeup.

The soul's number, or the heart's desire number, is the element that is at the core of a person's numerology chart. It is used to open up the numerology chart and remove the layers covering it. The soul number is responsible for unlocking the person that is kept hidden from the outside world—the spiritual and eternal person deep inside, the more intense and deeper person. When this personal code is opened and deciphered to reach its true meaning, then the true meaning of the person is made available to the outside world, what motivates the person on a spiritual level, the fears and passions, the urges and inner cravings, and the desires that are hidden deep in the core of the person. The guiding force behind exactly what the soul is expecting to experience on earth is the soul urge.

Life often begins once this number is revealed. The person's life begins to finally make sense as anxiety and depression begin to drift away. The soul can finally find meaning in the world, given the energy it needs to thrive and the ability to be nurtured and recognized. Using the methods of Pythagorean numerology, the number for the soul urge is determined by using only the vowels of the full name. The reason for this is that consonants are said with a sharp edge to them, and they have a definite end and a definite beginning. Consonants are considered to be the containers for the way people express themselves and for the traits that people reveal to the outside world, and consonants represent a person's public personality. Vowels are made from the timeless and formless essence inside of a person and formed from spirit and air. They are pronounced with a breath that flows freely.

Remove all of the consonants in the full name. Determine the values that are assigned to each letter and then add all of the numbers together. Keep adding and reducing until there is just one single digit. This is an example of determining a soul number:

A = 1, E = 5, I = 9, O = 6, U = 3, Y = 7

Mary Anne Smith

A + Y + A + E + I = 1+ 7+ 1+5+9 = 23 = 2+3 = 5

Mary Anne Smith's soul urge number is 5

"Y" is sometimes a vowel and sometimes a consonant. It is used as a vowel when it is the only sound in the syllable, like in the names Kylie or Terry. It is also used as a vowel when it comes before a vowel that is in the next syllable, and it makes a vowel sound, as in the names Mya or Hyacinth. The letter "Y" is considered to be a consonant when it is used to make the hard sound of a consonant like in the names Yulee or Yoda or when it comes after a vowel in the same syllable and does not make a vowel sound that is separate from the other vowel sound, like Maya or Grayson.

When all of the numbers are added together and condensed to the lowest possible number, that number is called the Master Number. When the numbers are being added together and a total of eleven or twenty-two is reached, that is where the adding stops. These are also considered to be Master Numbers. Once the soul number has been determined, the interpretation can be determined.

The Significance of Names

Analyzing a person's name using numerology is a way to provide them with knowledge about themselves by interpreting the energy that is represented by that person's name. The analysis can give a considerable amount of personal understanding when it is appropriately and accurately interpreted.

In focusing only on the name part of the analysis, the person's birth date is omitted, and the name is used. This will allow the name analysis to be clearer and deeper than a general numerology reading. When a name analysis is done, three name numbers are specifically analyzed. These three important name numbers are the personality number, the soul's urge or heart's desire number, and the destiny number.

The destiny number is determined from all of the letters in the person's full name given at birth. The soul's urge or heart's desire number is derived from all the vowels in the person's full birth name. And the personality number comes from the consonants in the person's full birth name. The destiny number is the number that tells how a person will live their life. The soul's urge number shows the person's real motivations and desires. The personality number will show the person how other people see them.

Number One – Number one people are all about moving forward. The number one person has leadership capabilities, independent nature, and the spirit of a pioneer. Sometimes, ones are boastful or bossy because they are using an inflated sense of self-importance to hide insecurities. Ones need to be careful not to become too lonely by always wanting to be first. Number ones still need to have the support of lovers, family, and friends.

Number Two – Two is aligned with harmony, balance, and sensitivity. Two takes on the position of the mediator in life, bringing together combating forces to create harmony by using kindness, empathy, and compassion. Twos have intuition and psychic abilities. Twos can sometimes feel unacknowledged or underappreciated because they are so sensitive. They need to realize that true validation lies within themselves and not look for it externally.

Number Three – The number three is the very essence of creation. It is two forces joined together to communicate. These people are gifted communicators who easily share concepts that are pioneering and innovative by using speaking, writing, and art. They love to make other people happy and their work uplifts, motivates, and inspires other people. But the number three person might withdraw from other people entirely because they feel misunderstood. Their imaginations tend to be overactive, so it is good for them to enjoy quiet times to recharge, restore, and reset.

Number Four – Four is a firm believer in the physical world and in building a legacy that lasts through a strong physical structure. Their energy is involved with strengthening their roots. They desire to support growth by creating logical systems by being responsible, hardworking, and practical. These people need to remember that rules were made to enhance situations and not to inhibit growth because the number four can quickly become rigid. Fours should take a few risks and try to think outside of the box to feel more inspired and liberated.

Number Five – Five is defined by the freedom that this progressive, adventurous, and free-thinking number enjoys. A number five will use all of their senses to explore the greater world. These people are known for their vivacious, impulsive, and playful spirit. Fives can become bored by the daily routine because they are always seeking excitement, and this can include personal and professional commitments.

Number Six – A number six person has an empathic, supportive, and nurturing nature. They can solve problems that are either physical or emotional. They help others with a gentle yet straightforward approach. They can communicate easily with animals or children. However, these people want to parent everyone and everything they come into contact with, and they need to learn that not every creature on earth needs a parent. They need to realize that all creatures need to follow their path.

Number Seven – These people are known for their analytical skills and their investigative abilities. A detail-oriented individual, they are also driven by strong inner wisdom. They have an inventive and humorous spirit and a keen eye for the flaws in any system. They tend to be perfectionists.

Number Eight – This number is aligned with financial success and material wealth. Their natural magnetism allows them to take charge easily in any situation because they are goal-oriented and ambitious. These people can easily become workaholics and can be excessively possessive and controlling. Eights will realize that the greater good lies in helping others and giving back to the world at large.

Number Nine – Number nines are old souls. These people can use incoming information to create a whole out of many little pieces. Nines want to reach an elevated level of consciousness and to help other people reach it too. These people are not afraid to change, but they must remember to keep themselves well-grounded in reality.

Master Number Eleven – This number has the energy of the number two. It uses it to heal other people with its high level of psychic abilities. Elevens often develop extrasensory talents because of extreme life events they have lived through. This number is aligned with philosophical balance, awareness, and spiritual enlightenment.

Master Number Twenty-Two – This number is often referred to as the Master Builder, and it expands on the energies of the number four. These people are inspired to transcend immediate realities by creating platforms within the physical realm. They like to join the powers of the intangible and the tangible. They are always looking for something to change and are dependable, creative, and diligent.

Fibonacci Numbers

The finding of Fibonacci numbers in human physiology as well as many other places in nature, is likewise not trivial. By denying their significance, I think we miss the point of their existence. Nature accomplishes things by logical extension. If such extension results in certain kinds of mathematic relationships like pi, the Fibonacci series, or any other mathematic relationships, then so be it. We must then look beneath these phenomena for the process that gives rise to these properties.

We see quartz crystals or snowflakes growing in their characteristic way related to the bond angles of the molecules from which they are formed. Are similar chemical patterns represented in biologic individuals, and does biologic evolution simply follow these kinds of biochemical templates? This question, first posed by Stuart Kaufman, may only find an answer in quantum mechanics itself—the field of physics related to particles and atoms.

Mario Livio has another perspective on this subject. In his article, The Golden Ratio—the Story of Phi, he states: "Physical systems usually settle into states that minimize the energy. The suggestions is therefore that phyllotaxis simply represents a state of minimal energy…" Fibonacci numbers may occur in biologic life because they represent the least energy, and the most order, of a biologic entity.

To deepen our inquiry about how phyllotaxis and Fibonacci numbers found their way into life's architecture, we must ask whether these patterns of organization are present even in particles and atoms: Are biologic forms simply copying more inorganic ones? Perhaps the only real solution lies hidden in the original patterns of organization laid down at the beginning of everything, before there was life, or chemicals, or even atoms; A time when the universe was just a sea of energy emerging from some great causative event.

Is this where everything in nature learned mathematics? Did evolution learn the art that we see expressed in physical and biologic structures, of building complex forms from simpler ones from an initial set of conditions present at the start of the universe? If so, what were those initial conditions? More questions, profoundly unanswered, are encountered in our search for the highest brain mechanism and the roots of consciousness.

Fibonacci Series

The Fibonacci series has been discovered in many natural processes, curiously dominating the framework of the human body. Could such a framework similarly be used to create musical scales? To this end, we again consider its numbers: 0,0,1,2,3,5,8,13,21...where each successive number in the series is formed by adding the two numbers that immediately precede it. This recursive series forms ratios, angles, and structural relationships between the adjacent elements of the series. The ratio is called the Golden Mean .6189339887....) also called Phi;) and its formulations is found below: The Golden Angle is 137.5 degrees (Phi times 360 degrees= 225. .5 degrees,. 360 minus 225.5 = 137.5.

When fractions are made from adjacent numbers of the Fibonacci series, they form slightly differing ratios from the beginning numbers of the series to the higher ones. The ratio between 0 and 1 (0 / 1) is zero, and the ratio between 1 and 0 (1 / 0) is a calculation that, though being virtually banned from our mathematics, still closes on infinity. The first two numbers of the series, 0 and 0, form ratios that we don't like to think about.

But from this point on, things get a little better. The numbers 1 and 2 form ratios of 1/2 and 2/1, both somewhat more respectable. If one were to multiply a note like C (frequency +261.63 cps), one gets nothing but octaves traveling up and down the keyboard from this calculation. C (261.63) times 1/2 creates descending octaves of C, and C (261.63) times 2 creates ascending octaves of C. There is a wave function—a mathematic equation describing the properties of how waves behave. There is also one of how various scale tones of a musical system interact.

The next two numbers in the series, 2 and 3, form ratios of 2/3 and 3/2. When these ratios are multiplied by C(261.63), two twelve-tone scales are formed in either direction that when modified to fit within a single octave and scale tone averages compensated for, form a Fibonacci twelve-tone scale that is quite similar to what we know of as the logarithmic tempered scale. This fourth-order Fibonacci scale, with (0:1/ 1:0, !:1/ 1:1, 1:2/ 2:1)being the first, second, and third order scales, is found below in the following diagram and its variances to the tempered twelve-tone scale noted in scale tunings deviations.

The Fibonacci series doesn't stop at 3, but keeps on going out to infinity. In successive orders of Fibonacci scales, having ratios 3/5: 5/3: and 5/8: 8/5, strange things start occurring. The number of tones that can be fit into the octave rapidly expands from 12 (in the 2/3:3/2 fourth-order scale) to 19 notes in a fifth-order scale (3:5/5:3), and to 28 notes in a sixth-order scale (5:8/8:5). But these Fibonacci scales don't keep increasing in the number of notes they generate endlessly, for in the higher order scales, the number of notes begins to diminish again. The Fibonacci ratios of these scales gradually wavers closer and closer to the calculated value of Phi, and the note counts of these scales finally settles down into an odd kind of scale having thirteen notes. These scale variations are described in the next few series of diagrams.

The Fibonacci scales don't exactly represent either strictly linear or logarithmic principles. They seem to range over a wide area of tonal landscapes, happily generating relationships between tonal intervals that we are familiar with, and some that we definitely are not. When we can corral these intervals into a single octave, they can be compared to the linear and logarithmic scales we have noted. But the Fibonacci scales are neither, for in their elaboration they span many octaves, and are best represented as a spiral of tones rather than as ladders. What really emerges from these scales are self-similar curvatures of a helical nature that travel in ascending and descending directions.

Lastly, ratios of the Fibonacci series gradually settle down into a single number: The Golden Mean. Phi.

Higher-order Fibonacci Scales

The above higher-order Fibonacci scale helixes approximate Phi (1.6180339887498948482045868343 65..., and it's reciprocal: 0.6180339887498948482045868343 65 ...) as they turn and spin their way through octaves of 4ths and 5ths. As we noted, these ratios generate recursive numbers that can be represented graphically as spirals, one of the primary patterns of Fibonacci numbers found in plants. These spirals, arising from any fundamental frequency, generate the same tonal series in either the ascending or descending direction they travel, enhancing, if nothing else, the amplitude of these tonal elements. In other words, tonal series based on the various orders of the Fibonacci scale, represent enhanced nodes of energy amplitudes. Such enhancements, seen only partially represented in other scale systems, such as the enharmonic scale, favor octaves, and less so other tonal combinations. Fibonacci scales represent the summation of scale-tone amplitudes that entrain the scale fundamental into an overarching logical system applicable not just to music, but to all vibrating energies. There is a wave function—a mathematic equation describing the properties of how waves behave, and there is one of how various scale tones of a musical system interact.

The underlying basis of harmony is founded not on what one tone may sound like in relation to some other tone, but on how all tones are related to an overall coherent system of tones: Coherent, a word defined most often as understandable, but yet having another meaning in energetic mechanisms. Coherent light such as emitted by a laser, is very ordered, and doesn't scatter because it is in phase. Their wave peaks and valleys are synchronistic.

Fibonacci scales describe this logic in music, and if this is a correct analysis, then these numbers describe the harmonic logic of energy in general. This logic is neither linear nor strictly logarithmic, but helical, and based on naturally occurring amplitudes of nodal energies present in any dynamic energy system.

For example, a musical scale based on middle C, having a fundamental frequency of 261.63 cps, multiplied by the above number and it's reciprocal (Phi), has no appreciable differentials in the ascending and descending scale intervals it generates. Both calculations wind up exactly on an octave of C and form a thirteen tonal scale. When we compare the intervals of this scale to the tempered scale, an interesting thing happens. There develops a kind of 'curvature" in the tonal relationships of this highest-order Fibonacci scale that, when compared with the tempered scale, has some 'wild-card' notes around the mid-scale region of F, F#, and Gas noted diagrams. These notes, in modern music, are sometimes called 'blue notes' because they are favorites in jazz and blues improvisations.

The significance of this ultimate termination of Fibonacci series and its associated thirteen-note musical scale is a quandary to I think has significance in the patterns they form, and add this scale to the overall puzzle of how Fibonacci numbers in general are written into the structures of nature.

What is Enneagram– Harmony Triads and Nine Types

Understanding personality is the key to understanding, not just other people, but ourselves as well. At times, we can be shocked by our behavior, unsure where the actions we've taken have come from. It is through becoming fully knowledgeable about our personality, are we able to fully grow. This is where the Enneagram of Personality comes in.

The Enneagram of Personality, or rather just Enneagram, has been taking the world by storm for the last quarter of a century, and yet, some are skeptical about it. They may have good reasons, but without the knowledge of what it is, it can become rather frightening.

Enneagram is derived from the Greek word ennea, which means "nine" and gramma, which means "written" or "drawn." It is called so since it is a personality test that takes into consideration nine different personality types. The exact origins of the enneagram are under dispute; however, the contemporary enneagram, the one that we see today, is said to have started in 1915 with various men and thinkers who had taken their part in making it what it is today.

Personality Types

The Enneagram is a diagram of nine separate personality types with each individual being born into one of those types dominating over all the others, something that comes out in childhood. This means that an individual does not change from one type to another for any reason, but rather, this is something that has a genetic predisposition.

The Reformer

The first personality type on the Enneagram diagram is called the Reformer. In some instances, it is also called the perfectionist as individuals that have this as their primary personality type work towards becoming idealistic with a very strong sense of right and wrong. These individuals pride themselves on being responsible, honest, and having common sense, getting annoyed with individuals who do not take life as seriously as they do.

This personality is characterized by the individual having a sense of a mission that they need to accomplish, which most of the time leads them to improve on the world around them.

Throughout history, these are the individuals that have left what seemed to be perfect and comfortable lives in order to accomplish a greater goal, such as Joan of Arc or Gandhi.

The Helper

Second, on the Enneagram personality diagram is The Helper, and their sole motivator is to feel loved. They are known as being caring and helpful. Individuals with this personality type are the most genuinely helpful, and if they find themselves less than fortunate health-wise, they still try to see themselves as the most helpful.

They work on being the most helpful in order to fulfill their need for acceptance, but also because it sincerely warms their hearts. Helpers consider themselves to be the richest when they've been able to be generous towards other people, which makes people gravitate towards them. This provides them with the need for the closeness of friendship and family.

On the other hand, due to their very nature, Helpers tend to become emotional sponges, soaking up the emotions of those around them, something they should be wary of. Since other's feelings cannot always be controlled or helped, people who fall into this personality type should be aware of the type of people they spend their time with to ensure that they are not soaking in too much negative emotion.

The Achiever

Type three, the Achiever, can also be called the Performer because when they are at their best, they can truly accomplish anything. Their strengths lie in being energetic and a high achiever which allows them to become very successful in life. To them, their own development, as well as that of others, is something that is valued the most. Most of the time, they are seen as the most popular person in the group because of their ability to stand in for others.

However, family or society defines success is what individuals with this personality type need to achieve in order to feel fulfilled, whether that is money or other status symbols. They learn to act in a way that will get them the praise and attention that they are always seeking.

The Achiever embodies the human need for attention and affirmation of value that most strive for, but not for the things that success can buy or the independence that will come with that. Instead, they strive for success because of their fear of being worthless and disappearing into some void which would only solidify that they hold no value.

The Individualist

The Individualist, or what is also known as the Romantic, is the fourth Enneagram personality type. This personality type is characterized by their belief that they are completely different from everyone else, making it impossible for anyone to understand or love them the way that they need. They have a strong conviction that they are in possession of singular gifts, but also that they are inherently flawed like no one else.

At their best, The Individualist is able to self-reflect and clearly see their motives and conflicts without trying to rationalize what they find, even if they do not like what they see. To them, there is no shame in admitting to things that may be shameful because they want to understand the experience in order to begin understanding who they are on a deeper level.

Unfortunately, their nature is such that they feel something missing from their lives or themselves, but they have trouble identifying what that something actually is. This leads the Individualist to admit that they do not necessarily have a clear picture of who they are; they lack a clear identity.

The Investigator

The fifth Enneagram personality type is the Investigator, or it can also be called the Observer because they are focused on amassing a large amount of intellectual knowledge. They always hunger for more information in an attempt to understand how the world works always testing things for themselves instead of taking information at face value.

Their need for knowledge often leads them to the life of a scholar or technical expert. An Investigator possesses a highly analytical mind with privacy and personal autonomy coming up at the forefront of what is most important to them.

An Investigator may be easily capable of detaching from the people around them, but that doesn't mean that they do not feel loneliness in that. Though they are highly intelligent and thirst for knowledge, relationships do not come easy. In order to continue on with their hunt for more information, they require adequate time alone, which means that time with family or friends will always come last.

The Loyalist

The Loyalist, the sixth personality type on the Enneagram, is the most loyal of all of the personality types. In other words, they will go down with the ship for their friends, hanging on to different relationships longer than most other personality types would. This loyalty extends beyond people into systems, thoughts, and ideas which they rarely challenge.

Loyalty may be a desirable trait; however, the Loyalist's main concern is not to become abandoned because they had different ideas than the people in their current relationships. Apart from loyalty, Loyalist also exhibits courage and giving attention to people as well as their problems.

On the other hand, they are also suspicious and pessimistic, which causes them to worry excessively. Overthinking causes them to be afraid to make any big decisions, but they also do not want anyone to make any decisions on their behalf.

The Enthusiast

Anyone who falls into this personality type can be described as enthusiastic, curious, and optimistic. Their wonderful sense of adventures means that they become enthralled with anything and everything that catches their attention. This overflow of enthusiasm for life ensures that they mingle in a couple of different projects at the same time, leaning towards those that will stimulate their brain to new things.

Defined as intelligent, they are very verbal with their thoughts even if they are not overly academic. Their brain's need for new stimulus makes them jump from one idea to the next with ease, giving them a great ability to brainstorm; however, they do not focus on the nitty-gritty of any topic. Instead, they thrive on being spontaneous, taking pleasure out of the general overview as opposed to an in-depth topic.

An Enthusiast quickly learns new things whether they are intellectual or manual, giving them the ability to become a master of many subjects. Unfortunately for them, their gift for learning gives them the problem of being lost—with so many things at their fingertips; an Enthusiast does not know what to do with themselves. Part of the problem is the ease with which they learn as it does not give them the time to appreciate a new skill they had to fight to learn.

The Challenger

Sometimes they are given the name of the Protector. The main component of this personality is how it got its name; they enjoy being challenged. They also enjoy challenging others and allowing them to reach their true potential. Individuals who are Challengers are charismatic, giving them the skills needed to get others to follow them.

To them, feeling alive comes from being able to use their strengths to bring changes to the world. In this, they also work on ensuring that though they are making changes to the world, they do not allow the world to hurt them in any way, as well as those they care about.

One of their priorities is fairness and justice since, in their world, a weakness can be exploited, and if they have been wronged in any way, they will fight back. This can be attributed to their fear of not wanting others to control them in any way. It doesn't matter to them what they become in life, whether it's the general of an army or the mother of five, they need to feel that they are in charge along with the added need to leave a mark upon the world which is unique to this personality type.

The Peacemaker

The ninth, and last, personality type on the Enneagram is the Peacemaker or Mediator. This personality is solely focused on finding the internal and external peace that can be applied to themselves as well as to others. They are often described as the glue that will hold a community together. The world is made up of mostly Peacemakers.

A Peacemaker has a strong desire to connect with the universe as a whole and work towards holding on to their peace of mind. Based on this, they are the most in touch with their physical bodies and the physical world, becoming out of touch with their own instincts.

Often being called the crown of the Enneagram, as it is placed at the very top, it seems to embody traits of all of the personality types below it. Most likely due to that fact, they do not have a strong sense of self, but instead, they melt into others. These characteristics of the Peacemaker means that they tend to try and numb themselves in order to find harmony, ignoring aspects of the world that they do not want to face.

How to Master the Spiritual Growth

A person is born on a specific time and day and is established into an astrological sign, house, cusp or other designation. To fully reflect on the traits and predilections of those under that category, you can investigate and strive to understand your relationship with the universe completely. This can be especially useful by raising your awareness of the past and the potential of the future, finessing your inner attunement with God. However, approaching astrology as a superstition can limit the use of this information and change this resource to a passive dependence on fate while you wait for the planets or stars to shift positions. Some people believe that religion and astrology cannot exist together as God is the only one who can have power or influence over your lifestyle, personality and future. Under this argument, if you are spiritual and can actually commune with God to receive answers on how you should behave and what your path is in life, there is no need for anything like astrology to guide you. Others believe that astrology can simply give you more information about your journey in this world and also with God, giving you further understanding and knowledge of yourself and those you interact with every day. Or it may separate from spirituality completely and use astrology as a way to dissect and study the universe, as it exists only through a cycle of cosmic principles and energy. Any of these approaches is a personal interpretation that everyone must make on their own. Aries: A Fire sign ruled by the planet Mars may need a physical spiritual practice, but with control. Yoga may be suited to this temperament, especially those types that are more energetic or vigorous in practice.

Taurus: the artistic Venus that brings out a gentle and creative approach to life. Most Taurus enjoy being in nature. This may lead them to feel a close connection to the Pagan religion. The celebrations throughout the year combining the spiritual with feasts and celebrations will speak directly to the heart of a Taurus. Having a close connection to the planet makes anyone under this Earth sign more enthusiastic.

Gemini: Gemini needs to be constantly mentally busy. This allows them to be more open to alternative approaches and spiritual discipline. The practice of mindful meditation, a Buddhist tradition, may help to quiet their mind and bring peace. With too much taxing the mind, the body can suffer as the nervous system can be pushed into insomnia and anxiety. The practice of turning off the brain and focusing on deeper connections is a great way to deal with stress.

Cancer: Cancer individuals can display a higher level of psychic awareness than other signs, especially if they have a history of family ancestors with similar abilities. Psychic pursuits, clairvoyance, aura readings and other similar fields may tune into the abilities and penchant of Cancer.

Leo: Leos have a lot of energy and need to be active daily. A spiritual practice that may appeal to them and that suits their temperament would be Tai Chi. Tai Chi is strongly linked to the Chinese philosophy and martial arts. It adds strength to the posture, deepens the breathing and has many health benefits. Leos will prefer Tai Chi classes to practicing alone as this will add a social aspect to it as well.

Virgo: Virgos need to be careful to engage in regular exercise and follow a diet. As their nervous system is an area of concern, they will benefit from regular practice. Alternative sources such as spiritual healing, aura reading or Reiki can be beneficial to this sign. Essentially, when participating in a spiritual activity, Virgos need activities that do not overly use their minds but can bring themselves out. It is assumed that among the twelve signs, Virgo is the natural healer. Virgo likes to give advice and service, so any spiritual or religious practice that includes doing good works would be close to their heart. However, any spiritual practice for a Virgo should allow them to recharge their mental batteries.

Libra: balance is their trademark. The study of auras might interest a Libra. Auras are the field that surrounds the physical body and are typically different colors which can display physical health, emotional well-being, and spirituality. The study and recognition of auras may allow a Libra to understand the actions of others better and teach them how to become more balanced when dealing with the other people in their lives. In turn, this may help them to build better relationships with people around them.

Scorpio: a spiritual journey will come as second nature to a Scorpio. During their lifetime, they may investigate a number of religions until they closely identify with one. With a drive to understand their life path and human psychology, they may experiment divination practices with Tarot to address the choices people face every day and properly decide on options that will make them move forward. The mysterious nature of the Tarot may appeal to a Scorpio to delve into the hidden aspects of the universe and life and to further understand the reason of why people live and thrive on Earth.

Sagittarius: this sign is known as the philosopher of the zodiac. They may be drawn to philosophy or a teaching role in whatever religion they choose. As they enjoy studying and exploring new ways of thinking and then sharing those words of wisdom, they may indeed venture into being a spiritual leader. Their journey into spirituality may involve Christianity, Hinduism, Buddhism or other alternative religion.

Capricorn: Although a materialistic sign, Capricorn does have the spiritual virtues that are required for a spiritual journey. Individuals under this sign need a spirituality that is going to last, combining both the need for being alone and spiritual advancement. Although less widely known, one option may be Shamanism. A Shaman alters the state of consciousness to communicate with the power of animals and the spirit world. Shamanism originates in central and northern Asia. This ancient and powerful spiritual practice takes time to learn, which will ensure a connection with Capricorn.

Aquarius: Aquarius is always looking up at the stars and to the future. Those under this sign may indeed be inclined to astrology. For those under this sign, astrology may be the key to self-understanding. Following astrology and finding the pattern through the planets and constellations may be a source of guidance to Aquarius. Once this pattern is revealed, Aquarius delves into a journey of joy and fulfillment and can take that lost knowledge to others.

Pisces: Pisces's personality constitutes their journey through their life and their spirituality. As the last sign of the zodiac, Pisces understands that we are just a small distance away from the next world. Pisces can contact the dead and possesses incredible psychic awareness. Pisces needs to learn self-discipline by energy cleaning and meditation. They are very sensitive with the surroundings and those that they come in with. To help steady their energy, it is best to give them some time to recuperate and be creative. This can lead them to a number of spiritual pursuits that connect them to that awareness such as Reiki healing, aura cleansing, meditation and more.

Aquarius, Pisces, Aries and Taurus

Aquarius — The Water Carrier

(January 20-February 18)

The first sign we will explore is Aquarius. Even though this sign is known as the water carrier, it actually falls under the air category. Air signs are thought to be social, communicative, rational and enjoy relationships with others. They are often quite friendly and intellectual. All positive traits come with some negative, and for Aquarius that is definitely the tendency to be somewhat superficial. The ruler of the Aquarius is the planet Uranus.

Pisces — The Fish

(February 19-March 20)

Unlike the water carrier symbol for the air element, Aquarius, the Pisces fish is a true water symbol. Their luckiest days of the week are Mondays and Thursdays. The ruler of Pisces is Neptune. They are generally compassionate, intuitive, wise and artistic. Pisces like, sleeping, spiritual themes, solitude, music and are usually quite romantic. They do not take criticism well, and loathe being witness to any kind of cruelty, or people who consider themselves a "know-it-all". Pisces also have a thing about the past coming back to haunt them, and often dwell on things that happened a long time ago. They are most compatible with Taurus, Cancer, Scorpio and Capricorn.

Pisceans are popular with just about any crowd because they are easygoing, and have a submissive nature about them that makes them less of a threat to those they associate with. They are most often selfless, and will help out others without expecting anything in return. As a water sign, they are quite empathetic and highly emotional. Pisceans are also compassionate, extremely faithful and caring individuals. A common trait that hurts their well-being is that they tend to concern themselves with the problems of others, rather than face and deal with their own.

This sign easily withdraws from reality, and prefers to spend a lot of time in fantasy worlds. There, they can do anything — from being rich and famous to living the life of a nomad; never settling down in one particular place. They often believe that their best work comes from the outside world, or the inspiration created by a muse. They find great pleasure in appreciating art, and yearn to travel to exotic places.

Downside to being a Pisces who can feel the emotions of others is that sometimes they worry themselves sick. They can also worry to the point that they are indecisive, and fear making a decision because they don't want others to disagree with them. This sign can easily forget to finish a task and might need a gentle reminder. They do not do well in managerial positions, but excel as support staff.

On the upside, Pisces are empathetic to the plight of others, and feel sorry for people whose lives are not going well. They usually believe what they are told, and try to reach out to those in need. They are caring people who feel deeply, even if it is not always apparent on the surface. They are creative and imaginative, and know no bounds when they are supported by their loved ones.

Aries — The Ram

(March 21 -April 20)

This fire sign is ruled by Mars. Aries are confident, optimistic, courageous, passionate and determined. They do well in leadership roles, and enjoy individual sports and physical challenges. They can also be impatient, aggressive, impulsive and short-tempered and will not find their calling in any role or job that they are not able to utilize their dynamic talents.

Although this sign begins in March, it is actually the first sign in the Zodiac. March 21 is the spring equinox, which is the beginning of the new zodiacal year, making Aries the sign of new beginnings. The ram is ambitious, impulsive, adventurous and energetic. They are usually very intelligent, and develop new ideas which they immediately want to put into action. They take on new challenges head on, but — because of their signature impatience — they can get agitated if results aren't immediate.

Aries make great, compassionate leaders in most fields. They are responsible, and have a genuine concern for their subordinates. Because they are a 'take charge' sign, they do not make good followers, and may actually be unwilling to submit to or obey directions.

Because this is the first sign in the Zodiac, Aries have a "lead-the-way-and-get-things-started" attitude. This also has to do with Mars being the ruling planet for this sign. Fire signs take action, sometimes before they've completely thought it through. Despite that, they have wonderful organizational skills, and don't like any sort of clutter in their environments.

Downside to this sign is when working a project, they focus solely on the goal alone, and can appear selfish to others. As mentioned, they are usually quite impatient, and if they are not promptly recognized for their hard work, they can become sarcastic and rude.

On the upside, this sign is highly energetic and willing to work long hours to complete a project. They generally take initiative, and in doing so, experience new discoveries and breakthroughs. Incredibly thorough, Aries have a knack for being precise. Their motto might just be, "live hard, play hard."

Taurus — The Bull

(April 21-May 20)

This sign falls under the Earth element, and is governed by Venus. Taurus are reliable, practical, devoted, stable and responsible. They are also known for their patience. With the bull as their animal, one might be led to believe that Taurus are aggressive when in fact, the opposite is true. Characteristically, Taurus are methodical and peaceful. Their actions are deliberate while relaxed, and they enjoy everything sensual. This includes food, sex, luxury and drink. Their love of luxury means that they will usually obtain it by working hard and purposefully. Taurus enjoy music, cooking, gardening and high-quality clothes. They are not fond of sudden change, insecurity or complications in work or life.

Taurus are incredibly stable, well-balanced and conservative. They are good citizens who obey the law and love peace. Because they love luxury, they are terrified to be in any serious debt, and will do everything they can to maintain their sense of security. This makes the Taurus hostile toward change. To them, the familiar is what keeps them in the lap of luxury, and they will always want to keep the status quo.

This sign is also very keen-witted, and often practical over intellectual. Once they've established an opinion, they are very unlikely to change it regardless of popular consensus. Their unwillingness to change their ideals makes them incredibly dependable and steadfast. They are just, and can keep their cool in the face of any difficulty.

On the downside, they are stubborn and unwilling to change the ideals they've adopted. This can make them quite difficult to get along with, especially when it comes to cooperating on a project in school or at work. In social situations, they are leaders that prefer to be held in high esteem. If they are not, they might refuse to work and could try to find ways to sabotage relationships or projects. Although they value the law and follow it, if they see an authoritative figure they deem unworthy to lead, the Taurus might seek to sabotage them as well.

On the upside, Taurus finish what they start. It is rare to see them leave something undone. They think deliberately, and when they make a decision, it tends to be the right one. If there is a reward of luxury or anything sensual, they can be adaptable. They are very family oriented, and love to spend time with their loved ones.

The best matches for Taurus are; Cancer, Capricorn Pisces and Virgo

Gemini, Cancer, Leo, Virgo, Libra, Scorpio, Sagittarius and Capricorn

Gemini — The Twins

(May 21-June 20)

Gemini and the Lovers

Number 6 is related to Gemini in Astrology, more popularly known as the "twins". You probably are a born communicator, and you do know how to speak your mind well.

Gemini is partly brainy, but could also be scatterbrained, and this is why you have to learn how to make use of introspection, and numerology to help yourself feel better. However, once you learn to know yourself better, you can be one of the funniest, most exciting people around.

You might also be quite flirty, and could be someone who tries to use his charm to get his way, or make his way out of certain things. One thing that you do have to remember, though, is that you have to learn how to slow down and calm your mind so that you won't easily be distracted of what's happening in your life.

In Tarot, this number is associated with The Lovers, which also says a lot about how you choose a partner in life.

What this means, though, is that whoever you decide to be intimate with, you should be fully committed. This is also why you have to "study your options" first so you'd be sure that you're with the right person, especially if a long-term relationship is in your mind.

Be mindful of the choices you'll make, especially if you know they're going to bring forth some discontent. Always learn to stick with your choice, and don't be too fickle-minded—or you just may hurt yourself and some people too.

Cancer — The Crab

(June 21-July 22)

The Number 7 is associated with the Cancer sign in Astrology. This means that you have the tendency to be quite sensitive, mostly because you are ruled by the emotional moon. While you have this tough exterior, you may also be the kind of person who keeps his feelings hidden just to avoid getting hurt, which may also mean that you're not really living life to the fullest, and thus, you're often said to be "crabby".

This could be changed, though, when you meet someone—or even a group of friends—who really gets you for who you are, and whom you can be sincere with. You may also be naturally protective, but at the same time, you may have crazy mood swings that you have to try to prevent from happening, if you can.

Try to manage and process these feelings first before reacting or you may just overreact.

Meanwhile, when it comes to the Tarot, this sign is connected to the Chariot, or someone who parades himself as a "hero" along the streets. What you have to understand is that even though you may be "on top" now, it doesn't necessarily mean that it's what's going to happen forever. Therefore, you have to learn how to be open to changes, and understand that life isn't always a constant thing. Learn how to be receptive to the new people in your life, as well. This way, you can "travel light", and just allow yourself to glide through life better.

Leo — The Lion

(July 23-August 22)

Next is number 8, which in Astrology is associated with the Leo sign. Leo stands for the Lion, which means that you could be quite fiery, and are someone who cannot easily be ignored. You are quite charming, and also has the love for drama, and naturally has a warm spirit, and is quite hospitable.

You are an actionable person—you don't like just to sit around and do nothing, and you often make sure that you do what you can to live life well. However, you could be quite attention-seeking and arrogant.

In Tarot, this number is related to Strength, which determines your nature in its most primal form.

You could be quite persuasive, especially when it comes to what you want in life. You also have to learn to distinguish your ego from your true self, and you should separate enlightened wisdom from self-interest. Have some integrity so you could influence others in the right manner, so that this way, you will succeed with whatever you have in mind, as long as it is good, of course!

Virgo — The Maiden

(August 23-September 22)

The Number 9 is related to Virgo in Astrology. Also known as the Virgin, this means that you can be quite analytical, detail-oriented, and ultimately hard-working, and you kind of get to see what's wrong with certain people or with their environments right away. However, the problem is that when some people start critiquing you, you do not take to it too lightly, and you may easily turn your back on them when this happens.

Therefore, you have to try to lessen the perfectionism and just try to be a realist—after all, no one is perfect, and it's always best to just do your best, instead of seeking to be "perfect" and destroying everything you have put your heart and soul into before.

In Tarot, this number is associated with the Hermit. This means that you're able to recognize those people who could teach you a thing or two about life—otherwise known as your life teachers or mentors. You are the kind of person who gains wisdom from your experiences in life, and from the people you meet, and who make an impact in your life.

One thing you have to remember, though, is that you have to try to think things through, and that you have to be careful of the way you think, as well. This way, you get to understand the more essential things in life, and learn to see the bigger picture. You also need alone time, so do not be scared to tell people that you need to be alone for a while, think, and then just get your ducks in a row.

Libra — The Scales

(September 23-October 22)

Duality (Masculine Feminine) - Assertive

Element - Air

Quality - Cardinal

Ruling Planet – Venus: Just like the name of the famous Goddess, this planet is linked to pleasure and beauty. In addition to aesthetics, this also includes sociability, harmony, attraction, and eroticism. Venus changes signs every four to five weeks.

Dominant Keyword - I BALANCE

Polarity - Yang (+) Libras are very level-headed and do not get angry easily, so when they do, it is usually for a good reason.

Part of the body - Kidneys, Skin, Lower Back, Buttocks

Lucky Day - FRIDAY

Lucky Numbers - 7, 20, 55, 77 and 86

Magical Birthstone - Chrysolite

Special Colors - Pink and blue

Flowers -Rose

The danger for the people with that sign – Financial success is not a priority to Libras, and they will have many ups and downs when it comes to their careers because of this. Libras place more value on peace and justice in their lives.

Scorpio — The Scorpion

(October 23-November 21)

Duality (Masculine Feminine) - Passive

Element - Water

Quality - Fixed

Ruling Planet - Mars (ancient) and Pluto (modern): This tiny planet represents how people cope with power, both their own and other people's. Pluto is associated with transformation and rebirth, which also includes the cycle of death and regeneration. Pluto's orbit causes it to change signs every twelve to fifteen years. However, this can vary.

Dominant Keyword - I DESIRE

Polarity - Yin (-) When Scorpios are young, they are often religious and virtuous, but when they reach their twenties, they will undergo a dramatic shift. Many of the greatest saints were born under this sign. Even though it is common for a Scorpio's mind to change and for them to seek new experiences and paths, sometimes they dedicate themselves to their faith and feel as though they found their purpose early on.

Part of the body ruled by Taurus - Reproductive System, Sexual Organs

Lucky Day - TUESDAY

Lucky Numbers - 27, 29, 45, 53 and 89.

Magical Birthstone - Beryl

Special Colors - Black

Flowers - Chrysanthemum

Metal -Water

The danger for the people with that sign - they are infamous for procrastinating and will look for any excuse to put something off until a later date. This is not the best habit to have in the business world, so they must learn to adhere to a schedule if they want to be successful. However, once they overcome this obstacle, they are usually very successful in the career they choose.

Sagittarius — The Centaur

(November 22-December 21)

Duality (Masculine Feminine) - Assertive

Element (Fire, water [..]) - Fire

Quality - Mutable

Ruling Planet – Jupiter: Jupiter embodies hope, faith, luck, spirituality, justice, and purpose. Jupiter also represents spiritual growth and wisdom, and it changes signs every twelve to thirteen months.

Dominant Keyword - I SEE

Polarity - Yang (+) Sagittarius love to travel and learn as much as they can, they find it enlightening and fun. They are also known to be carefree and independent, but for the right partner, will make love a priority in their busy lives.

Part of the body - Hips, Thighs, Liver

Lucky Day - THURSDAY

Lucky Numbers - 6, 16, 23, 60, and 81

Magical Birthstone - Citrine

Special Colors - Purple

Flowers - Narcissus

The danger for the people with that sign - This sign is prone to restlessness because they have trouble sitting down and relaxing. They get bored easily and prefer instant gratification where they can get it. When a Sagittarius faces a task or goal that takes longer than anticipated to accomplish they move onto something else altogether and forget about the initial task. Even when they are 'relaxing,' they are making plans, and it is for this reason that they are so good in a crisis.

Capricorn — The Mountain Sea-Goat

(December 22-January 19)

Duality (Masculine Feminine) - Passive

Element (Fire, water [..]) - Earth

Quality - Cardinal

Ruling Planet — Saturn: This planet represents our limitations and boundaries. It explains the way a person experiences "reality," and the places they meet resistance in their lives. Saturn is also associated with laws, rules, morals, and our conscience, and whether we choose to abide by laws or regulations. Saturn is also connected to our concentration and our powers of endurance, including reserve and caution. Saturn only crosses through a sign every two or three years.

Dominant Keyword - I USE

Polarity - Yin (-) Those born under this sign are eyes on the prize types that let nothing stand in the way of them fulfilling their purpose. They take the concept of destiny and work very seriously and put great faith in their own abilities. They are mentally sound and strong, but often not understood by others. They excel at government work or business ventures but do not do very well being at the bottom of the corporate ladder.

Part of the body - Joints, Skeletal System

Lucky Day - SATURDAY

Lucky Numbers - 3, 21, 66, 83, 84.

Magical Birthstone - Ruby

Special Colors - Brown and grey

Flowers -Carnation

The danger for the people with that sign - Fear is at the root of a Capricorn's troubles; this is a life-long battle they fight with themselves. Learning to cope and overcome their fears is something that they must learn to do. However, this does not always come easily, and part of it is usually finding the patience and inner calm to allow themselves to begin the long process of chipping away at these fears and frustrations. Everyone has different fears, but for a Capricorn, it generally deals with failure, living without purpose, and feelings of loneliness.

Celestial Sphere

If on a clear night we turn our eyes to the sky, we will see an incredible number of stars, bright and not very, and it seems that there are so many of them that it is not possible to make out something in the sky. But if we take a closer look at the set of diamond points in the sky, we will notice that some of them form separate groups1. How to navigate the starry sky map

In antiquity, people distinguished groups of stars: the imagination of a certain sage gave these groups diverse forms. There are purely geometric shapes, but more often people used the shapes of animals, people, or objects. Then the name "constellation" appeared. In the northern hemisphere there are special constellations that shine only for Europe; There are special constellations in the southern hemisphere, on the other side of the equator.

Star route 1 Description of stars and constellations. A star is a part of the constellation that could be distinguished.

It is worth noting that in addition to stars that invariably appear in the sky, there are moving celestial bodies, the path of which passes through the constellations. This is the Sun and the Moon in the first place, we will talk about other planets later. Let us linger briefly on the external manifestations that the Sun and Moon project onto the Earth.

We will notice that most of their movements are due to the movement of the Earth, but for now we will leave it so as not to get confused.

Thus, people noticed that on its way through the sky the Sun crosses the constellations, each time the same; they also noted that the moon moves on the same principle as all other wandering stars or planets.

Zodiac

This path along which the heavenly wanderers move is called the path of heavenly animals, or the divine starry path, or the zodiac. The zodiac consists of twelve constellations. Knowledge of the zodiac is essential for both the astronomer and the astrologer.

Sky division

All celestial bodies are divided into two large categories: motionless stars, from which constellations are formed, and wandering stars, which move through the twelve signs of the zodiac.

Motionless stars

In fact, motionless stars can only be called relatively: they really do not move independently - this distinguishes them from wandering stars. But the sky moves around the Heavenly Pole; therefore, ancient people believed that the sky is like a huge ocean, in which the constellations rise and go.

Celestial sphere

The set of astronomical observations, both ancient and modern, is based on the sunrise and sunset of the constellations.

Celestial sphere according to the ancient system of Ptolemy

To navigate the sea, people divided the celestial sphere into parts by analogy with the division of the Earth. Between the two poles and through the center passes the celestial equator; The zodiac, which acts as an ecliptic in the sky, divides the equator into two parts so that the six signs of the zodiac are above the equator, closer to the Arctic pole, and the remaining six signs are below the equator, closer to the Antarctic pole. The northernmost sign of the zodiac is Cancer, the southernmost is Capricorn.

In the sky, in addition to the equator and latitudinal parallels, there is another belt that passes through the sign of Capricorn and is called the Tropic of Capricorn. The two aforementioned zodiac signs, Cancer and Capricorn, are the northern and southern extreme points of the zodiac, respectively, and form the line of the winter and summer solstices; the other two signs, eastern Aries and western Libra, make up the line of the spring and autumn equinox.

Four corners symbolize the beginning of the four seasons. Now you need to remember the order and names of the zodiac signs. Please note that the astrological year begins in March.

Aries (A) March 20 ... ... April 20

Taurus (B) April 20 ... ... May 20

Gemini (C) May 21 .... June 20

Cancer (D) June 21 .... July 22

Leo (E) July 23 .... August 22

Virgo (F) August 23 .... September 22

Libra (G) September 23 .... October 22

Scorpio (H) October 23 .... November 21

Sagittarius (I) November 22 .... December 21

Capricorn (J) December 22 .... January 20

Aquarius (K) January 21st .... February 18th

Pisces (L) February 19 .... March 19.

These dates indicate the entry of the Sun into other signs in 1916.

In small portions you will learn the sequence of zodiac signs, which is extremely necessary for astrology.

For a better understanding of the arrangement of the zodiac signs, we recommend using a special mnemonic reader:

OV - TE - BLI - RA

LEO - DE - WEIGHT - SPORTS STRE - KO - WATER - PY

Each of the twelve signs of the zodiac is a group of closely spaced stars, enclosed in a geometric shape. In antiquity, signs were assigned symbolic images of animals, characters, or objects that they were like. In addition, each sign was assigned a symbolic image, and we advise the reader to remember them.

We will continue, but let's learn what we have already learned about the signs of the zodiac. This knowledge gives us the opportunity to consider them further in the future.

How each Planet's Astrology Directly Affects every Zodiac Sign

In astrology, zodiac signs get a lot of attention— after all, to read the regular horoscope, all you need is a sun sign. But the field of astrology is big, light, and majestic, and if you want to see what the stars are trying to do in astrology, you need to get an understanding of what planets mean. It's not a surprising news that planets are something in the field of astrology— after all, it is precisely what astrology is. To perceive the passage of planets and other celestial bodies through the heavens (and zodiac). Yet knowing the planets will help you make so much more sense of things like your signals of sun and moon, and in the next moment, someone rants about Mercury going backward again, or their location of Venus ruining their life of love.

You are undoubtedly still familiar with the planets of the old solar system (shouting out to teachers of primary school science around the world). Nevertheless, you have a seat back at your office, as planets in astrology can vary a bit from what you discovered from Bill Nye, the Science Guy. Next, both the sun and the moon are called planets in astrology. Although in the astronomical sense they may not be stars, they are vitally critical celestial bodies for all of we earth dwellers and therefore called planets as far as astrology is concerned. Pluto is also a satellite in astrology. While astronomers may have demoted it a few years ago to a mere dwarf planet, it's still a full-fledged planet in astrology— and it's just as strong. Finally, scratch the Earth from the list of planets in astrology— I mean, it's essential, but we also live on it, so from our Earthly point of view, it doesn't travel through the sky like the other celestial objects. All in all, ten main planets are made up of that.

Through astrology, each planet represents a different set of qualities and characteristics and rules another part of our lives— each taking their unique vibes with them. "Each planet symbolizes another part of life, another form of energy," Astro Library explained. "In psychological terms, we might call them' needs' or' drives.'" The planets ranging from the earth to Mars are known as' inner planets.' We pass relatively quickly from sign to sign, thereby providing greater control over every day, shorter-term problems. "Outer planets," ranging from Jupiter to Pluto, travel even slowly through the zodiac table, thus affecting higher parts of your life and yourself. And when someone names a planet "beneficial," it refers to their association with delivering perfect vibes (Jupiter and Venus are regarded as beneficial). On the other hand, "malefic" planets like Saturn and Mars are believed to have stronger, more destructive energy (although we love them and still need them!).

Okay, it depends on where they are located to learn how the planets impact us. Planets pass through numerous signals, and their energy works out differently depending on their location. If you want to learn where your birth planets are, your birth chart will need to be checked out (if you have your precise birth date, you can find it online, or ask a qualified astrologer to help). The birth map consists of twelve astrological houses and twelve signs of the zodiac that correspond with those houses. But there are stars in all these signs and buildings. "That house provides the planets living there with a home — giving the planet a place to practice its unique energy," Insightful Astrology explained. But planets do not affect anything themselves— it's more about where they are located and how they communicate with other parts of your map.

Sun

Naturally rules: Leo

The sun is our universe's nucleus. It's what the world around us paints, the light around which we revolve, and that brings us beauty. That's part of why, and who we are, our sun signs are so crucial to our astrology! "The Sun is our conscience, our life-force, what we are motivated to do," Stardust says to Bustle. The sun is the driving force behind our hearts, and people who can accept their sun placement tend to feel happy and satisfied.

Moon

Naturally rules: Cancer

The sweet, emotion-driven moon is seriously our Astro mom (I know I'm a mad Lil' witch and all, but I practically welcome the moon with a "Hello, mum!" when I see her in the night sky.) "The Moon reflects our inner feelings, the pieces within us which we cannot communicate," says Stardust. "It also reflects our maternal side, our parents, our memories, and what foods we love." Nurturing, receptive, and governing over matters of survival, the moon rules over the dark, more fragile aspects of ourselves, as well as the factors we need to feel safe and comfortable.

Mercury

Naturally rules: Gemini & Virgo

You probably know this world more than anything else for its notorious retrograde cycles, but in truth, this fast-witted master of contact is cool when it doesn't turn anything upside down in your life. "Mercury impacts how we interact, communicate and travel information," McGarry says to Bustle. Mercury is known as the gods' messenger, so it makes sense that it is its jam to connect, share information, and fly.

Venus

Naturally rules: Taurus & Libra

Beautiful Venus, a flowery, sensual, and heart-flutteringly wonderful world of all things. Named after the divine goddess herself, Venus enjoys life and is absorbed in the world's aestheticism and aesthetics. Venus is also synonymous with money— especially the money we spend on things that offer us pleasure and joy more frivolously. "Venus portrays love affairs, passion, elegance, fine wines, and rich food," Stardust says. "Venus always embodies self-esteem and wealth." She's kind of like the planet's Valentine's day — think of a romantic evening full of chocolates, champagne, red rose petals, and a warm bubble bath.

Mars

Naturally rules: Aries

Wild fiery Mars is strong, motivated, and full of raw, unbridled, animalistic fire, named after the god of war. "Mars is the way we fight and show ourselves," McGarry states to Bustle. The so-called Red Planet, with its red-hot strength and zeal, definitely lives up to its name. And you might have noticed "Mars guys, Venus women," right? Okay, we all have a delicate balance of both, so while erotic passion is the domain of Venus, Mars rules over our sexual drive and attraction that is more animalistic. In our gut and feel, Venus is the butterflies, while Mars is the primitive physical impulse.

Jupiter

Naturally rules: Sagittarius

The bigger the head, the closer to heaven, the larger the world, the closer to sweet, sweet peace, as the saying goes. Jupiter is considered particularly auspicious, carrying with it its vast presence of prosperity, positivity, potential, and good vibes. "The greater benefit of Jupiter is an opportunity, prosperity, travel, spirituality, schooling, teaching, and expansion," says Stardust to Bustle. This big boy is a positive and good luck spreader, so always welcome the peachy vibes of Jupiter.

Saturn

Naturally rules: Capricorn

If the moon is our celestial mother, then Saturn is our cosmic lord altogether. Speak of this world as the harsh father who is a little too rigid, oppressive, and strict. "Saturn is the biggest malefic, representing limits, boundaries, limitations, and parental partnership," Stardust states. About the notorious return of Saturn, which happens to everyone around their late twenties (cue utter existential breakdown), you may be familiar with Saturn. Saturn's all about tough love— but mind, it's just harsh on us because we want to learn and grow.

Uranus

Naturally rules: Aquarius

Look forward to the unpredictable with Uranus as this planet is about shaking up the standards. It is radical, forward-thinking, hyper-creative, but susceptible to abrupt changes and transitions as well. "Uranus is known as the' Great Awakener' as it shakes the universe on a universal level through revolutions and creativity," says Stardust. For nostalgia, Uranus doesn't care about tradition— it cares about being pioneering, bright, and unique. The world is sometimes compared to a beam of light because it surprises us with unexpected discoveries and inspirations.

Neptune

Naturally rules: Pisces

Dreamy, Neptune, otherworldly. The origins of this world are as profound as their color is blue, as they reflect psychic imagination and spiritual attainment, as well as visions and artistic expression. As Stardust states, "Neptune reflects visions, imagination, and myth." Because of its dreams, inter-dimensional existence, it also appears to separate itself a little bit from reality. But if you can avoid falling into this planet's escapist habits, it will offer a positive resilience and spiritual power.

Pluto

Naturally rules: Scorpio

Scientists back in 2006 may have stripped Pluto of his planethood — indeed a cruel move, particularly to the planet named after the king of the underworld. Yet Pluto is as planet like as it can be in astrology. As McGarry tells Bustle, "Pluto includes the transition force." Transition covers a lot of ground — think of the energy of light and darkness, death and rebirth, day to night, culminating in the beginning. Like Anne Welles said in the Valley of the Dolls, "You have to scale Mount Everest to reach the Valley of the Dolls." And if the Valley of the Dolls is your inner reality, then hey, brace for the daunting so dangerous yet exciting war that Pluto insists on, because it is undoubtedly for the ultimate good.

Oracle Cards and Psycards

Oracle Cards

Oracle cards are very similar to Tarot cards, with one exception—there are no rules to follow with oracle cards. Much like with Tarot, these cards are used to gain clarity, inspiration, insight, and answers. These cards are just more modern than Tarot. Like with Tarot decks, there are many different styles of oracle decks to choose from, and you should pick one that resonates with you and that you can connect with.

Since oracle cards do not have any rules, it is a very freeform way of getting guidance, checking if you are on the correct path, receiving clarity and inspiration, and getting questions answered. Oracle cards are all about how you feel when you look at the words and imagery on the cards, and both are equally important. There is no set number of cards you need to draw, no set-in-stone meaning—all of this is so that the interpretation is completely up to the reader. Many find it helpful to write in a journal while pulling cards in order to keep a flowing stream of consciousness. Many find this allows them to get what they want out of reading more easily.

A historian, Caitlín Matthews, is very familiar with oracle cards, particularly the 36-card Lenormand deck that was named after Mademoiselle Marie Anne Lenormand, a famous card reader from the 18th and 19th century. The cards were not published with her name until after her death, and the two oldest Lenormand-style decks in Matthews' collection are the French Daveluy from the 1860s and the Viennese Zauberkarten from 1864. The Zauberkarten decks were some of the first divination decks that used chromolithography to produce the imagery on the cards.

Oracle decks rely on a visual language that is more direct than those that traditional Tarot cards use. Most fortune-telling decks, like thee Lenormand deck, focus less on archetypes and tend to use straightforward imagery that keeps the conversation more direct, as opposed to Tarot cards that speak in a universal language that is broader.

A woman by the name of Mary Greer found that there was a predecessor to the Lenormand cards called "les Amusements des Allemands" or the German Entertainment. These were created by a British firm, and the Lenormand decks heavily resembled their style.

Popular oracle cards are:

- The Angel Blessings Oracle Card Deck
- The Deck of Shadows Oracle Card Deck
- The Earth Magic Oracle Card Deck
- The Magical Unicorn Oracle Card Deck
- The Wisdom of Avalon Oracle Card Deck
- The Mystic Art Medicine Oracle Card Deck
- The Sacred Path Oracle Card Deck
- The Black Power Tarot Oracle Card Deck
- The Animal Kin Oracle Card Deck
- The Spirit de la Lune Oracle Card Deck
- The Cosmic Mother Oracle Card Deck
- The Illest Oracle Card Deck
- The Rebel Oracle Card Deck
- The Ancient Animal Wisdom Oracle Card Deck
- The Angel Answers Oracle Card Deck
- The Cards of Alchemy Oracle Card Deck
- The Celtic Oracle Card Deck
- The Moonology Oracle Card Deck
- The Wild Offering Oracle Card Deck
- The Goddess Power Oracle Card Deck
- The Earth Magic Oracle Card Deck
- The Precious Gems Oracle Card Deck

- The Every Day Oracle Card Deck
- The Whispers of Lord Ganesha Oracle Card Deck
- The Goddess Guidance Oracle Card Deck
- The Wisdom of the Oracle Divination Card Deck
- The Sacred Rebels Oracle Card Deck

Psycards

Psycards were influenced by Carl Jung's work in psychotherapy and can be used to get answers and guidance, help with one's growth and self-improvement, and deal with a question that has been on your mind for a while. They were created by Nick Hobson and Maggie Keen in the 1980s.

These cards work similarly to Tarot, but this deck only has 40 cards instead of 78. The cards do resemble the Major Arcana, but they are separated into 6 groups:

- Directions
- Happenings
- Characters
- Fundamentals
- Archetypes
- Symbols

The symbols are used to link the unconscious and the conscious mind, allowing you to get answers to direct questions and receive general guidance. If you do prefer to receive general information, there is a simple spread you can do:

- Shuffle your cards
- Draw 7 cards and put 2 in a row on top, 3 below that, and 2 on the bottom
- the top row represents what you should aspire to.
- the middle row shows the past, present, and future.
- the bottom row shows the forces that are unconsciously driving you forward.

Performing Tarot Readings

There are a few differences between reading for yourself and reading for someone else, so these will be covered before we get into the process of a Tarot reading.

Reading for Yourself

Some Tarot readers will tell you that you cannot read for yourself, but it holds little merit if you believe that the Tarot is simply there to help you tap into the information that you already subconsciously know.

When you are reading for yourself, it can be a useful tool in personal self-discovery and development. When you are first starting out, reading your own Tarot is a great way to learn and familiarize yourself with the cards. A great idea is reading your own Tarot every day and keeping notes over those readings in your Tarot journal.

Since you are reading for yourself, though, it can be difficult to remain objective and emotionally removed. Doing this, however, is incredibly important, as your emotions and attachments to the situation can hinder your ability to read correctly the cards you draw. Meditating beforehand, whether to clear your mind completely or simply focus on the question you have, can do wonders for the remaining objective. You can also choose to use an inanimate object to represent yourself and set it across from you (where your client would sit if you were doing a reading for them), and tell yourself that the reading you are doing is for this "'you," sitting opposite you.

Many people, especially those who are just starting out, find it beneficial to do their reading out loud, just as they would do with a client because it enables them to see things that they may have missed by just looking over them in their head.

Reading for Others

When reading for others, the rules are similar but different. Instead of shuffling the cards yourself, it can be more beneficial for the querent to shuffle them. This is because it gives them the opportunity to infuse their own energy into the cards while thinking about the question they want to be answered.

When you decide to read for others, you will have to keep in mind that their skepticism can play a big role in how well the reading goes. If a person is a non-believer, that doubt can skew the cards or make them useless (unreadable) gibberish. It can also end up being a waste of time if the querent believes the reading does not relate to them or that the things the cards have said will not happen. The best thing to do in situations like this is to end the reading, as it is not benefitting anyone, not you or the client.

It is also important that you take into consideration what the client or querent can and cannot handle. This was covered in ethics, but it is an important consideration to keep in mind. Your job is never to lie to the querent if there is bad news; simply determine the best way to tell them in a way that will not crush them. Putting a positive spin on something or offering them options to fix the situation will always soften such blows.

For example, if someone's reading produces the Death Tarot card, assure the client that it often means death in the way of an ending, but all endings happen to make room for new beginnings. There is typically always a way to put a positive twist on a reading or particular card, and it is the reader's job to ensure that the querent leaves feeling empowered and not beaten down.

If you happen to get stuck in a reading, it will typically resolve itself as you look at the other cards, so if you need to skip a Tarot card and come back to it, that is completely acceptable. Often, doing this actually makes the once confusing card make perfect sense, and all you needed was a bit more context clues to figure it out. If that is not the case, and you are still stuck, you can use the tips that are listed:

- First impressions
- Describing the Tarot cards
- Searching for patterns
- Drawing a clarifying card
- Giving yourself or the querent time

Reading for Family or Friends

After having practiced on yourself for a while, you may want to spread your wings a bit and branch out to a few people you are close to so that you can practice in a judgment-free environment. Being able to practice on family and friends who are close to you is definitely a benefit, as it gives you more practice and exposure to the cards, but there can be a few hindrances that come along with that as well.

Since these people are typically close to you, you tend to know their stories, and you know what is going on in their lives, making it difficult to remain detached in the way that you should in order to perform the most accurate reading. Much like when you are reading for yourself, reading for those whom you are close to can be difficult because of the emotional ties you have to the situation, even if you are not directly linked to the question they want to be answered.

Meditating and clearing your mind can help you remove yourself from the situation while reminding yourself to be objective can also do more than you might imagine.

Reading for Strangers

If you decide to read for others in a business sense, you will often do readings for people whom you do not know. Now, this can be both more or less ideal or easy, depending on who you ask or what kind of person you are.

The emotions and connections that you have with family and friends can make it pretty difficult to give a good, accurate reading, but there is the level of comfort that comes with it that some could find as a plus.

Reading for strangers certainly eliminates the emotional connection, as you will not know anything about their life. This typically makes it significantly easier to interpret the story that the cards are attempting to get across to you, as they are not being blocked by bias or non-objectivity. You are free to use your intuition to determine what the cards are trying to say and the wisdom they are trying to impart upon the one who seek.

Note for Readings for Others

When you start doing readings for others, whether your family, friends, or clients, you will move through the five numbers of their Core Profile, and there are some important things to keep in mind.

Always start with the Life Path Number, and explain to your participant why it is the most important number in their profile. Then, move on to the Soul Number, to reveal what their heart wants: This is the private, more intimate side of them that only those very close to them get to see. Touch on compatibility by explaining Soul Stress Numbers (here).

From there, look at the Personality, Destiny, and Birthday Numbers. These all have a profound effect on career and how one makes a living. Discuss the special gifts, talents, and abilities this numerical energy grants them.

Follow with the Attitude Number, explaining this is where first impressions and judgments are born. Finish with the Maturity Number, which becomes more relevant depending on the person's age.

While you are doing the reading, pay special attention to the placement and influence of each number. If there are repeating numbers in the chart, discuss those intensities. Repetition can significantly change the meaning of the information you relay.

Explain Karmic Lessons and Debt as they are revealed, and always offer gentle guidance about how to learn lessons and pay the cosmic bank. Empower them with the tools to resolve karma during their lifetime.

Close with the cycles and timing of their Personal Years, Months, and Days in order to give them awareness of the opportunities, possibilities, and challenges that may come their way.

BE SENSITIVE AND RESPECTFUL

Doing readings for others comes with immense responsibility. Think about who usually asks for a reading—generally, people seek help in times of despair or when at an important crossroads. They are looking to the spiritual world for guidance. Consider it an honor and a privilege to provide guidance during such times.

Clients, friends, and family might make important decisions based on the information and insights you provide. Because of this, you must be careful with your words and never project your personal feelings, judgments, or opinions into the reading. Remember that you are just a conduit for the intelligence the numbers provide.

Keep it positive. Avoid creating self-fulfilling prophecies for your clients or friends. For example, if you find markers for divorce in a chart, don't doom the person to give up on a relationship as soon as it gets hard (there's always room for interpretation: this is also the marker for someone who is widowed or has lost a parent at a young age). Instead, explain they may experience some harsh lessons around love. You never know exactly how the numbers will play out in another person's life. As the always inspiring Maya Angelou said, "Words are things, I'm convinced. You must be careful." You cannot undo the power of a word once spoken. Bring kindness, empathy, and compassion; these traits will be some of your greatest assets as a reader.

If you choose to showcase your new knowledge as a party trick, be respectful of the science. Always make sure you are accurate and have a clear mind (math and alcohol don't usually mix well). Many intuitive believe that if the gift is abused or used in the wrong way, their abilities will be decreased or even blocked.

Some clients will take everything to heart; others will struggle against it. Free will is always involved, and people will heal only when they are ready.

I cannot emphasize this enough: Ground your energy. You do not want to take on someone else's problems or toxic energy, so implement boundaries. There are many effective techniques and crystals that offer protection. Continue with your own research and find a method that works for you.

To quote Numerologist Hans Decoz, "Numerology is a difficult, but intensely rewarding profession." Motivate, inspire, elevate, provide insight, and always tell the truth, and your readings will be fabulous!

DEVELOPING YOUR INTUITION

Your intuition will continue to evolve and expand along with your awareness and confidence. Understanding and developing intuition is deeply personal and happens differently for everyone.

Early in my Numerology career, I was taught the concept of "blah"—basically, receiving a very strong message that you blurt or "blah" out (which stands for "bring love and healing"). This phenomenon has created some of my most meaningful and heartfelt connections with clients. Several stories come to mind, but I'll share just one:

That nagging message came to me as the words "blue plaid shirt, blue plaid shirt." I tried to dismiss it, but it was relentless, as messages from the Universe tend to be. Eventually, I asked the client the significance of this image. They had no immediate answer, so I continued on with the reading. By the end of our time together, her face lit up and she ran out to her truck to get something to show me, a program from her father-in-law's memorial. It had a photo of him in a blue plaid shirt.

I still get chills when I think about how emotional this was for her.

Finding the balance between kindness, honesty, and censorship will be crucial. Check your ego, keep everything confidential, and deliver your intuitive readings with compassion and love.

CRACKING THE CODE

Whether you choose to reveal your new ability is up to you. People can get strangely secretive about their birth date (or even provide inaccurate information) when they feel you could reveal something that they'd rather keep private. With experience, you will likely know when this is the case. Never push someone to share their numbers with you. Always be open to learning, respect boundaries, and keep an open mind.

Eventually they'll understand what you know after reading this: that life can be easier, decisions and timing less confusing, and relationships more harmonious and greater opportunities can be seized through Numerology.

Embrace the magic of the Universe. I've often said that if everyone had just a little Numerology in their lives, the world would be a more magical, understanding, and compassionate place.

Congratulations on your newfound wisdom.

Tarot 101- Getting Started

Now that you're ready to get a Tarot deck and begin the learning process, the first thing you must do is find your own Tarot deck and make it your own. You can then start to develop a personal connection with those cards and build a foundation that will provide you with guidance and insight for years to come.

- Choosing a Tarot Deck

Because there are so many Tarot decks now available, it can be difficult when first deciding which deck to use. Don't worry about choosing the wrong deck, as anything that calls to you is going to the right fit. You aren't limited to just having one deck either, you can and probably will end up with multiple decks that you use for various reasons. Some will keep one deck private, and only use it when they are reading cards for themselves. Others will use one deck for everything. Most teachers of Tarot recommend that you find a deck that you resonate with and use it to practice and learn with. Once you are comfortable enough to perform readings for others, you will know if you require a new deck for that purpose or if the one you already have will work.

No matter which deck you end up choosing, having a sense of connection with it is crucial. Take your time and browse all the options available to you. If you find a deck and decide that you don't really have any relationship with the images, find a new deck. You're not held to any commitment with the Tarot. Once you locate a deck that you like, you'll want to clear the energies that might exist around it and cleanse the deck. If that sounds a little too metaphysical for you, think about as introducing yourself to the deck and starting fresh.

- Sorting

To begin, you will want to sort out your cards and pay attention to any energies that you might pick up from them. On a clean table or area, sort your cards out in front of you in order. Start with the Major Arcana cards and then sort the Suits of the Minor Arcana. Take a brief look at each card while doing this. This is a way of ensuring that you have all the cards in your deck as well as taking note of the illustrations for the first time. When dealing with the Minor Arcana cards, sort the Suits by type and then by number. You start with sorting in order from Ace through Ten followed by the Page, the Knight, the Queen, and finally the King card.

For the purposes of learning, you may want to sort your cards into the Major Arcana and the Minor Arcana and put one or the other away in the place you dedicate for storage. When we focus on either one of these specifically, we allow space for further insight and development. For example, it's quite common to start with the Minor Arcana and to develop a good sense of what each Suit, Number or Court card is telling us. It makes us focus solely on a limited number of cards so that we can use the repetition to build on our original thoughts and impressions.

- Cleansing Energies

Once you have looked at each individual card and have it sorted you can use a smudging wand such as sage or sweetgrass to clear any stored energy in the cards. This is particularly useful if you have cards that have been used before, but it's also a great starting point for new decks. At this point, you may want to meditate on the cards and visualize energy coming from you and moving towards and into the cards. If you're familiar with guided meditation or visualization techniques, you may want to use them to create a protective circle of while light that encompasses you and the cards. This can be a powerful cleansing and connection exercise.

There are energy cleansing techniques that are much more involved such as salt burials, moon bathing, or water clearing. If you feel your cards have any negative energies associated or clinging to them, take the time to perform a cleansing ritual with them. For beginners though, a simple sorting and pause in contemplation should suffice. It's recommended that you do some sort of energy clearing, however small, before performing any readings to concentrate on the questions at hand and the client.

- Making the cards your Own

When you are satisfied with the energy, pick them all up and shuffle them to impart your own energy into the cards. Continue shuffling and reshuffling any way you like to achieve this. Maybe you want to shuffle a certain lucky amount of times or randomly select cards to put on top or at the bottom of the deck. Whatever works for you will get your deck ready for its first use. When your deck is not being used, you should consider where you will store them. Many people find the box that they came in completely okay while others have a dedicated, specialized space just for them. Silk is associated with magical properties due to how it's created and is widely accepted as the fabric of choice when wrapping cards before placing in a box. While it's fine to do what feels right for you, keep in mind that Tarot is an ancient art that deserves our respect and reverence.

Develop a Personal Connection

Now you are ready to work with your cards and develop a personal connection to them. This connection should be with every single card in the Tarot deck. You may choose to begin with the Minor Arcana and develop a sense of what each Suit represents. You may decide to start with the Major Arcana and develop an understanding with the illustrations found there. However, you go about learning the cards for the first time, you'll want to associate meaning to each one. You will begin to develop a relationship with your cards, which is why working with a deck you like and resonate with is so crucial. You're basically bonding with the deck and noting how you feel when using it.

You don't have to memorize the meaning of each card, only develop a basic sense of what the card represents at first. You will inherently acquire a sense of what they mean as you continue to work with them. Keep in mind that you will at one point want to express what they represent to other people so work on creating associations that are easily recognized, repeated, and deciphered. This should be fun for you, so if you feel that it's becoming too much information just take a step back and return when you are ready. You don't have to learn the whole deck right away; you can pull one card and sit with it until you feel ready to move on. Some people select only one card and meditate on it and learn everything they can from it for an entire month. This can take a very long time but if you are serious about using Tarot for deeper insight, it's a practice that is highly recommended. Remember that you can do this as you practice daily.

For now, any symbolism and representation that you find in each card are completely fine. Lay out all the cards and with a birds-eye-view take note of any patterns that emerge. Keep a journal of themes that the cards share and feelings that they give you. Refer to your journal throughout your learning to build upon your relationship with them. The interpretations of each card are only activated when you are interacting with them. When you have a need for the indications, you will be ready to find them and use them. Use this time you are spending bonding with your Tarot cards to develop your own opinions about them. The deck you chose essentially becomes an extension of your voice. Be honest with anyone that might approach you for a reading early on. Let me know that you can do it for fun but that they shouldn't take anything that comes across seriously as you are just learning. Remember, these meanings are hypothetical and not necessarily prophetic. You and the people you may do readings for are safe from harm.

Shuffling

Learn to Shuffle your Tarot deck. Unless it's very small, shuffling a deck can be difficult. This is because the cards are larger and thicker. There are many ways to shuffle a deck successfully- just keep in mind that if you are spreading them out and circulating them repeatedly that you do so on a clean surface where they will not be damaged. You can attempt to shuffle them like a regular playing card deck, or try shuffling half of them at a time, etc. You can cut them repeatedly, or have your client cut them. The goal is to have the cards be completely randomized while you're contemplating the questions being asked. This is the difference between getting a meaningful reading and not just random cards to interpret.

When you are performing a reading for someone else, consider letting them shuffle the deck so that they can get in tune with their energies. If that's not something you're comfortable with, that's okay! Maybe you can compromise by letting them cut the deck as many times as they want to without ever fully handling your cards. Discover where your boundaries are regarding your cards and demand they be respected.

You can always pick up a spread and reshuffle the deck and re-spread them. If you are not connecting with the person asking the questions, or you are not in a headspace to interpret the cards you'll find that reading the Tarot cards is hard to do. Clear the energy around you and on your cards and begin again. You do not have to pull meaning out of the cards forcefully. This should take exertion on your part as the cards will provide the insight you are looking for just by sight. You can develop intuitive reading quickly through practice!

Decks for Experienced Readers, Collectors, and Tarot Lovers

Tarot de Marseilles

This traditional French medieval style deck is a must-have for any collector who loves history. It is one of the oldest deck designs still in popular circulation; its earliest version may have been produced as early as the year 1500; there is a copy of this deck still in existence that was made in 1650. In the Tarot de Marseilles, illustrations of the Major Arcana cards are somehow cartoonish simplistic and hauntingly beautiful at the same time. The only reason this deck is not ideal for beginners is the design of the numbered suit cards; while they are beautiful and intricate, they often feature geometric designs rather than illustrations and can be difficult for novices to interpret.

Mother peace Tarot

This is one of the most popular and distinctive modern decks around. It was designed in the 1970s to update the classic Tarot imagery to something better suited to new-wave feminist ideals, particularly inspired by the Goddess movement. The cards are round rather than rectangular; their shape symbolizes the moon and feminine energy. This is a wonderful deck for those who crave a diverse, intersectional, feminist update to Tarot imagery and symbolism. The deck even has its own unique spread of eleven cards laid out in a circular shape.

The Hermetic Tarot

Another great deck for history lovers and those with a special interest in the esoteric side of Tarot. This deck features a great deal of symbolism from the Secret or Hermetic Order of the Golden Dawn, an occultist group that was popular in Europe at the turn of the twentieth century and still survives to this day (though it boasts lesser numbers currently). While the current Golden Dawn movement may have some unfortunate connections to fascist and racist ideologies, the Hermetic order was primarily concerned with the preservation of ancient alchemical, cabalistic, and arcane knowledge; current leaders of the Hermetic Order claim no connection or alignment whatsoever with the modern Golden Dawn movement. This deck is a wonderful tool to further your study of individual card meanings, as the images feature clues to elemental, astrological, Kabbalistic, numerical, and geomantic connections for many cards. The entire deck is drawn in only black and white, with highly detailed illustrations; you'll want to stare at these spreads for hours.

Aquarian Tarot

This deck is breathtakingly beautiful, featuring art deco and art nouveau inspired illustrations and a modern color scheme. The symbolism is a bit more complex than a standard deck, and this isn't ideal for a novice cartomancer, but for a reader who has some experience with a traditional deck, it will be easy to transition into this style.

Shadowscapes Tarot

This is a gorgeous deck, with finely detailed, ethereal illustrations. In fact, the beautiful imagery is the only reason this deck might not work for beginners--it can be a distraction, and furthermore, some of it is quite abstract. This is a great deck for anyone who loves fantasy, Norse mythology, and faeries.

The Wild Unknown Tarot

This beautiful deck is gaining a large modern following. It may not be best for novices, as many of the illustrations are minimalist, featuring nature and animals rather than human characters, but the artist's interpretations of card meanings are profound and inspiring.

Starchild Tarot

A perfect deck for the modern-minded wiccan, this deck uses a gorgeous pastel, new-age color scheme, and photo-collage art to create some truly breathtaking imagery. This deck draws heavily on cosmic spirituality, sacred geometry, metaphysical healing philosophies and ancient mystery schools for symbolism.

Fountain Tarot

Another wonderful modern deck, the Fountain Tarot features original oil paintings by Jonathan Saiz that beautifully capture the concepts of Tarot, updating them for the internet age while retaining a sense of mystery and appreciation for its historical legacy. It's a must-have for modern metaphysical practitioners, energy healers, and contemporary art lovers, too.

Visconti-Sforza Deck

This deck is about as old as the Tarot de Marseilles design, and another wonderful deck for history lovers, with illustrations drawn in more of a medieval style, barely hinting at the dawning of the Renaissance. The original Visconti deck is missing four cards--the Tower, the Devil, the Three of Swords and the Knight of Coins--so for modern prints, these four cards have been recreated in a similar style to the rest of the deck. Many of the original cards survive to this day, in museums and private collections; they were often created using precious materials, such as gold leaf for the card's borders, and show us not only that Tarot was valued by the wealthy and powerful, but also provide us a glimpse into the daily life and value structure of the Italian nobility of the 15th century through its detailed imagery.

Caring for your cards

However, you acquire your deck (or decks), you'll want to store them in a silk cloth or bag, in a cool, dry place. Ideally, you'll want to store them out of direct sunlight, but also avoid storing them in perpetual darkness (basements, dark corners, etc.). If you believe in metaphysical power, then be sure to protect your cards from negative energies, either by storing with a crystal that can combat negativity, keeping the deck within a protection grid or by regularly cleansing the cards.

In order to bond the cards of the deck to your personal spirit, see to it that nobody touches the cards except yourself--even those people whose questions prompt your readings. For this reason, it might be wise to purchase another deck for practice after receiving your first as a gift; that way, you can work with another novice to familiarize yourself with card readings.

Some cartomancers believe that Tarot decks, even when wrapped in silk and out of use, possess the metaphysical energy needed to weaken or even open portals between realms easily; for this reason, some warn that Tarot cards should not be used or even touched during pregnancy, or while a woman is menstruating, and that decks should also be avoided on All Hallow's Eve, on nights with no moon, and any evening after ten o'clock at night, if the reader wishes to avoid communion with any negative energies or malicious spirits.

How to cleanse your cards

Especially after practice or heavy use, you'll want to make sure that you cleanse your decks to remove any negative energy and prevent muddled clarity in the messages you receive from the cards. If you aren't using your Tarot decks frequently, you'll still want to put them through a routine cleanse about once a month; get into the habit of cleansing every new moon, or every full moon if you prefer to use moonlight for cleansing.

To cleanse with moonlight, spread your cards out beneath the light of a full moon and give them time to soak up those moonbeams--at least an hour per card--before wrapping them in silk again. Another popular cleansing method is smudging, which is a ritual cleansing with smoke. This can be done by burning smudge sticks made of bundled sage leaves, rosemary, or any other dried herb with a scent that you particularly enjoy. Run the cards over the smoke, being sure to separate them so that the smoke can reach every single card, on all surfaces.

Alternatively, some cartomancers prefer to slip their decks into plastic bags or airtight containers before burying the sealed deck in salt (ideally, sea salt or rock salt, but table salt will also work in a pinch), making sure the deck is entirely submerged, and remains buried for several days before being used again. This method takes longer, as the salt will slowly draw negative and stagnant energies from the deck as it would draw moisture from a piece of preserved meat. Be sure to keep the cards protected in an airtight container, as salt and moisture may damage the cards over time.

Awakening your intuition

One of the first steps towards enhancing your intuitive powers is to learn how to recognize them. Many of us make the mistake of thinking that intuition happens in the head or mind, as part of a thought process; that is intellect, not intuition. Intuition happens within the body and subconscious. It often displays itself as strong emotions or physical sensations. An inexplicable sense of optimism, a melancholy mood, or a sudden sharp pain in the gut--these experiences can all be interpreted as intuitive messages. Meditation and mindfulness practices are excellent tools to heighten your awareness of intuitive experiences and can help to transform you into an astute and insightful card reader, as well as helping you to become the best possible version of yourself in other walks of life.

Lots of people are imbued with many more intuitive gifts than they give themselves credit for, especially since modern life and technologies often encourage us to disconnect from and deny our gut instincts, suppressing physical manifestations of emotion. This being the case, it is usually a good idea for a novice cartomancer to spend some time reflecting upon the imagery in their first deck before they begin a formal study of Tarot. Go through each card in the deck; examine the illustrations; maybe even grip each card with both hands, creating an energetic channel, close your eyes, and breathe. How does the card make you feel? What messages can you divine from it without external guidance? Different decks have different energetic vibes, so while this will speak to the most commonly accepted interpretations of popular decks, you may find that your cards depict the mysteries of life in a different light, or capture them from a different angle. The colors and shapes used in card illustrations will impact you on a visceral level, and these initial impressions will resonate even more strongly with a reader who gets to know their deck without any preconceived notions or expectations.

Many card practitioners find that they benefit from ritual practices to deepen their connection to their favorite deck, leading to more accurate and insightful readings. You might incorporate your deck into a daily, weekly, or monthly meditation practice, holding the entire deck or just a single selected card as you meditate on its imagery and divine meaning. You might also adopt the practice of sleeping with your deck underneath your pillow (wrapped in silk for protection, of course!) to connect your dreaming, subconscious mind to the cards.

Dream journaling can be extraordinarily helpful in enhancing your awareness of your intuitive mind; it can also aid the novice cartomancer to get into the practice of interpreting imagery and symbolism in abstract sequence. Spending time in nature, relaxing, and regular sleep cycles are immensely important for divination; without a healthy, well-rested mind, even the most experienced card-reader is liable to misunderstand the messages of the divine and their own subconscious.

Sense isolation can be a useful practice for recognizing and honing your sixth sense. Sensory deprivation chambers can provide this experience for a cost, but you needn't shell out any cash to experiment with this practice. Try using makeshift blindfolds, earplugs or nose plugs, or keeping your hands bundled in oven mitts to learn how acute your senses can grow when one or more of the others are diminished. This can help you to recognize where your sensational feelings are coming from, and root out those that have no rational or obvious explanation.

For those who struggle to quiet the mind during meditation, repetitive actions or tasks may be able to provide a similar transcendent experience. This could be running, practicing the performance of one particular song on the guitar or piano and striving for perfection, chopping vegetables to prep meals for the week, doodling, juggling, dancing, or creating origami sculptures. These repetitive motions can lead you into a sort of self-induced hypnosis.

The Effect of Numerology on Your Life

You have taken the journey of finding out how Numerology and specific numbers impact you as a person. Numerology doesn't just affect you, though, it also affects the things in your life as well. It has an influence on what paths or choices you may make in regard to life, career, and love.

Influence on Life Path

Your life path is the essence of your life. Every challenge, opportunity, and lesson during the span of your life is related to the Numerology behind the life path number. If you want to know where your life is essentially going to go and what you are going to face, your reading with your life path number can tell you.

Influence on Your Personality

Your personality is the DNA of who you are. The personality number that Numerology uncovers about us it the core of who we are as a person. Every action we take, every situation we face, and how we handle it, all aspects of our personality. Numerology readings regarding your personality show you exactly who you are as a person, and no matter how we try to fight it, our personality is something we were born with and it is impossible to deny it.

Influence on Career

Choosing a career path is influenced directly and indirectly by our Numerology. We are people who are composed of so many different traits that once our reading is complete, it can show us where we were naturally born to rule. Think of it in terms of those tests that we were all made to take in high school. The ones that supposedly shows you what profession you are supposedly made for. Your Numerology numbers do something like this but consider your total person, not just who you are on the surface.

Influence on Our Interests

Because we are all composed of different traits, we are naturally made to enjoy certain things while detesting others. This works the same vice versa. When we know who we are and who we are meant to be based on our numerological makeup, it is easier to accept and explain the things that other people may find abnormal in our lives.

Influence on Attitude

The first thing that people tend to notice about another person is their attitude. There is a good chance that the way you come across to other people can be explained in greater detail based on your numerology reading. We are all composed of different numbers and paths, which can have a severe influence on our attitudes. Someone may interpret an attitude that is strong-willed as being defiant when in reality, you are simply focused on your goals.

Influence on Relationships and Compatibility

Besides the incompatibility that you learned with the Zodiac, there are also incompatibilities that occur with the Numerology numbers as well. There are a lot of things that are required to make a relationship with someone else work, and sometimes what happens is that we are simply just not compatible. Personalities can clash just like the courses we want to take with our lives can clash. It would not be any one person's fault if the incompatibility were naturally destined to happen due to the incompatibility of Numerology readings.

Influence on Location

It is proven that every city and state have their own numerological vibration, which means that if you have ever felt out of place somewhere, chances are you were not compatible with the numbers. Before changing your scenery, it might be worth talking to an expert numerologist to find out about the vibrations of the place you are thinking of moving. Much like relationships, it is not your fault for feeling averse to a place. You are just not numerically wired to belong there.

Influence on a Home

Just like the vibrations, a location can possess, the same can apply to your new address. Your home or apartment can have its own numerical vibrations, and if you are not compatible with it, you may never feel at home. It might be worth your time to get a Numerology reading for your potential home just to make sure that you are compatibly going to be comfortable.

Influence on Pets

Your pet is a person too, so in the same way that you have numerical vibes, so does your pet. The name you choose can have a huge influence on their personality, thanks to the vibrations from the name and the astrological values predestined for them. You can find out your pet's reading by using the same Numerology calculations done on your own name.

Influence on Business Ventures

The name of your business can be converted into a numerological reading as well. Just like you and your pet, the path that your business name falls under will be an indicator of the success or wealth it may attain. If you and your business's life path numbers are compatible, it can prove to be extremely prosperous for you.

How to Read Astrological Chart

Simply put, an astrological chart is the projection of the sky on the Earth's plane. Of course, that the Earth is not a plane, but this is not the question here because we approximate the image of the sky onto ourselves as if we were the center of the world. And if we "catch" the image of the sky at the same moment we were born, then we have the "natal chart". The same is applicable for the charts of the animals, buildings, companies, business deals, events like weddings, receptions and anything you can think of. These are all natal charts and they all describe the potential for good and bad events, which can happen further on, depending on some other factors.

The main one of those "other factors" are planetary transits. They are the most important fact in western astrology; while the Vedic school favors divisional charts, which is an arrangement of the planets and sensitive points in the chart calculated through some geometrical and mathematical rules. To avoid confusion, you should know that Vedic or sidereal astrology deals with sidereal positions of the planets in the sky, while western astrology deals with tropical positions or the projection of planets on the Earth's plane. In simple words, for example, the first day of spring is March 21st. We know this because day and night are equal and this is called the spring equinox. The Sun enters into the sign of Aries and the new cycle begins. You know that this is the equinox; you know that spring is here, but if you go to the observatory and look at the Sun through a telescope, you will see that Sun is still in the constellation of Pisces. This "effect" is happening due to the precession of the equinoxes; however, for now this concept is beyond the basics of astrology.

The most important thing you have to know is that both astrological schools are right, they have their precise prediction systems, which differ, but they both work. The quality of the prediction depends on the quality of chosen astrologer, not the school which is selected for the reading.

Let's get back to planetary transits. This is the term which describes the image of the current or upcoming planetary arrangement in the sky. If you, for instance, overlap the transit chart over your natal chart, you will be able to see the areas where you are challenged, blessed, where can you grow, in what to invest, from what or who to beware and so on. Sometimes the warning signs are extremely obvious if you know how to read those two sets of planetary arrangements together.

The same applies to your partner's charts, whether they can show the development and the outcome of love, business or any other relationship. All you need to do is to overlap those two charts and to read mutual aspects that the planets make.

GENERAL ASTROLOGY RULES

First, you have to know the meaning of each planet and the meaning of each astrological sign. Then you have to know the basic aspects planets make together.

The chart in the western astrology style is presented as a circle divided into 12 parts, each one representing astrological houses. The most important points are the Ascendant – Descendant (Asc-Dsc) line, which is a horizontal line in the chart and the Medium Coeli – Imum Coeli (MC-IC) line, which is showing the highest and the lowest points of your chart. Those are four of the most important points you have to pay attention to. Ascendant is your rising sign, describing just you. Descendant is how you deal with your love, business or any other partner and how you project yourself into the world. IC is your origin, while MC is your highest accomplishment.

A circle with the cross in it, it is so simple, and the whole life in it.

The image of your natal chart will look like this circle, but with the snapshot of the planetary arrangements at the moment you were born. This snapshot holds the potentials which will develop to a greater or a lesser degree, depending on upcoming planetary transits during your life. Whether those potentials and life's events are good or bad, you will know by reading the aspects the planets make.

PLANETARY ASPECTS

Whenever celestial body moves through the heavens, it creates a motion, frequency, and sound. Any relation between celestial bodies creates a mutual aspect and all together they make the music of the spheres. However, the aspects considered as the most important in astrology are conjunction, sextile, square, and trine and opposition.

Conjunction happens when the two planets are placed close to each other so their influences are mixed. If there are three or more planets involved, then this is called stellium. Are the planets forming conjunction or stellium? This depends on their orbs of influences. Bigger bodies have greater orbs and for the Sun, Moon, Jupiter, and Saturn, this can extend to 15 degrees because they are big planets with great strength. Also, depending on the planets involved, conjunction can be considered as good or bad.

Sextile is formed between planets when they form the 60-degree angle between them looking from the center point of an astrological circle or a chart. Generally speaking, this is a good aspect and suggests that planets are active and can result in a positive outcome.

Square happens when two planets form a 90-degree angle in the chart and squares are often perceived as bad aspects because they can bring very challenging situations in our lives. But, at the same time, they force us to change and to grow in attempts to overcome or resolve our problems.

Trine is seen as the exceptionally auspicious aspect and it happens when two planets form a 120-degree angle between them. Although beneficial, trines can sometimes produce a lazy attitude, so there is really nothing just black and white going on in the sky.

An opposition is another "bad" aspect because two celestial bodies are forming 180-degrees angle and they are directly opposing each other. This is challenging too, causing open war between opposite sides, frictional, but at the same time, it provokes the search for a better option or solution.

ZODIAC SIGNS AND HOUSES

Now that we have learned the general meaning of planets and aspects in the chart, we should take the closer look at the astrological signs and houses. As you already know, the horoscope is divided into four sectors (remember the cross in the circle?) and twelve "houses" or main areas of life. In Vedic astrology, those houses are equal. Each one extends to 30 degrees. However, in the western school, this is not the case, because the geometry of the point on Earth where you were born, for instance, is calculated through various systems. This is something which is beyond the basics, but you should know that today, Placidus house system is mostly used and it shows the best results, except in the case that person was born in the areas of polar circles.

The main rule of astrology is that each Zodiac sign has the meaning of the same house. Translated, this rule can be easily explained looking at the signs. Aries is the first sign in the Zodiac belt, so the first house of any horoscope has the general meaning of the sign of Aries; the second house has the meaning of Taurus and so on until we reach to the Pisces or twelfth house.

For instance, you can be born in the sign of Gemini and this means that you were born on the 21st of May until 20th of June. However, if you were born, let's say, during the afternoon hours, your rising sign or your Ascendant could be placed in the sign of Scorpio. This is just an example; we will have to know the exact time to see where the Ascendant is placed.

Now, you have your natal Sun in Gemini, but your rising sign is Scorpio. This means that your first house is placed in the sign of Scorpio, but at the same time, this means that you will have all the traits of Aries (first house) through the characteristics of Scorpio. In this case, also, the Sun is placed in Gemini, but in the eighth house of the horoscope, which again carries the symbolism of the sign of Scorpio. Add to this mix the position of your natal Moon and you will have the basic understanding of your character and appearance.

It can sound a bit complicated for an absolute beginner, but in time and with the little practice, you will start using those "double" systems, not even thinking about them while applying the rules.

True Purpose of the Zodiac Sign in Life

The signs of the Zodiac can give us incredible experiences in our everyday lives, just as the numerous gifts and uncommon characteristics we have. You can find a lot of important data about yourself by finding out about your Zodiac sign. In this article, we'll disclose to you how you can utilize the data gave by your sign so as to improve your life.

The term zodiac indicates a yearly cycle of twelve stations along the way of the sun. Astrologists utilize galactic perceptions of the developments in the night sky for divinatory purposes. Each star sign has a different significance, and your astrological chart is comprised of the sun signs and their traits, and the position of the planets in the place of your exceptional chart.

Your Sun Sign could be either sign since the date changes marginally from year to year. If you were conceived inside 2 days of the sign change dates, you might need to counsel an astrologer to discover your actual Sun Sign.

Every zodiac sign mirrors a different side of your own encounters and character, despite the fact that some of them are more underlined than others. In view of the date of birth, a spot of birth and time of birth, astrologer can give you an extremely exact representation of your character, just as reveal to you numerous things about your past and future, gifts and difficulties. Individuals from all societies accept that astrology is one of the absolute best devices that there is for understanding a person's latent capacity, qualities, and shortcomings.

Every one of the Zodiac signs is additionally designated into components. How these components identify with each other is particularly significant when utilizing astrology to decide an adoration coordinate. Astrologists accept that every individual is good or incongruent with others dependent on their introduction to the world dates. To characterize this similarity, your component bunch is contrasted with the other component bunches in the zodiac chart.

Those brought into the world under the Zodiac signs Aries, Leo, or Sagittarius have a place with the component of fire which speaks to excitement and solid will. The earth component incorporates Taurus, Virgo, and Capricorn, which speaks to useful and material concerns.

Aquarius, Gemini, Libra, and emanates from the air part and address ratiocination. The water component incorporates Cancer, Scorpio and Pieces and speaks to sentiments, feelings, and sympathy.

Your Zodiac sign can give data that can assist you with having a more joyful existence by drawing out into the open your qualities and shortcomings. If your sign makes you inclined to envy, you can deal with being additionally trusting.

If you're destined to be a pioneer, you can concentrate on excelling expertly. Numerous individuals start their day by counseling their horoscope to perceive what the day will bring. That demonstrates that the intensity of the Zodiac is still particularly alive.

The Most Effective Method to Understand Your Horoscope

As you likely know, a horoscope is a guide of the sky at the time you were conceived. Your horoscope gives the astrologer what indications your planets are in. It uncovers every one of your propensities, dispositions, dissatisfactions, gifts, and life reasons. Also, significantly more!

Be that as it may, you don't have to make sense of this to discover what your Mars implies. Simply ask an astrologer.

Suppose I took a glance at your horoscope and discovered that your Mars is in the sign of Cancer. Here's a simple method to get this:

Mars = enthusiasm and want to make a move

Cancer = a sign that identifies with nourishment, heating, bread, land, home, family, stomach, mothering and supporting

Presently, put a portion of these implications together with Mars, and you will think of a few things you truly have the energy for. At that point, you basically solicit "Which one of these things, that identify with my energy, do I feel the most grounded about?"

You may state that you have solid energy for cabinetmaking, which identifies with building homes. Or on the other hand you could have solid energy for land or running a bread shop. Regardless, your Mars in Cancer shows that your enthusiasm is firmly related to the everyday issues that identify with that sign.

Here's another model:

Your Mercury is in Aquarius. Mercury = thinking and correspondences.

Aquarius = identifies with cutting edge innovation, PCs, airship, space travel, astrology, designing, melodic structure, and kinships.

If you have your Mercury in Aquarius, you will consistently move toward data from a specialized or propelled level of awareness. The Aquarian signs bestow a sharp capacity to look past the undeniable and search out radical types of articulation. A portion of our most noteworthy pioneers, designers, and authors had Mercury in Aquarius.

If your Mercury is in Aquarius, the entirety of this will sound good to you.

Don't you discover it very astounding that the sky can uncover such a lot of data about you?

We should take one more model.

Your Venus is in Leo. Venus = gratefulness, fascination, what you like. Leo = sign of expressions of the human experience, imagination in all structures, love, sentiment, sports, theater, painting music, the heart, and kids.

If your Venus is in Leo, you are genuinely sentimental. You love the round of adoration, exploring every available opportunity, and conveying everything that needs to be conveyed imaginatively. You have a caring heart and you need to give that feeling to other people. At the point when you join the planets with the signs, think about the planet as want and the sign as a disposition. At that point, your horoscope will start to sound good to you.

Clearly, your horoscope is definitely more mind-boggling than this, yet I have indicated you in an exceptionally basic manner how the planets and signs uncover what your identity is.

Astrological Terminologies and Their Meaning

If you are new to astrology, then it is fundamental to get familiar with a portion of the essential terms that are utilized in astrology. This would assist you with understanding and pursue your introduction to the world chart. Each term decides some importance. Here are the terms and what it signifies given in a point by point way. The air horoscope image is the signs of Gemini, Libra, and Aquarius. Ascendant is the term signifying the rising sign. This is the horoscope image on the cusp of the principal place of the birth chart. Relative is the cusp of the seventh house in the birth chart. The horoscope image of Taurus, Virgo, and Capricorn are called Earth signs. Components, which are outstanding to all and it is said to be Fire, Earth, Air, and Water.

Aries, Capricorn, Cancer, and Libra, symbols are referred to as 'cardinal signs'. The horoscope image of Cancer, Scorpio, and Pisces are water signs. Aries, Sagittarius, and Leo symbols are referred to as 'fire signs.' Gemini, Virgo, Sagittarius, and Pisces symbols are referred to as 'variable signs.' The horoscope image of Taurus, Leo, Scorpio, and Aquarius are said to be a fixed horoscope image. Cancer, Capricorn, Pisces, Scorpio, Taurus, and Virgo are referred to as 'feminine signs.' The other Zodiac signs are referred to as a 'masculine horoscope image.'

Every one of these signs has its own highlights. In the horoscope, a few divisions are seen; it includes twelve in number. The paradise is separated into 12. These are called the houses and each house is managed by specific planets which are called planetary rulers. Each house likewise signifies some specific everyday issues. What is referred to as the luminaries are the Sun and the Moon? A cusp of a sign is said to be the degree when one sign closures and different starts.

The cusp of the principal, fourth, seventh, and tenth houses are said to be the quadrants. Zodiac is a hover of 360 degrees. The 360 degrees variant of Birth chart is partitioned into 12 equivalent divisions of 30 degrees each. You can see this plainly in any birth chart. It is difficult for a non-specialist to comprehend these terms. An astrological individual has total information on what these terms allude to. Nowadays, CDs are accessible in the market which gives data about these astrological sciences. Indeed, even online channels assume a significant job as it gives a wide range of astrological data at the fingertips. However, the opportune individual must be counseled who might be the best source to control you altogether.

Expression Number

One

An individual with the number one is often very skilled in the world of business. They have a natural tact for entrepreneurship and often have grand ideas for new businesses they want to start. This individual will probably have many successful (and a few failed) businesses in their lifetime. They greatly enjoy being their own boss and many are known to find ways to live from home. Individuals with this number can also be very hypercritical of themselves or others. This can help create a quality business or organization, but if the individual does not keep this trait in check, they can push away those around them. People may find them overly judgmental or too harsh of a critic. Paying attention to this trait and learning to reign in their opinion will help maintain good, comfortable relationships with coworkers.

Two

Individuals with this number put a lot of weight on social prowess. They tend to be very skilled in the world of manners and elegance. These individuals usually have very high social skills and are very talented at marketing themselves and others. These people usually make brilliant marketing professionals and excel in the world of advertising. The hardest pill for this person to swallow is the fact that not everyone is going to like or get along with them. These individuals want to be friends with everyone and often cannot handle it when someone either clearly or secretly dislikes them. It would be beneficial for this person to remember that sometimes there is nothing you can do to make someone like you. These individuals may need to try and let it go if someone simply isn't getting along with them.

Three

Individuals with this number usually have increased skill in communication with others. Because of this, they tend to make brilliant writers, actors, and artists. They can often communicate feelings and emotions in a beautiful and elegant way that can be understood across a wide array of platforms and media. These individuals are often found in careers that involve some sort of self-expression because that is what they love to do. The flaw often found in these individuals is that they may have difficulty concentrating their thoughts into clear and concise information. They tend to go off on tangents and ramble for long periods. An individual with this number usually has to do a lot of editing to their writing and can often end up with mass amounts of cut material that has almost nothing to do with the end product. These individuals would benefit from thinking more clearly about what they are going to include in their projects and taking a moment to consider more deeply if it connects properly to what they are trying to convey.

Four

Individuals with this number often have skills in management and organization. They are often fair and impartial leaders who thrive in structure. These individuals are known for being reliable and consistent in their lives. These individuals tend to reject the unconventional and like to live in stable, structured environments. These people tend to find themselves in nine to five jobs where they have some sort of managerial status. Risk takers, these individuals are not. They are not likely to take jobs for companies that are up and coming or that appear to be rapidly growing or shrinking; they prefer to find employment within a well-established company. These individuals are faithful and loyal to those close to them. The biggest negative to this person is their tendency to focus too hard on the things that are outside their grasp. They tend to get caught up on the barriers that block them from things that they want and would benefit from focusing more on the things that are within their capabilities.

Five

These individuals are quite the separation from their neighbor, number four. These people live for adventure and love excitement. They practically ooze curiosity and are known to throw themselves into every new mini obsession they develop. They despise structured and organized careers and would rip their hair out in a typical nine to five job. These individuals crave freedom and constant stimulation. These individuals' greatest talents are their ability to pick up random unusual skills seemingly out of the blue. By working hard, these individuals can learn how to do anything from fixing a car to juggling. Because of their charismatic and energetic demeanor (and their love of travel), these individuals often have a large group of friends from very different cultural and geographic backgrounds. Fives, unfortunately, tend to have a higher chance of becoming addicted to things like alcohol, drugs, and even sex. Their need to experience new and interesting things can often have consequences that they either don't notice or outright ignore at that moment.

Six

Individuals with this number are often very committed to speaking up for the underdog. They usually are the pushers of political movements and have a talent of getting others to agree with them purely through their conviction. These individuals are often known to be extremely passionate about the things that they are involved in. They are usually representatives or heads of nonprofits. From time to time, these individuals tend to put others before themselves too much. That is to say – they tend to push their needs and skills to the side to accommodate those which they believe to need help more. It would be beneficial to these individuals to remember that they are important as well and should focus more time and energy towards themselves.

Seven

These individuals are often very analytical and usually quite skilled at finding answers to complex questions. They usually make brilliant scientists or engineers. These people are usually very skilled at mathematics and science because they have a rare ability to see every detail and remember every last part of a process. These individuals are known for having a strong urge to seek the truth in everyday life. They are constantly asking questions about why things happen and are usually inclined to find the answer no matter what. These individuals are very determined to understand the world around them and often find that if they have not found the answers they seek, by a certain age, they may sink into a difficult depression. These individuals would benefit from remembering that some things in life are not meant to be understood.

Eight

Individuals with this number have only one goal in life: to win. These individuals are extremely competitive in almost everything that they do. They want to be number one in everything and are willing to fight hard for it. These are the type of people to turn everything into a competition, but they are also the type to work the absolute hardest for something they want. The greatest skill of this individual is their ability to focus on an end goal and push themselves past their current fatigue to reach that goal. These individuals care very little about their own comfort in a given situation. These individuals sometimes tend to work a little too hard and should remind themselves that it is often more important to take a break than to finish something.

Nine

Individuals with this number are often described as being philanthropic and a humanitarian. They are often very passionate about the activities they are involved in. These individuals are very powerful in their belief in themselves. These people often believe so strongly that they can accomplish anything that they usually do. It is these individuals' pure willpower that sets them apart from the crowd. They are often their own champions and have no trouble cheering themselves on their whole life. With this strong high can sometimes mean a strong low as well. This means that while these individuals believe very strongly that they can do anything, if they are not able to do something important to them, they may fall into a deep depressive state.

Life Paths

Life path number

This number is the negotiator and the arbitrator of any cause and effect that occurs in your life. This number determines you experiences in the world and can also be described as the way by which you project yourself in the universal currents. You will be able to decide how you can affect the operations of your life. This number carries both positive and negative attributes since no human being can carry only positive vibes.

Your life path is always permanent since it is dependent on the date of birth. Your name can always be changed but this does not change the effect of the life path number. You will need to conform to the rules set by your life path number but will always go about it in a different way.

Life path one

If your life path is the number one, you have numerous positive qualities of which leadership, self – motivation and assertiveness are a few. You are also an energetic person and always look for new projects to take on. You have a unique sense of life and are always determined to reach newer heights. You are someone who is ambitious and is always curious to learn more! While you have these many positives, there are certain negatives too! You are someone who is egocentric or passive – aggressive and may lack in self – esteem. You are arrogant and are uncooperative and can often be perceived as a bully!

Life path two

As a person with a life path number two, you will find yourself with the qualities of being sensitive, diplomatic, organized and even intuitive. You are someone who is friendly and is often at harmony that leaves you as a great mediator. You are a person who is compassionate and has the tact to deal with matters. You are someone who is loyal and intuitive. As a two, you may be shy, careless and sometimes timid. You may find yourself self – centered and will find it extremely difficult to let go of certain emotional attachments that will leave you overly sentimental. You are someone who can never work on a team and are sometimes dogmatic.

Life path three

If you are a person who has the number three, you will be charming and charismatic. When you enter a room, you will be able to create an energetic vibe that helps in drawing the crowd towards you. You are a person who is artistic, sensual, witty and intelligent. Since you have the charm, you have the confidence that helps you in communicating with the people around you. There are a few negatives to having this number as well. You are someone who is scattered and can be bored easily. You can never be trusted since your attention flits by the second who is when you leave thing s undone and expect people to clean up after you. You are someone who is insecure and is hard to understand at times.

Life path four

If you are a person with the life path four will always be reliable and is down – to – earth. You are someone who always works hard and is loyal and practical. You will be family oriented and will be systematic and methodical. You will ensure that you are a loyal person with a practical approach to life that will leave you focused. You will be someone who is arrogant and biased. Since you have a practical approach you would never choose to take another person's idea leaving you to react in ways that may sometimes be cruel and abusive. You are a person who is highly opinionated and will ensure that he has his way. You will always try your best to defend what it is that you have said or done.

Life path five

If you are someone who has the life path number five, you will be a charming person who is entertaining and is sensual. You will love freedom and are curious about understanding your thoughts. You are someone who is adventurous and is always looking at undertaking activities that are thrilling and enticing. But, there are certain negative aspects as well. You will be an irresponsible person and will find yourself over indulging in activities that will leave you unfaithful and restless. You will find yourself frustrated with life and will always be looking for something more! You may be addictive since you will tend to love activities that excite you and drive you wild!

Life Path six

If you are someone who has the life path six, you will find yourself being responsible and gentle. You will be someone who is kind, romantic and is compassionate. The best part about you is that you are someone who is very loyal and will always work towards servicing people in your community. You are someone who always works towards nurturing people and will ensure that you protect the people you love most. You are a perfectionist and a little nosy when it comes to work since you want everything to be the way you had imagined it! You are someone who is moody and is a busybody who tries to control any given situation. You will also be someone who is somewhat smothering due to your habit to nurture and protect people.

Life path seven

As a person who has the life path seven, you will find yourself very intelligent and philosophical. You are someone who is studious and is always seeking the truth. You are a rational person and are always dignified and efficient. You are somewhat fearful and distant and try to stay aloof on most occasions and can be perceived as a snob. You are reliable but never trust another person since you do not place your faith on anybody else. You are sometimes discriminative and argumentative leaving you to close yourself off emotionally.

Life path eight

As a person with a life path number eight, you will be tenacious, focused powerful. You are someone who can always walk the talk and is a born leader. Organizing any meeting or succeeding at anything is simple for you since you are adaptable and find it easy to assume authority which will leave you in charge of the happenings in your surroundings. You are a generous person and sometimes are also a spendthrift. Since you are authoritative, you tend to become controlling and power hungry and will be easily frustrated when things do not go your way. You are stubborn and will never tolerate it when someone crosses you.

Life path nine

As a person who has the life path nine, you will find yourself to be artistic, intuitive, creative and imaginative. You will be a person who can be approached by anybody since you are easy going and exude a sense of friendliness. You are someone who is oriented towards a future and re always thorough with what you do. As a person who is caring and loving and compassionate, you find romance with ease and are quite gentle with your partner. You are someone who needs to be dependent on someone else and may sometimes lack self – confidence. You will probably begin to take on another person's problems since you are too helpful which will lead people around you to take you for a ride. You are a dreamer and may sometimes limit yourself from achieving your full potential. You sometimes procrastinate since you cannot get yourself to finish things on time.

Life path eleven

As a person with the life path eleven, you will be approachable and friendly which will leave people with a sense of calm and they will come to you like you are a plant with nectar in it and they are the bees! You are imaginative, intuitive and are hypnotic. Your charm is what brings you together with different kinds of people that feed your need for different interests. You have a superiority complex that leaves you disrespectful at times which may make you antisocial. You are someone who can be perceived to be blunt as well.

Life path twenty two

As a person with a life path numbers as twenty-two, you will find yourself charming and idealistic. You are someone who is intelligent beyond his years and will be someone who is innovative and creative. You work towards creating mass awareness and always work towards ensuring that you achieve your dream. You are tireless and will always ensure that you produce results as soon as you can. You may sometimes have the feeling of being invulnerable. You are someone who may be unfair and is selfish and could never be satiated no matter what goal you have achieved.

Life Path Cycles

Your life path is built on three cycles called the sub – cycles each of which have their very own tone of vibration. These cycles are what form the backdrop against how the vibrations in a year pan out for you. You will also be able to understand what challenges you may find yourself presented with and how you should meet and overcome those challenges. The sub paths or the life path cycles are based on the numeric values of the three components of your life path that are the birthday, month and year!

You will always have to understand how and when your life path will change. Your life path cycles all run in a sequence. They all gave a very deep connection with two cycles in astrology called the Return of the Progressed Moon and Saturn Return.

1. The formative cycle starts at the year of birth and ends at the beginning of the next cycle that is called the cycle of productivity.

2. The productive cycle begins during your first personal year and is closest to your 28th birthday. In most cases, the first personal year may fall before the 28th birthday that would imply that the beginning of the cycle is never felt until your 28th birthday. There are certain events that may correspond to the nature of the next cycle that will always be set into motion in the period of transition.

3.   The harvest cycle always begins on the first personal year that is closest to your 57th birthday. In most cases, the first personal year may fall before the 57th birthday, which would imply that the beginning of the cycle is never felt until your 57th birthday. There are certain events that may correspond to the nature of the next cycle that will always be set into motion in the period of transition. This number is called the maturity number since this is the point at which there will be changes in your life!

The sub paths are extremely important since they leave you with opportunities that help you achieve goals and also help you enjoy your personal happiness when you operate in your positive modes. When you start operating on your negative modes, you will learn some important lessons in your life, which will help you, open the positive aspects of your life. When these cycles change, people tend to mysteriously switch from one career path to the next since they have a different way of living life at the moment. They have certain expectations and find it difficult to live the way they used to. They also change the way they live.

Kundalini

Kundalini Rising – What Is It?

Kundalini Rising (a.k.a. Kundalini Awakening) is based on the idea that all humans contain some sort of energy within the base of their spine called "Kundalini". The idea is that through vigorous meditation and yoga, this energy can be "Awakened" and thus travel up and down the spine through the body. This energy is often represented as a coiled snake at the base of the spine, which matches with its name which roughly translates into "coiled". The results of this awakening are said to cause states of extreme bliss and enlightenment. To reach this period, it is said that the Kundalini needs to pass through several chakra points inside the human body and along the spine. It is believed that once this energy is awakened, it does not ever return to its coiled state but will ebb and flow throughout the lifetime of that individual.

Kundalini in History

The roots of the Kundalini idea trace their way back to Ancient India, in the Indus Valley, Ancient Egypt, and Sumerian civilizations. Most notably we can see this in the Ancient Vedic texts in which numerous Rig-Veda hymns praise a liquid known as "Soma" that many believe to be a metaphor for this energy within us all. Kundalini has strong ties with the ancient god known as Lord Shiva, for Lord Shiva is always seen with a serpent wrapped around his neck which some argue represents Kundalini. Possibly the most notable allegorical record of Kundalini is an ancient Ramayana tale which tells the tale of a noble and his beautiful wife. In this tale, the noble, who goes by the name Rama, and his wife, who goes by the name Sita, are caught in escort with an evil demon called Ravana. Ravana kidnaps Sita, who is meant to encapsulate the ideal woman and perfect femininity, and imprisons her in an island fortress called "Lanka". It is well known within this tale that Lanka is meant to represent a physical human body and Sita is meant to represent the Kundalini energy. Ravana, on the other hand, is meant to represent the five senses and the five organs of action which are believed to lead man towards desire and away from their spirituality. He represents this symbolically with his ten heads. Rama is meant to represent the consciousness, and through powerful expertise, "releases" Sita, a very clear metaphor for the releasing of Kundalini within a human.

Kundalini Yoga

Yoga, in recent years, has come to the forefront of modern physical fitness. With its image as the skinny girl who can do the splits and balance perfectly with her leg over her head, it has become a very popular form of physical workout. While Kundalini Yoga does offer some form of physical exertion, it has a taste of spirituality to go along with it. Kundalini Yoga is often performed with a more worship-like air about it. Often taking place in almost complete silence and rarely in a gym, this workout is definitely different from many others. One of these differences is its vast spiritual history. This yoga is old and has managed to stay with almost the same principles for centuries. This is partially due to the fact that Kundalini does not have any overwhelming strict or suffocating dogmas to steer away practitioners. Kundalini allows itself not to be a strict religion but simply to be a tool one can use to find their inner spirituality. In ancient times, yoga was not confined by the definition of physical activity but, in fact, was considered simply a connection to one's spiritual self through their bodies. They had no goals of physical fitness but rather a connection to the energy they believe lives within us all – and for this connection, they stressed the fact that no buffer was necessary. No prayer or food or special dance – simply to practice and focus. In fact, it is recorded that the first Kundalini sessions consisted of almost entirely no physical activity whatsoever. Disciples simply sat in front of their master and listened to their revelations about spirit. This practice was very common in Ancient Vedic times and was later replicated in religious figures known as Buddha and Jesus. Throughout the years, this method of spirituality evolved until it began to include the physical acting out of the spiritual visions. This then evolved into what we know as yoga today. One of the reasons that this form of spiritual expression is not commonly known or spoken of today is due to its secretiveness throughout history. For thousands of years, the study of Kundalini was kept secret and sacred, known only by an inner group of spiritualists and their students. This was often explained through the idea that the public was not ready or prepared for such incredible knowledge and that the awakening of Kundalini amongst the average folk would cause chaos and destruction. Kundalini would still be mostly lost to western society if not for the teachings of a man known as "Yogi Bahjan". Yogi chose to impart his wisdom upon the youth of the United States due to the uprising of the hippie movement in the late 1960s. He came to America and found hundreds of youth desperately wanting to be closer to their spiritual side and going about it in all the wrong ways through drugs and mysticism. He taught over 8,000 yoga classes. At the beginning of his career, he is also credited with establishing the Healthy, Happy, Holy Organization. Without this man, Kundalini Yoga and subsequent Awakening would never have reached the States.

Kundalini Rising and You

Now that you fully understand the origins of Kundalini and how it has reached us, it is time to learn how you too can awaken the energy within. With the internet today, anyone can find hundreds and hundreds of ways to awaken the energy within them. However, the average person must approach these with caution, as this energy is extremely powerful, and without the learned expertise, over time they may harm themselves or their chakra balances.

Warning: we highly recommend that the reader consults with an expert regarding the awakening of their energy for their life before attempting to do so.

1) The first step to awakening your chakra energy is to practice mindful breathing exercises. To begin, you will want to relax and take several cleansing breaths in and out. You will want to begin to practice a sort of soft abdominal breathing – these are soft, calm breaths within you that eventually bring your abdomen and lungs to an equilibrium of gases.

2) Now, you will want to find with your mind's eye (this is easiest done with your eyes closed) the location of your kidneys. This may sound strange, but you simply have to visualize it in the lower back of your body are your two kidneys. Visualize them and imagine their location.

3) You will want to "massage" the kidneys by releasing several breaths of air that expel all the air from your lungs and the bag within your abdomen.

4) At this point, to help with your breathing, you will want to begin chanting the phrase "Num Mum Yum Pa 'Hum." As you exhale, you will want to focus and try to feel for the vibration of the right Adrenal, the Right Kidney and then the subsequent left Adrenal or Left Kidney.

5) If you are having difficulty feeling the vibration in your kidneys, you can rub your lower back to promote the activity.

6) You will now want to make sure that you are in a comfortable position.

7) You will physically want to lift your arms above your head with your thumbs out. You will want to make sure your shoulders are rotated down and back. Rotating your thumbs back and forth, you should be able to feel the connection of your thumbs to your lungs.

8) You will now want to reach your index finger towards the sky and feel the large intestine connect to the ribcage.

9) You will want to lift your collarbones and feel a responding suspension of the kidneys.

10) Think back with your mind's eye to the airbags and their connection to the kidneys.

11) You will now want to tuck the chin and release a small bit of air from the diaphragm.

12) Inhale deeply, feel the air bags, and make sure that the chin, tongue, palate, and sinuses are stacked neatly with a connection to the spinal cord.

13) Exhale slowly. You should feel the top of your lungs buoy upwards.

14) Inhale again touching the top of the chest and bottom of the abdomen.

15) Exhale and feel the chakra point at the top of the nose.

16) Breathe again, letting the chakra point expand.

17) Feel the vertebrae of your spinal cord lift and extend upwards slightly.

Practicing this meditation system on a regular basis can help guide you to your own Kundalini Awakening.

Now we will describe some of the common side effects and positive as well as negative experiences of those who have awakened their own energy within themselves. Kundalini energy is often described as a sensation of electricity or internal lightning bolts within the person at the sight of the awakening. People are often described to shake or jerk their body parts or limbs. This is usually completely out of the control of the individual who is awakening their energy. You may also feel upon the awakening of this energy a sensation of insects crawling along your spinal cord, along with feelings of either intense heat or intense cold. The individual in question may also feel an intense moment of pleasure that sometimes leads to an orgasmic state. They also may experience sudden and unexplainable mood swings, far beyond normal highs and lows. As a result of this awakening, people often report having much more empathetic bonds with those around them. They have also said that this increased level of empathy results in telepathic or psychic abilities. Aging has been said to slow as a result of the rising of Kundalini as well as the increase in creative ability and charismatic personality traits. These individuals often say that the great mysteries of life are no longer mysteries; they are connected more deeply to all that is and ever was.

An individual in search of the enlightenment that comes with the awakening of Kundalini is strongly urged to consult with professionals and support groups on the matter. Trying to find an experienced Kundalini yoga instructor who has experienced an awakening themselves will greatly help someone who's desire it is to awaken this incredible power. Attempting to awaken this power on your own can result in terrible consequences as well as simply not working at all. Many support groups can be found online, and Kundalini Yoga instructors are common in larger cities. If you have trouble finding one in your local area, many online instructors openly give their knowledge to the public. They can be found on YouTube, Pinterest, and blog sites. Many YouTube videos have been made on the process of awakening the Kundalini as well as how to cope with the aftermath. If you have experienced an awakening or would like to, we would highly recommend searching through these.

Kundalini Yoga Poses

Kundalini yoga poses are also called asanas. Asanas generally apply pressure on your nerves and acupressure points in your body, which reflexes to the brain and body to allow for certain effects. These poses are generally to help with stimulating the organs and glands for better body awareness.

(Sukhasana) Easy Pose

To perform the easy pose, cross feet allowing your ankles to touch, or place both feet flat on the floor. Press your bottom most point of your spine up and keep your back straight.

(Siddhasana) Perfect Pose

Start with sukasana and at the perineum, press into it with the heel on your right foot, the sole of your foot should be resting on the left upper thigh. Place the heel of your left foot over the top of the right foot so that you are pressing upward with your toes tucked between the thigh and calf muscle. Your knees should be resting on the ground with your heels directly above one another. This is the most comfortable asana position and is considered to be the one to promote the most psychic power.

(Padmasana) Lotus Pose

Starting with the easy pose, lift your left foot up and onto the upper part of the thigh on your right leg. Then your left foot should be resting on the upper part of your left thigh. Make sure to keep them near your body as possible. This is a safe posture that is simpler than it sounds, and it is a good way to enhance deep meditative states. Make sure that you always have your right leg on top.

(Vajrasana) Rock Pose

Kneel, sitting on the back of your heels. The top of your feet should be flat on the floor. Make sure that the heels are pressing into the nerves that are positioned in the middle of your rear end. They called this the rock pose because of its help in the digestive process.

Hero (Celibate) Pose

Along with your feet positioned equidistant to your hips, go down on your knees and sit in sandwiched between your feet. Hero (celibate) pose helps channel sensual power up the spinal column.

Deep Breathing Techniques (Pranayama)

For practitioners of Kundalini that have been doing the deep breathing techniques for many years, it is a natural thing that occurs for them. A lot of the time, a newer student will fill the lower abdomen area of the lungs and then try to fill the chest area but do not keep the right pressure, and the complete breath is only obtained in the chest cavity. This is not the diaphragm breathing that is needed.

Long Deep Breathing

Long deep breathing is a good way to relax and is often the first breathing technique that is taught when starting Kundalini. This also helps those who have lung-related issues with building up their lung capacity.

You begin by sitting with your legs crossed. You then take in a deep breath filling the abdominal area by pushing the air downward, then pressing the air into the lower areas. By arching your body somewhat forward and resting your palms on your knees, your chest cavity can begin to open forward. This allows you to keep pressure on the lungs and the abdominal area.

Once your lungs have been completely filled, hold the breath for a moment while pushing your shoulders back to expand the chest outward. You should feel the full pressure of the diaphragm at this point. Once you feel this, contract your diaphragm and push out the air.

The purpose of breathing this way through the nose for several of these breaths is to help the flow of energy and consciousness. This also helps with the blood circulation because of the involvement of the lungs and the deep breaths that circulate through them.

Once this type of deep breathing has been accomplished several times, you will find that it becomes a lot more natural. You will also begin to feel the motion that the entire diaphragm is involved during the whole breathing cycle.

Breath of Fire (Agni-Prasanna)

The breath of fire is an energizing breath that is cleansing to the body, and that is powered through spasms of the abdomen.

Once the long deep breathing technique has been mastered and you can feel the diaphragm, then you can begin the breath of fire technique. This begins with the long deep breathing technique. Once you take the air in, you do not hold; you immediately let it out. Once it has been let out, you immediately bring in another breath. You keep doing this process. It is reminiscent of a locomotive engine lurching on the tracks.

With each breath, you replace it with another until a nice rhythm begins to form out of the breathing. The breath of fire is meant to help charge the nervous system. It allows your glands to secrete the hormones you need and the blood to purify. Using this breathing technique for periods of time can help strengthen the mind and allows the body to become more connected to the mind.

The Language of Energy

Astrology is self-considered to be the language of energy that is exerted by the Planets, Elements, Signs, houses, and aspects. The astrological birth chart of an individual shows the pattern of energy which influences them in doing work and progress. Often the exaltation of energy may have a negative impact on the personality of an individual. Each element, sign, Planet, houses exert vibrant energy which is experienced by an individual such:

The Planets regulate the flow of energy and their dimensions in which this energy is experienced.

The Signs in the zodiac wheel show the pattern of energy and the quality of energy experienced by an individual

The Elements like Air, Fire, Earth, and Water considered as the substance of energy.

The houses in the zodiac wheel represent the field in which these energies were experienced.

The energy that we experience is directly reflected in the personality of an individual's life. The energy can be malefic or beneficial means it can be constructive or destructive. In astrology, we deal with different energies and their interaction and mutual relation with the other pattern of energy. The birth chart or an astrological chart shows the precise form of energy and its nature for us. Astrology is concerned with the three basic forms of energy which are as follows;

- The Constellation's energy by which the Sun is posited during the time of birth.
- The ascendant energy or the rising sign energy is where a man responses.
- The physical form of energy is the one governed by the Moon.
- The energy of a particular sign with which a person is born has a great significance on its own.
- The energy act as an indicator of present problems that are related to the quality of the individual. It expresses the activity during the incarnation and governs the fact (if I could express it), whereas, the ascendant/rising sign shows the flow of energy

in the line used to fulfill the desires and governs the fact that (of course I can do it if handled rightly).

- The power also holds future secrets and symbolizes the understanding which can be utilized to solve the problems and achieve success. It shows positive, vibrant energy.

The Moon exerts a steady-state form of energy which uses inertia. It indicates the body type and quality of energy, which pushes the person towards goals. The energy comes from the experience which is expressed physically.

The month of birth is indicative of the opportunity in which the soul comes into existence with the quality of energy and nature of the force to be experienced from that. Though the energy is neither destructive, it will start from the same end where you have left.

The energy of the Sun in the solar system has vital importance. It exerts a type of force which pushes you to the extent of origin and beginning just like a flower comes out the bud. Thus, considering the birth chart of an individual location of Planets, Signs, the ascendants, and house. These all speak in the form of energy which exerts its influence in the person's life. Considering the circle of the solar system on which our horoscope is based affects the soul, which is considered as the point of spiritual energy also. The sign falls in particular Elements like Earth, Fire, Air, and Water. These are the thoughts to be the person living below the diaphragm that use the energy of the lower body parts to perceive life.

The meditation also developed the energy from the inner soul which can be used for spiritual connection and turns into the positive vibes and by mantric words that can be used by the person in governing the power of their soul in a positive way.

To an extent when the energy of two different constellations collides in the same sign or house, then the person has two different forms of energies which sometimes creates complications and also makes a smoother life. In the modern astrological concept, physical and spiritual energy is the keywords of the astrological chart.

Thus, the point to be noticed is that astrology is self-concerned about the language of energy. The energy is directly concerned with the work form, which has to be done to fulfill the desires and our role in the physical as well as spiritual life.

The Test Enneagram Instructions

There are many Enneagram tests available online. Whatever Enneagram test you decide to take, the most important thing that you must do is to read the instructions carefully before you complete the test. Just like any other exam, an Enneagram test is very important, but it is also fun and stimulating.

The following nine paragraphs give a full description of each of the different personality types. No personality type is considered to be superior to the others, and each description represents a simple snapshot of each personality type on the Enneagram. Note that no paragraph is intended to give a deeper description of an individual type than the others.

Carefully read through each description and select three paragraphs that you agree fit your individual personality best. Once you have identified these three paragraphs, number them in order of the most fitting to the least fitting description of you. That is, the one the describes you best ranks 1 and the least ranks 3. These are the three that are highly likely to contribute to your personality.

Note that each one of the nine descriptions may be like you to a certain extent but select only the three that are most like you. It is important that you consider each paragraph as a whole rather than dismissing it all together by just reading a single sentence.

Before selecting a paragraph, ask yourself, "Is this paragraph a better description of me than the others?"

You may find it difficult to select three paragraphs. In this case, think about what a close friend would say when describing you. Remember that personality patterns are often quite evident in adult life.

How to record your selection: Once you have read, understood, and selected the three paragraphs that best describe you, record them as first choice, second choice, and third choice. Then refer to the answers below to determine what personality type is represented in each paragraph.

Enneagram Test

These are the nine Enneagram descriptions for the nine essential personality types.

A.   I approach things that really matter to me with an all-or-nothing method. I place emphasis mainly on strength, honesty, and reliability. In other words, what you see is what you get in return. I find it hard to trust people easily until they have proven themselves to be dependable. I prefer when people are straight up with me. I can tell when someone is being cunning, exploitative, or lying. I struggle with weaknesses in people unless I completely understand the reason underlying their weaknesses, or when they are striving to overcome them.

I find it hard to follow people's directives, especially when I have no respect for their authority. I prefer taking charge myself. When I am angry, I display my feelings and am always ready to stand up for my friends and family in unjust conditions. I may not win every fight, but people know that I have been there, done that!

B.   I have high standards of correctness and I expect people to abide by those standards. It is quite easy for me to see when things are going wrong and find ways to improve the situation. People often perceive me as being overly critical and a perfectionist. However, I find it hard to overlook things when they are not being handled in the right way. I take responsibility for all things assigned to me and am sure to do them right.

Often, I resent people when they fail to do things the right way or act irresponsibly/unfairly. In such a case, I do not show them my opinions openly. I prioritize work over pleasure; I often suppress my selfish interests to ensure that work gets done.

C.   I see people's points of view with ease. Because of my ability to perceive both pros and cons of something, sometimes I may come across as indecisive. Being able to appreciate both sides of a situation lets me help people resolve conflicts. However, this same ability makes me aware of how people's personal priorities, agendas, and positions differ from mine.

I become easily distracted and I get off course from the things am trying to achieve. When this happens, I concern myself with things that are trivial. I find it difficult to determine what is important. To avoid conflicts, I choose to agree with the majority; because of this people consider me to be easy-going, agreeable, and people-pleasing. It takes a lot of effort to get me to show my anger at someone in a direct way.

D.   I am sensitive about people's feelings, and I can perceive their needs even if they don't open up to me. It can be frustrating to know what people need because I am not able to do as much for them as I want. I easily say yes to people and wish that sometimes I would say no; I often end up using so much effort and energy taking care of others that I forget to take care of myself.

It hurts me when people think that my actions mean that I am manipulative or controlling, I am just trying to understand them so that I can better help. I like it when people consider me to be warmhearted and kind. If not, I become demanding and emotional. Good relationships are very important to me, and I strive to make them happen.

E.   I am strongly motivated to be the best at what I do. Because of this, I have received lots of recognition for my accomplishments over the years. I ensure that I do a lot and I am always successful at everything I do. I strongly identify with what I do, mainly because I consider success and recognition as measures of self-worth. I take on more tasks than will fit in the time available. When that happens, I push aside my feelings so that I can concentrate on getting things done.

Because I always have something to do, I do not have time to sit around or be idle. I grow impatient when people waste my time. In some cases, I prefer taking over a task that someone else is doing because they are going too slow for my liking. I feel good when I stay "on top of things." While I like working independently to complete tasks, I am also a great team player.

F.   I consider myself quiet and analytical. I prefer spending more time alone than most people. When people are engaging in conversations or discussions, I prefer being an observer rather than taking part. I don't like it when people place too many expectations on me. I get in touch with my inner person and feelings alone better than when I am in a crowd or with people.

I don't get bored when I am alone because I possess a strong mental life. I protect my time and energy, which allows me to live a simple life without complications, thus feeling self-sufficient.

G.   I possess a vivid imagination, especially concerning matters to do with safety and security. I can spot danger and harm from afar and this triggers extreme fear, as though it were happening in real time. I either face danger or try to avoid it. Because of my imagination, I have a good sense of humor.

I would prefer if life were full of certainty, but this makes me doubt the people around me. When someone is sharing their views, I can see disadvantages and pitfalls and this makes people consider me to be someone who are very astute.

I'm always suspicious of authority and am uncomfortable when people see me as an authority. When I commit myself to something or someone, I am very loyal.

H. People consider me a very optimistic person. I enjoy creating new interests and ideas of things to do. My mind is very active and I am constantly analyzing different ideas. I like to have a big picture of how the ideas I come up with fit together. I get excited when concepts connect eventually, even when they seemed not to at first. I devote a lot of effort and energy into the things that interest me and find it very hard to stick to things that are unrewarding, including routine tasks.

I prefer being part of a project at the very inception, during planning and implementation because these things are interesting. However, once my interest is exhausted, I find it difficult to stay focused, and I move on to the next thing that captivates me. If something lowers my mood, I prefer focusing on things that bring me pleasure because I believe everyone deserves an enjoyable life.

I. I am a very sensitive person and possess some intense feelings. I feel different from other people, and most of them misunderstand me or alienate me as a loner. Others consider my behavior to be dramatic. People criticize me as being overly sensitive. Inside, I have a nostalgia to connect with people emotionally and establish a sense of belonging and relationship. I often want what I cannot have, and this makes it hard for me to appreciate the uniqueness of each relationship.

My quest for emotional connection has been my desire my whole life. The absence of this is the reason I get melancholic and depressed. I often wonder why people have much better, healthier, and happier relationships than I do.

Enneagram Test Outcome

Which three of the above paragraphs best describe your personality?

These are the outcomes of each of the paragraph descriptions above. Use this table to identify what personality type you are.

- A-Type 8
- B-Type 1
- C-Type 9
- D-Type 2
- E-Type 3
- F-Type 5
- G-Type 6
- H-Type 7
- I-Type 4

Decoding the Nine-Value Code

LIFE TABLES

Own energy

1. Energy draws from other sources, often beyond measure. A refined egoist. Physically weak, quickly tired.

2. Close to the egoist (all the time he praises himself as if for sale).

3. Good, compliant character.

4. Sometimes compliant, but more often achieves the goal.

5. Strong-willed, strong character.

6. It seems that you are a dictator, a very strong-willed character.

7. A person is cruel, but at the same time for the loved one can do the impossible. It's very difficult with him.

Energy from nature, bioenergy.

0. This person has a good attitude towards others, is very responsive to changes in atmospheric pressure, often prone to colds.

1. Hypersensitivity to atmospheric phenomena, it is advisable to go in for sports, a contrast shower is useful.

2. Bioenergy is enough. It rarely happens without mood.

3. The tendency to extrasensory perception.

4. People around them are drawn. Their presence softens the atmosphere. They react to changes in atmospheric phenomena. They can be good doctors, masseurs. If you don't give this energy away, frequent headaches can bother you.--

5. A person can develop remarkable strength, but if you do not physically engage, energy can move into another sphere.-

6. A person can develop remarkable strength, but if you do not engage physically, energy can move into another sphere. It has a great energy effect on others, subordinating them to their will.-

The energy of space

0. A man likes to talk, moderately accurate. It is difficult for him to give exact sciences.

1. Man of mood (I want to do, I want not).

2. Propensity for exact sciences.

3. Remarkable physicists, mathematicians, chemists, a humanitarian bias is possible.-

4. Intuition can be the meaning of life. These people often anticipate events, a good analytical mind.

Health energy

There is no health energy. A painful condition, especially with a small amount of bioenergy.

1. The tendency to disease in old age.

2. Health is normal and even elevated temperament.

3. The body will be resistant to physical illnesses, but the psyche may be weak.

4. Excellent health.

Energy of intuition:

A person is always trying to do something, to prove something, always a head in thought, himself in an experiment. Life experience shows that many mistakes will be made by this person. All that is given to him - he "punches his head."--

1. The channel of intuition is open; these people make fewer mistakes in decision making.

2. Good intuition. You can be an investigator, a lawyer. Rarely mistaken.

3. Almost clairvoyant, these people know what they are doing.

4. Clairvoyants, everything that is happening around them is clear to them and do not try to convince them. There are times when they are outside of space and spatial time.--

Energy performance, grounding.

There is no tendency to physical labor. Physical work is performed as necessary, and not as desired.

1. A man loves physical labor, he needs it, but you can think about learning.

2. Love of physical labor.

3. Very charming, elevated temperament, a person cannot live without physical labor. Your partner should be with lots of bioenergy.-

4. A man works a lot. For him there is no severity of labor (physical), he always works.

The energy of talent.

It's hard for a person to live and earn money, talent will come in subsequent transformations.

1. A capable, inventive person. There is talent, but dimly expressed. Endowed with artistic and musical taste.-

2. If you develop abilities, then a person is musical, has a good artistic taste, draws well, and is endowed with everything: bad and good. There will be no closed doors for him. From childhood, you need to prepare yourself to disinterestedly act in favor of others, regardless of your personal interests.

3. You have to face serious difficulties.

4. You should remember caution.

Energy binding.

A person is not always punctual and obligatory.

1. A person with a developed sense of duty. Mandatory, punctual.-

2. A sense of duty is very developed, there is always a desire to help.

3. A very big responsibility, service to the people.

4. A person with parapsychological abilities, with knowledge of the exact sciences.-

The energy of the mind.

1. Mental abilities can make themselves felt in the second half of life, after accumulating experience.

2. As a rule, these people can easily study and there is no need to "cram" the material.-

3. From birth, a smart head, but reluctantly learns.

4. Smart by nature, everything is given to him.

5. A rare mind, but rudeness and mercy interfere.

Conclusion

Now, as you have to go through, now you will come to know how you can read and construct your natal charts and their deeper meanings. This must have explained all the basics of astrology; the history and origin of the astrology make you familiar with the concept of astrological predictions. It has explained all the related tools of astrology that is used by the astrologer for making a prediction. If you are a beginner, you will be able to deal with the astrological aspect.

The main aim of this was to make you aware of the basic concept of astrology and how to use them in the prediction of an individual's birth chart and their personality. It has explained all the possible facts of astrology that you people like the most. I am sure this will definitely help you in learning astrology in a better and easy way.

As you all that the celestial objects present in the universe emit different kind of energy which is directly or indirectly concerned with our daily life activity but mostly, we are not aware of these and neglected by us most of the time. The purpose of this is to tell you about the techniques and tools that are used in astrology to predict the circumstances in your life. The content of this opens your eyes towards the astrological aspects and meaning of each and every celestial object in your life.

The Enneagram sheds light on self-awareness and personal growth. Considering this is a new year, make the decision to look deep inside yourself for the things you like most and the things you would like to change to be a better version of yourself. Learning about your Enneagram personality type is an excellent catalyst to making a positive change in your life. So, what is it going to be for you in 2020? Take a bold step and make a difference in your life. You will thank the Enneagram for aiding in successful personal growth later.

The more that you invest in understanding yourself through crafts like numerology, the easier it is for you to develop yourself along this journey. It is important to understand that tools like numerology are only meant to be used as a guide and not as a strict rule in your life. As you read through your chart and reflect on it, remember that you may find areas where you do not resonate with your chart simply because you are a unique individual. You may find that you can find an even deeper resonance by going back to the double-digit number before the single digit number to help you resonate even deeper. In other numbers, you may completely identify with the primary number and find that it tells you plenty. To summarize, there is so much to be learned about yourself through numerology, but the ultimate learning comes from reflecting on it and seeing how it actually relates to you in your lifetime. This way, you can learn not only about numerology, but about yourself, too.

It is a good idea to write your chart down on paper or in a document so that you can reflect back on it whenever you need to. Many people find that their charts become valuable to them at many points in life, and they reference back to it frequently. As a result, they are able to get great information about how they can move through different phases of their life, what they can expect from the people around them, and how they make better decisions. Regularly reflecting back on your chart can be a valuable opportunity for you to move in alignment with your true soul, which is the biggest benefit of numerology.

Book 4

Astrology

Introduction

Zodiac, Astrology, and other practices of divinity are everywhere – but just how much are these horoscopes truly connected to the original practices? Historically, these practices of Divinity helped people make decisions regarding agriculture, love, and war strategies. In modern day, horoscopes and the like are primarily treated like fortune cookies – fun, cute, but mostly unappreciated. The truth of the matter is that these practices have deep roots within our history as a society. In addition to this history, they also have much more complicated values and beliefs than just the surface level we see in the media. To give you, the reader, some background, here is a quick, comprehensive history of each branch of divinity.

Since the beginning of human thought and consciousness, one part of the human existence has connected all of life. It is a part of everyday life that all humans have experienced – past, present, and future. It has brought about wonder and amazement upon all generations and all cultures and people. This is, of course, the sky. The night sky has been the subject of many a love song, or an incredible story, and is generally a magical experience. The sky above us has been used for centuries as a scientific tool, a navigational map, and (possibly the most important) a source of emotional and spiritual thought. It is due to this incredible phenomenon that we call a "sky" that we now have modern-day Astrology. However, how did we get here? To fully understand this, we have to start at the beginning – the beginning of Astrology as a thought process, that is.

The earliest observations of the night sky began with ancient Mesopotamia. The early civilizations of Mesopotamia saw the first names of our most prominent constellations and the five wandering stars. When added with the sun and the moon, these form the seven original planets. It is within this early civilization that we find the early Babylonians beginning the very science known as Astronomy (not to be confused with Astrology). It is through the studies of these ancient people that the very first studies of the "Zodiac" are produced. The Zodiac originally was a map-like distinction of the night sky – breaking up the different constellations to help judge the time of the year based on the location of certain "Wandering" stars within each constellation. Not only was this very useful from a scientific standpoint, but the different portions of the sky were also connected to different gods; thus, giving them different personality traits. This is the origin of the 12 Zodiac signs as we know them today.

The origin of modern-day Tarot cards goes back much farther than the average person may realize. The actual origin of these mystical decks is widely debated among historians, but one of the most common beliefs is that they first appeared in the 14th century in Turkey. At this time, they were most likely known as Mamluk game cards but later received their modern name from an Italian game known as "Tarrochi Appropriati", which later shortened to the modern term "Tarot".

The history of Numerology is long and widespread – almost every civilization with a hand in the formulation of mathematics connects some form of meaning to numbers. We will focus on the three most common forms of numerology: Kabbalic, Chaldean, and Pythagorean. Kabbalic numerology originates from Hebrew mysticism with a connection to the original Hebrew alphabet. This form of Numerology is usually used to interpret names. The original Hebrew alphabet, having 22 letters, gives more significance to the Tarot deck of 22 trump cards. Chaldean Numerology is more closely related to Astrology due to its origin in ancient Mesopotamia, which we know is the ultimate origin of modern-day Astrology. Within Chaldean Numerology, each number is believed to have its own vibration and is given a level of energy from one to eight based on its energy. The final and most commonly used system of Numerology is the Pythagorean numerology, which was developed by the Greek mathematician Pythagoras. In this system of Numerology, numbers are given to the letters in the Greek alphabet based on location. This system also uses a system of vibrations but, unlike the Chaldean Numerology system, the Pythagorean system uses numbers one through nine and 11 through 22.

Kundalini Rising is certainly one of the lesser-known of the four divinities but has very powerful ideals and origins. The actual origin of the Kundalini idea is somewhat unclear in a historical context – not much is understood of who first theorized about Kundalini and how the awakening within a person may affect them. What's found, though, is the written record of several Vedic and Tantric texts that describe Kundalini. The earliest known currently is a record by a man named Adi Sankaracharya, who lived around the seventh to eighth century AD and gave his record here: "Having filled the pathway of the Nadis with the streaming shower of nectar flowing from the Lotus feet, having resumed thine own position from out of the resplendent Lunar regions and Thyself assuming the form of a serpent of three and a half coils, sleepest thou, in the hollow of Kula Kunda (Kula Kunda means the hollow of Mooladhara Sacrum bone)."

Clearly, we can see from this that the historical context of these practices alone is much more than we make them out to be. Throughout this text, you will learn in depth about the practice and meaning behind each of these forms of Divinity. Along the way, you will find information that may help you navigate your own life through the understanding of these practices. The information regarded in the practices can help you understand why you feel the way you do, why other people may act certain ways towards you, and how to respond in certain situations to yield the most positive impact for you as an individual.

The Beginning of Astrology

Astrology was based on the notion that the relationship between the position of the planets and the nature of the person who was born at the same time exists. The foundation of this idea is the fundamental idea that the Universe and all its components are not separate but inherently linked in a single whole. What happens in a very large, macrocosm, or Earth also happens in a very small microcosm or human being simultaneous.

It's not so much that now the planets influence the individual, as people generally believe in astrology, although the Sun and Moon definitely do. Therefore, the position of the planets and the essence of individuals are a reflection and a manifestation of the same universal force acting on them. So when the process is known, what the location of the planets can see will tell us something about the existence of the person Birthed in the same moment as well. A simple analogy is how we tell the time using clocks. We can read the time on a clock and know much about what will happen in the world at that moment without actually having to witness it.

The full art of astrology has several essential components. This needs time and place for an occurrence that is normally a person's birth. When this event takes place, Astrology then considers the position of the planets in the sky, the signs, the houses, and the aspects (or links) between the planets.

Astrology's first part is The Planets. In all, ten planetary bodies are commonly accepted, with some new ones still discussed by astrologers. The Mercury, Sun, Mars, Venus, Saturn, Jupiter, Neptune, Uranus, and Pluto. They're all here. The Earth is also an essential part of astrology because it is used to draw up that sign and houses we will address.

Throughout astrological thinking, there is no coincidence or pure chance of the planets, but there are the underlying purpose and importance of the Universe. Each celestial body reflects particular energy in the world, some of which would call it angelic power. This is supported by many years of observation, literature, mythology, and even common words in our language.

For example, Mars is often known as a god of war and energy and battle. People would call upon this God to inspire victory for them. The red color of the world represents power, sexuality, and inspiration. We derive terms such as martial from which war, discipline, and military order have been linked. Mercury was, on the other hand, known as a communicator and trickster in Roman mythology, because he could move so much faster than anyone else. He is often portrayed on his feet with wings. Mercury was the gods' envoy. Mercury is the fastest planet in our Universe to orbit the Sun. The metal is used to say the temperature because it adjusts very rapidly and receptively. This is also where we can change the word mercurial meaning. It is also called Quicksilver, which reinforces the idea of pace and transition. Jupiter gave rise to Jovial's terms. It is a huge planet with many moon orbits, much like a king or queen with many subjects. It was always considered a vast, inspiring, optimistic, fortunate force in mythology. In reality, the Earth has been saved several times from meteors, drawn by Jupiter, and absorbed on its surface.

We understand the different ideas of all planets, but how does this affect us, individuals? The Universe is a whole and not separate, as we said, so as the planets embody such energy forces, the individual also has these forces in his nature. Some of us, like Jupiter, are larger than life and inspirational, others like Mercury, many major athletes, and warriors, or even despots, as embodied in the Martian theory.

According to astrology, it is about where the planets are at birth in the Zodiac. This brings us to the second area of astrology—the signs.

The planets are traveling along a fixed path with the stars as far backdrop along the night sky since the stars are farther than the planets. These star clusters along the path of the planets contain twelve equally large sets of stars known as zodiac signs. From the end of March, Taurus, signs are Aries, Mercury, Gemini, Virgo, Leo, Scorpio, Libra, Capricorn, Sagittarius, Sun and Aquarius. Although they don't correspond exactly with the constellations named in the sky. The Zodiac is the background or screen to see the planets. For example, at the time of someone's birth, Mars could have been in the constellation of Aries. This essentially means that the backdrop of the stars behind Mars, from the viewpoint of the Earth, would be that of the Aries part of the Zodiac. In the same way, each planet would have a star background when someone was born, and each planet could lie in any of the twelve zodiacal signs. Conventional astrology only includes the constellation in which the Sun lies when you are born. I.e., She is a Leo would mean the Sun is laying before the constellation of Leo at the time of her birth even if we didn't advise you to see!

What are the Zodiacal signs all about? The zodiacal constellations are like a filter that colors and affects the energies represented by a planet and are expressed in some way just as the planets represent various forces.

For instance, Aries is the Zodiac's first sign. It is related to the spring and rebirth season after the long, sleeping winter. New life is to be seen everywhere, optimism after the bleak time still exists. Aries is about new starts with vivid, free-flowing heat, and it is the first of the signs of flame. It's very much about innocence and childhood and a little naivety as the first sign of the Zodiac. It's the start of an adventure. It is conveyed mainly through practice. But if we look at cancer, it's a whole different message. This is a water sign for the family, the past, the home, and the nursing family, and expresses itself mainly in feelings and emotions. Now, if we take the planet Mars, which we mentioned before, when the planets are described, this is the strength of personal energy or will and the ability to hold your position and strive for what you want in life. If Mars is present in Aries at the time of the birth of a child, the flow of energy is represented by practice. as you will see in an athlete, military commander, or a person with such a temper., they would be competitive and uninhibited. When we discovered Mars in cancer, however, the energy would be emotionally conveyed. It is less apparent and more subdued, and the energy will psychological overreaction or psychological manipulation, or surface if only a friend or a family member is threatened.

Each of the ten planets may lie in such a specific sign of the Zodiac. However, there is a wide, wide range of combinations. Due to this fact and the connection between planetary positions and peoples, one can see one of the main reasons why so many different personalities inhabit our planet. Astrology, in turn, does not believe that personalities are formed exclusively through the growing process; it believes that the fundamental components of a person are already there waiting for their expression at birth.

Besides this astrology, Houses has the idea. This will be the third area of art used in astrology. We said before how much the planetary energy is processed by a sign-in, which they are. However, the position of the house adds to that by saying in what areas of life these energies are mainly expressed. The houses are between one and twelve. In the Ascendant, which is the eastern horizon of the chart, the first house begins. The place of the Ascendant depends on the person's location at birth. As you go around the chart, the number of the house goes up to the twelfth and final house.

Astrology and the Planets

Sun

Sun is the lord/ ruler of the zodiac.

Sun in Aries – Sun is exalted in Aries as Mars the ruler of Aries is compatible with Sun.

Sun in Taurus – Taurus is ruled by Venus and so Sun is in conflict in Taurus.

Sun in Gemini – Gemini is ruled by Mercury and Sun is compatible with mercury. A native having this combination in his chart will be educated and knowledgeable.

Sun in Cancer - They're compatible and a native having both sun and moon together in his chart must've been born on a new moon day.

Sun in Leo- Leo is ruled by sun. The natives who ahs sun in Leo in their chart will be strong willed and become leaders.

Sun in Virgo – Same as Gemini.

Sun in Libra- Sun is weak in Libra since Libra is ruled by Venus; so is powerless.

Sun in Scorpio – Scorpio is ruled by Mars and Pluto.

Sun in Sagittarius – He may become a scientist.

Sun in Capricorn- Capricorn is ruled by Saturn, so Sun is subdued in Capricorn.

Sun in Aquarius – Aquarius is ruled by Saturn (ancient astrology) and Uranus (modern astrology).

Sun in Pisces – Neptune is the ruler of Pisces. He's the lord of dreams, illusions and inspiration and psychic powers.

Moon

The moon rules the mind and can create mental illness if not placed well in a chart. The moon is considered to be feminine and has sex appeal.

Moon in Aries – The natives having moon in Aries in natal chart will be attached to their father and will also own fixed assets like house and land.

Moon in Taurus – The native with this combination is sure to become a film star. Taurus is ruled by Venus the lord of luxury and comfort and the combination of moon makes the native creative and artistic.

Moon in Gemini – These natives are great communicators.

Moon in Cancer – In its own house the person will be attractive, beautiful with pleasing personality.

Moon in Leo – Since Leo is the house of Sun the moon is muted in Leo.

Moon in Virgo – You're a prim and proper kind of person.

Moon in Libra – Ruled by Venus, Libra is the house of love. You enjoy all the pleasures of life.

Moon in Scorpio – The moon is weak in Scorpio. If there is no favorable planet aspecting it the native is likely to lead a troubled life.

Moon in Sagittarius – This native is likely to be passionate, optimistic and posses a positive approach to life.

Moon in Capricorn – You're a strong personality and have an innate sense of righteousness.

Moon in Aquarius – The people born with moon in Aquarius don't mingle well and like to keep to them. They're egoistic and eccentric loners.

Moon in Pisces – A person born with moon in Pisces is psychic and intuitive. He's spiritual and seeks to achieve a higher plane of consciousness. They're sensitive, caring and creative in nature.

Mercury

It is the planet for money, communication and creativity.

Mercury in Aries – Mercury in Aries makes a person romantic and passionate in love. They're good with people and make successful builders and real estate agents.

Mercury in Taurus – They make a good team. A native having Mercury placed in Taurus will be a traveler and enjoy all the pleasures of life.

Mercury in Gemini- Being its own sign Mercury makes the native attractive, flirty and beautiful.

Mercury in Cancer – Mercury in Moon sign of Cancer makes a person emotional. They become moody and are sensitive.

Mercury in Leo – This positioning leads to higher knowledge and education. Mercury positioned in Sun's house gives the native a high paying job.

Mercury in Virgo – Mercury is exalted in Virgo. This position leads to power, wealth and success in all aspects of life.

Mercury in Libra- Mercury residing in the house of Venus leads to fame, name and popularity in creative arts like theater and cinema.

Mercury in Scorpio – The positioning of Mercury in Scorpio makes the person temperamental and angry.

Mercury in Sagittarius – Residing in the house of Jupiter, the knowledge giver the natives do well in studies and acquire multiple degrees in the field of education.

Mercury in Capricorn – The house of Saturn welcomes Mercury and shows effects that are aspected to the house.

Mercury in Aquarius - Same as above.

Mercury in Pisces – Neptune, the lord of Pisces along with Mercury makes the person dreamer and excels in creative pursuits.

Venus

Venus is the closest planet to earth and is the lord of romance, love, comfort and luxury.

Venus in Aries – Such a person will have a troubled life especially in relationships unless there is Jupiter aspecting or positioned together.

Venus in Taurus – Since it is its own sign the native will be good looking and enjoy all the pleasures of life.

Venus in Gemini – Such a native will have an amazing life full of happiness and victory. This aspect is favorable as Mercury and Venus are compatible.

Venus in Cancer – Moon is the lord of Cancer and it has no enemies. Yet Venus repels Moon. So having Venus in Cancer may not be beneficial.

Venus in Leo – Venus is hostile to Sun the lord of Leo. So there is conflict and the native will not get favorable results.

Venus in Virgo – Venus is weak in Virgo. Due to this the native will be a flirt, cheat on his spouse and always be sick.

Venus in Libra – this is Venus's own house and so the native will enjoy all the benefits, comforts and luxury in life.

Venus in Scorpio – since Venus is in conflict with the lord of Scorpio, Mars the results may not be favorable. If there is another planet along with it then the effect gets neutralized.

Venus in Sagittarius - Sagittarius is the house of Jupiter. Positioning of Venus there has neutral gains.

Venus in Capricorn – Saturn the lord of Capricorn is compatible with Venus and showers multiple benefits to natives who have Venus in Capricorn. They offer brilliant results.

Venus in Aquarius – Same as above.

Venus in Pisces – Pisces the dreamer combines with Venus to offer brilliant results to the natives.

Mars

Mars is a fiery planet that is also close to earth. It is smaller in size than earth and double the size of moon

Mars in Aries – Aries is the house of Mars and so the native will be showered with good personality and leadership qualities. The native will exude arrogance and will focus in achieving success and prosperity.

Mars in Gemini – Being in an airy sign these natives spit venom and often are on short fuse. They're restless and always have to be occupied with work.

Mars in Cancer – Mars is weak /debilitated in Cancer. These natives have passive aggression. They resist change or anything new.

Mars in Leo – mars residing in the house of Sun leads to the native becoming an engineer and lead the way to innovation.

Mars in Virgo- The natives having Mars in Virgo have a knack of getting their work done.

Mars in Libra - Mars in Libra enables the person to act without thinking.

Mars in Scorpio – These natives like to attain the impossible. Since it is Mars's own sign the natives are strong and have a brilliant personality. They're sturdy and take their own decisions.

Mars in Sagittarius – They've loads of energy that needs to be spent. Taking up a sport will be ideal for these natives. They love fooling around and being fun loving. They are very lucky and blessed.

Mars in Capricorn – These natives enjoy all the wealth and pleasures of life. They are successful in whatever they set out to do. High achievers these natives are focused and ambitious.

Mars in Aquarius- They're secretive and enjoy surprises. They turn towards spirituality to seek answers They are quite clever and succeed in whatever they set out to do.

Mars in Pisces – These natives are moody, angry and don't know what they want out of life. They go with the flow and they scheme to get what they want.

Jupiter

. It is considered to be the most positive planet in a horoscope. Jupiter is also considered powerful as per Greek mythology- Zeus = the father of gods.

Yellow is the favorable color and their element is sky. Jupiter is a friendly planet. Its powers are tremendous.

Jupiter in Aries – Enthusiastic and warm Jupiter in Aries makes the person knowledge driver and ambitious. They do well in academics.

Jupiter in Taurus – These natives look after themselves well and do well in life. They're self sufficient. These natives are pleasantly mannered and practical.

Jupiter in Gemini – The natives who have this combination are impatient and highly energized to start something new all the time. They love to learn everything under the Sun and be knowledgeable.

Jupiter in Cancer – Jupiter is exalted in Cancer. The natives are highly educated and become scientists and technocrats. They also have a leaning towards religion, philosophy and spirituality.

Jupiter in Leo – Jupiter in the house of Sun makes these natives family oriented and responsible towards their children. Domesticated and caring they love sports.

Jupiter in Virgo – These natives are caring and helpful. In case of any emergency these people are highly dependable. They're talented and are good at social work and healthcare.

Jupiter in Libra –   They make good teachers, lawyers and judges. They are also kind and civilized people.

Jupiter in Scorpio – The native will be competent and hard working. They are good with numbers and often end up being financial professionals

Jupiter in Sagittarius -   They're well mannered, dependable and never lie. They're also liberal, broad minded and loyal in relationships. After middle age these natives develop an interest for occult and philosophical matters.

Jupiter in Capricorn – Jupiter is debilitated in Capricorn. Hence the natives are not as successful as they dream to be. Yet they're courteous, polite and sincere to others. Honest and truthful they wish to succeed in whatever they set out to do.

Jupiter in Aquarius – Many social activists have Jupiter in Aquarius. These natives are charitable, think about serving the society and brotherhood in general.

Jupiter in Pisces – . They seek a higher plane of consciousness to understand the meaning of life. Highly intuitive these natives are visionaries.

Saturn

According to astrology Saturn stands for justice, detachment and spiritual value. The color of Saturn is blue with three golden rings around it.

Saturn in Aries – Saturn is weak/ debilitated in Aries..

Saturn in Taurus –You're conscious about material comforts and try to lead a lazy life. You learn to work hard and continue to keep focus on security. Material possessions matter to you.

Saturn in Gemini – You're keen to learn and enjoy doing everything to achieve happiness

Saturn in Cancer – You're a very caring person for whom relationships matter.

Saturn in Leo – In the sign of Sun, Saturn is subdued. The effect is less as sun dominates in Leo.

Saturn in Virgo – This placement makes a person hard working and steadfast. They're truthful, capable, reasonable and prompt.

Saturn in Libra – In Libra, Saturn is exalted and he showers the native with all the choicest material and monetary comforts.

Saturn in Scorpio- You're a self disciplined person who does things with intensity. You may possess psychic abilities

Saturn in Sagittarius – You're a philanthropist who is generous in your approach to life. You've intuition and help people with your insights.

Saturn in Capricorn – This is Saturn's own house and the native who has this placement is matured, practical and moody.

Saturn in Aquarius – The combination of Neptune and Saturn as lords of Aquarius gives a philosophical edge to your personality.

Saturn in Pisces – Jupiter and Pluto, the lords of Pisces give you an added advantage to aim towards world peace and brotherhood.

Neptune/ Uranus/ Pluto

Since these three planets are newly added into western astrology there are no specific predictions attached to them.

Understanding the Zodiac Signs

Aries

March 21 - April 19

Element - Fire

Lucky Numbers - 6, 18, 41, 77 and 83

Magical Birthstone - Bloodstone

Special Colors –Red

The danger for the people with that sign - Aries lack caution and are very quick in action and thought. This is a double-edged sword for them because sometimes it is the right decision and sometimes it isn't. This means that it is easy for them to make enemies and friends, depending on the circumstances. Aries are very ambitious, and it is easy for them to gain both money and position.

Taurus

April 20 - May 20

Element - Earth

Lucky Numbers - 5, 35, 50, 57, and 82

Magical Birthstone - Sapphire

Special Colors - Green

The danger for the people with that sign - One of the faults of a Taurus is that they have a jealous streak that is difficult for them to control. They are incredibly loyal, but their cautious nature makes them wonder if the same can be said for their partners. More often than they care to admit, this can lead to an exhibition of a temper, another fault. They feel sorry for this afterward and is usually not difficult for them to overcome because, in the end, this is a very level-headed sign. They will almost always fall back on their sense of practicality and inner strength.

Gemini

May 21 - June 20

Element - Air

Lucky Numbers - 1, 10, 18, 35 and 86

Magical Birthstone - Agate

Special Colors - Yellow

The danger for the people with that sign - They are natural gamblers which can work for or against them depending on the situation.

Cancer

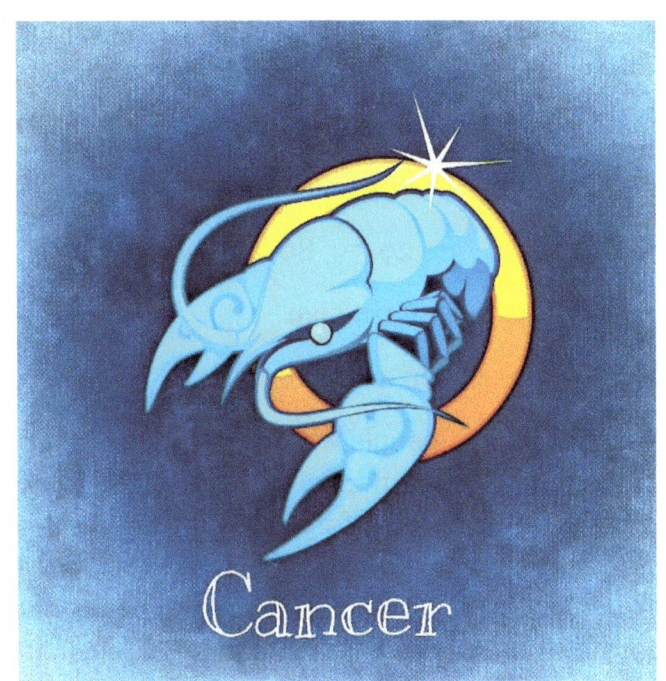

June 21 - July 22

Element - Water .

Lucky Numbers - 1, 21, 24, 58, and 66

Magical Birthstone - Emerald

Special Colors - White and silver

The danger for the people with that sign - One of the disadvantages of being so sensitive is that Cancers learn how to hide it from people, simply because our world forces them to feel like they must. They often appear more put together and confident than they feel. This façade makes it difficult for them to make friends, but once they do, they make solid, strong friendships. This sign excels at many different careers, but because they are nurturers, careers such as nursing, social work, teaching, or even being a lawyer suit them well because they like setting an example and feeling as though they are helping people.

Leo

July 23 - August 22

Element - Fire

Lucky Numbers - 6, 24, 39, 59, and 83

Magical Birthstone - Onyx

Special Colors - Gold

The danger for the people with that sign - They are not the best at managing their finances, usually because they haven't had to be, being lucky in money matters. Leos might find themselves getting money from surprising sources, which feels somewhat normal to them. It is because of this that so many Leos have not had to learn to manage their finances properly. This is something that comes to them with time and experience, though but can cause some problems early on in their lives.

Virgo

August 23 - September 22

Element - Earth

Lucky Numbers - 16, 29, 79, 80, and 90

Magical Birthstone - Carnelian

Special Colors - Green and brown

The danger for the people with that sign – Sometimes Virgos can come off as insensitive or selfish and need to learn to keep themselves in check when this happens. Even when it does, they are not doing it out of malice; they are just simply so detail-oriented they can lose sight of the big picture. Of all the signs, Virgos hold the most potential for going to extremes regarding good and evil. This is just the result of them being too smart for their own good; Virgos have the uncanny ability to justify almost anything if they feel it is for the greater good.

Libra

September 23 - October 22

Element - Air

Lucky Numbers - 7, 20, 55, 77 and 86

Magical Birthstone - Chrysolite

Special Colors - Pink and blue

The danger for the people with that sign – Financial success is not a priority to Libras, and they will have many ups and downs when it comes to their careers because of this. Libras place more value on peace and justice in their lives.

Scorpio

October 23 - November 21

Element - Water

Lucky Numbers - 27, 29, 45, 53 and 89.

Magical Birthstone - Beryl

Special Colors - Black

The danger for the people with that sign - they are infamous for procrastinating and will look for any excuse to put something off until a later date. This is not the best habit to have in the business world, so they must learn to adhere to a schedule if they want to be successful. However, once they overcome this obstacle, they are usually very successful in the career they choose.

Sagittarius

November 22 - December 21

Element (Fire, water [..]) - Fire

Lucky Numbers - 6, 16, 23, 60, and 81

Magical Birthstone - Citrine

Special Colors - Purple

The danger for the people with that sign - This sign is prone to restlessness because they have trouble sitting down and relaxing. They get bored easily and prefer instant gratification where they can get it. When a Sagittarius faces a task or goal that takes longer than anticipated to accomplish they move onto something else altogether and forget about the initial task. Even when they are 'relaxing,' they are making plans, and it is for this reason that they are so good in a crisis.

Capricorn

December 22 - January 19

Element (Fire, water [..]) - Earth

Lucky Numbers - 3, 21, 66, 83, 84.

Magical Birthstone - Ruby

Special Colors - Brown and grey

The danger for the people with that sign - Fear is at the root of a Capricorn's troubles; this is a life-long battle they fight with themselves. Learning to cope and overcome their fears is something that they must learn to do. However, this does not always come easily, and part of it is usually finding the patience and inner calm to allow themselves to begin the long process of chipping away at these fears and frustrations. Everyone has different fears, but for a Capricorn, it generally deals with failure, living without purpose, and feelings of loneliness.

Aquarius

January 20 - February 18

Element - Air

Lucky Numbers - 17, 40, 46, 61, and 76

Magical Birthstone - Garnet

Special Colors – Blue

The danger for the people with that sign - No one would call an Aquarius boring, as they are full of surprises. The water bearer symbol perfectly represents this sign; one vessel is holding water that is alive and the other dead. This symbolizes the separation of good and evil, and the fine line between the two, that Aquarians so often find themselves on.

Pisces

Element - Water

Lucky Numbers - 8, 10, 27, 56 and 69.

Magical Birthstone - Amethyst

Special Colors - Light green

The danger for the people with that sign - This is another sign that enjoys luxury and beautiful things, which does not help them with learning to budget properly. This can pose a real problem when they are younger and still learning to take the time to think about their decisions. Even if they are not sure of their purpose early on, when they find it, they rise to the challenge in a way only a Pisces can.

Horoscope

Many people may consult astrologers about sorting out a relationship issue, changing jobs or changing careers, opening a new business and becoming self-employed.

People usually make changes to improve their earning potential.

We will look at areas of income that relate to other people's resources — for example, bank loans, business partnerships, inheritance, and gifted money.

We will study the indicators in the natal horoscope. I will be using an example that I have imaginary come up with to illustrate well how Horoscope can change your life even financially. By studying one horoscope, we will clearly see the natal configurations sensitive to career and financial changes.

Let's start with the indicators of financial improvement in the horoscope. We want to see solar arc or transit activity from Jupiter, Uranus or Pluto in 8th harmonic hard aspect -- conjunction, semi square (45 degrees), square, sesquiquadrate (135 degrees) and opposition - to the ruler of the 2nd house (money) and planets located in the 2nd house. We want to focus as well on the ruler of the 8th house or planets in the 8th house since this area concerns other people's resources.

Jupiter is a beneficial planet. It augments and expands whatever it touches. Uranus represents sudden changes, upsetting the status quo, bringing in new and exciting developments.

And Pluto signifies empowerment and transformation.

We are not interested in transiting Neptune. If for example transiting Neptune is in hard aspect to the planet ruling the 2nd house, it can suggest confusion, doubt, insecurity even deception with finances.

Neptune generally is not going to be a positive influence, as well with Saturn in hard aspect to a planet ruling the 2nd or 8th house. Saturn tends to be controlling and restrictive. So, we want to focus on Jupiter, Uranus and Pluto.

We want to look for solar arcs or transits from Jupiter, Uranus or Pluto in hard aspect to the angles of the horoscope. The Midheaven (MC) reflects a change of status, career developments and recognition. As well, in hard aspect to the planet ruling the 10th house or located in the 10th house. Same for the 11th house as well, since it represents income and recognition from the profession.

Another essential combination in solar arc (SA) or transit activity is Pluto or Uranus to Jupiter, and vice-versa such as Jupiter in hard aspect to Pluto or Uranus, or Pluto in hard aspect to Jupiter, or Uranus in hard aspect to Jupiter.

Jupiter to Uranus or Uranus to Jupiter suggests exciting opportunities, success, becoming independent, and heading to where the grass is greener. It is optimism and intensifies (Uranus) reward (Jupiter). Likewise, Jupiter to Pluto or Pluto to Jupiter symbolizes success, wealth, establishing new perspectives of opportunity, leadership, influence, and resourcefulness.

The reward cycle of transiting Jupiter conjunct the Sun, occurs every twelve years. When you test someone's past through this cycle, you should see a theme reoccurring every twelve years of success or reward.

For example, that I had started a business venture every twelve years.

If transiting Jupiter conjunct the Sun does not manifest as reward, there are usually other mitigating measurements or factors that trump or negate Jupiter. For example, transiting Pluto to Saturn, or transiting Neptune to the Sun or angle of the horoscope can be challenging.

Usually however, transiting Jupiter conjunct the Sun marks a time of promotion, reward and recognition.

We also want to look for solar arc or transiting Uranus to Saturn. This suggests a wake-up call of ambition. Imagine cheerleaders on the sidelines at a football game, jumping up and down. It's time to get things going, to pick up the pace.

It intensifies ambition, bringing in exciting new developments. It can also suggest making changes that will afford the person more freedom or individuality. Sometimes it can be about freedom in relationships leading to a separation, but at the same time, career developments can occur simultaneously. Check your horoscope when solar arc or transiting Uranus was in hard aspect with natal Saturn and see what manifested then.

Another measurement susceptible to career developments is solar arc or transiting Saturn conjunct, square or opposed the natal Moon. This occurs approximately every seven years by transit. This registers as advancement in one's work. Astrologer Noel Tyl calls this configuration 'the architecture of advance.' Look to see what house the Moon is situated in and what house it rules.

This will help determine what areas of life may be involved. It is a very reliable measurement every seven years for career developments.

Similar is the Secondary Progressed Moon (SP Moon) conjunct, square or opposed natal Saturn occurring approximately every seven years. This is a strong time for ambitious planning and strategizing, when the person gets a kick to get things moving. It is so powerful it usually kicks in six months before the aspect is exact, and 6 months after exact - about one year of ambitious activity.

These four measurements are vital for career advancement, changes and promotions.

Let's begin by studying an example of horoscope using an imaginary sample of you as a reader to make you understand how the Horoscope works, for career developments and improved finances. It is interesting to see natal aspect configurations come alive through solar arc development. This is when progress happens. I want to show you the sensitive areas in your horoscope.

First, we look at the 10th house. You were born with the Sun conjunct the Midheaven (MC) so whenever the MC is hit off by transit, so is the natal Sun. They work as a pair.

When Uranus or Mercury is hit off by transits, we should expect developments that affect the profession and finances.

The third natal aspect is Venus square to the Moon in the 2nd house. Venus sits in the 11th house of career recognition. It rules the Ascendant and 6th house. When a planet rules an angle of the horoscope, it has significant importance.

Let's say you were 24 to 25 years old when taking out a bank loan to start a business as a computer consultant.

A bank loan in your horoscope would be affiliated with Jupiter ruler of the 8th house. Since you didn't have the collateral for the loan, one of your parents co-signed.

Looking at the solar arc activity first, we see SA Ascendant conjunct the Moon in the 2nd house. SA Jupiter was sesquiquadrate Mars in the 2nd house. SA Venus was square Jupiter ruler of the 8th house, and SA Uranus was in hard aspect to the Midheaven.

Transiting Pluto was square the Midheaven suggesting something big was brewing professionally. It's like a volcano bubbling with lava about to erupt. Events are building through this transit.

Transiting Saturn was opposed the Ascendant. When Saturn comes up above the horizon to transit through houses 7 through 12, it represents a time of increased responsibilities with the outer world. There is a sense of release from the past fourteen years when transiting Saturn was below the horizon. The person is now more visible.

Transiting Jupiter was conjunct your Midheaven and Sun. Because transiting Jupiter moves relative quickly it would also conjunct Mercury in the 10th house and oppose Uranus in the 4th house.

Then it would move on to oppose Pluto.

We can see the houses involved with this activity in the right column of the chart: the 2nd house, 3rd house (the Moon rules the 3rd), 7th house, 8th house and 10th house.

In continuation with our example, in 1987-1988, about one year after you become self-employed tension was building financially. What was over your head now is the idea that paying back the loan is a short time period while trying to grow your business with new clients. Let's say now you were forced to work for another company in sales while you built your business as well.

We see SA Venus square Jupiter, and the following year, SA Moon opposed Jupiter. The natal configuration of Venus square Moon has now arced to Jupiter. At the time you went to work in this company in sales (Moon rules the 3rd), and your mother (Moon) helped you pay off the loan. This clearly shows the importance of the mother (Venus square Moon) with 8th house resources of others (Jupiter). Within this time period, SA Uranus arced to the MC and also the Sun. The Sun rules the 4th house.

You were working from an office space in your home. Transiting Uranus was opposed the Moon, and square Venus. It was a time of reprogramming into other directions (in sales for this company). Transiting Saturn was in hard aspect to the Moon in the 2nd house. Transiting Jupiter was square the Moon, then square the MC, Sun, Mercury and Uranus. Here we see transiting Jupiter hit off all three natal configurations sensitive to career and finances.

If we see a tight conjunction, square or opposition in the natal horoscope such as Venus square the Moon in this example, then a solar arc planet will aspect both the Moon (at 23 Gemini) and Venus (at 24 Pisces) within a space of one year. In solar arc development, one degree is equivalent to one year of life.

The same applies to the natal Sun conjunct the Midheaven. In the aspect grid, it is two degrees apart or two years apart in solar arc development. Uranus opposed Mercury is about 2 ½ years apart (2 degrees 32').

Also, let's put it that you changed jobs in 1989 to make more money working for a new company in sales and you continued with your small business on the side. We see SA Uranus approaching a square to the Moon. The following year, 1990-1991, SA Uranus would oppose Venus.

Notice in 1987-1988 SA Sun=Jupiter, a successful combination. In 1989, SA Mercury ruler of the 2nd house was semi square the Midheaven with transiting Jupiter in the 2nd house conjunct the Moon. All of this fits nicely together with the essential natal aspect configurations in your horoscope.

In 1990-1991, you did a complete turnaround in every direction of your life. Transiting Saturn was approaching a conjunction with the Midheaven. It had just passed conjunction with natal Saturn, your Saturn Return, in 1990 occurring in the 9th house.

In spring 1990 around May, you give up your job. You decided you were done working with large corporations and you wanted to change your life. You no longer wanted to live in a specific country.

You worked in the area of accounting, finance and administration. In 1990-1991, SA Midheaven=Jupiter in your 9th house of internationalism and foreign countries.

SA Uranus was opposed Venus ruler of your Ascendant. You can feel the exciting, exhilarating change. Uranus rules your 10th house. It carries 10th house concerns with it as it moves in solar arc development.

The Secondary Progressed Moon opposed Saturn. Transiting Saturn would conjunct the Midheaven and the Sun. It's time to take on more responsibilities and move into the height of one's profession.

Transiting Jupiter at the 4th house cusp was opposing the MC and Sun. Whenever a planet comes to the IC, the 4th house cusp, by solar arc or transit activity, it carries a new start feel. This was a time of significant changes in every area of your life. You were promoted quickly in April and October 1991.

In 1992, transiting Jupiter was conjunct Mercury and opposed Uranus ruler of the 10th house. The Jupiter-Uranus combination paid off. You were promoted to work in Europe and other parts of the world. In 1992, you worked in two different countries.

At the end of 1994 with SA Jupiter opposed Uranus, you received the promotion you had been working toward over the past four years. You became financial controller, responsible for the administrative and commercial areas of the resort. You had reached your goal.

Birth Chart

An astrological birth chart is a map that has been put together to show where all the planets are in their rotation around the Sun, from our current point on Earth at the exact moment of a person's birth. This is also called a natal chart. A reading of this chart can tell a person a lot of things about their life. Strengths and weaknesses in character can be identified, timing for important moves and decisions, and the opportunities for soul growth within a specific person are identified.

Calculating your birth chart calls for some very specific and personal information.

- The date of your birth
- The exact time of your birth
- The exact place of your birth

If you are missing any of the vital information, like place or time, it will be hard to give an accurate reading. The ascendant (rising sign) of your birth cannot be accurately measured. You won't be able to accurately know which of the houses the planets fall into on your chart without this information. However, you can still get a lot of useful information from your birth chart without this information.

An astrologer is going to use the information to look for a few key items from your specific birth chart:

- Which of the twelve houses and which zodiac sign each of the planets lie in on the chart
- Venus, the Moon, and Mars' zodiac signs and the house of love
- Jupiter and where you could be lucky
- Saturn for where you may need to work harder
- The angles formed between two planets
- A grouping of three planets in any given sector which could indicate a heavy concentration on a specific energy
- The elemental balance

- The balance of the qualities in the chart
- The patterns formed by the planets on the chart

The astrologer will take all of this information that has been gathered and tally up a score. This score will help them advise you on what aspects of your life need more concentration and how to equal it all out.

Planetary Connections

The Sun

The Sun is the most important planetary body in your birth chart. The link is masculine and connected to your father. The sun represents your ego, your interests, your vitality, your likes and dislikes in basic terms, what motivates you, and what expresses and identifies you as a person. The Sun gives you the "I am" mindset.

The Moon

The Moon is what controls your emotions, so consequently, the mindset that it implies is the "I feel" concept. If you ever notice people and some of them need more assurance than others, look to their moon sign for the answers. The Moon is the governor of all the representations of intuition, habits, feelings of security, and instincts.

The Moon also rules over all the emotions you try to hide from other people as well. These can be things like anger, jealousy, and fear. You like to keep this side hidden, and it is only shown to those who are closest to you.

Mercury

Mercury rules your curiosity. The mindset given to this planet is "I think." Mercury is your communication style; it is how you learn, what sparks your curiosity, problem-solving skills, and your general interests. Someone who is born during Mercury retrograde is often intuitive and a thinker. They rarely rush before thinking something through. If stationary during your birth, Mercury makes you a talkative thinker.

Venus

The planet, Venus, rules your romantic relationships. The mindset associated with Venus is "I love." Venus plays a big role in who you attract, how you interact socially, how you interpret beauty, what you look for in a partner, and how you spend and earn your money.

If Venus was in retrograde when you were born, you find yourself most comfortable in the company of the people you know. You may have lived a limited financial and love life when you were younger, but as time goes on, you will increase in both areas.

If the planet was stationary during your birth, you are a social butterfly. You revere love as an importance and finding a partner as well. You have the capability of having a successful financial life.

Mars

Mars is about your motivation and your initiative. The association of "I act" is used in the description of a Mars mindset. Mars is your driving force in the areas of confidence, aggression, strength, and stamina, and how much of a risk-taker you are. Mars is also synonymous with your sex drive and what you search for when pursuing one.

When you were born, if Mars was in retrograde, you direct your energy inward so that you can avoid all confrontation. If Mars was stationary, you are all about taking action and going after what you want.

Jupiter

"I grow" is the planetary mindset of Jupiter. This planet is the one that rules your ethical decisions, how you feel about life, what areas you show caution in, where you find your luck at, the areas you want to learn, and what you need to do to gain that knowledge. Jupiter is about searching for truths, which is why it is the best planet for governing law and religion, education, and philosophy.

If you were born while Jupiter was in retrograde, you are a reserved philosopher. If it was stationary, you are outspoken on your point of view and your principles.

Saturn

There is no surprise that Saturn is the governing planet of the Capricorn zodiac. The principle of "I achieve" is what Saturn describes in their lives. Ambition, major life decisions, restrictions, limitations, boundaries, feelings of inadequacy, safety, practicality, and hard work theories are what Saturn fuels in a person. Saturn oversees the achievements in your chart that deal with career, wealth, and business.

If Saturn was in retrograde when you were born, you find yourself solely responsible for your own successes and failures. If it was stationary, you are of a more goal-oriented mind that is set on succeeding.

Uranus

Uranus is about rebellion and seeking out the unexpected. The principle of "I evolve" could not be truer for this planet. This planet is where you stand out from the crowd, what areas you will do the unexpected in, where you will find changes, and encompasses the accidents that can happen in your life. It is the "aha" moment that occurs in your life or when you just know something that has happened. The feeling of déjà vu.

Neptune

Neptune is both inspiration and illusion. "I dream" is a concept that can both be helpful or deceptive. Neptune is the reason for this. It is the all encompassment of illusion and confusion versus imagination and creativity. It is like the devil and the angel sitting on your shoulder at any given time, pushing you toward something. Neptune is also what determines the addictions you may develop in life. Drugs, alcohol, gambling, and any other blind spots that can take you by surprise in your life.

If Neptune was in retrograde when you were born, you might have a higher tendency to try to escape your reality. If it was a stationary planet on your chart, you may be artistic but lack the sense of anything realistic.

Pluto

"I empower" is the Pluto mindset. This is the planet that can help you clear out the old to make way for the new in your life. It helps you understand when you feel powerless and how to take charge of that feeling to find your power. It is representative of how your inner beliefs can change over time but that you can choose the positive over the negative and vice versa. It's in your hands.

Did you notice that Earth does not have a place amongst the planets listed above? Never fear, this was not an accident, but intentional. A birth chart is from the viewpoint of the Earth because you were born on Earth. So basically, the interpretation is that your birth represents Earth on the birth chart.

The Ascendant

Ascendant In Aries Or Aries Rising

You probably have a sturdy, muscular frame with a lively, energetic face. You make intense and direct eye contact with others, and may well have been told off for staring at people as a child because of this. You are probably of medium height and can show amazing feats of strength when necessary. Red hair is common with those with Aries on the Ascendant.

Always in a hurry, this can lead to your being accident-prone, especially with injuries to the head or face. A hasty temper turned inwards produces headaches or even migraines. Sporting activities or any form of physical exercise is an excellent release for this.

You meet life in a straightforward and energetic manner. You want to have control over your life, and a feeling of lack of control will manifest itself as illness. You often express yourself through dramatic outbursts, many times in anger or even other forms of self-destructive behaviour.

Ascendant In Taurus Or Taurus Rising

Taurus is the sign of the bull, and this may reflected in your body shape. Your well-shaped body displays a warm attractiveness and ripeness. In your later years, you may need to watch the tendency to gain weight too easily. Your strong broad shoulders support either a long slender neck, or else you have a very large neck size. Your most outstanding feature is your eyes and your gentle smile and voice. You may be big-boned. You enjoy dressing well, preferring soft colours.

You need to have your feet planted firmly on the ground whilst you aim for the stars, because you like to be able to see concrete results for your efforts. However high you aim, you like to remain in contact with the earthy and material side of life. This can have its drawbacks in as much as you have a tendency to hang on to people, things and experiences out of habit and a feeling of security, when there is no longer any need to. It is important for you to learn to distinguish between when it is necessary to hang on, and when you should let go. When you head towards your goals you like to have plans and a structure to systematically work around.

You may need to consciously develop better habits with looking after your body and its requirements.

Ascendant In Gemini Or Gemini Rising

You are the most youthful-looking of the zodiac with veritable Peter Pan looks. You may have neat, sharp facial features and a wiry frame. You are able to wear bright colours, mix patterns and fabrics and may love bizarre jewellery. You are lithe and agile with slender hands. Some people may think that you can look like two different people at different times.

Your ability to communicate, in fact your need to communicate, contributes to your sense of identity. You are extremely observant and are able to follow two or more conversations at once. You are a fast talker and may use your hands a lot. In any case, you always seem to have a lot to say. You are an excellent mimic and may also have a flair for languages.

You love to find out how people and things work and are quite clever at taking things apart and putting them back together again. Your curiosity makes you versatile and adaptable, but you may suffer from an over-abundance of diverse interests. In any case, you dislike being committed to only one thing, because you hate to lose alternatives.

Your abundance of nervous energy means that you are always on the move. You may appear highly strung. You are often in two minds about the situations that you are involved in.

Ascendant In Cancer Or Cancer Rising

Your face is rounded with beautiful round, sensitive eyes that show concern and innocence. Your whole appearance speaks of softness and tenderness. You may not be that energetic, and you need to watch weight gain later in life. Fluid retention can also be a problem. As a female, you may be quite big-breasted. As a male, you may have quite a broad and fleshy chest in comparison with the rest of your body, especially your hips. You don't dress for glamour or to impress, instead you tend to prefer your old comfortable clothes rather than following uncomfortable fashion styles.

Growth in self-awareness comes to you through fully acknowledging, experiencing and respecting your true feelings, and developing the nurturing and caring side to your personality. You may feel overwhelmed at times by the depth of emotion that you feel. It is difficult for you to simply let go of a strongly felt emotion, unless you have another feeling just as powerful to take its place.

It is very healthy for you to play the mothering role, whether to a group of people, in the context of a business, or by nurturing a strongly felt cause. On the other hand, if you shun the role of nurturer, your aim will be to find someone else to mother you. You will constantly be looking for the ideal mother type. There is also the possibility that you over-identify with your mother and find it hard to break away from the family unit.

You tend to approach issues and situations from a sideways angle and in a non-confrontational manner rather than head-on.

Ascendant In Leo Or Leo Rising

You have great presence with a strong-featured face and a sunny glow of inner self-confidence. You display a regal quality in your posture and carriage, holding your head proudly, back straight, walking slowly and deliberately. You are probably well-built and taller than average. You have an eye for design and glamour. You are comfortable wearing strong colours and patterns. You may be quite vain about your hair.

You tend to feel that anything is better than being ordinary. You are preoccupied with emerging as an individual in your own right, and to do this you need to develop your own sense of power and authority and exercise your creative expression.

Ascendant In Virgo Or Virgo Rising

With Virgo on the Ascendant your body is probably neat and wiry, and you tend to use neat and economical movements. Your well-groomed appearance is mirrored in your cool and classic way of dressing, good posture, fine bone structure and animated expression. Physically, you possess good stamina. You tend to look younger than you really are, all the way through into your later years.

In creating and defining yourself, you use self-criticism, mental analysis and discrimination, focussing on very specific points of your personality. It is important for you to settle the practical management of the everyday necessities of daily life before you embark on your grander aims in life.

You are very conscious of making sure that your body functions smoothly and well. You are very good at analysing yourself and life in general, but you need to develop the ability to jettison anything that is destructive to yourself. The danger exists that too much analysis can box you in to an existence that is overly rigid and tight. If you over-emphasise and become obsessive about order, correctness and precision, you may lose touch with your spontaneity and natural sense of flow.

Ascendant In Libra Or Libra Rising

You are extremely attractive and have a warm and charming nature. Your features are usually refined, your bones delicate and your skin fair. Your movements are very graceful. You are aware of your attractiveness, but be careful that you don't fall into the trap of being vain and judging others by how beautiful they may look.

You are indecisive and tend to always sit on the fence. This is because you can always see the other's viewpoint. In fact, you are able see the viewpoint of everybody else around you. You must learn to force yourself to make choices and be prepared to take the consequences. Don't take the easy option of letting others decide for you. You are able to objectively and fairly assess any situation.

Ascendant In Scorpio Or Scorpio Rising

You most likely have dark, brooding looks with thick, abundant hair and strongly marked eyebrows that frame the most important feature of your face, your eyes. Your eyes have a piercing, penetrating quality, so much so that many people are unable to meet the directness of your gaze. Overall, you give the impression of quietly contained power. Your movements are controlled, and your clothes are chosen for their dramatic value. With your commanding personality, you are able to instil fear and apprehension if you wish. There is an air of mystery about you, as well as veiled but potent sexuality.

Ascendant In Sagittarius Or Sagittarius Rising

The Ascendant reveals how you present yourself to the outside world and the style in which you meet new experiences and life in general. When people first meet you, they meet your Ascendant rather than your Sun sign. The Ascendant may also indicate your physical characteristics.

Although you may not be tall, your legs are probably long and gangling. As a child, you may have been quite clumsy. Your long legs give you a jaunty way of walking, which you exercise, restlessly pacing up and down when you need to think. Your most outstanding feature is your wide brilliant smile, shining out of your open face. Although you prefer dressing casually most times, when you do dress up, you can look absolutely stunning.

Ascendant In Capricorn Or Capricorn Rising

Your bone structure is distinctive, and you probably have good teeth. Your shoulders may be rounded, and physically you tend towards a wiry and lean frame. There may even be a certain devilish look to your face. Just as your life improves after the age of roughly forty, so do your looks lighten up, and you seem younger and more frivolous than years earlier. As a child, you looked serious and old for your years, but as you grow older, you seem to grow younger and more good-looking. You feel better and happier with every passing year.

Ascendant In Aquarius Or Aquarius Rising

You are most likely tall and slim with good bone structure and clear, open and refined features. Your eyes are extraordinary, helping to give you an electric or magnetic aura. Your distinguishing feature is your hair, or if you are male, your beard perhaps. Your dress sense can add to your sometimes bizarre appearance, but even more conservatively dressed, you are always arresting. You tend to prefer bright electric colours over the more conservative and quiet shades.

Ascendant In Pisces Or Pisces Rising

Your beautiful eyes are one of your most attractive features. Your complexion has a translucent quality, very pale if you are fair-skinned, or ripe and lush if you are dark-skinned. The clothes that you choose don't call attention to you, and they are soft and comfortable rather than fashionably gimmicky. Your feet tend to be large and your hair hard to manage.

Astrology for Relationships - Sun Sign Compatibility, Rising Sign Compatibility

Sun Sign Compatibility

Your Sun sign—aka your zodiac sign, star sign, the answer you give when asked "What's your sign?"—represents the foundation of who you are. It's your ego, your sense of creativity, and your core traits. Each planet in your birth chart represents a facet of your personality. They revolve around your Sun sign—the epicenter of your self. The Sun is at its strongest in Leo and Aries and at its weakest in Libra and Aquarius, but regardless of the sign, it's one of the most important components of anyone's birth chart! Most pop-astrology books and horoscopes will list out the birth dates for each sign, but it's important to know that the sign's birth dates are not set in stone. Astrology doesn't line up with our calendar year perfectly, so there's a bit of wiggle room for Sun sign birth dates—also, there's no such thing as a "cusp," either, period. That's why it's important to know your time of birth to be certain of your Sun sign if you were born at the very end or beginning of a sign.

Moon Sign Compatibility

The Moon represents your emotions, your inner self, what makes you feel nurtured, and how you nurture others. The brightest lights in the sky are the Sun and the Moon, the two luminaries. Where the Sun represents your ego or spirit, the Moon represents the "reflection" of your Sun sign, so it rules your health and physical body, too. Your Moon is key to how you operate on an emotional level.

Rising Sign Compatibility

The Ascendant, or Rising, sign is the sign that was on the horizon at the exact moment of your birth (that's why you need an exact birth time and location to create a birth chart). It's commonly described as the mask you wear for the world and the sign people see upon first impressions, but it's much more than that—it's the starting point of your horoscope and determines the positions of each of your chart's twelve houses, and it acts as a filter. It's the lens through which you see the world and it determines how you express yourself. The Rising sign is also used to describe your physical appearance, style, and self-image. The Rising sign is, without a doubt, just as important as your Sun and Moon signs in your birth chart (some might argue the Rising sign is more important) and is a major component of determining astrological compatibility.

A person is born on a specific time and day and is established into an astrological sign, house, cusp or other designation. To fully reflect on the traits and predilections of those under that category, you can investigate and strive to understand your relationship with the universe completely. This can be especially useful by raising your awareness of the past and the potential of the future, finessing your inner attunement with God. However, approaching astrology as a superstition can limit the use of this information and change this resource to a passive dependence on fate while you wait for the planets or stars to shift positions. Some people believe that religion and astrology cannot exist together as God is the only one who can have power or influence over your lifestyle, personality and future. Under this argument, if you are spiritual and can actually commune with God to receive answers on how you should behave and what your path is in life, there is no need for anything like astrology to guide you. Others believe that astrology can simply give you more information about your journey in this world and also with God, giving you further understanding and knowledge of yourself and those you interact with every day. Or it may separate from spirituality completely and use astrology as a way to dissect and study the universe, as it exists only through a cycle of cosmic principles and energy. Any of these approaches is a personal interpretation that everyone must make on their own.

Aries: The planet Mars may need a physical spiritual practice, but with control. Yoga may be suited to this temperament, especially those types that are more energetic or vigorous in practice.

Taurus: The artistic Venus that brings out a gentle and creative approach to life. Most Taurus enjoy being in nature. This may lead them to feel a close connection to the Pagan religion. The celebrations throughout the year combining the spiritual with feasts and celebrations will speak directly to the heart of a Taurus. Having a close connection to the planet makes anyone under this Earth sign more enthusiastic.

Gemini: Gemini needs to be constantly mentally busy. This allows them to be more open to alternative approaches and spiritual discipline. The practice of mindful meditation, a Buddhist tradition, may help to quiet their mind and bring peace. With too much taxing the mind, the body can suffer as the nervous system can be pushed into insomnia and anxiety. The practice of turning off the brain and focusing on deeper connections is a great way to deal with stress.

Cancer: Cancer individuals can display a higher level of psychic awareness than other signs, especially if they have a history of family ancestors with similar abilities. Psychic pursuits, clairvoyance, aura readings and other similar fields may tune into the abilities and penchant of Cancer.

Leo: Leos have a lot of energy and need to be active daily. A spiritual practice that may appeal to them and that suits their temperament would be Tai Chi. Tai Chi is strongly linked to the Chinese philosophy and martial arts. It adds strength to the posture, deepens the breathing and has many health benefits. Leos will prefer Tai Chi classes to practicing alone as this will add a social aspect to it as well.

Virgo: Virgos need to be careful to engage in regular exercise and follow a diet. As their nervous system is an area of concern, they will benefit from regular practice. Alternative sources such as spiritual healing, aura reading or Reiki can be beneficial to this sign. Essentially, when participating in a spiritual activity, Virgos need activities that do not overly use their minds but can bring themselves out. It is assumed that among the twelve signs, Virgo is the natural healer. Virgo likes to give advice and service, so any spiritual or religious practice that includes doing good works would be close to their heart. However, any spiritual practice for a Virgo should allow them to recharge their mental batteries.

Libra: Balance is their trademark of libra. The study of auras might interest a Libra. Auras are the field that surrounds the physical body and are typically different colors which can display physical health, emotional well-being, and spirituality. The study and recognition of auras may allow a Libra to understand the actions of others better and teach them how to become more balanced when dealing with the other people in their lives. In turn, this may help them to build better relationships with people around them.

Scorpio: A spiritual journey will come as second nature to a Scorpio. During their lifetime, they may investigate a number of religions until they closely identify with one. With a drive to understand their life path and human psychology, they may experiment divination practices with Tarot to address the choices people face every day and properly decide on options that will make them move forward. The mysterious nature of the Tarot may appeal to a Scorpio to delve into the hidden aspects of the universe and life and to further understand the reason of why people live and thrive on Earth.

Sagittarius: A sign is known as the philosopher of the zodiac. They may be drawn to philosophy or a teaching role in whatever religion they choose. As they enjoy studying and exploring new ways of thinking and then sharing those words of wisdom, they may indeed venture into being a spiritual leader. Their journey into spirituality may involve Christianity, Hinduism, Buddhism or other alternative religion.

Capricorn: Although a materialistic sign, Capricorn does have the spiritual virtues that are required for a spiritual journey. Individuals under this sign need a spirituality that is going to last, combining both the need for being alone and spiritual advancement. Although less widely known, one option may be Shamanism. A Shaman alters the state of consciousness to communicate with the power of animals and the spirit world. Shamanism originates in central and northern Asia. This ancient and powerful spiritual practice takes time to learn, which will ensure a connection with Capricorn.

Aquarius: Aquarius is always looking up at the stars and to the future. Those under this sign may indeed be inclined to astrology. For those under this sign, astrology may be the key to self-understanding. Following astrology and finding the pattern through the planets and constellations may be a source of guidance to Aquarius. Once this pattern is revealed, Aquarius delves into a journey of joy and fulfillment and can take that lost knowledge to others.

Pisces: A Pisces's personality constitutes their journey through their life and their spirituality. As the last sign of the zodiac, Pisces understands that we are just a small distance away from the next world. Pisces can contact the dead and possesses incredible psychic awareness. Pisces needs to learn self-discipline by energy cleaning and meditation. They are very sensitive with the surroundings and those that they come in with. To help steady their energy, it is best to give them some time to recuperate and be creative. This can lead them to a number of spiritual pursuits that connect them to that awareness such as Reiki healing, aura cleansing, meditation and more.

Tarot Basics

- **Choosing a Tarot Deck**

Because there are so many Tarot decks now available, it can be difficult when first deciding which deck to use. Don't worry about choosing the wrong deck, as anything that calls to you is going to the right fit. You aren't limited to just having one deck either, you can and probably will end up with multiple decks that you use for various reasons. Some will keep one deck private, and only use it when they are reading cards for themselves. Others will use one deck for everything. Most teachers of Tarot recommend that you find a deck that you resonate with and use it to practice and learn with. Once you are comfortable enough to perform readings for others, you will know if you require a new deck for that purpose or if the one you already have will work.

No matter which deck you end up choosing, having a sense of connection with it is crucial. Take your time and browse all the options available to you. If you find a deck and decide that you don't really have any relationship with the images, find a new deck. You're not held to any commitment with the Tarot. Once you locate a deck that you like, you'll want to clear the energies that might exist around it and cleanse the deck. If that sounds a little too metaphysical for you, think about as introducing yourself to the deck and starting fresh.

- **Sorting**

To begin, you will want to sort out your cards and pay attention to any energies that you might pick up from them. On a clean table or area, sort your cards out in front of you in order. Start with the Major Arcana cards and then sort the Suits of the Minor Arcana. Take a brief look at each card while doing this. This is a way of ensuring that you have all the cards in your deck as well as taking note of the illustrations for the first time. When dealing with the Minor Arcana cards, sort the Suits by type and then by number. You start with sorting in order from Ace through Ten followed by the Page, the Knight, the Queen, and finally the King card.

For the purposes of learning, you may want to sort your cards into the Major Arcana and the Minor Arcana and put one or the other away in the place you dedicate for storage. When we focus on either one of these specifically, we allow space for further insight and development with that section. For example, it's quite common to start with the Minor Arcana and to develop a good sense of what each Suit, Number or Court card is telling us. It makes us focus solely on a limited number of cards so that we can use the repetition to build on our original thoughts and impressions.

- **Cleansing Energies**

Once you have looked at each individual card and have it sorted you can use a smudging wand such as sage or sweetgrass to clear any stored energy in the cards. This is particularly useful if you have cards that have been used before, but it's also a great starting point for new decks. At this point, you may want to meditate on the cards and visualize energy coming from you and moving towards and into the cards. If you're familiar with guided meditation or visualization techniques, you may want to use them to create a protective circle of while light that encompasses you and the cards. This can be a powerful cleansing and connection exercise.

There are energy cleansing techniques that are much more involved such as salt burials, moon bathing, or water clearing. If you feel your cards have any negative energies associated or clinging to them, take the time to perform a cleansing ritual with them. For beginners though, a simple sorting and pause in contemplation should suffice. It's recommended that you do some sort of energy clearing, however small, before performing any readings to concentrate on the questions at hand and the client.

- **Making the cards your Own**

When you are satisfied with the energy, pick them all up and shuffle them to impart your own energy into the cards. Continue shuffling and reshuffling any way you like to achieve this. Maybe you want to shuffle a certain lucky amount of times or randomly select cards to put on top or at the bottom of the deck. Whatever works for you will get your deck ready for its first use. When your deck is not being used, you should consider where you will store them. Many people find the box that they came in completely okay while others have a dedicated, specialized space just for them. Silk is associated with magical properties due to how it's created and is widely accepted as the fabric of choice when wrapping cards before placing in a box. While it's fine to do what feels right for you, keep in mind that Tarot is an ancient artform that deserves our respect and reverence.

Develop a Personal Connection

Now you are ready to work with your cards and develop a personal connection to them. This connection should be with every single card in the Tarot deck. You may choose to begin with the Minor Arcana and develop a sense of what each Suit represents. You may decide to start with the Major Arcana and develop an understanding with the illustrations found there. However, you go about learning the cards for the first time, you'll want to associate meaning to each one. You will begin to develop a relationship with your cards, which is why working with a deck you like and resonate with is so crucial. You're basically bonding with the deck and noting how you feel when using it.

You don't have to memorize the meaning of each card, only develop a basic sense of what the card represents at first. You will inherently acquire a sense of what they mean as you continue to work with them. Keep in mind that you will at one point want to express what they represent to other people so work on creating associations that are easily recognized, repeated, and deciphered. This should be fun for you, so if you feel that it's becoming too much information just take a step back and return when you are ready. You don't have to learn the whole deck right away; you can pull one card and sit with it until you feel ready to move on. Some people select only one card and meditate on it and learn everything they can from it for an entire month. This can take a very long time but if you are serious about using Tarot for deeper insight, it's a practice that is highly recommended. Remember that you can do this as you practice daily.

For now, any symbolism and representation that you find in each card are completely fine. Lay out all the cards and with a birds-eye-view take note of any patterns that emerge. Keep a journal of themes that the cards share and feelings that they give you. Refer to your journal throughout your learning to build upon your relationship with them. The interpretations of each card are only activated when you are interacting with them. When you have a need for the indications, you will be ready to find them and use them. Use this time you are spending bonding with your Tarot cards to develop your own opinions about them. The deck you chose essentially becomes an extension of your voice. Be honest with anyone that might approach you for a reading early on. Let me know that you can do it for fun but that they shouldn't take anything that comes across seriously as you are just learning. Remember, these meanings are hypothetical and not necessarily prophetic. You and the people you may do readings for are safe from harm.

Shuffling

Learn to Shuffle your Tarot deck. Unless it's very small, shuffling a deck can be difficult. This is because the cards are larger and thicker. There are many ways to shuffle a deck successfully- just keep in mind that if you are spreading them out and circulating them repeatedly that you do so on a clean surface where they will not be damaged. You can attempt to shuffle them like a regular playing card deck, or try shuffling half of them at a time, etc. You can cut them repeatedly, or have your client cut them. The goal is to have the cards be completely randomized while you're contemplating the questions being asked. This is the difference between getting a meaningful reading and not just random cards to interpret.

When you are performing a reading for someone else, consider letting them shuffle the deck so that they can get in tune with their energies. If that's not something you're comfortable with, that's okay! Maybe you can compromise by letting them cut the deck as many times as they want to without ever fully handling your cards. Discover where your boundaries are regarding your cards and demand they be respected.

You can always pick up a spread and reshuffle the deck and re-spread them. If you are not connecting with the person asking the questions, or you are not in a headspace to interpret the cards you'll find that reading the Tarot cards is hard to do. Clear the energy around you and on your cards and begin again. You do not have to pull meaning out of the cards forcefully. This should take exertion on your part as the cards will provide the insight you are looking for just by sight. You can develop intuitive reading quickly through practice!

What is Numerology?

The History and Origin of Numerology

Numerology is an art form that has been in existence since the very earliest days when mathematics was first discovered. Those who practice numerology can use numbers, names, and words to reveal divine meanings because the alphabet is so easily applied to numbers.

Numerology has three major forms, known as Pythagorean, Chaldean, and Kabbalah. All three forms can be used in any combination to create a numerology reading, but it is best to pick one of the versions and use it exclusively. Any of the three are acceptable; the one that draws a person's attention is the best one for them.

A numerology portrait is a person's guide to their life. It will reveal who a person will become and their weaknesses and strengths. A numerology portrait is something of a cheat sheet for mystical interpretations of a person's life path. Numerology uses a simple formula to determine a person's numerological chart, which can also be known as a person's numerological portrait. The numbers used are the three numbers from the letters of the name of the person, which will determine the power number, personality number, and the urge of the soul, along with three numbers from the actual birth date, which will determine the person's attitude number, life path number, and birth number.

Kabbalic numerology has its basis in the Hebrew alphabet and old Hebrew mysticism. It was first developed for the Hebrew alphabet and then later was adapted to the Greek alphabet and then the Roman alphabet. The word itself, Kabbalah, means that knowledge does not come from the body or the senses but rather from the mind. The goal of the Kabbalic method of numerology is to bring elevated levels of intelligence and knowledge by elevating personal levels of self-awareness. Only the person's name is analyzed in Kabbalic numerology. Many numerologists feel that Kabbalic numerology is less accurate than the other forms of numerology because of this.

In the Kabbalic method, every letter of the alphabet is assigned a number. According to Kabbalah studies, it is possible to have up to four-hundred different life path numbers, but Kabbalic numerology focuses only on the most popular numbers. It may not seem to be that much different from the other forms of numerology at first glance. But the other two methods use a person's date of birth, along with their name to learn their life path number. The alphabet in Kabbalah is assigned a corresponding number different than the other two systems. Many of the letters do not correspond directly to the letters of the other two methods of numerology.

The Chaldean method is believed to have originated in Babylon, south of Mesopotamia, which is now known as Iraq when the area was inhabited by the Chaldeans. It is the oldest system of numerology. Many people consider the Chaldean method to be more accurate than the Pythagorean method, although the latter method is more widely known and used more often. In the Chaldean system of numerology, every letter is given its own numerical value between one and eight. The big difference between this method and the other two methods is in the name that is used to calculate a person's numbers.

All three methods use a person's name to determine the life path number. However, the method in Kabbalic and Pythagorean numerology is to use the name that is marked on the birth certificate. Chaldean numerology will use the name that the person is known by the most. This could be the name on the birth certificate, or it could be a married name or a nickname. In Chaldean numerology, the numbers used are never single-digit numbers but double-digit numbers. In this method, the single-digit number is considered to be the number that represents the way other people see the person and the outside influences of the greater world. Double-digit numbers, also known as compound numbers, represent the hidden influences that have a specific influence of one's life. Chaldean numerology does have a closer relationship with astrology.

Pythagoras developed Pythagorean numerology before the time of Christ in ancient Greece. Pythagoras believed that numbers could be used to explain all things in the universe. He used mathematics for spiritual matters. This method of numerology is often referred to as modern numerology because it is the most recently developed method, and it has come to be the method most widely used in modern times, particularly in the Western world. Popular legend states that Pythagoras used the practice of numerology to use name-changing as a way to alter the destiny of an individual, predict what events would take place at certain locations, and determine the future fates of individuals. In this system, the letters of the alphabet are assigned a corresponding number based on their position in the alphabet. Both the date of birth and the name are used in Pythagorean Numerology, and the relationships between the two are studied.

This method uses the full name that is given at birth because that is the name that will determine an individual's numerical makeup. The birth name will tell what impression a person is most likely to make on other people, what the person naturally expresses the best, and what motivates a person, mentally and psychologically. The other most important number in Pythagorean numerology is the actual date of birth, which is used to determine the number of the life path of the individual.

Those who subscribed to the Pythagorean method of numerology were not simply interested in applying the science of numbers to determining the individual strengths and weaknesses of people. They believed that numbers were present in vast quantities in the natural world and that most things in life were ruled by a series of numbers. They firmly believed that numbers possessed mystical abilities and properties and the "all is number" meaning that anything in the world can be described in terms of proportions and numbers and everything in the world can be measured. This belief is the basic foundation of the practice of numerology.

Every letter in the alphabet has a numeric value, and every number has its related cosmic vibration. When the letters in a person's name and the date on which the person was born are combined in a particular formula, this will give an insight into how the vibrations are related to each other. This formula will give information to the person's purpose in life as a part of the overall plan of the cosmos. It will also reveal details of a person's motivations, natural talents, weaknesses, strengths, and character tendencies. Numerology is one of the best tools in use today that will help an individual develop a better insight into their overall physiological and cosmic makeup.

What is Wicca – Magic, Tools, Exercise and Magical Techniques

Wicca refers to a kind of modern paganism, and of course, looking at its background, it is recorded that it was found to be a tradition that was founded in England, that was in the mid-20th century, and its source or origin claims to be derived from the pre (before) Christian religions.

Wicca was developed by some fraternities in the great country, England, it was a secretive coven in nature, it was recorded that those who practice it, based their beliefs, faith, on what they discovered through the readings of an historical witch cult.

The Beginning of the Goddess Religion Wicca is a religion of Mysteries and nature worship with its beliefs practices and deep philosophy focused on Paganism.

When Wicca came out of the mist and went around the world, countless people began to identify with this religious manifestation why it was the only one until that moment that had a female central deity as Creator. This was in the mid-1950s and extended into the 1970s and early 1970s to the 80s. From its inception in 1951, Wicca has acquired new expectations and has undergone significant transformations, being hugged by the movements feminist and environmental, earning a new face, much more MA trifocal and Goddess-oriented than in the beginning of their history. That it's understandable, since the Sacred male was revered by thousands of years, while the Goddess was mutilated and forgotten. It was in 1970 that the feminist movement embraced Wicca as their religion.

Magic, Rituals, Religion And Spells

In Wicca the most common way to do magic is through spells. The word spell comes from the Greek "Facturus" which means action on the future. When we perform a spell we try to channel and put the energy to our around in action to bring about change according to our will. Forget all the things you have heard so far about spells. They don't part of the legends created around black wizards who perform macabre rituals in the dead of night, even because Witches don't use their magical powers to harm others. All spells practiced in Wicca aim to establish a connection between the Warlock and the Gods to attract health, harmony and success. There is a tradition in Wicca that every spell done will return to its emitter triple.

This means that whoever desires good will receive blessings and who desires evil, will get back what he wanted. One of the Wiccan taboos is also not to interfere with one's free will.

So even some seemingly good spells can be unethical. That applies for example to love spells made to conquer a person in private. This is manipulative magic and consequently you will be interfering in the free will of a person, often wishing for something that he does not desire for you. So be ethical and respect the free will of others when performing an enchantment, always taking into consideration the main Wiccan principle:

Do what you want as long as it doesn't hurt anything or anyone. Spells are forces used to create favorable circumstances so that the we wish to materialize. The biggest tool to make it happen is your personal power and your imagination. This will create channel between you and the Gods for your will to be fully realized. We often use candles, herbs, incense sticks and some magic instruments to perform a spell. This obviously will not make your spell more powerful or work miraculously but serves as a focus and brings an added magical power and vital energy of the very elements used for your enchantment.

Wicca spells most often use elements found in Wicca nature and the Witch's own will. This is more than enough for performing any enchantment. Animal sacrifices are abhorred by every serious Wiccan, which means that using an animal's blood, for example, is not acceptable at Wicca! There are some practices where it is even acceptable for you to use your own blood. To serve as a testimony, as in the making of a spell. But for these cases you can use a piece of your nail, a strand of hair or a cotton soaked in your saliva or sweat which means the blood is not essential and yes one of the many possible alternatives. If you choose to use your own blood, a drop from a pin prick is more than that's enough and nothing more than that. Be aware and always take in consideration the danger you will be in by mutilating yourself with an object of non-sterile metal. I highly discourage this kind of thing for anyone!

Know that the universe does not remain inert waiting for your spell to be project to set the energies in motion. Remember that the universe is a living being. And carries within itself many energies and powers, sometimes operating in opposed to your will and desire. For this very reason, you may have to perform a ritual or spell over and over for favorable results.

A spell can be performed as part of a Sabbath rite or practice. Devotional and you can also simply cast a Magic Circle to your around and then carry it out. For a spell to materialize satisfactorily you must act in harmony with nature. According to Wiccan philosophy there is a time and phase right lunar for everything, including working desires through a spell. For all who are new to the Wiccan religion, it is sufficient to consider two factors: the moon phase and the days of the week.

For Wiccans the moon phases are considered the manifestations themselves. Of the faces of the Goddess who presents herself as the Maiden, Mother and Elder on rising, full and waning respectively. All beings in nature react to the lunar phases. The seas, plantations and Women's menstruation are all governed by the cycles of the moon.

The magical power also changes according to the lunar phases and so when we want to do a ritual or spell properly we must follow the period lunar most suitable. See below the phases of the moon and their respective matches:

Crescent Moon

it is the ideal time for enchantments aimed at the growth, strengthening and strengthening and new beginnings. This is the ideal lunar phase for us to do spells related to planning, changes, birth, achievements and news.

Full Moon

it is the ideal time to make spells linked to abundance, success, prosperity,

fertility and marriages. It is also linked to peace, spiritual direction, intuition and

protection in every way.

Waning Moon

it is the ideal time for spells related to wisdom, knowledge, transformation, elimination of addictions, overcoming obstacles. It is also the period ideal for ending relationships, jobs or friendships that are ending.

New Moon

In the first 3 days of this lunation it is traditional not to work magically.

After this period begins a positive phase to reflect on our fears, shadows and fears. It is the ideal phase for facing the unknown parts of our being. On average every two to three days the moon will be "off course" for a few hours. It is believed that no ritual or project should be started during these hours Consult an astrological or lunar calendar for dates and times. Where the moon is in this period.

Crystal Protective Circle

Crystals can also be used to create a circle of power and protection. For this take several crystal tips and create with them a large circle in clockwise. Have the stones touch each other so that the circle is fully closed. Whenever you need to recharge your energy batteries, enter the circle and sit inside for a few minutes.

Herbs And Plants

Like stones, each herb has a vibration and energy. They are gifts from Mother Earth capable of healing, purifying, blessing, and attracting luck and success.

Herbs can also be used in conjunction with stones, complementing each other ideally you would plant and harvest your own herbs. But how can this be a little difficult in modern days, the most common is to buy them in stores specialized.

Herbs are widely used in Wiccan practices. They are burned in the cauldron as offerings, used to make cleansing baths or as filling talismans.

A pot of herbs can be made by mixing several of them with stones. When this pot is placed in an environment, serves as an energy filter and is capable of ward off the negative influences that are nearby.

Get to know some of the most commonly used herbs in Wicca and their magical properties.

ARRUDA: Used to protect and ward off all kinds of evil. It is linked to the planet Mars.

ARTEMISIA: Used to develop extrasensory psychic gifts. It is linked to the moon

ASSAFRON: Brightens the mind and stimulates the sexual and loving life. It is linked to Venus and the Sun.

BENJOIM: Attracts physical and magical energy. It is linked to the planet Mercury

CALENDULA: Attracts health, prophetic dreams, comfort and love. It is linked to the sun.

Cinnamon: Cinnamon favors physical energy, love and prosperity. Weed on in the sun.

CAMPHORA: purifying and energizing, is also used to ensure the faithfulness. It is directly linked to the moon.

OAK: Brings us centering and power in all its manifestations. It is connected to the planet Jupiter

CEDRO: favors self-control and spirituality. Planet sun.

CYPRUS: attracts health and tranquility. It is linked to Saturn.

Indian cloves: protects, drives away evil and attracts protection. It is connected to the sun and Jupiter

GINGER: enhancer of enchantments and spells. Your powder can be used. To fend off enemies. It is linked to Mars.

JASMINE: Suitable for attracting harmony, peace and tranquility. It is linked to Venus and Mercury.

JUNIPERO: protective and purifying herb, besides being used for the physical recovery. It is linked to the sun.

BLONDE: attracts vitality, success, prosperity, psychic knowledge and purification. This herb is linked to the sun.

BASIL: Brings awareness, joy, peace and money. It is connected to Mars and Venus

NUTTY: Attracts magical energy, prosperity, wealth and expansion. It is linked to Jupiter

ROSES: It attracts love in all its manifestations. It is strongly linked to Venus

SANDAL: Used to achieve all desires. It is connected to the moon.

VERBENA: It attracts love and is used to break spells. It is linked with Mercury.

VETIVER: Great for love spells. It is linked to the planet Venus.

Astrology vs. Astronomy– What is the Difference?

Despite the fact that space science and astrology may sound comparative, they are essentially different subjects contemplated by individuals. There are a couple of fundamental likenesses, however, which may befuddle a few people about the uniqueness of the two branches. For instance, both the subjects manage the perception of the nearby planetary group and planetary developments. The pathways of the sun and the moon are significant in both the examinations.

Understanding the idea of time is additionally the fundamental necessities of both the fields. Besides, in the antiquated world, eyewitnesses and ministers used to consolidate the two fields to chalk up their fates and furthermore comprehend different cataclysms and their celebrations.

In any case, enormous differentiations are there among stargazing and astrology. Cosmology is a piece of no-nonsense science. Whatever ends that are drawn from the different perceptions of the things around us have sound thinking and evidence behind them. Space science is fundamentally close identified with another branch called astronomy, which serves the underlying hypotheses and suspicions of different inquiries encompassing our planet. Space experts affirmed the legitimacy of those hypotheses, careful down to earth perceptions and thinking.

Astrology, then again, lingers behind cosmology in only one viewpoint, scientific thinking. Astrologers study the sun, the moon, and a portion of the stars to foresee the fate of individuals, to comprehend individuals' inclinations and trademark waterways. Since a great many people accept these days that there is no straight association between the heavenly items and our introduction to the world, it is considered as pseudoscience. Additionally, the absence of sorted out scientific information likewise adds to individuals' skepticism. In any case, that doesn't belittle the prominence of astrology in numerous nations, particularly in the Far East.

Astrological Rising Sign

At the point when your Astrological Chart is drawn up by the astrologer as per the data you have given of your introduction to the world date, time of birth and furthermore the spot of the birth, it shows up as a huge round circle with a little one in the middle where the individual is emblematically set. The bigger hover of 360° is normally similarly partitioned into 12 sections of 30° like equivalent cuts of a cake. Every one of the 12 fragments is known as a 'house' with the first being that on the left and just beneath the skyline or level in the chart. Enumerating anticlockwise, the 12 houses are spoken to in arrangement and named by their numerical spot - First House, Second House, etc. Once in a while, the Rising Sign may show up as just a couple of degrees over the skyline and, on different occasions, 28° or more. At the point when it is sharing the impact of the following sign ascending as in these last degrees to the 30° it is designated "on the cusp" and the attributes of that Rising Sign are modified by those of the one after. The Rising sign is most grounded in its basic qualities the closer it is to the 15° or the halfway point.

The zodiacal sign where the Sun is set at your introduction to the world is what is usually called your Sun Sign, Birth Sign, or astrological sign. The image for the Sun is promptly set suitably in the sign and the degree that it involved right now of your introduction to the world. All different planets will likewise beset by their real cosmic position.

Toward the start of each house is one of the zodiacal signs which commands that specific house. The decision or prevailing sign administering the primary house, when it has been set up by cosmic estimation, is put on the Chart on the left-hand flat, and this is called your 'Rising Sign.' Just an astrological chart drawn with scientific exactness can decide the definite level of the Rising Sign.

For instance, let us call that zodiacal Rising Sign, Aries. The remainder of the zodiacal signs are then put in their normal request, and in anticlockwise design around the hover of the Chart, to complete with the sign, Pisces appeared as administering the twelfth House, arranged over the skyline, similarly as Aries is underneath.

Fundamentally this implies when you start to consider your own make-up, there are two principal components to consider, not simply the one. Despite the fact that your Sun sign (your realized Birth Sign) might be Cancer, you should consider that Aries will likewise assume a predominant job in your inclination, especially with respect to your physical appearance, your external character, and a large number of your intuitive responses to life occasions. For this situation, despite the fact that you might be exceptionally passionate, as showed by Cancer, you will have extremely solid, friendly energies and demeanors that are certain and altogether different from the more delicate individual you are inside. You will have an external appearance of mighty, immediate and braver character than the calmer soul you know as your actual nature.

The vast majority of us start life with these two different and regularly contradicting impacts inborn as a part of our character and in our potential mental gear. Our Rising sign is different from our Sun sign. We need to come to comprehend this blend of impacts and ingest the best of the energies of each into our very own keen mix of attributes. We should make an investigation of both these signs in our first endeavor to see how astrology uncovers our primary character characteristics, as they speak to the constituents in our interesting and complex formula of human instinct.

Obviously, there are likewise numerous situations where both the Sun sign and the Rising sign, in light of galactic setups, will be the equivalent. In this case, there is an intensification of the considerable number of characteristics and no directing impacts and a Taurean individual with Taurus additionally as the Rising sign will show traditional excellencies and issues of a Taurean - a twofold Taurean so to state! It is sure that such an individual will know that the signs to his inclination and his life will be found through investigation of the Taurean energies and standards.

It is the level of the Rising Sign which accents or conservatives the qualities relationship with that sign, as per the separation between its neighboring signs. So with 1 degree, Aries ascending, there would be as yet the solid impact of Pisces. As the characteristics of Pisces are totally different from Aries, in character investigation, this factor would need to be thought about. With 28-30° Aries rising, one would need to include the solid, exceptional impact of Taurus which, for this situation would add some alert to the thoughtlessness of the Aries nature.

The factor of the Sun Sign and the Rising Sign and their appropriate translation is a fascinating subject that has been the focal point of a lot of research in the course of the only remaining century or somewhere in the vicinity. There is sufficient proof to show that specific, unequivocal highlights and conditions will be regular to those people having comparable factors in their introduction to the world charts. This encourages you to feel sure when looking to clarify specific subtleties.

Many come to realize that the Sun sign is the thing that you appear on the scene within regards to your gifts, soul purposes, and profound demeanors, and the Rising Sign is the marker of our physical appearance and external character - the instrument through which our spirit communicates.

The Rising sign firmly impacts a few parts of our appearance (with respect to whether we are reasonable, dull, and some impact over the extent and facial highlights). It influences our wellbeing, giving us obviously characterized physical qualities and shortcomings. It emphasizes all character likes, aversions, dispositions, and credits to as often as possible depict how different a character you are contrasted and your kin - who were conceived at different occasions and now and then different spots.

So it is astute to ponder the energies and impacts of both the Rising Sign and the Sun Sign in the blend, so as to see which factors you feel precisely depict your own makeup. It is great to know at the beginning what the restricting or clashing components in your character are probably going to be. It is additionally useful to know the positive, reciprocal characteristics which you can use in a creative and positive way.

Dissecting someone else's horoscope is particularly similar to attempting to recognize the flavorings in a perplexing formula of a cake - a portion of the different fixings may in time be identified, yet a definitive flavor and taste are past any investigation, similarly as crafted by planning and using the different astrological energies is altogether an issue for the individual himself.

Breaking down your own Chart is totally different from perusing the report of an expert. It expects you to be without inclination, which is practically unthinkable aside from in regards to occasions and conditions. Anyway, such activity has numerous prizes. It can make you mindful of your characteristics, both great and awful, and support self-improvement.

Deciphering astrological energies is a difficult assignment, which is the reason numerous astrologers remain, to some degree detached from individual contact with the subject, liking to utilize PC helps for the scientific planning and to depend upon just a single individual interview for a perusing.

Others compare it to brain science and their work of understanding to the relationship of making requests out of bits of a jigsaw - with each factor being simply one more piece to discover a spot for in the perplexing example of the character. It can't be accentuated enough, that Astrology is both a science and a quality.

If you earnestly wish to comprehend the subject, there are numerous books covering different angles and a few courses which take you from an investigation of the zodiacal signs and their related characteristics, to the situation of different planets, the significance of the Moon upon your passionate nature, the connection between the planets in the birth chart, the regular connection with guardians and friends and family, wellbeing matters, great and terrible luck, connections, premiums and occasions and obviously that which intrigues numerous individuals, their future. One must be wary of paying heed to the general and regularly shallow remarks in astrological paper segments. These regularly serve to criticize science.

Each expert astrologer ought to be knowledgeable in setting up your own chart, giving you have a record of the specific time and the spot of birth. Every individual astrologer has his very own techniques and arrangement of translating your Chart. Many represent considerable authority, specifically viewpoints, for example, wellbeing, connections, character, future occasions, and significantly climate forecast. It is critical to locate a decent expert with extensive involvement with the field of your own advantage. Meanwhile, know when perusing of issues identified with your Birth Sign or Sun Sign that you should likewise contemplate the characteristics of your Rising Sign.

The Basics of Astrology

Let's dig a little deeper and get to know the basics of what there is to know on creating a birth chart. It is a time sensitive, data based chart consisting of one of the Four Elements (fire, water, earth and air) combined with either one of Three Qualities which could either be the Fixed, the Cardinal or the Mutable quality, this shows us the connection between all things breathing and have matter on this Earth and how we are tied in together in the bigger picture. It shows us that we are part of a cycle.

It is not to say that this is the end all and be all of your persona, personality or being. There are good and a bad characteristic that you will see on each of the four elements but it does not describe you in completion. What Astrology is an outline, if you must, of your capabilities, potential and weaknesses and how you the study can you recognize some of these traits and evolve. It essentially helps you learn more about yourself and what you can do to either overcome or enhance in your life.

These are the basic precepts you will need to know in order to be able to make calculated decisions about any given event at any given time of your life. We will go over the foundation of astrology and learn about the signs, planetary houses, the role of the sun and the moon to us.

Discover your own sign to be privy to your weaknesses - so as to be able to make adjustments and realize your "limitations" and be empowered to overcome your own fears which you feel may be holding you back. Confirm your strengths and gain the knowledge of your sleeping self and allow these traits innate to you be awakened to help enhance your life and being. Have a deeper sense of perception of yourself and get a clearer picture of what you are to help you get to where you want to be.

In the end we are given free will and the choice is for us to make on which of these traits, negative or positive alike, we will build up or tone down. The essence in fact is not to put down the individual but help the individual realize these elemental powers and how we can use them for good and how we can transform and evolve from the negative aspects into a more near-perfect being.

Join us for a brief look into the celestial bodies that we look upon to give us clearer insight of our being and let's discover what they each mean and how looking up allows us a better understanding of events in our lives but more importantly - a look into ourselves.

The Four Elements and What They Mean

Each of these elements is neither good nor bad but neutral. It is the individual who inherently gives way to disrupting the harmony and balance of the elements and man who develops in himself the good and bad traits. So this is exactly why we are looking into the strengths of each individual sign and element - it is not to make you feel less than you are but to have you understand that and make the necessary adjustments, and to understand that we do have limitations and some of those limitations are things we can overcome.

The signs falling under Fire are known as extroverts or are also called the masculine traits. Water and Earth signs are more feminine in qualities and sometimes referred to as negative traits.

Some of the positive qualities of the signs which fall under the Fire element include their enthusiasm and vigor. They are a courageous bunch with zeal. This element delivers creativity and they are known for being brave. On the other hand, the not-so-positive qualities of the signs classified under the Fire element include tendency to excess, jealousy, violence, anger, hate. They tend to destroy and are vindictive; they get easily irritated and are quite quarrelsome. They are voracious and lean toward violence. Some of the signs which are categorized under the Fire Elements are Leo, Aries and Sagittarius.

The positive qualities of the Air element includes being mild in manner, and watchful. They display and a trusting nature, they are known for being kind hearted and devoted. They display clarity, dexterity and are optimists. Those who fall under this element are independent, as well as diligent. They are a pretty joyful bunch. On the other hand the negative traits of those who fall under the Air element is their tendency to gossip. Signs under this element can be quite cunning. They can be quite sensitive and touchy. They can also be inconsistent, with a lack of perseverance and dishonest. Libra, Aquarius and Gemini are the signs which fall under the Air Element.

Earth, is a female or introvert element and the signs of Virgo, Taurus and Capricorn fall under this category. The signs that fall under this element are known for being persevering. Signs under this element are also known for their consistency, mindfulness, ambition, and straight-forwardness. They are responsible and steadfast known for punctuality and reliability. On the other hand the negative traits of signs under this element show that they lack consciousness, and scorn. They can be quite timid and cumbersome, known also to be lazy, indifferent and superficial.

Some of the stronger traits of those who fall under the element of Water are that they are a trusting bunch by nature; they are placid, understanding, and mild in manner. They are a forgiving lot who are compassionate who are devoted. They like to internalize and enjoy the company of their thoughts as they are meditative. Those signs falling under the Water Element category are modest and do things with fervor. On the other hand they can be quite indifferent and heartless with circumstances and situations they may find unsavory. They aren't exactly the most daring bunch, and tend to be a tad lazy. They tend to display dejection, can be pretty unstable and tend to display lack of concern and instability. Cancer, Pisces and Scorpio are signs which fall under the category of the Water Element.

What is Chakra?

Words Chakra was originated from the Sanskrit word chakra meaning "wheel." Words refer to a spinning wheel of light or a wheel or time, as well as stands for celestial peace as well as order. The Chakra system was first defined in the ancient Hindu message Vedas, the earliest written practice in India. It is believed, that the Chakra system is an approach that originated from the Aryans, the Indo-European invaders of India.

The Chakras defined in Hindu customs are recognized as the key Chakras. These Chakras have no particular kinds or locations and are believed to be symbolic. In the western world, a different Chakra system dominates; it is called the New Age Chakra system.

New Age Chakras, unlike their primary counterparts, have certain types and locations in the body. They stand for energy centers, power joints, and points of power entrance in the body.

The New Age Chakra system consists of Chakras situated along the back cord. Each Chakra represents a specific shade, which describes the visible light range linked with it.

Chakras are not physical items but rather power patterns shaped like funnels and are frequently explained as "whirlpools of power."

Researchers considering that Einstein (that theorized that all issues are power as well as whatever in the cosmos is accumulated by internet of interconnecting energy) have actually understood concerning and also researched power fields. Sheldrake's Morphogenic Resonance Theory, the clinical research of individuals like Einthoven and also Berger, who have developed those body organs, such as the heart and brain, create bioelectric areas.

When conductors like cords or living cells lug electric currents, the surrounding space produces a magnetic field. The space around the living cells of the human body is currently being called the biomagnetic fields. Or more simply - energy fields.

Within these biomagnetic fields are rotating whirlpools of this energy. And there are plenty of varieties of these throughout the body- all feeding right into the 7 biggest vortices. These seven are what we generally call the Chakras, and they have been associated with the colors of the light range.

Each chakra properly attracts right into the body's power area energy from the 'interconnecting internet' Einstein talked of, as well as after that sucks out 'old' power from our bodies. They are a little bit like just how air-conditioning works.

If our chakras functioned effectively constantly after that, we would certainly all be delighted and also completely healthy and balanced. The trouble is they do not, so we aren't.

Frequently the chakras end up being blocked by the particles of our lives- emotions, environmental stress, physical misuse like toxic substances in our food. They all include up to those spinning vortexes not spinning the way they should.

So, just like our body needs to be cleaned up of particles by bathing, so the chakra system requires to be cleaned up as well as free from the particles that quit it performing its task properly.

There are a whole new type of healers who are dealing with the power fields to cause optimal wellness, and also, a great deal of their job entails these chakras.

Vibrational Medicine or Energy healing might appear a little bit airy-fairy, but the more we discover these energy areas as well as just how they function, the more the feeling behind these new kinds of holistic healing approaches makes.

However, you do not have to go to a specialist to remain healthy and balanced, although it's probably a great suggestion to see an excellent power healer if you aren't healthy to start with. It functions actually well in combination with traditional clinical practices.

To keep your chakras, you can work with yourself vigorously by picturing these chakras and picturing them being cleansed. Those that have an idea in a Higher Power, such as Angels, can request their assistance to clear them.

The fact is, there is a great deal of high vibrational energy 'muscle' available simply waiting to help us with our power job. It's only a matter of requesting assistance, and also locating the most effective means that works for you.

There Are Seven Major Chakras In The Human Body.

We all have seven major chakras, as well as several minor chakras. Each chakra is associated with organs or parts of each demand and also the body to be looked after and balanced routinely. You can function on each chakra individually, starting with the base chakra, after that, bring them all right into equilibrium, or you can work on all the chakras at the same time.

All chakras connect with one another. Each chakra corresponds to a certain color frequency and also with a certain gland or body organ.

In a healthy and balanced body, the chakras distribute and also soak up color power evenly, while in an undesirable person, contaminants might begin to collect triggering physical, psychological, and psychological troubles.

Each chakra can be stabilized, making use of colors, crystals, necessary oils, songs, affirmations, or altering what you do. It is additionally valuable to have a chakra balance to bring them all back into equilibrium. This can be done in your home on your own, or you can go to a crystal specialist or color specialist to have it done.

When all your chakras are well balanced - you should be healthy and also well balanced.

It is very important to have all your chakras in equilibrium; often, when people begin on the spiritual path, they focus on the pineal eye. However, it is essential to begin near the bottom. Our body is like a structure; you require to obtain the structures right before you deal with the top floors. So make sure your bottom chakras are well balanced as well as operating effectively.

- The First Chakra lies at the base of the spinal column and also stands for survival and also physical vigor. It is associated with the shade RED.

- The Second Chakra is located at the sacral as well as stands for a wish and also sexual power. It is connected with the shade ORANGE.

- The Third Chakra lies at the solar plexus and represents self-image. It is connected with the color YELLOW.

- The Fourth Chakra is located at heart and represents love, empathy, as well as compassion. It is associated with the color GREEN.

- The Fifth Chakra is situated at the pit of the throat and stands for interaction and liberty of expression. It is related to the shade BLUE.

- The Sixth Chakra lies at the forehead (typically called the 3rd eye) as well as stands for psychic vision. It is linked with the shade INDIGO.

- The Seventh Chakra lies at the crown of the head and also stands for the completeness of the being as well as spiritual perfection. It is connected with the color VIOLET.

The seven Chakras align in the spine. Energy normally moves upwards in the body, depending upon a person's specific life experience. The lower Chakras represent the physical existence, and also power ascends as a person participates in more spiritual features.

The Chakra system is a holistic entity that suggests that when the one chakra is interrupted, the energy circulation of the whole system is affected. An unbalanced Chakra system causes an unbalanced life; it causes poor physical, psychological, psychological, and spiritual wellness.

Energy healing is a topic that often concerns those who understand the importance of maintaining a stable chakra network. There are several examples and theories of how the chakra mechanism is restored. However, all lead to total well-being, as a balanced chakra system represents the complete harmony of body and spirit.

How Chakras Work

A great way to believe in your chakra energy is like a collection of linked swimming pools in a creek-- in some cases, the round flow of a pool can come to be blocked or reduce down due to points that drop in — the very same puts on each swirling chakra. By resolving the blockages and also living a healthy and balanced and also satisfied way of living, energy will certainly move between them, and equilibrium will certainly return to your life.

You can open your power flow in each chakra using several methods. We'll cover a few of those strategies below.

Every person has their very own specific energy flow, and how you live your life influences your circulation. With several life conditions, there isn't one detailed treatment that can be applied.

The Chakra system is a part of a much larger system, our power system. This is the system that enables you, the private stimulate of divine awareness, to experience living right here in this globe, on Mother Earth. The Energy system is linked to your spirit, the power systems of the Earth, and the solar system and also deep space, so that although we are different in lots of ways, we are likewise deeply linked to a much bigger area than we recognize.

The Chakra system is a system of sites, doorways that access your spirit as well as deep space as well as various facets of your experience here in the world. Each chakra resonates at a various vibrational price, and through this vibration is tuned right into a details element of yourself and your experience. So for instance, one chakra will certainly focus on your experience of security and security (money, food, etc.) whilst an additional will be concentrated on the all-important 'love,' all sort of love from romantic love to the relationship as well as so on.

It is simplest to imagine the Chakras as rotating rounds of colored light. There are a lot more exact descriptions than this, at an introductory degree, the rotating ball picture is still really efficient as well as gives you the chance of working with the chakras without overloading you with info.

The chakras are additionally interactive, which means that they can be influenced and altered by your experience, and they, in turn, influence and also change your experience. If you can see their chakras, they are generally distorted, usually filled up with filth (negative or stationary power), and also not functioning well at all. This suggests that all incoming information goes through these harmed chakras (unles the chakra in inquiry has shut down altogether).

Choosing Your Candles

One well-balanced tool that is directly symbolic of the elements is the candle. This is because each element is present throughout the use of a candle. The element of air is ever-present in the form of oxygen, and oxygen is necessary to keep the flame alive and burning. The earth element is represented by the wax of the candle, as well as the fibers used to make the wick. The wax also represents the element of water as it transforms from solid to liquid when it melts, as the element of water is characterized by its shape-shifting abilities. And, of course, the literal flame of the candle represents the element of fire. By charging the candle with your intent, you create a small yet powerful tool that embodies the entire Universe because when you change your candle, you add that last very important element: spirit.

Types of Candles

Candles come in all shapes and sizes. You will find a wide variety among different occultist shops, body shops, or even grocery stores. It helps, however, to buy from shops that specialize in magical intent so that if you have any questions, there will be somebody there who likely knows what they are talking about, compared to an average grocery store clerk.

The majority of witches and those who practice magic rituals will tell you that the size of the candle is not important, but if the candle is too big and takes three days to burn out, you may not want to use those in a spell that requires the candle to burn all the way down naturally, which is a requirement in most spells. Therefore, a giant, bulky candle can actually be counterproductive.

The main types of candles are tea lights, votives, tapers, columns, encased pillars, and free-standing pillars. All of these types can be used interchangeably, but the best kinds of candles to use in spells that require them to be burned all the way are votives and tapers. This is because their wicks are typically short, and they are generally the easiest to control. One of the most popular candle types are the menorah candles, which are about four inches in length and are sold in bulk at easily accessed places, such as the grocery store. They are white, thin, and unscented, which make them perfect for most kinds of spell work.

In a few cases, a spell or ritual may need a specific kind of candle, such as a candle shaped like a certain figure to represent a specific person or a seven-day candle. Below is a short list containing the intent of a few commonly used candles in these cases.

Female figure: This is used to attract or repel someone specific but can also be used to represent someone close to you who identifies as female.

Male figure: This is used to attract or repel someone specific but can also be used to represent someone close to you who identifies as male.

Couple: Candles shaped like a couple are used to bring a married couple closer together.

Genitalia: This one is pretty straight forward. It is used for arousal, passion, sexual desire, and fertility.

Buddha: Good fortune, abundance, and luck

Devil: A devil-shaped candle is used for temptations, whether to encourage or banish them.

The Cat: This is used specifically for money spells, luck, or even protection.

Skull: This candle shape is used to repel unwanted feelings or thoughts. It is also used for healing spells or cleansing.

Knob Candle: The seven knobs that make up the body of this candle represent seven wishes.

It is highly suggested that you use a candle that has never been used for spell work. Don't just pick up a candle that you burned for your nighttime bath and use it in a money spell because you do not have anything else. If you do not feel like going out and buying a new candle that day, you should save your spell work for another day. According to most magical beliefs, a candle, once lit, absorbs the vibrations caused by the many items around it. It is believed that this may lead to a negative or ineffective magical outcome, so you must exercise caution.

Colors and What They Mean to a Wiccan

In our world, colors have many purposes. They are used in art to express a certain intention or mood, to stimulate the mind with subtle or winding patterns, or even to organize. To a Wiccan, colors play a vital role in spell casting and intent. Each color has a role and intention for our everyday lives. Certain days, feelings, and even numbers have a connection to a certain color.

Candles, with their superb symbolic qualities, allow us to work directly with the magical properties that they possess. For hundreds of years, humans have associated different colors with certain qualities or events. For example, passion and love have always been associated with the color red, as it is the color of blood and the heart. The color green is ever-present during the growing season of the earth and, therefore, has long been associated with abundance and prosperity.

In order to accurately cast the spells highlighted, you will need to choose your candle's color carefully, and, ideally, perform the spells on the day of the week in which the intent is clear. Utilizing these color and time correspondences in your magic reinforces the intent of your spell and makes it more potent.

Red: Red is a symbol of vitality, passion, intense emotions, fertility, desire, sexuality, and strength.

White: White represents purity, healing, the beginning of a phase, the ridding of malicious spirits, peace, and innocence.

Pink: Pink is the color of love, friendship, affection, reconciliation, and harmony.

Purple: Purple represents spirituality, wisdom, idealism, devotion, and spiritual strength, insight, and emotion.

Black: This color rids negativity. It represents protection, stability, dignity, and the end (but also seed to a new beginning).

Blue: Blue symbolizes healing, truth, wisdom, protection, spirit, and patience.

Brown: Brown represents solidarity, grounding, strength, endurance, and unity with nature.

Yellow: This color symbolizes happiness, achievement, inspiration, knowledge, completeness, and imagination.

Green: The color green represents abundance, wealth, growth, prosperity, employment, balance, and renewal.

Gold: Gold represents integrity, inner strength, self-realization, intuition, and understanding.

Silver: Silver is the color of intuition, vision, purity, healing, capacity, memory, and intelligence.

Orange: This color represents energy, stimulation, vitality, communication, happiness, and attraction.

Grey: Grey symbolizes contemplation, stability, reserve, and neutrality.

The Intent Behind the Days of the Week

Monday: Monday is ruled by the moon, and deals with fertility, insight, wisdom, beauty, illusion, emotions, and dreams. The colors best used on this day are blue, white, and silver.

Tuesday: Tuesday is ruled by Mars, and deals with victory, success, courage, defense, logic, vitality, conviction. It is a good day to cast problem-solving spells. The colors best used on this day are black, red, and orange.

Wednesday: Wednesday is ruled by Mercury, and deals with luck, change, fortune, creativity, education, insight, and self-improvement. The colors best used on this day are orange, purple, and grey.

Thursday: Thursday is ruled by Jupiter, and deals with prosperity, wealth, healing, abundance, and protection. The best colors to use on this day are purple, green, and blue.

Friday: Friday is ruled by Venus, and deals with love, fertility, birth, romance, passion, friendship, and pregnancy. The best colors to use on this day are green, pink, and blue.

Saturday: Saturday is ruled by Saturn, and deals with wisdom, change, cleansing, motivation, and spirituality. The best colors to use on this day are black, purple, and brown.

Sunday: Sunday is ruled by the Sun, and deals with promotion, success, fame, prosperity, and wealth. It is a good day to cast money spells. The best colors to use this day are gold, yellow, green, and orange.

Now that the days and the colors have been covered, it is time to choose a candle. To choose the color, it is best to correlate your intentions with the color you pick and the day that you cast the spell. For example, if you want to cast a spell that will multiply your wealth, you will want to use gold, yellow, or green candle and cast a spell on a Sunday.

The potency of your desired spell entirely depends on how you choose to organize it. The closer you cast the spell to the intended day and with the right color, the more potent it will be. This is why it is of dire importance to choose your candle with deep thought and preparation.

Most candle spells require the candle's flame to burn all the way down naturally, on its own, without being disturbed. However, it is hardly a good idea to leave a flame unattended, even in the form of a candle. Staying with the candle as it burns down could take hours, depending on the kind of candle one uses, and most do not have the time to spare. If you absolutely must leave your candle, simply place it in a safe place away from any flammable objects. An empty tub or sink are examples of safe places to leave the candle while you go about your daily business. It is also important to note that many oils used for anointing can be highly flammable and must be used with care. Some spells require the candles to be snuffed out, and it is easy for one to forget that there is oil on their fingers as they try to pinch the candle out. Handle these oils with extra caution.

As you explore and practice the magical qualities of candles, you will soon take note that if you exercise the appropriate cautions and keep your focus, as well as a sincere intent, with harm to none, of course, you will begin to see your spell work flourish with success.

Horoscope Matches – Why is it Important?

Any modern person definitely finds it difficult to grasp the entire concept of zodiac signs and horoscope matches. In fact, most people do not think horoscopes or planets have anything to do with our lives these days. While the west faith strongly suggests that our shortcomings and circumstances in life are all we have to blame for are ourselves and the poor choices we make, the people of the East think differently.

Eastern culture has always been about the mystical –something that can not be explained by human knowledge and skill or events beyond our control.

Eastern culture believes that there is a greater force than us and is responsible for doing things in our lives. It determines who we are, asks us what we are, and even guides us towards the right person that we should marry and spend the rest of our lives with.

In comparison to the way people see marriage in Western countries, Eastern ideology sees marriage as one of the most precious and important things in one's life. It is so valuable that you can't make mistakes by marrying the wrong person. But then again, there is no guarantee, particularly when they are from different backgrounds, cultures, religions, and lifestyles, that the marriage of two different people works. The Hindu tradition offers a solution to this dilemma-with the horoscope matches. The success rate of marriage can be determined in advance. Horoscopes are considered Kundali under the Hindu tradition. A kundali is made shortly after the birth of a child. In order to make a kundali, essential natal information such as the date, time, and place of birth is necessary. Such information is presented and evaluated in accordance with the relations between the three. Whatever the result, she will speak about the future life of the child, including schooling, health, income, marriage, the number of children, and so forth. Horoscopes are very important predictive factors during a wedding. These are actually so critical that priests and astrologers must first be consulted before the wedding plans are enforced.

If you think it is easy to fit horoscopes, you are terribly wrong. In reality, the process of finding horoscope matches is both complicated and comprehensive. In the first stages of wedding planning, the horoscopes of couples are usually balanced and will determine whether the man and the woman will bind under the everlasting bond of sacred marriage. There are eight factors deciding whether a man and a woman will have a good marriage or not. If the eight variables fit-up, the pair are expected to live together happily. Each of the eight factors has its own importance in the life of a couple, such as spiritual compatibility, character, and temperament. Find out whether the couple fit in these areas will say whether or not they are happy in life.

Nonetheless, there are many situations where emotions often get in the way of rationality. It must be pointed out. This means that a person or a couple can choose to ignore the analysis of the horoscope compatibility test. The usual reason is that one or both partners are so loved that they dare to continue with the relationship even if there is no good future for the heavenly bodies upon which the horoscope is founded. It is always the couples themselves who decide their fate under these circumstances. If the relationships continue, they will brace for the likelihood of traumatic breakups and other similar incidents. The defiance of horoscope signs may be bad for the person or the couple.

This is why compatibility is best practiced well before a relationship gets deeper. A couple may think that they can already do this at the next point, marriage because they have been together for a relatively long time. You have to remember that marriage is completely different from dating or courtship. In reality, during the marriage, couples who used to enjoy so much romance would realize that after all, they weren't meant for one another. In addition, this is a tragedy that must be avoided.

The best way to prevent these disasters is to know about horoscope matches even before you and the person you have mutual attraction find a serious relationship. This will ensure that you do not take further steps towards higher expectations. It is a fact that the majority of those who are deeply affected by failed relationships are also those who demand them too much. It will definitely be hard for you to conquer suffering when your relationship ends if you believe you will be with your loved one as long as you live. On the other hand, people who take their interpersonal relations lightly do not face these possibilities. Nonetheless, this doesn't mean you shouldn't be serious about your relationship. You only have to make sure that you and your partner are truly compatible before you reach a higher level of partnership.

While the use of the horoscope for the study of compatibility may not seem empirical to people in the West, the East will draw attention to many examples to prove its accuracy. However, if you do not fully believe in the concept, you have the right to do so. Nonetheless, you should always note that the main aim is to ensure that couples are happy before taking the next major step in their relationship. It is definitely a very scientific concept. Therefore, you should still remember this as your relationship with your loved one continues to grow.

Horoscope Sign Compatibility: Does It Work?

What is the accuracy of the horoscope sign? Will indications and portents tell me whether anybody else is supposed to be a happy partner? What if all the astrologers are correct? Even if you have concerns about compatibility with horoscope signs, you may well find out what the stars might have to say about your love life and perhaps even your friends and business connections. Why would it hurt, after all?

What is Symbol Accuracy Horoscope?

Everybody has a zodiacal sun sign, depending on the date of birth. While a natal chart will give you more information based on the exact time, date, and where you were born, you just have to start with your sun sign. It's easy to find out if you don't know what your horoscope sign is. There are many great sites that can clarify your sign and give you a fantastic insight into your personality.

Now that you know your own sign of the horoscope, it is time to look for additional facts. When you know the birthday of the other guy, you can also figure out what his or her sign is. Fitted with this knowledge, it is easy to find out if your horoscopes are compatible or not!

Different levels of compatibility You will discover whether you are compatible with another person and the extent of compatibility of the horoscope signals. Many people are extremely compatible. For example, Capricorn and Virgo, Leo and Aries, Aquarian, and Libra. Examples of these are:

Some people can get along well, but on the way, they may have trouble. Check out your own compatibility to find out who fits into this category in your life; you may be surprised!

Finally, some sun signs seldom click. For starters, an Aquarius and cancer will seldom be a good match. Would you wonder if this relates to your life relationships? It's easy to find out. When you wonder even more with the answers you hear, it might be a good idea to plan a birth chart so that you can learn even more interesting things about yourself and the people you encounter in your life and how to make the most of the time.

Make the most Horoscope sign compatibility. There are plenty of online resources to help you do just that if you want to know more about your Zodiac Sun sign. Comprising various sun signs that lead you to a deeper knowledge of the people in your life, and while some horoscopes are dumb, others are prepared by people who have turned the art and science of understanding astrology into a way of life.

It may seem strange at first to consult an astrologer, but once you stop thinking about it, it makes sense! Historical figures, great leaders, and people of all kinds of respected astrological guidance and flourished in love and other fields of life. Why wonder? Why wonder? Find out more today about the compatibility of your horoscope signs and other important astrological evidence.

The History of the Horoscope Signs System

In the past, ancient civilizations used the sun and moon positions and the presence of different constellations to perform various activities such as seasonal planting as well as navigation practices. The horoscope signs were thought to come from the ancient Greeks, who believed that the placement of the Moon, the Sun, and other celestial bodies determined and forecast a person's life. We used to look at the constellation's location when a person was born to assess the signs of Zodiac that the individual was born.

The scheme of horoscope signs is divided into twelve parts based on the time of year and the dominant constellation. These are personalized according to the day, date, and year of birth. The typical zodiacs include Aries (21March-19 April) Taurus (20 April220 May) Gemini (21 May-20 June) Cancer (21 June-22 July) Leo (23 July-22 August) Leo (22August-22 September) Libra (23September-22 October) Scorpio (23October-22 November), Capricorn (22December-19 January) Aquarius (20January-20 February) and Mercury (20February-20 March)

In the horoscope, there is a relation between the temperament of the individual and the astrological characteristics, and it is understood that the zodiac signs have both positive and negative characteristics. Since these characteristics have long been in use, they have evolved over the years, and that is why these unique features are known for a certain zodiac. The horoscope reading is based on an individual's birth chart that includes the planet under which it was born, planets operating on the birth planet, and other forces in the sky.

The horoscope reading is still popular in today's world, as many cultures still practice it. Others come with different variants, such as the Chinese and the Mayan systems. Most people use this system to help them understand more about their daily lives and future relations. Across various sources, such as the internet and regular newspapers, magazines, and consumers, the information about the zodiac system can also be found across fortune-tellers and astrologers to learn more about their horoscopes.

Kundalini Rising

What is Kundalini?

Kundalini is a Sanskrit term from ancient India that identifies the arising of a form of energy and consciousness that remains coiled at the base of our backbone from birth, and is the source of the life force that everyone holds within himself - depending on of culture this force is identified with different names, for example pranic energy, Chi energy or bio-energy.

Yogic science suggests that this energy is responsible for the formation of the baby in the womb, and after birth it remains coiled at the base of the spine in order to keep the energy intact in stasis until death, when it unwinds and returns to its source.

However, Kundalini can also deviate or unwind from the base of the spine as a result of certain spiritual practices, or in response to life events. When this happens, it can be moved little by little, unrolling like a snake, or quickly and explosively, involving the intestine, heart or head. This event can be surprising and chaotic, frightening or blissful, and usually triggers months and years of new sensations and changes in the person who awakens this energy.

You can clearly perceive the balance of the body moving and failing, and it takes time to adapt. Awakening Kundalini is a practice considered in the East very significant for the spiritual realization of each individual, but it is rarely recognized as such in Western traditions, and perhaps for this reason Western peoples are more easily affected by energy or physical problems related to the malfunction of this energy.

The awakening of the Kundalini is able to trigger phenomena and changes that can be as positive as they are negative, and that occur both on the physical and psychological and spiritual levels. You can both feel inspired, full of energy and creative, and exhausted, tired and stressed beyond measure. Very often these phenomena are also accompanied by sensations and movements of the body that are completely unknown to us, such as sudden vibrations of the limbs, momentary visions, mirages and agitation.

For this reason it is very important to awaken the Kundalini in the correct and unhurried way, taking care to do it in the calmest and most relaxed state of mind possible.

The awakening of the Kundalini offers a profound opportunity for those who are called to follow a spiritual path: it is thanks to it that we are able to get rid of our preconceptions, disappointments and ghosts of the past.

Like any energy of creation (prana, electricity, atoms) it can be abused incorrectly by those who are not spiritually motivated or have not completed a path of personal growth, and therefore are not free from their mental constraints. In order to be ready for his awakening, we need to fully understand our mind and not be impatient or nervous.

Therefore, the activation of kundalini can also take place thanks to various spiritual practices. It may also happen that his awakening is not desired but occurs after some life events. You can awaken the slow mode or, overwhelmingly. Not everyone experiences kundalini activation in the same way and for many it can turn into a frightening experience. The changes it implements are manifold and it can take years to know what has happened.

The rise of the Kundalini allows you to experience, in full awareness, new states of consciousness, accompanied by a series of phenomena of a physical, sensory and perceptual nature. When awakened, Kundalini manifests itself through knowledge of the past, present and future, with a strong awareness, in addition to an expansion of consciousness. Thanks to the beneficial action that Kundalini meditation exerts on the chakras, and on the subtle in general, the practitioner is able to achieve a state of complete well-being, a sense of unconditional joy and harmony. This energy is also related to the reserve of sexual energy. Kundalini conveys sexual energy in its radical form, converting it into high frequency spiritual energy, which allows the development and activation of paranormal activities such as telepathy, matter / energy conversion and communication with other entities.

The symbol most used to represent the Kundalini is the snake, a symbol of knowledge. Since ancient times, the snake has been considered synonymous with transformation, thanks to its ability to change the skin. Also the Rod of Asclepius or Caduceus of Hermes, symbol of modern medicine, presents a snake wrapped around a stick. Some meanings of the three windings are: the past, the present and the future; waking, sleeping and dreaming; subjective, sensory experience and absence of experience; harmony, action and matter.

The awakening of the Kundalini starts from our perineum, rises along the entire spine, until it reaches the heart and finally the top of the head. This flow of vital energy naturally produces a sense of well-being and healing on all levels and gives us great strength and clarity.

Many also experience an extraordinary sense of synchronicity with the universe, sometimes accompanied by visions and achievements on important issues in their lives.

However, not being generally accustomed to this release of vital energy, the awakening of Kundalini can be a very intense experience and can bring to light unresolved issues of our life. For this reason it is important to start gradually, learning to know yourself and how to overcome your limits one step at a time.

By faithfully following the practice of Kundalini Yoga and the teacher's instructions, you can experience the benefits of Kundalini Yoga in a completely safe way.

Kundalini Yoga is the legacy of technical and spiritual knowledge traditionally passed on for thousands of years.

It is a sacred science that combines form, breathing, movement, meditation, relaxation. It is the art of sequence, rhythm and sound.

It is the Yoga of awareness.

Its power derives from unleashing that potential, traditionally called Kundalini, that reserve of latent energy which represents itself as a sleeping snake or a curl twisted three and a half times at the base of the vertebral column. It is a potential that is generally untapped, just asleep, which awakened and traced back along the column, activates rebalancing them at a higher level of consciousness, all our chakras.

Kundalini yoga works on the body (but it is not gymnastics) with kriyas, sequences of postures and movements associated with particular breathing. Through physical practice, blood circulation is stimulated, tissues and organs are purified and fortified, the glandular system is balanced, the nervous system strengthened. With Kundalini Yoga we act on the central and peripheral nervous system, relaxing the tensions created by daily stress and helping to contain its deleterious effects; on the internal organs by massaging them and improving their physiological functions; on the body in general, which finds a new flexibility and tone; on the control of emotions, allowing us to act in the newspaper with renewed tranquility; strength, beauty, sense of well-being; high sense of awareness, increased intuition; elimination of negative habits, creativity. In this way one experiences a sense of vitality and awareness of one's body accompanied by a gradually increasing sense of self-awareness.

In addition to and at the same time as the work of balance on the body, through relaxation, breathing and meditation, Kundalini Yoga acts with a progressive process also on mental energy and concentration, giving the experience of a deep inner calm. It broadens the radiance which in turn improves our impact on the outside world. It helps to recognize our negative patterns and patterns, to dissolve anxiety, depression, frustration in a deeper, real and subtle (spiritual) vision of our existence.

Indications of a Kundalini Rising

Singular encounters of Kundalini process shift extensively, however the essential indications of a Kundalini rising that an individual may encounter include:

– feeling unique, not fitting in

– a profound disappointment or a longing for internal improvement

– internal impressions of light, solid, current, or warmth

– an elevated inward or external mindfulness; expanded affectability

– sentiments of vitality streaming or vibrating inside

– unique capacities, limits, and gifts

– non-standard marvels; adjusted states

– unconstrained substantial developments or breathing examples

– enthusiastic variances; mental issues approaching

– atypical sensations or sensitivities

– an enthusiasm for otherworldly development or in power or the recondite

– sympathy and a craving to help other people

– a feeling that something non-customary, transformative, or blessed is going on inside

– self-improvement, and ideally, profound change and acknowledgment

Kundalini Shakti's endeavors to improve her status can influence the inconspicuous body (psyche and vitality), causing an assortment of encounters, including unpretentious body exercises that vibe physical. Individuals can have a Kundalini discharge sooner or later in their lives, or they can start this lifetime brought into the world with a functioning Kundalini process. They might know about something extraordinary going on, or they may not understand it until the procedure matures sometime down the road. Kundalini procedure can be experienced as wonderful and delicate or as sensational and awkward. One need not be having an "otherworldly crisis" to have a profound Kundalini process.

Despite the fact that there are plainly discernable examples to Kundalini process, Kundalini risings offer a boundless cluster of conceivable outcomes, and each is extraordinary. A Kundalini rising doesn't really bring about programmed sacredness, ideals, virtuoso, unique capacities, remarkable encounters, or particular distresses. Numerous individuals have risings that produce not many momentous show attributes other than some type of affectability and longing and an ability or quality that stands apart somewhat. Such an individual is progressively mindful of the unobtrusive parts of life and is sufficiently unsatisfied to look for additional from life. This may form into an exceptional aching that inclinations the person to discover reason, which means, and profound life, on the off chance that they are not unduly diverted into less fulfilling transitory substitutes meanwhile.

With right direction, an experiencer can appropriately bolster Kundalini Shakti's endeavors for otherworldly headway, and progress can be securely improved, yielding individual change and profound development. On the off chance that an individual doesn't have a clue how to effectively bolster their procedure and on the off chance that they take part in undesirable and unspiritual way of life practices, their imperative vitality may get dispersed or misled. This can pressure the unobtrusive body, potentially yield inevitable awkward outcomes and defer otherworldly advancement.

Eclipses

You have read about the North Node and how it affects a person's life. Different astrologers have varied opinions regards to the North Node by which they deliver predictions.

Now, we will discuss regards to eclipses, which plays an essential role in both astrology and human life.

The eclipses occur when any of the Planet or Moon comes in the path of the Sun's light. In Planet Earth, two types of eclipses occur solar and lunar eclipses.

Comparison of Solar and Lunar Eclipses

In the event of the solar and lunar eclipses, three celestial bodies are involved that is the Sun, Moon, and the Earth.

On the Earth, lunar eclipses occur when the Earth comes between the Sun and the Moon. In this, the shadow of the Sun obscures the Moon.

However, the Moon doesn't have its light, and it only shines when its surface reflects the rays of the Sun. It only occurs during a full Moon.

Effects of Lunar Eclipses

According to NASA scientists, they haven't found any evidence which states that lunar eclipse has some impact on the people. But they have found that it has some physiological effects which can lead to effects on the human according to their belief.

Wildlife and Lunar Eclipses

Many centuries ago, people claimed that during lunar eclipses, the animals behave differently. To prove this, the University of Pennsylvania Department of Anthropology conducted a study on owls and stated that their activities get changed and come to the conclusion that older people were right.

Eventually, the main reason for the change is the light level of the lunar eclipses changes as it proceeds.

Now, if you talk about astrology, it has a very big concept regards to lunar eclipses.

Astrologers think that this open sky shows something mysterious for the human being. These two celestial bodies, the Sun, and the Moon have an essential place in human nature and imagination. And indeed, both solar and lunar eclipses.

This is the time when these two events become all the more crucial in Indian astrology. As it is said that lunar eclipses have a profound effect on the human that's why Indian astrologers give beforehand warning to the various classes of people according to their age and situations.

What not to do during lunar eclipses?

- According to the astrologers, both men and women don't eat food and drink water
- Don't keep the airs open
- Don't engage yourself in intercourse
- Don't brush your teeth, wash clothes, and open locks
- Sleeping at the time of eclipse means you are inviting illness
- Don't pluck flowers, leaves, branches, plants, grass
- Never do any good work at the time of eclipses

What to do at the time of lunar eclipses?

- An individual should take a bath before eclipse starts and worship god

- An individual has to chant guru mantra at the time of lunar eclipse as it will offer positive energy to you

- After lunar eclipse gets the end, you have to take a bath and offer some donation to the brahmins

- All the stored Water should be replaced by freshwater

- The person can take food or drink something only after eclipse gets over

- At the time eclipse, one should wash all the clothes which they touched during a lunar eclipse

- It is said that after eclipse gets over a person should feed cows, birds, and donate something useful to the needy people as it is considered to be very beneficial which multiplies in the coming future

- Precautions for pregnant women at the time of eclipses

- According to astrology, it is very harmful to both pregnant women and fetus as it damages the body organs of the child

- During the eclipses, a pregnant lady should apply cow dung or basil leaves on the stomach, and it is believed that this shield keeps the Rahu-Ketu away from the child

- During eclipses, the women should not ever cut anything with a knife or scissors and sewing clothes

On the other hand, solar eclipse is the phenomenon in which the Moon passes between the Earth and the Sun. It only happens during the new Moon when three celestial bodies form the same line.

Every year, there are 2-5 solar eclipses which can be categorized into three types. They are:

1. Total Solar Eclipse

It happened when the Moon completely covers the Sun as an individual sees from the Earth. It is said that don't look at the solar eclipse from the naked eye as it will severely harm it.

2. Partial Solar Eclipse

It occurs when the Moon partially covers the disk of the Sun.

3. Hybrid Solar Eclipses

This solar eclipse occurs very rarely in the world, which gradually changes from an annular to total solar eclipses moving along its path.

Effects of Solar Eclipses on the Human Body

People get very excited to see the rare occasion of solar eclipse as it occurs 2-3 times in a year. However, our ancient legends have described the effects of the solar eclipse on the human body.

If you talk about the effects of the solar eclipse in terms of astrology, then it has a very deep meaning as the Sun is closely related to life, ego, personality, and many more things. Moreover, the positive energy of the Sun in the individual birth chart signifies growth after meeting various challenges of life.

Now let's put some light on the effects of the solar eclipse on the human body:

1. People can feel tired or lethargic

If you talk in regards to spiritual research by the great astrologers, the total solar eclipse can cause tiredness or sickness to the human body. It is advisable that don't take any essential decisions during the time of the solar eclipse.

2. Pregnancy gets affected

Our Indian experts in astrology recommended that pregnant women have to take certain precautions during a solar eclipse. And it is said that during a total solar eclipse-the child might be born with certain abnormalities.

But, behind this theory, there is no scientific proof, but still, it is a very predominant thing.

3. Might get eye abnormalities

It happens when an individual directly sees the solar eclipse. This recommendation is scientifically proven, which can harm the person's eye up to a great extent. However, this can cause permanent damage to the retina and also cause blindness. So, never see the total solar eclipse with naked eyes but if you are interested in watching the solar eclipse, wear glasses which are specially meant to see the eclipse.

4. Can have digestion problem

Solar eclipse might cause digestion problems to some individuals. That's why many spiritual people don't eat or drink anything during solar eclipse time.

5. Individual emotions get out of whack

As solar eclipse occurs very rare, so it affects the psychological thinking of the person. There are shreds of evidence that during solar eclipse behavior of the individual changes they feel very agitated, unusual dreams come, creativity gets boosted, and not the least sometimes solar eclipse often makes relationships difficult.

Furthermore, if you want to know about the difference between the two, then let's move forward, and I will make you clear that. The main and most crucial difference is solar eclipse occurs during the day, and the former happens during the night.

If you talk the duration, then solar eclipse comes just for 5-7 minutes, and lunar eclipse comes for an hour affecting every aspect of life.

Taking you to the frequency of the solar eclipse it happens once in every 18 months, and a lunar eclipse occurs twice in a year. Moreover, a lunar eclipse can be seen in innumerable places in the world but, solar eclipse rarely seen in some places which are told by science or our astrology experts by calculating everything.

Nonetheless, astrologers can also tell us in what degrees solar or lunar eclipse can affect humans, animals, or Earth. Astrology is a vast subject which can tell everything from your birth till death by calculating but still some people don't believe it as they think that it is just wastage of time and the path of earning money.

Tarot and Western Astrology

Every sign of the zodiac in Western astrology relates with an archetypal energy from the tarot deck. This section will show you how to recognize those relations, since they are admittedly less than obvious. It's not so simple to say that Aries links with the Magician because they're both #1 in their respective areas of study. It's not so simple at all but worry not! I'll guide you through the associations, and it will be accessible enough in no time.

Tarot Looks at Aries...

...and sees the Emperor card from the Major Arcana. Both have energies of determination, commitment, applied authority, motivation, loyalty, and reliability. If you're an Aries conducting a reading for yourself (or if you're reading for someone else who's an Aries), choose the Emperor card to represent yourself (or the Aries querent in question) if the reading asks for a card of this type. Additionally, if the Emperor card arises in an Aries person's spread, it likely represents that person him or herself.

Tarot Looks at Taurus...

...and sees the Hierophant card from the Major Arcana. Both are intense and piercing, they cannot be superficial, and they're deeply involved in truth as a tradition. If you're a Taurus conducting a reading for yourself (or if you're reading for someone else who's a Taurus), choose the Hierophant card to represent yourself (or the Taurus querent in question) if the reading asks for a card of this type. Additionally, if the Hierophant card arises in a Taurus person's spread, it likely represents that person him or herself.

Tarot Looks at Gemini...

...and sees the Lovers card from the Major Arcana. Both are involved with turning points, weighty decisions, careful proceedings, and maintaining personal integrity. If you're a Gemini conducting a reading for yourself (or if you're reading for someone else who's a Gemini), choose the Lovers card to represent yourself (or the Gemini querent in question) if the reading asks for a card of this type. Additionally, if the Lovers card arises in a Gemini person's spread, it likely represents that person him or herself.

Tarot Looks at Cancer...

...and sees the Chariot card from the Major Arcana. Both are transcendent, steady, security-seeking, partially-protected or -shielded freedom-loving, intuitive, and road-opening. If you're a Cancer conducting a reading for yourself (or if you're reading for someone else who's a Cancer), choose the Chariot card to represent yourself (or the Cancer querent in question) if the reading asks for a card of this type. Additionally, if the Chariot card arises in a Cancer person's spread, it likely represents that person him or herself.

Tarot Looks at Leo...

...and sees the Strength card from the Major Arcana. Both are strong, emotional, mental, courageous, and physical. They both prefer to face their problems with grace rather than avoid them entirely. If you're a Leo conducting a reading for yourself (or if you're reading for someone who's a Leo), choose the Strength card to represent yourself (or the Leo querent in question) if the reading asks for a card of this type. Additionally, if the Strength card arises in a Leo person's spread, it likely represents that person him or herself.

Tarot Looks at Virgo...

...and sees the Hermit card from the Major Arcana. Both are purposeful yet slow, wary yet innocent, experienced and wise yet young at heart, exploratory but only on the inside, and open to the world yet guarded. If you're a Virgo conducting a reading for yourself (or if you're reading for someone who's a Virgo), choose the Hermit card to represent yourself (or the Virgo querent in question) if the reading asks for a card of this type. Additionally, if the Hermit card arises in a Virgo person's spread, it likely represents that person him or herself.

Tarot Looks at Libra...

...and sees the Justice card from the Major Arcana. Both are desirous, emotional, light-hearted, righteous, fair, and justice-oriented. Both also should be careful to note the difference between what is desire versus what is need. If you're a Libra conducting a reading for yourself (or if you're reading for someone else who's a Libra), choose the Justice card to represent yourself (or the Libra querent in question) if the reading asks for a card of this type. Additionally, if the Justice card arises in a Libra person's spread, it likely represents that person him or herself.

Tarot Looks at Scorpio...

...and sees the Death card from the Major Arcana. Both are intense, fascinated by transformation, interested in rebirth, enigmatic, changeable, and introspective. They can both also be extremely personal or utterly detached, for they contain so many extremes. If you're a Scorpio conducting a reading for yourself (or if you're reading for someone else who's a Scorpio), choose the Death card to represent yourself (or the Scorpio querent in question) if the reading asks for a card of this type. Additionally, if the Death card arises in a Scorpio person's spread, it likely represents that person him or herself.

Tarot Looks at Sagittarius...

...and sees the Temperance card from the Major Arcana. Both are gifted mediators and social balancers, understanding leaders, and conscious adventurers. If you're a Sagittarius conducting a reading for yourself (or if you're reading for someone who's a Sagittarius), choose the Temperance card to represent yourself (or the Sagittarius querent in question) if the reading asks for a card of this type. Additionally, if the Temperance card arises in a Sagittarius person's spread, it likely represents that person him or herself.

Tarot Looks at Capricorn...

...and sees the Devil card from the Major Arcana. Both are shadowy yet skilled, guarded yet knowledgeable, intense yet internally playful, reflective yet confident, and restrictive yet protective of others. If you're a Capricorn conducting a reading for yourself (or if you're reading for someone who's a Capricorn), choose the Devil card to represent yourself (or the Capricorn querent in question) if the reading asks for a card of this type. Additionally, if the Devil card arises in a Capricorn person's spread, it likely represents that person him or herself.

Tarot Looks at Aquarius...

...and sees the Star card from the Major Arcana. Both are enlightened, optimistic, spiritual, leaders, altruistic, and humanitarian. If you're an Aquarius conducting a reading for yourself (or if you're reading for someone else who's an Aquarius), choose the Star card to represent yourself (or the Aquarius querent in question) if the reading asks for a card of this type. Additionally, if the Star card arises in an Aquarius person's spread, it likely represents that person him or herself.

Tarot Looks at Pisces...

...and sees the Moon card from the Major Arcana. Both are dreamy, idealistic, potentially deluded, intuitive, emotional, strong, compassionate, creative, moody, and subtle. If you're a Pisces conducting a reading for yourself (or if you're reading for some else who's a Pisces), choose the Moon card to represent yourself (or the Pisces querent in question) if the reading asks for a card of this type. Additionally, if the Moon card arises in a Pisces person's spread, it likely represents that person him or herself.

Tarot Looks at Water Signs…

…and sees the suit of Cups. Whether your wateriness comes from your Western zodiac sign (Cancer, Scorpio, and Pisces are water signs), your Eastern zodiac sign (Rat and Pig are water signs), your internal Ayurvedic constitution (a.k.a. – your Dosha (Pitta and Kapha constitutions are water-influenced), or otherwise, those associated with the element of water will connect best with the suit of Cups. If Cups arise for you in a reading, they will signify positivity and alignment on your soul mission or life path. If you're looking for a card to demonstrate yourself as a water sign, choose any of the water sign cards (the Chariot, Death, or the Moon), or choose one of the court/face cards in the suit of Cups.

Tarot Looks at Fire Signs…

…and sees the suit of Wands. Whether your fire energy comes from your Western zodiac sign (Aries, Leo, and Sagittarius are fire signs), your Eastern zodiac sign (Snake and Horse are fire signs), your internal Ayurvedic constitution or Dosha (Pitta is primarily fire-influenced), or otherwise, those associated with the element of fire will connect best with the suit of Wands. If Wands arise for you in a reading, they will signify positivity and alignment on your soul mission or life path. If you're looking for a card to demonstrate yourself as a fire sign, choose any of the fire sign cards (the Emperor, Strength, or Temperance), or choose one of the court cards in the suit of wands.

Tarot Looks at Air Signs…

…and sees the suit of Swords. Whether your airiness comes from your Western zodiac sign (Gemini, Libra, and Aquarius are air signs), your internal Ayurvedic constitution or Dosha (Vata is primarily air-influenced), or otherwise (the Eastern zodiac has no alignment with the element of air; they substitute for elements of metal and wood instead), those associated with the element of air will connect best with the suit of Swords. If Swords arise for you in a reading, they will signify positivity and alignment on your soul mission or life path. If you're looking for a card to demonstrate yourself as an air sign, choose any of the air sign cards (the Lovers, Justice, and the Star), or choose one of the court cards in the suit of Swords.

Tarot Looks at Earth Signs…

…and sees the suit of Pentacles. Whether your earthiness comes from your Western zodiac sign (Taurus, Virgo, and Capricorn are earth signs), your Eastern zodiac sign (Dog, Sheep, Ox, and Dragon are earth signs), your internal Ayurvedic constitution or Dosha (Kapha is primarily earth-influenced), or otherwise, those associated with the element of Earth will connect best with the suit of Pentacles. If Pentacles arise for you in a reading, they will signify positivity and alignment on your soul mission or life path. If you're looking for a card to demonstrate yourself as an earth sign, choose any of the earth sign cards (the Hierophant, the Hermit, or the Devil), or choose one of the court cards in the suit of Pentacles.

Wiccan Beliefs

Deities

Wiccan practices focus on two aspects of divine energy: The Goddess and the God. These represent the feminine and masculine energies of the Universe. You can choose to work with specific goddesses and gods, or you can choose to honor the basic feminine and masculine energies they represent simply. The Goddess and the God each have three aspects that reflect the main stages seen in life and in Nature: Maiden, Mother, and Crone for the Goddess and Warrior, Father, and Sage for the God. Many Wiccans only focus on the Goddess in their magical practices due to the overwhelming male influence in deities seen in most modern religions, but it is important to honor both in your magical practices. Wicca is a path of balance in all things, and that includes a balance between feminine and masculine energies in the divine and in yourself. Ignoring one in favor of the other only harms your practices and your progress on your magical journey. When setting up your altar, the Goddess is typically symbolized by the chalice and the color silver. The God is symbolized by the athame and the color gold. You can also add small statues or figurines in honor of the divine feminine and masculine if you have space for it.

Working with the Elements

Along with a Goddess and God, Wiccans work with the energies and spirits of the four basic elements: air, fire, water, and earth. Each of these elements governs different types of energies and has different colors associated with it. Air is related to the cardinal direction of east and the color yellow. It governs the realms of creativity and abstract thought. Air is represented by Zephyrs when working in the spirit realm. Fire is related to the cardinal direction of the south and the color red. It governs the realms of passion and love. Fire is represented by Salamanders when working in the spirit realm. Water is related to the cardinal direction of the west and the color blue. It governs the realms of emotion and compassion. Water is represented by Undines when working in the spirit realm. Earth is related to the cardinal direction of north and the color green. It governs the realms of stability and grounding. Earth is represented by Gnomes when working in the spirit realm.

When setting up your altar, you should have symbols related to each element in the quadrant facing the direction that element is associated with. There is no one single answer when it comes to what symbol you should use; anything associated with that element will work. Traditionally these symbols have been wands for air, swords or daggers (not the athame) for fire, cups (not the chalice) for water, and pentacles for the earth. However, the more personal the symbols you use, the more effective they will be. You could choose to have a feather in the east for air, a candle or a piece of wood from a campfire in the south for fire, a seashell in the west for water, and a pinecone in the north for the earth. Be creative and find what works best for you! The primary direction your altar faces (the element that is at the top of it when you are facing it) is the one that is going to be strongest in your magical workings, so keep that in mind when you are choosing a place to set your altar up.

Wiccan Practices

Spells

Spells lie at the base of all Wiccan magical practices. This is the way witches manifest their desires into real-world outcomes. Spells can be simple or elaborate, depending on the specific magic being worked and the desires of the particular witch. One is not necessarily better than the other; more than they are different ways of achieving similar outcomes. Elaborate spells can increase the strength of the magic worked because of the inclusion of various tools that will each add their own stored magical potential to the spell. In taking the time to plan an elaborate spell and acquire the implements needed, you can help yourself focus on the outcome and the increased focus will assist in directing the energies you raise during your working more effectively. Simple spells are not less effective, but they require stronger focus and visualization of the outcomes that are desired from them. This can be difficult for someone just starting out, but the more you practice your magic the better you will become at it.

Rituals

Rituals can be thought of as similar to spells, but they are quite a lot stronger and are usually conducted for specific celebrations or observations, or when the magic being worked is especially difficult or needs to be particularly strong. Rituals are a major focal point of Wiccan holiday celebrations and are used to observe and utilize the energies of the full and new moon. Rituals require quite a bit of preparation and include many of the magical tools that can be found in a witch's cabinet. All rituals start by casting a circle, which is a protected place to work magic in. This has the dual effect of amplifying the magical energies raised during the ritual and keeping out negative energies or entities that may disrupt the magic being worked. Since a witch opens themselves up to the Universe and the spirit realm when working magic, they can be vulnerable to the harmful effects of this as well as the beneficial ones that aid in magical practices. A ritual will also involve invoking deities to add their energy to the working, typically both a Goddess and a God. Many witches will have specific deities that they work with most often, but this is not always the case. If not, the witch can simply call on the Goddess and God as representations of the feminine and masculine divine energies that flow through the Universe. After this, the elements will be called in through their respective quarters. Most of the time this begins in the north or the east and continues clockwise, but you can choose to start with whichever element is most appropriate for the focus of ritual you are conducting. Once the circle has been cast and the divine and elemental energies have been called to attend, the ritual itself can begin. Upon completion of the ritual, the elements and deities must be released from the circle to go back to their natural place in the Universe and the circle must be uncast. Leaving these aspects in place beyond what is necessary can have unintended effects. Usually, this is an ineffective ritual at best or negative occurrences at worst. Rituals invoke and utilize very powerful energies, so these are not to be taken lightly and must be respected at all times.

Personal Growth and Self Esteem

Personal Growth

These barriers are only removed when the person understands how to use the powerful tools that turn challenges into strengths. Our biggest challenge in changing is our own mind; therefore, we have to do more to understand the different barriers that we are trying to break down to allow that growth to happen.

- Fear Personal Growth Barriers: This is the biggest barrier to personal growth. The most extraordinary thing that happens when we face that fear is that we are able to face it head-on and break it down bit by bit. In the end, there is a great sense of liberation once we break the barrier down.

- The Barriers of No Support: This barrier is found if you find yourself lacking in support of your family or friends in your endeavor to remove any barriers. This is a tough one because it causes the person to evaluate the type of people that they are in company with. And in some instances, it might be time to move on from other people, especially if you find that your personality types are so out of sync, you are unable to move past them.

- Hurt and Pride Barriers: Anything that happened in the past that caused any hurt or pride to surface is a great barrier to personal growth and personal development. This is something that the person may not even remember because it becomes so ingrained in the personality. This may make the person come off as aloof or distant when, in reality, they are trying to protect themselves.

- Barriers of Isolation: In some way, everyone on this planet is inter-dependent on one another. It is able to ask for assistance that can actually become quite liberating even if it may seem like a very daunting task. This will require the person to step out of their own comfort zone to be able to overcome the barrier and ask when they find themselves in need of help.

- Victimization Barrier: This means that the individual is blaming others and constantly feeling like a victim. This is a huge barrier to personal growth because it means that the individual is not taking any responsibility for themselves and their own actions.

- Barriers of Selfishness: People are automatically built-in with a barrier that causes them to be selfish to some degree. What needs to be understood is that the more that we give, the more that tends to return to us.

- Distrust and Cynicism Barrier: Because of past experiences, it becomes very easy for someone to become distrustful and cynical. This barrier means that we have hardened over time and in some way, is a little more instinctual than the rest of the personality.

- Guilt Barriers: Guilt presents itself in many different ways, and each way is a barrier to personal growth. It may be that people feel guilty because they have broken a set of moral standards, most likely their own, or because there is still a "voice" in their head that tells them that they should be, such as that of a past authority figure.

- Time Personal Growth Barriers: Time and financial barriers are cousins to one another. Often, the fact that we believe we do not have time is becoming an excuse not to work on oneself; however, it is very important to make time for growth, even if it is a little bit at a time.

- Financial Barrier: Is the cousin to time. There are times where people start believing that they do not have the financial means to work on themselves. But money is not necessarily the answer to this as growth can happen without having to spend any money.

- Perfectionism Barriers: This is the idea of not being good enough which makes this barrier a very vicious cycle. Whenever something like trying to work personal growth is presented with an obstacle or frustration, it becomes easy to quit believing that it is either not going right, or we don't have the skills to do it.

The different barriers that are present within a person have many effects on how we work on our own personal growth. Not everyone has the same barriers, and one person does not necessarily have all of them at once, but no matter how many there are, they are always a challenge. By taking the Enneagram personality types, it becomes easier to understand how the personality functions and the barriers that it will face which need to be overcome to get past the barriers and go up on the levels of the Enneagram development.

Self-Esteem

Self-esteem is something that develops naturally, which is determined by how you view yourself. The key to remember with self-esteem is that one has to take a truthful view of oneself, but also not to place too many limitations. Though this can fluctuate daily, most of the time it stays within a certain range.

Knowing the Enneagram personality type can help with figuring out what limitations have been placed that leave self-esteem where it should be. It also assists in breaking down those limitations so that the individual can make an accurate evaluation of their self-esteem.

It is in the best interest of anyone taking the Enneagram test to be as truthful as possible so that those limitations may be well known. At that point, it will be much easier to evaluate self-esteem and determine ways to help it if that is what is needed. Different types of self-esteem present different challenges in life.

Low Self-Esteem, common problems:

- Relationship problems
- Depression
- Anxiety
- Anti-social behavior
- Employment issues
- Sexual difficulties
- Communication challenges
- Issues with boundaries
- Destructive behaviors

Self-esteem is something that originates in the messages that we give to ourselves. Whether those messages are positive, or negative are what ultimately affect our self-esteem and the way that we view ourselves.

Sometimes it is the past circumstances that we have lived through that prove how our self-esteem will be. If as a child, the individual had received the appropriate amount of attention, people who were authority figures listened to them, such as parents and teachers. They will have higher self-esteem as they believe that they are worthy individuals. For others, who have had quite the opposite experience, may find that their self-esteem has not grown as high as they would like.

Those messages that we received at the beginning of our lives are also something that we have internalized. They are the messages that we continue to give to ourselves, which either help or hurt our self-esteem. Understanding the personality type that the Enneagram has determined can be very eye-opening in how someone responds to particular situations or stimuli, allowing them to make the conscious effort to change those messages.

Opening Your Numerology Center

If with time your ability to connect with numbers betters, then you can consider becoming a numerologist.

As you know, a numerologist is one who uses numbers to predict a person's future. You too can start looking at people's name and life path numbers and predict what lies in their future. But, you have to take a few steps in the right direction before opening up your center. Here is a look at the steps.

Hone your skill

First things first, you should hone your skills before you start a business. It is important for you to be near perfect and not leave any room for doubt. Once you hone your skills, you will develop the confidence to start your business and pursue it whole-heartedly. If you are unsure about something, then look it up first and ensure that you are well educated on the topic and capable of starting and running a business.

Make a plan

The next step is to etch a plan for the business. You have to come up with a business model that will help you get started with your numerology business. The plan should be such that it allows you not just to get started but also help you in remaining put with the business. You can consider consulting someone who will help you get started. The plan should include all the details of how the business will begin and the steps you will take towards setting it up and running it. If you plan on having a partner then the two of you should sit down and plan it out together for better results.

Raise capital

The next step is to raise capital for the business. Capital is probably the most important element when it comes to setting up a business and you need enough to fund the company's functioning. How much capital you raise will depend on how much you need for your business. The scale of your business will determine the money that you will require. You can use your own money or borrow from a relative or a friend. You can also raise the capital through a loan.

Find the place

It is important for you to find the right place for your business. Where you set it up will determine how your business will run. It is best for you to start small and that can mean opening up the business in your own house. If you have a spare room or an empty garage then you can consider it as a potential space to open up your business. The place should also be convenient for you to entertain your clients. If you wish to seek privacy then you can choose a room that is attached to your house from the outside so that people don't gain entry into your house.

Decide on fees

The next step is to decide on the fees that you will be charging for your services. As you know, you will need the money to keep your business going and must consider setting a limit that is high enough to leave you with enough money to operate your business smoothly. The best thing is to find out what other numerologists in your area are charging for their services and then base yours on it. Giving an initial discount can be a good strategy to acquire new clients.

Add in the décor

You have to decorate your room in such a way that it instantly appeals to the clients. They should be taken in by the décor and get into the right mood. But don't overdo anything. Keep it mellowed down and subtle. You can also display any certificates that you might have attained for numerology, which will tell them you are a bona fide numerologist.

License

You might have to acquire a license for your work in order to carry it out. You have to look for the right place to apply for the license, especially if it is mandatory in your state. It might take some time for your license to be approved and you should remain patient. Once it is, you can collect it, have it framed and hang it in your office space for others to see.

Test it

Before you open up your office, you might want to test out your skills first. You can call your friends and family members over and read out their numbers. They will give you a fair analysis of your skill and presentation and tell you what you can do to better yourself. You can also have a test session with some random customers and ask them for a feedback. Depending on what you get, you can change your presentation accordingly.

Advertise

You have to advertise your business then and let others know about it. You can make use of social media to tell others about your business. You can also get your family members and friends to spread the word about it and advertise your business in the best possible manner. The more people that hear about it, the more business will come your way. You can also advertise the traditional way by using flyers that you can post on streets to tell people about your business.

Start your business

The next step is to start your business. You have to put in efforts to make it good and use your skill to acquire newer clients. Growth should be your motto and also to give people an accurate reading. You can set yourself goals that will help you attain the best.

Expand it

You must plan on expanding your business in order to help it reach its true potential. Business expansion is a must for all businesses in order to bring out the best in them. You can decide to get a bigger place to conduct the business and also plan on the budget you will need for it.

These are the different steps you have to take in order to start your numerology business.

Lucky and Unlucky Numbers

As you know, there are both lucky and unlucky numbers in this world. However, it is difficult to categorize them into these two broad categories, as what is lucky for one might be unlucky for another and vice versa. However, one can attempt to understand why these labels are lent to numbers and whether they will prove to be lucky or unlucky for you. Let us look at them in detail. Note that most of these are based on Chinese traditions.

Number 2

Number 2 is believed to be a lucky number as per Chinese traditions. They believe that anything in pairs is lucky as it doubles the luck. Therefore, they prefer to do things in pairs like hanging decorations in pairs, burning incense in pairs etc. they associate the number 2 with happiness and believe that it is possible to reel in good luck by mentioning two. Many companies mention their names twice as a means to affect their luck. You too can do things in pairs as it can bring about good luck.

Number 3

Although many people think 3 is not a lucky number, the Chinese share a different opinion. Number 3 is not necessarily a bad number and can signify a lot of positivity. It stands for health and happiness. Number 3 also signifies life and birth. So it is associated with children and healthy babies. Number 3 is also a big part of the Buddhist culture that relates it to the three jewels of life. Many people prefer to have this as their life path number and also consider making it a part of their nameplate.

Number 4

Number 4 is viewed as an unlucky number. Its Chinese pronunciation rhymes with the word Shi, which signifies death. It is a big taboo to have 4 as a part of any endeavor in china. They try to avoid it as much as they can including not using it in their name plates, elevators etc. in fact, any house that has the number 4 attached to it will be purchased at a lesser value as compared to places that do not have a 4. This peculiar characteristic also extends to certain other Asian countries, where people prefer to shun the number 4. However, as per numerology, the number 4 is a lucky number and having your life path number as 4 can help you attain the best out of life.

Number 5

Number 5 is generally regarded as being both lucky and unlucky. You can view it as a lucky or an unlucky number based on how you interpret its meaning. The word closest to 4 in Chinese stands for without or not, which can be judged as a negative aspect. On the other hand, the Chinese attach several positive attributes to this number, which can make it a lucky number for some. The number 5 is generally associated with the 5 elements in Chinese tradition, which can promote creativity.

Number 7

The number 7 is regarded as being both a lucky and an unlucky number. The word for 7 sounds similar to starting or rising, which can signify the start of something new. It is also regarded as an important number when you wish to begin a new relationship. So going on a date on the 7th or picking 7 pm as the meeting time can help you reel in luck. However, the term also sounds like he word for cheat, which might signify bad luck. The Chinese believe that ghosts rise from hell on the 7th month of each year, which is not necessarily a bad thing. These ghosts might bring in luck to the people who celebrate the ghost festival.

Number 8

As per the Chinese, 8 is the luckiest number in the whole context of numbers. In fact, they prefer to feature 8 wherever possible owing to the luck it brings about. And it is not just the Chinese that are obsessed with this number. Many Indians also view the number as being lucky and incorporate it in several aspects of their life such as business ventures. Some people prefer to keep an eight on their desk to invite good luck.

Number 9

The number 9 is considered to be quite lucky as per Chinese traditions. It stands for prosperity and eternity, both of which are desirable aspects of life. Number 9 is incorporated in several ways. Many people use it as their door number even if theirs is not 9. The same goes for vehicle numbers.

How to Embrace Your Gift

As you have read, being an empath is physically and emotionally exhausting, which can cause you to feel as if you don't have a gift but a burden. Feeling this burden is the first step towards embracing your gift. You will now need to learn how to look after yourself so that you can embrace your gift without feeling exhausted. This is an extremely important process and you should invest time and effort into mastering the best techniques for effective coping mechanisms. Once you learn how to cope and function as an empath, you can use your gift to better yourself and your environment.

Due to the constant feelings of overwhelming emotions and stress, you must go to great lengths to eliminate the negative energy that you can attract. The techniques that you learn should become a part of your daily routine and will open your eyes to the true value of the gift that you have been blessed with.

Even though being an empath is not a disease or a curse, it is controversial. It can cause you to feel so uncomfortable that you will try to suppress it. In alcoholics or narcotics anonymous their slogan is the first step to cure is to admit that you have a problem. The same applies to you as an empath; the first step towards embracing your gift is admitting that you are indeed an empath and that you are proud of it. Although this is a small step, it will make a great difference, as you will eliminate a lot of the stress associated with hiding your gift.

For you to feel relieved from the struggles of being an empath, you must get enough rest. The most effective method of doing so is to set a regular sleep-wake cycle and do what you can to ensure that you have a restful sleep throughout the night. You should also take regular breaks throughout the day for relaxation and deep breathing exercises to rid yourself of some of the stress that has built up throughout the day. Such exercises will provide you with immediate relief

Take care that you do not place yourself in environments that are overly stimulating regularly. It can be difficult to avoid them completely; however, you should endeavor to avoid them as much as you can. If you know that you are going to be in an overly stimulating environment, make sure that you prepare yourself emotionally and mentally beforehand. This will enable you to quickly rid yourself of any of the stress that you feel as a result of the energy that you are surrounded by.

Social media and the internet in general are extremely stimulating environments. It is advised that you often take a break from the energy that is emitted through the internet. You don't have to be in the physical presence of someone to absorb their energy.

It is also advised that you have a routine in place for stress relief. What you do depends on what you find relaxing. You might enjoy reading motivational books, getting a massage, going to a spa, using aromatherapy or taking a warm bath.

Here Are Some Helpful Tips to Assist You in Fully Embracing Your Gift:

APPRECIATE AND HONOR YOUR STATE OF CONSCIOUSNESS

Empaths often feel pressure because they are different. Being different brings many challenges because the world expects you to conform to its norms and values. When you are misunderstood by others, it is easy to take their disapproval personal and carry it as a burden. It is normal to be emphatic and a gift to be in tune with yourself physically and spiritually. I would go as far as saying that it is essential that you have this gift to survive because it puts you on high alert when danger is surrounding you or your family.

IDENTIFY THE DIFFERENCE BETWEEN THOUGHT CONSCIOUSNESS AND EMPHATIC CONSCIOUSNESS

You can observe the difference between day and night because you can see it. It is difficult to identify emphatic awareness because you can't see it. It is something that is felt and experienced on the inside. Once you can identify this difference, you will begin to see your gift as a blessing instead of a curse. You attain self-knowledge when you know when the mind and its thoughts are dominating. Feelings and thoughts are different, and when you recognize these differences, you will feel liberated. This knowledge will give you the power to defend yourself against energetic tides instead of being pulled into them.

TRUST IN YOUR INTUITION

This does not mean that you should fully understand or embrace the feeling. You may not have complete knowledge of the situation. Still, the feeling is real, and you should embrace the deeper communication that is happening within.

UNDERSTANDING ENERGY

Once an empath starts to embrace their gift and understand that they don't have to carry other people's energy around with them, a natural curiosity about energy sets in. Through your symptoms and experiences, you are aware of how powerfully energy can affect you negatively. If this is the case, it is also possible that energy can have a positive effect on you.

Once you have learned how to deal with the stress of carrying energy, it then frees you to learn how you can use energy positively. Learning how energy works is an exciting adventure, and it can take you to places in life that you didn't think existed. As you have read, many empaths become healers; these are the people who have learned how to embrace their gift because they understand how their energy can have a positive effect on others.

The first step in learning about energy is to understand how to ground yourself from different energy. This will help you to avoid becoming overwhelmed by the energy that you can feel. One of the most popular grounding techniques is through visualization. This is where you consciously imagine yourself being grounded; here are some steps to get you started:

Sit comfortably in a chair and position both of your feet firmly on the ground with your palms facing upwards. Don't force yourself into a certain position; simply allow your body to relax into the chair. Imagine that a piercing white light is radiating from the sun and through your crown chakra and leaving the bottom of your spine and then into the earth's center. Imagine that as your body is being filled with the white light, negative black energy is being released through your palms. When your entire body has been filled with the white light you will naturally relax knowing that you are now filled with positive and peaceful energy.

You should practice visualization regularly as a strategy to keep you grounded to the earth underneath you, to release the negative energy that has attached itself to you and to enhance your empath gift.

Working confidently with energy will cause you to stop feeling as if you are out of control. It will enable you to protect yourself and heal yourself and the people who are placed in your path. Ultimately, it will give you the ability to control the energy that is directly affecting you.

There are many things that you can excel in when you learn to effectively handle energy, which is one of the reasons it is so attractive to many. It is your divine right to learn how to navigate this powerful terrain of energy so that you can use it in a way that benefits you and others

PSYCHIC ABILITIES

Empaths are capable of sensing things before they manifest; the psychic ability is strongly connected to your ability to "just know." You will often have visions or premonitions about things before them happening. You can't learn to have visions or premonitions, but you can train yourself to have them whenever you need to. This provides you with the wonderful and powerful ability to be able to predict future events. You may not have experienced any premonitions or visions yet, but this doesn't mean that you can't operate in that gift; it may be that you haven't tapped into it yet. As you learn how to control this gift, you will find it easy and exciting to predict the future.

ENERGY PROJECTION

One of the things that you may not be aware of as an empath is that you can send energy to people. And when you do it you are giving that individual the particular sensation or vibe that you want them to experience. This is a skill that is used for remote healing, where empaths are capable of healing people when they are not even in their presence. Others use this as a way of praying for people and sending good energy and thoughts in the direction of another person to help them to get through a difficult time when they are unable to be there personally. Sending energy is not limited to empaths; everyone can do this if they put their mind to it. However, when empaths send energy the recipient is more likely to feel it because they have a powerful connection to the energy source.

HEALING

Empaths understand the connection that energy and people have, this is referred to as an energy body, and it can become inflicted with illness or pain. When you are trained in energy healing, you learn how you can work with your own or another person's energy body to induce healing to create a healthy energy body.

Tarot Cards and Their Association to Specific Subjects

When you are asking the Tarot a question about a specific subject (love, career, travel, etc.), there are certain cards that you should keep an eye on.

Love

•   The Lovers: This is the ultimate card for love and embodies a deep connection or bond between people. If this card shows up in your reading, it signifies a relationship that is authentic and based on respect and trust.

•   Two of Cups: This card represents a bond between two people that is particularly strong. It often portrays a committed, monogamous relationship.

•   Ten of Cups: This card is typical when dealing with a loving, warm home with a happy family. This card embodies a feeling of being complete, having strong familial values, and having a great partner and children.

- Four of Wands: This is the card that represents a secure and safe home environment along with the celebration. Having this card in a reading often reflects an engagement, wedding, or something like a serious relationship.

- Ten of Pentacles: This card embodies a relationship, typically a marriage, that is well-established with strong family life.

- Ace of Cups: Getting This card, during a reading, reflects a budding relationship with joy, excitement, and happiness. This is like the feeling of your first love.

- Knight of Cups: When this card appears in a reading, it represents being romanced by their "knight in shining armor."

- The Empress: This card embodies the sensual nature of a relationship and points to a deep connection between partners.

- The Emperor: This card embodies a strong male partner and can be indicative of a long-term relationship.

- The Hierophant: Getting this card during a reading can represent marriage or relationship that is fairly traditional.

Professional Development

- Ace of Pentacles: If you draw this card during a reading, it is likely that promotion, pay raise, or a new job is coming your way.

- Two of Wands: This card represents foresight and career planning.

- The Chariot: Drawing this card during a reading could be indicative of tackling a challenge with the determination needed to overcome it.

- Ten of Pentacles: Drawing this card represents that great success or accomplishment is coming your way.

- Eight of Wands: Drawing this card during a reading could be indicative of traveling for business or experiencing international travel.

- Six of Wands: Drawing this card during a reading could represent receiving recognition or success from the work you are doing.

- Eight of Pentacles: This card represents training, skill development, and education.

- The Emperor: This card is indicative of being respected by your coworkers.

- Two of Cups: Drawing this card could be indicative of an upcoming employment contract or a business deal coming to fruition.

- Three of Pentacles: Drawing this card during a reading means that a large amount of collaboration is needed for success in the venture in question.

Tension and Conflict

- Two of Swords: This card represents a conflict of a passive-aggressive nature.

- Five of Swords: This card is indicative of the loss of a relationship or the loss of trust in that relationship.

- Five of Wands: Drawing this card during a reading is indicative of the fact that people are speaking, but no one is listening.

- Temperance (Reversed): Drawing this card during a reading could be indicative of an upcoming conflict between two people who used to be harmonious.

- The Tower: This card represents utter chaos and destruction.

- Seven of Wands: This card represents the feeling of being attacked.

- Three of Swords: Drawing this card during a reading represents having said things that hurt to cause emotional pain.

Decision-Making

- Queen of Swords: Drawing this card during a reading reflects the need for thinking with one's head, not the heart.

- Justice: This card represents finding out the truth to determine what is wrong and right.

- Two of Wands: Drawing this card during a reading suggests that long-term planning will ease the decision-making process.

- Ace of Swords: This card represents a jolt of clarity.

- Two of Swords: This card represents the feeling of being caught in the middle of two choices and the indecision that comes with that.

- The Hanged Man: Drawing this card during a reading signifies that you are at the mercy of the actions of others.

- Seven of Cups: This card symbolizes the indecision that comes with having multiple options.
- The Emperor: Drawing this card during a reading means that you should do what you know is the best decision.
- Judgment: Drawing this card during a reading symbolizes a point where you will be evaluating the actions you have taken.
- The Chariot: Drawing this card during a reading means that you need to stay strong, remain committed, and use your will power.

Finance

- Ace of Pentacle: Drawing this card during a reading signifies an upcoming opportunity.
- Four of Pentacles: This card represents saving more and spending less.
- Seven of Pentacles: Drawing this card during a reading could be indicative of paying an allowance into long-term investments.
- Nine of Pentacles: This card represents luxurious lifestyles and an abundance of material goods.
- Ten of Pentacles: Drawing this card during a reading could be indicative of accumulating enough wealth that it can be shared.
- Nine of Cups: This card represents the law of attraction
- Wheel of Fortune: Drawing this card during a reading signifies an upcoming streak of good luck or a surprising gift.
- Page of Pentacles: Drawing this card during a reading can be indicative of a chance to earn a bit of side money with a new venture.
- Six of Wands: This card represents rewards being earned by hard work.
- The Sun: Drawing this card during a reading signifies a positive outcome to the question, usually in the form of investments pulling in a high earning.

Goals, Long-Term Planning, and Vision

- Two of Wands: This card represents decision-making based on personal growth.

- Three of Wands: Drawing this card during a reading indicates an expansion in one's goals.

- Page of Pentacles: This card represents the value of forward-planning in achieving goals.

- Ace of Swords: This card represents a breakthrough.

- The Chariot: This card represents standing up to opposition with strength.

- King of Wands: This card represents the setting of goals for others who would like to join in your success.

- The Magician: This card represents talent for manifesting and making plans.

Healing

- Death: Drawing this card during a reading signifies the need to accept that something has ended.

- The Star: This card represents the Universe being behind us in both good and bad times.

- The Hermit: This card inspires introspection on one's journey.

- Temperance: Drawing this card during a reading indicates that healing will likely be a long process, but it is in the works.

- Judgment: This card represents learning while we move forward.

- Ace of Cups: Drawing this card during a reading indicates you should not be afraid to let your emotions out.

- Three of Cups: This card represents the ability your loved ones and friends have to support you while you are healing.

- Five of Cups: This card represents the ability to trust and love again after forgiveness.

- Four of Swords: This card represents the importance of allowing yourself space and time to heal.

- Six of Swords: Drawing this card during a reading indicates the need to continue forward, though you are still sad.

Mental Illness

It is important to note that these are not diagnoses.

- The Devil: Drawing this card during a reading could indicate an unhealthy attachment or addiction (drugs, alcohol, etc.)

- The Moon (Reversed): Drawing this card during a reading could indicate that there are undiscovered mental health issues.

- Temperance (Reversed): Drawing this card during a reading could potentially mean that there is a form of chemical imbalance.

- The Tower: This card represents a series of panic attacks or a breakdown that is fairly major.

- The Star (Reversed): This card represents a feeling of general hopelessness and lack of faith.

- Nine of Wands (Reversed): This card represents the feeling that everyone is against you.

- Nine of Cups (Reversed): Drawing this card during a reading indicates that your needs are not being met emotionally.

- Five of Cups (Reversed): This card represents depression that often accompanies loss.

- Five of Pentacles: This card represents that anxiety surrounding financial struggles or losing a job.

- Nine of Swords: drawing This card indicates that the depression and anxiety you are experiencing is egged on negative self-talk.

Relationship Breakups

- The Tower: Drawing this card during a reading indicates the potential for major change or period of great upset.

- Death: Drawing This card, during a reading, indicates the need to embrace the future and let go of past hurt.

- The Hermit: Drawing this card during a reading indicates the need for personal time and solitude.

- Three of Swords: This card represents sorrow, grief, and heartbreak.

- Ten of Swords: Drawing this card can be indicative of an unexpected or dramatic ending.

- Two of Cups (Reversed): Drawing this card can be indicative of making the hard decision to separate.

- Five of Swords: This card represents a battle fought and lost.

- Five of Pentacles: Drawing this card during a reading indicates that a time of feeling isolation is upcoming.

- Ten of Pentacles (Reversed): Drawing this card during a reading indicates the end of a relationship and the division of assets.

- Three of Cups (Reversed): Drawing this card during a reading could be indicative of a partner who is unfaithful or a love triangle.

Spiritual Development

- The Hierophant: Drawing this card during a reading indicates that it may be useful to receive guidance from a leader of spiritual nature.

- The High Priestess: Drawing this card during a reading indicates the need to trust one's intuition to connect to the inner spirit.

- The Hermit: Drawing this card during a reading indicates the need for contemplation over the chosen spiritual path.

- The Tower: This card represents the destruction that enables you to have a new view of your life.

- The Hanged Man: Drawing this card during a reading indicates the need to be more selfless.

- Five of Pentacles: Drawing this card during a reading indicates the need to put more worth on spiritual abundance than material abundance.

- Eight of Pentacles: This card represents seeing one's path as a lifetime journey.

- Four of Cups: Drawing this card during a reading indicates the need to reflect inwardly and discover what stabilizes you.

- Ace of Wands: This card represents the energy spurt needed to start your journey.

Courage and Strength

- **Strength:** This card represents the strength that comes from compassion, peace, and surrender.
- **The Emperor:** This card represents being unafraid of conflict and having authority over others.
- **The Star:** This card represents faith and hope in the Universe.
- **The Lovers:** Drawing this card encourages decision-making based on your values regardless of a challenging path.
- **Six of Wands:** This card represents operating from a place of high self-esteem and confidence.
- **The Kings:** These cards represent the courage and strength that comes from authority and power.
- **The Knights:** Drawing this card encourages pursuing things that are meaningful and committing to those goals.
- **Nine of Wands:** This card represents persevering in the presence of adversity.
- **Seven of Wands:** This card represents facing odds with courage and strength.
- **Six of Swords:** Drawing this card during a reading encourages having the strength to let go of what no longer serves you.

Education and Study

- **The High Priestess:** Drawing this card during a reading is indicative of receiving intuitive or mystical knowledge.
- **The Chariot:** This card represents focus, determination, and concentration.
- **The Hermit:** This card represents the knowledge and education that comes from within.
- **The Fool:** This card represents being a student of life and continuing to learn.
- **The Hierophant:** Drawing this card during a reading indicates that a teacher will appear when you are ready for one.
- **Page of Pentacles:** This card represents a new direction or skill.

- Eight of Pentacles: drawing this card during a reading indicates that the querent should be prepared to begin learning.

Wiccan Tools

Altars and Altar Tools

Wiccans maintain an altar. An altar is is a sacred space cultivated by a Wiccan for meditation, prayer, offerings, spells, and divination. The altar can also be a space to connect with and worship deities. Altars are decorated with tools, crystals, art, and other things to make them unique and to help them channel the desired energies. Some Wiccans maintain multiple altars for different purposes.

The altar is the heart of one's sacred space. It is an area of concentrated energy, the seat of a Wiccan's worship. While in most organized religions the altar is found at the front of a congregation, inaccessible to the congregants, the altar in Wicca is very personal. The altar is not shared with a whole community; it is a place for private worship and solitary devotion to the sacred.

Building your first altar can seem daunting, but it is an opportunity to create something unique. For some it is so intimidating that it is put off. Your altar doesn't have to mimic anyone else's or have significance to anyone except for you. As long as the items on your altar are meaningful to you, that is all that matters.

Conversely, over-excitement can lead to a crowded altar covered with distracting trinkets that will only serve to collect dust. You want your altar to contain useful things. Altars are dynamic as well; what may be useful on your altar at first may eventually have fully served its purpose and need to be replaced as your beliefs and Craft develop.

Athames

An athame is a special dagger used for magickal rituals. The athame often is double-edged, with a pointed, sharp tip. Athames should be used with great care to prevent harm during use. Respect the athame as you would any other kind of knife. The handle of the athame is often inscribed with symbols or sigils. These carvings can vary depending on which tradition the practitioner is a part of.

The purpose of the athames are not to cut things, but rather to direct energy during the ritual. Cutting is considered a mundane task, and athames are reserved for the sacred. The athame represents the fire element. It is used to cast circles by outlining their circumference. The athame wards off negative energies and spirits during magickal work.

Bolines

A boline is a ritual knife used for more mundane tasks than the athame. Traditionally the blade is one-sided and straight, but it is becoming more and more common to find them in a crescent shape to invoke the moon and the Triple Goddess. The boline has a white handle rather than a black one, and is usually smaller than an athame. The boline is used to cut herbs and cord, and to carve wands and candles.

Pentacles

While the pentacle and the pentagram are related, they are not the same. To use the words interchangeably is incorrect, and it is important to know the difference.

The pentagram symbol is a five-pointed star contained in a circle. It is a type of talisman and can also be worn as an amulet. The five points on the pentagram represent many things. They represent the five elements. For Wiccans who worship The Horned God and The Triple Goddess, the five points also represent the two horns of the God and the three forms of the Goddess.

However, a ritual pentacle is different from the simple symbol pentagram. The pentacle is drawn as a pentagram, but also includes other writing. A ritual pentagram is often the centerpiece of the altar. It can be used to summon spirits or energies. The pentagram can be made from many natural materials, such as wood or paper. Within the pentagram, the words and symbols of whatever is being summoned are drawn.

Chalices

A chalice is a cup used for ritual purposes, often resembling a goblet. A chalice my be filled with wine, whiskey, beer, water, or some other fluids with magickal properties depending on what the ritual is for. The ancient Romans would drink from chalices at banquets and feasts, and at the dawn of Christianity vessels were used for ritual purposes.

The vessel represents the element of water, and represents the womb. If one worships a female deity, it could represent the womb of that deity and be used to encourage fertility. The base of the vessel represents the physical world. The stem of the vessel symbolizes the connection between the mind, the body, and the spirit. The rim is that from which we receive spiritual energy, if the chalice is used to drink from.

When used in combination with an athame, the chalice and the athame together represent the feminine womb of the Goddess and the masculine phallus of the God coming together to create.

Wands

A wand is a thin, straight carved piece of wood, ivory, metal, or even crystal. The wand is meant to be hand-held. Originally, wands were supposed to stretch from the tip of the middle finger to the elbow, but as tradition has evolved wands have become smaller. Wand traditions trace back to ancient Egypt, where wands were buried in tombs for souls to use in the afterlife. The Hellenistic God Hermes/Mercury is also depicted as having used a wand.

Wands are commonly carved from wood of sacred trees, such as willow, elder, and oak. However, with new technology wands can be made from many materials. Some modern wands are made entirely of crystal or have crystal tips attached.

While the most effective wands are handcrafted, store-bought wands also work if you feel a connection with them.

Candles

Candles are a primary tool for Wiccans, and their different colors are used for different purposes. During a ritual they are placed at the four corners of the ritual circle to represent the presence of the four elements Fire, Wind, Earth, and Water (Aether is represented by the practitioners themselves).

Candles can be consecrated and charged for use by cleansing and anointing them with concentrated essential oils. Always do your research before using an oil, because some are more flammable than others, and you don't want an out of control blaze on your hands. Many Wiccans also sprinkle dried herbs over the candles to invoke their properties.

The colors of the candles are very important to for rituals and spells. Luckily, candles can often be found for low prices at your local dollar store, or in bulk online. Below is a brief review of the various candle colors and what they represent and invoke.

White: unity; spiritual truth; strength; peace and purity; breaking curses; meditation; purification

Yellow: persuasion; creativity; confidence and charisma; improving memory and studying

Green: nature, renewal, and fertility; healing; money and prosperity; emotional soothing and balance

Pink: love and strengthening friendships; femininity; spiritual healing; warding away evil

Red: strength and vitality; power; sexuality; passion; protection; the cycle of reincarnation

Orange: strength, courage, and authority; concentration; encouragement

Blue: psychic powers and spiritual awareness; wisdom and intelligence; harmony and balance; dreams of prophecy; protection while sleeping

Purple: mysticism; ambition; inspiration and idealism; heightening psychic abilities; breaking curses

Brown: animal healing; protection of animals; attracting money; solving domestic issues; finding lost objects

Gold: masculinity; intuition; persuasion and charm; protection; gaining luck and fortune quickly

Silver: removing negativity and encouraging stability; neutrality; developing psychic ability

Black: loss, grief, disappointment, and sadness; depression; absorbing and destroying evil and discord; protection from retribution

If a spell calls for a candle color you don't currently have, white candles are often used as a neutral acceptable replacement. It helps to carve a sigil in the candle to endow it with the energy of the colored candle you are replacing.

Incense

Incense is another important tool for many Wiccans. Incense is a substance, usually found in the form of a stick of infused herbs, which can be burned to release a fragrant smoke. Thought to have originally been used by Egyptians, the practice spread far and wide, adopted by Romans and Greeks and pagans worldwide.

Incense represents four elements at once. It is created from materials from the Earth by soaking them in Water. Then it is ignited with Fire, upon which time it wafts smoke through the Air. Some Wiccans consider its connection to Air to be the strongest, because it is an aesthetic representation of Air and helps us see the movement of the air around us.

Incense is held in a special container called a censer. This can take many forms. It could be a flat, straight piece of wood or other material upon which the ash can fall. Some witches fill a ceramic or metal cauldron with coal and burn incense within the cauldron. For certain rituals, ashes are important, so often the ashes are saved to use in other spells and rituals.

Types of Altars

One of the first steps to building your own altar is choosing what kind of altar you want. This will help you decide what should be present and what can be left out and used for other purposes.

Shrines

A shrine is an altar created to venerate a deity, or less commonly for ancestor worship. A shrine is the perfect place to pray, commune with your deity, and make offerings. Making offerings, such as flowers, herbs, or alcohol, brings you closer to the deity. Offerings also encourage the deity to guide you in general, or to help you with a specific task.

Shrines are typically simple, because they are a focal point and therefore should have a bright, focused energy. A representation of the focus of the shrine is usually used, whether its a statue or a drawing or photograph. Candles are placed on the shrine to "activate" the energy of the shrine. Small decorations such as vases are good ways to keep fresh offerings present, and also an excellent way to remember Wiccan veneration of all that is natural.

Ritual Altars

A ritual altar is more elaborately done because it includes the tools necessary to perform the ritual. Ritual altars are used for occasions such as Esbats or festivals. A full ritual altar often includes an athame, wand, cup, pentagram, and candles (often many of them in different colors).

Because of all the tools that are usually present during a full-blown ritual, these altars are usually quite large and often temporary. Ritual altars are typically constructed outdoors, where the connection with nature is most robust.

Working Altar

A working altar is an altar that is prepared for functional, practical magickal use. While some work can be completed in a single session, other ritual sessions or spells may require you to return to the altar multiple times. Thus, these altars are often more permanent than ritual altars.

This type of altar should be extremely focused and contain no more pieces than is absolutely necessary for the work being done. Excess tools and trinkets will distract from the magickal work and divert energy to other places.

Personal Altar

A personal altar is more permanent, although the pieces included on the altar will change over time as your needs change. This kind of altar is often elaborately decorated with images, cloths, photos, crystals, candles, incense, and flowers. A personal altar is used to generate the desired vibrations. It can be focused on one particular energy, but in this case it does not have to be.

With any type of altar one should be cautious of clutter. Don't hold onto items that don't have meaning to you, or that have worn out their usefulness. It's easy to become attached to material things, but this is contradictory to the Wiccan path. It is not the material things a Wiccan owns that gives them power. The power comes from within. If you're having trouble with materialism, take time to enjoy nature and remember the real roots of Wicca.

Wiccan Moon

The Horned God / the Sun God

The masculine god is often seen or referred to as the horned god. Horns are a traditional symbol of masculinity, representing qualities such as strength, sex drive, and energy.

During the Wiccan year, the horned god will adopt different personalities. For half of the year he can be referred to as the Oak King and for the other half, the Holly King. He is also referred to as the Sun God who is worshipped on the Sabbat of Lughnasadh. Some Wiccans believe that these are all different gods and will worship each of them separately and other Wiccans have them all fall under the God.

The Goddess / the Triple Goddess

The Goddess is the Feminine deity. Like the horns represent the masculine god, the Goddess is represented by three phases of the moon. This is why she is also called the Triple Goddess. Each phase of the moon represents a different form of the Goddess. The waxing moon represents creation and inspiration, the full moon represents sustenance and the waning moon represents fulfillment. The three forms of the Goddess are as follows:

The Maiden - The maiden is young, full of beauty and innocence. Her future is promising and filled with potential. She is associated with beginnings and the new moon.

The Mother - The mother is experienced and mature. She is protective, nurturing and selfless.

The Crone - The crone is full of wisdom, a leader and respected. She reminds us of our mortality and that our bodies will one day return to the earth. Despite this, she does not have a negative connotation. In fact, she is seen as a guide and her wisdom can help us through difficult times.

The Wheel of the Year

The Wheel of the Year is the Wiccan calendar if you will. It represents the annual cycle of the Earth and is derived from the seasons. Wiccans believe that time is cyclical, a continuous cycle. This is why the festivals (or Sabbats) are represented by a wheel.

The wheel also represents the progression of life. We are born, we grow, we live, we decline and then we die.

This period of birth, life, and death is represented by the life of the Horned God during different seasons. The cycle of fertility (virginity, pregnancy, and birth) is represented in different seasons by the Triple Goddess.

The Sabbats

Yule: December 20-23. Yule is the winter solstice. The Goddess (in the form of the mother) gives birth to the sun god.

Imbolc: February 2. Candles are used to celebrate this Sabbat. They are to encourage the sun to shine brighter. The sun god at this stage is an infant and feeds from the breast of his mother, the Goddess. This also represents the end of winter because the earth is starting to feel the warmth of the infant sun.

Ostara: March 20-23. Ostara is the spring equinox. The God is now a child, and the Goddess will take on the form of the maiden. She acts as the God's playmate and they play in the fields to encourage the flowers to bloom.

Here is where beginner Wiccans might get confused. The Goddess has now taken on two forms simultaneously. She is both the playmate of the child God (as a maiden) and the nurturing (mother) of the child. She will continue the year changing from two forms as needed in order to serve the life cycle of the God.

Beltane: May 1. The Maiden Goddess and the Sun God are now young adults. They are fertile and ready to procreate. For this reason, Beltane is viewed by Wiccans as a sacred night for sex. Fertility also represents the upcoming crops. The Sun God will impregnate the maiden here and she will turn from the maiden to the pregnant mother. The Goddess is now both the pregnant lover of the God as well as his nurturing mother.

Litha: June 20-23. Litha is the peak of the Sun God's life, he is now full of strength and masculinity. Litha is when the Sun God and the pregnant Goddess will get married.

Lughnasadh: August 1. Autumn is upon the earth. The leaves are turning brown and the temperature is cooling. The Sun God is dying. The God will begin preparations for his death and make sure that his unborn child and the pregnant Goddess are taken care of. The Sun God knows that winter is upon the earth and it will be a challenge to survive it. He knows that his strength and light can only be renewed if he willingly offers himself up as a sacrifice. He will do this to become one with the earth to provide sustenance. His sacrifice will be the wheat that is harvested for the winter.

Mabon: September 20-23. Time with the Sun God has nearly ended. Preparation for his death and the winter are in full swing. Knowing of losing her son, the nurturing mother transitions into the crone. Her wisdom and experience will help guide us through the mourning of the Sun God.

Samhain: October 31. The Sun God dies. Many Wiccans believe that this is when the Sun God is referred to as the Horn God. He is animal-like, he is one with the earth.

During Samhain, the crone and the pregnant mother goddess mourn the God's death. Samhain is the start of the New Year for Wiccans and many Wiccans view Samhain as the most important Sabbat. Samhain is a day to remember those who have passed on, including ancestors, family and even animals that were either pets or used on a farm. Samhain rituals celebrate darkness.

Although it is considered the beginning of the year, it also marks the end of the previous year in which rituals celebrate and commemorate last year's harvest and the accomplishments that were made.

Samhain also represents a promise of new life. The pregnant mother holds the seed of the reincarnated Son God who will be born at Yule.

Yule: December 20-23. The Goddess gives birth and the Sun God is reborn, thus re-starting the cycle.

The Greater Sabbats and the Lesser Sabbats

The eight Sabbats are divided in half making four of them greater Sabbats and the other four, lesser Sabbats. The divide is as follows:

Greater Sabbats:

Samhain (October 31)

Imbolc (February 2)

Beltane (May 1)

Lughnasadh (August 1)

Lesser Sabbats:

Yule (December 20-23)

Ostara (March 20-23)

Litha (June 20-23)

Mabon (September 20-23)

The four lesser Sabbats mark the end of one season and the beginning of the next while the four greater Sabbats are the middle or the peak of the season. These days are considered days of power.

Reincarnation

Unlike Christians, Wiccans do not believe in the idea of heaven and hell, but we do believe in an afterlife, or a place where the soul can live without the physical body.

As a witch on this earth, your purpose is to better yourself, better your environment and help others. You are to go through life's ups and downs, learn from your mistakes, collect wisdom and grow as a person. This is the same purpose that your soul has.
Your soul is meant to experience the physical world, die, reflect on the life it lived and then be reincarnated into a new physical life. The goal is that each physical life is lived better than the last. For this reason, we can assume that people who are immoral and mistreat others are "new souls" who have not yet lived many lives and learned how to be good.

The Afterlife

Every time your soul lives life and reflects upon it in The Afterlife, it will live a more moral and spiritually satisfying physical life the next time it is reincarnated. It's like your soul is on a mission to live the perfect physical life and it takes numerous tries for this to happen.

So, what is the Afterlife? The Afterlife is a place (similar to the idea of heaven) where your soul can go and rest before it is reincarnated into a new physical body. Unlike heaven, however, this place is not a place where your soul will be judged. While you are in The Afterlife, you can communicate with the other souls, the deities and reflect on the physical life you just lived. If you lived a bad life, you would follow the guidance of the Goddess and the God in hopes that your next life will be more spiritually satisfying. Once your soul has satisfied the physical life's purpose, it will remain in The Afterlife for all eternity.

The God and Goddess (or Lord and Lady)

Wicca acknowledges both the masculine god and the feminine goddess. They both represent unique but essential characteristics and are seen as equal. Now for Christians, the deities in Wicca can be confusing, I know it was for me! This is because Christianity focuses on a very rigid set of beliefs, but Wiccans have the ability to interpret things on their own.

Some Wiccans view the God and Goddess as two gods. Other Wiccans believe there are many different masculine deities which collectively would be referred to as the God or Horned God and that there would also be many feminine deities that all together would be referred to as the Goddess or Triple Goddess.

To compare this to Christianity, we can use God, Jesus, and the Holy Spirit. In Christianity you would consider all three of those entities to be "God", but they can either be broken down into individual entities or referred to as a whole.

In Wicca, you have the ability to choose whether you want to refer to the God and Goddess as a whole or if you'd like to worship the individual deities and break them down further. I will outline the basic overview of the God and Goddess, but I recommend delving deeper into this on your own.

The Elements

Throughout the history of humanity and magic across Europe, as well as the Middle East and Asia, the discussion and study of the four elements has been a topic of passion, speculation and mystery. These are not elements to be found on the periodic table—they are the "nature" of things, the inherent quality in every aspect of life. When you feel comfortable enough to begin crafting and writing your own spells, taking the elements into consideration will help increase the emphasis of your magic, as well as add to its power.

Earth

The duality of the God and the Goddess can also be found in the elements, as well as their nature. Earth is considered a feminine element, which makes sense when you consider the Goddess is the Earth. She is our planet and giver of life. The element of Earth is stable, bountiful and useful when we are working with magic regarding abundance, prosperity and foundations. It is also essential when working on personal growth, growth of an idea or project, or even a business. Anything that involves change in stages can be well-served by incorporating the element of Earth. When we are working with the Earth element, we're keeping an eye to the future, but with roots firmly planted in the present. We can also tap into our past, our legacies given to us by our ancestors and family tree. Two tarot cards that personify the element of Earth are the Empress and the Queen of Pentacles.

Some Earthly symbolic guides include wolf and stag, beetle, bull and fox. Gods to incorporate into your Earth magic include Cernunnos, the Horned God, the Green Man, Ochosi and Lugh. Earth goddesses such as Demeter, Gaea and Pomona can be especially helpful when working with Earth magic.

Winter, as well as the direction North, are connected to the element of Earth, as are Capricorn, Taurus and Virgo of the western zodiac. The Earth element is connected with midnight.

All crystals, stones and metals are linked to Earth in some way, but the ones especially significant include salt, pyrite, amber, onyx, iron, diamond and petrified wood. Earth elemental herbs include sage, rue, oak, pennyroyal, cinquefoil and yarrow.

Invoke the guardians of Earth when you need to become more grounded, for stability, protection, solace, healing and courage. The element of Earth is also useful for garden magic.

Air

The element of Air symbolizes communication, messages, logic, speech, poetry, divination and the intellect. This is a masculine energy, as well as being a direct energy: in other words, it moves, it changes, it is never still. The location on the compass rose for Air is the East and we may think of the East winds and their importance in fable and song. Travel, contracts, agreements, platonic unions, legal issues, freedom, personal journeys, are all blessed by the element of Air.

Air spirit guides and animals include the eagle, the dove, angels, spirits, crows, dragonflies and butterflies. Airy gods include Ellegua, Mercury, Thoth, Cupid and the Thunderbird. Goddesses connected to air include Oya, Nuit, Athena and Ariada, as well as Hecate.

The element of Air is represented by the season of Spring. Aquarius, Libra and Gemini are the airy zodiac signs and Air is represented by dawn, each day.

Crystals representative of the element of Air include topaz, amethyst, citrine, Herkimer diamond and labradorite. Herbs of the Air element include lavender, dandelion, jasmine, rose and thyme.

Call upon the guardians and guides of the Air element for swift communication, good news, luck, opportunities and change. Air can bring your need for miracles to the universe's attention.

Fire

The Fire element symbolizes passion, excitement, inner strength, desire, the divine spark, creativity and inspiration. Out of all of the elements, Fire is the only one we cannot physically touch and yet we still depend on it to keep us alive in the months of Winter.

Unlike Air, Earth and Water, Fire did not come easily to us, which is why we think of it as a gift from the God and the Goddess. With Fire we are able to change fire creates chemical processes, through which metal is forged into steel, potions are brewed, medicine extracted, ingredients blended.

Not only that, but the constantly-churning core of our planet—filled with metals—is on fire and because of its never-ending activity, our planet is able to produce a magnetic field which protects us from the violent energy of the Sun. As witches, we adore watching fire: from the dancing flame of a single candle to the roaring heat of a bonfire. Fire is magic that we can see.

The energy of Fire is considered masculine and mutable. It is connected with the suit of Wands in the minor arcana of the tarot deck. We may use Fire in our magical work to ignite, inspire, release pent-up energies, but when we do so we must be careful. Fire un-contained can level forests. It is an energy that will run rampant if we allow it to.

Fire is connected to the direction of the South, as well as the time of day of noon.

Spirit guides and animals symbolized by Fire include the phoenix, salamander, dragon, as well as any red or orange creature. Gods connected to Fire include Ogun, Ra, Hephaestus and Chango. Goddesses linked to fire include Brigid, Sehkmet, Pele, Hestia and Amaterasu.

Crystals, gems and metals linked to the element of Fire include yellow jade, ruby, garnet, copper and tiger's eye. Herbs and plants of Fire include cinnamon, basil, black pepper, garlic, stinging nettle and thistle.

Call upon the Guardians of the element of Fire when you are in need of inspiration, passion and a rekindling of your energy. Do not use Fire to punish, as this will backfire on you (notice how the word backfire contains this element). Use Fire reverently and respect its power and it will light up your life.

Water

Water is the calmest element at first glance, but it, too, has a destructive side. Tsunamis can topple the tallest towers and the patience of rivers has carved canyons that are one of the wonders of the natural world. Water is essential to us: it is the most important thing our bodies need and comprises most of our body's ingredients. Water is the embodiment of emotion. It rules memory, empathy and medicine. Herbalists and plant witches need water to keep their gardens flourishing. When paired with Earth, Water becomes more stable and full of potential and growth. The two elements naturally complement each other.

Water is also divinely linked to the phases of the Moon. Moon magic should always have an amount of water nearby, whether you choose to cast your circle beside a running stream, or simply keep a goblet filled with water on your altar as you cast your spell beneath the moon's magical light.

It is challenging to craft medicine without water. The healing nature of water guides our empathy and gives us the instinct to soothe someone who is in pain. Water elemental magic can be powerful, but unlike Fire, it will not rebel against the witch: it is solace incarnate and sacred to the Goddess. As such, Water is considered a feminine element and is mutable, meaning that it changes and can create change.

Spirit guides and animals of the element of Water include nyads, water snakes, turtles, dolphins, whales and undines. Gods of water include Olokun, Hapi, Freyr, Poseidon. Goddesses of water include Sarasvati, Tefnut, Oshun and Yemaya.

The season of the year connected to Water is Autumn and the zodiac signs it represents are Scorpio, Cancer and Pisces. The time of day sacred to Water is dusk.

Getting Started with Meditation

Now that you've determined the chakras on which you want to focus, it's time to turn your attention to meditation.

Choosing a Meditation

Before deciding which meditation, you want to practice, you'll first need to determine which chakras you'll focus your energy on, which chakra to start with, and in which order to address the other chakras. You'll also want to evaluate the timeframe you have to work with for the day and then set aside time in your schedule for meditation.

One Chakra or Many

You may want to work on one chakra at a time or multiple chakras. If you've identified multiple chakras to address, you'll first need to figure out where to begin.

The order won't negatively affect any of your other chakras. However, an excellent general rule is to work on the chakra with the most issues first. I recommend that you listen to your intuition to determine which chakra is giving you the most trouble.

Some chakra experts prefer to work from the center out, because the central chakras—heart and solar plexus—tend to become "stuck" due to their locations. Another option is to start with the root space and then move up to the crown. Opening these end chakras usually will bring about a significant shift, so your energy can flow, and balance can naturally return.

I prefer to work on the heart chakra first because this chakra is the ultimate connection to your infinite being. I usually find that once the heart chakra is cleared, energy issues within other chakras are more comfortable to resolve. For example, say I am experiencing emotional pain from a breakup, and because I have not dealt with those feelings, I am also experiencing anxiety and back pain. My solar plexus is being affected as well as my heart space. I would first want to focus on heart-based healing and then on my solar plexus to address my physical symptoms.

TIME AS A FACTOR

The meditations fit into 5-, 15-, or 30-minute timeframes to make finding a meditation that will suit your schedule easy. The five-minute meditations are an excellent way to dip your toes in the water before you get into the deep end. They are also perfect for energetic maintenance. The longer meditations will help you unlock your creativity and examine personal connections in deep and profound ways. They will yield great insights, clarity, and focus and make your practice more meaningful.

To really clear a chakra on your own, without Reiki or the use of other energy modalities, you'll want to sit with that specific chakra for a minimum of 30 to 45 minutes. You'll have the option to extend all of the meditations with additional breathing and visualization exercises. Time is of the essence, so choose your meditation wisely and commit to it for the minimum suggested length to receive the full benefits.

WHAT'S YOUR INTENTION?

Setting an intention before you begin meditating is the perfect way to formalize what you want to achieve. An intention also improves your odds of successfully making your wish a reality. For example, you may want to achieve balance. Maybe you want a more harmonious relationship with yourself or another person. Perhaps you have an urgent health issue. Maybe you're tackling a more significant issue, such as what you want most out of your life.

Whatever your need, just remember that a restorative or preventative long-term practice will look and feel different than a practice that directly addresses an immediate need, such as a health crisis. Be sure to check in with yourself before you start each meditation in order to determine your goals. If your intention shifts once you get started, simply adjust. Being open and flexible is how all seasoned meditators achieve the most significant results.

The Elements of Guided Meditation

Building a meditation practice is easy.

There are many ways to explore your meditation practice, including mantras, visualizations, breathe work, and reflections. You may find it beneficial to begin by practicing a few meditations with a friend. You may also find it beneficial to record yourself reading the meditation instructions so you can play them back whenever you need a reminder.

If you feel called to make one of the mantras the focus of your meditation, you could potentially do a full sit with that mantra and challenge yourself with a timer. You don't have to pair any meditation elements in order for a meditation to be coherent and successful. Once you learn the foundational elements of meditation, you can put them together however you see fit. The beauty of this practice is that it is yours.

MANTRAS AND MUDRA

In Sanskrit, the word mantra can be broken into two parts: man, which means "mind," and tra, which means "vehicle." Therefore, a mantra is primarily a vehicle of the mind, a type of spiritual formula used to take you into a deep state of meditation quickly.

Mantras help you alter your state of consciousness. Chanting a powerful word or phrase, every syllable of which is specifically designed to affect subconscious impulses and habits, helps you transcend thought and heighten your awareness.

Mudras are hand postures or gestures that are practiced with your fingers, and their origins are rooted in Hinduism and Buddhism. Because your hand is mapped to your brain, mudras target the reflex points important for unlocking specific biological signals such as relaxation, metabolic rate, or circulation. Adding mudras to your meditations is not necessary but can complement and enhance your practice.

VISUALIZATION

Many meditations include some type of visualization. Some visualizations involve specific colors or ask you to use your imagination to enhance your experience. But the emphasis should always be on the feeling that the visualization evokes.

Visualization is a powerful meditation tool that's used to influence the physical body as well as desired outcomes, particularly when those outcomes involve health. Deepak Chopra teaches whatever the focus of our attention, it grows stronger; whatever we withdraw our attention from diminishes. Therefore, visualizing wellness creates more of it.

Visualizations are known to manifest specific results with startling accuracy. Creating a mental image of desired feelings and situations helps you elicit them. Use this practice to live in ways that support your desired goals.

Everything is created twice. First in the mind, and then in reality.

—ROBIN S. SHARMA

MEDITATION

For each chakra, I'll guide you through meditations that are 5, 15, and 30 minutes in length and that instruct you to link your breath with color and other visualizations. The bulk of the meditations focus on the areas, systems, and organs of the body that each chakra governs. By regularly practicing these meditations, you'll get to know each chakra intimately, and you'll create your desired healing effect.

I'll be asking a lot of you in these meditations, especially if you're practicing chakra healing for the first time. But don't worry—I'll provide tips. I'll also explain how to expand the shorter meditations.

CLOSING REFLECTION

Reflection is an opportunity to review what transpired during your sit. Engaging in reflection will help you get comfortable with building your awareness so you can be more in tune with your body and your mind.

After your meditation has concluded, spend about five minutes putting ideas or thoughts that you need to process onto paper. You could also sit with the newly created space of awareness that comes up during meditation. Either way is fine.

Although you won't be cued to spend time in reflection after every meditation, it's a good idea to set two timers: one for the length of the meditation and one for five minutes longer, to give yourself a little buffer before coming back to the real world.

Monkey Mind

The mind can be a land mine of distractions and activity. Your thoughts can race around—much like monkeys swinging from tree to tree. The trees in this case are your emotions and thoughts that are attempting to gain your attention. Originally a Buddhist term meaning "unsettled," "restless," or "indecisive," monkey mind can refer to any mind chatter.

Meditation is not about stopping the chatter—rather, it's about making a choice. Each time you drop into meditation, you have a choice: Allow distractions to pull you out of your space or show up for yourself and go deeper into that space. Instead of jumping from branch to branch, giving anything and everything your attention, make the choice to be present and quiet the chaos.

That choice doesn't mean that you should ignore the chatter. In fact, acknowledging your thoughts can neutralize them, particularly when they include self-doubt.

Giving your mind a task is a good way to transcend thought patterns and processes. One simple technique is to focus on your breath moving in and out of your body. If you become overwhelmed by monkey mind, try incorporating a mantra into your meditation.

Over time, you'll become better at being in the moment. With practice, your thoughts will become less disruptive. Consistency is key here. It's all about training your monkey mind so you can swing gracefully through the trees with patience, compassion, and control.

Before You Begin

Before jumping into your healing practice, there are a few steps that need to be covered. Some of these may seem a bit obvious, but I wouldn't be doing my due diligence as a healer if I didn't include them.

Clearing some time for your meditation is imperative to ensure that your practice is successful. Try setting a daily reminder on your phone to help you establish a meditation habit. Make sure you are comfortable. Eliminate distractions and plan time for reflection before your meditation starts. I'll go over these steps in more detail below.

Do a general check-in with yourself to connect with your current emotions. Make note of any issues so you can develop a loving attitude of self-acceptance each time you practice meditation. And don't worry about whether you're doing it wrong, because there is no wrong way to meditate—I promise!

Forecasting

Being able to anticipate the future or see into future events has been a desirable power of the human mind for millennia. The idea that the timeline can somehow be tapped into and manipulated may seem like something out of a comic book, but these concepts have been around for all of written history. While this practice is very mysterious, it has been practiced successfully for centuries.

Have you ever felt that someone was going to call and then they call soon after you had that thought? This is a subtle taste of how we can sense the future. Somehow our minds are not subject to the confines of time the way our bodies are, this very intriguing most of the population. But how can we practice this amazing power with purpose and intellect? Some science has been used to attempt to capture these powers but rarely see consistent results.

Many tools have been used over the years to help us tap into our potential to predict future events, among them runes, tea leaves, crystals, pendulums, stones, and water. Numerology, astrology and tarot. These techniques have been around for thousands of years, but to what end? Science is very valuable but tends to write off these ancient practices as superstition or parlor tricks. Let's look deeper at divination and forecasting.

What is divination or forecasting?

Divination is an attempt to find meaningful insight into the future by using ritual or esoteric techniques. There are many forms as mentioned above, but the most popular are astrology and tarot, numerology being a key part of these other two arts. These forecasting systems have stood the test of time over millennia and are still used today, even in our materialist and science-driven society.

The idea of finding love, treasure, cures and other incredible things all motivated our ancestors to use divination to achieve greatness or predict catastrophe. Nostradamus comes to mind as a famous practitioner of the divinatory arts.

Defining this practice may be simple, but its practice can take a lifetime to master. These techniques require intense focus and dedication to be used to the fullest extent.

History and Use

The idea of oracles and divination is well recorded in Alexander the Great's success as he tore through Egypt. The Oracle of Amun was visited by Alexander and spoke of his success and inevitable downfall. Although Christianity forbids these practices, the Bible contains plenty of events that would fall under the category of divination. Ancient Greece and Roman mythology are filled with plenty of divinatory events. These oracles and seers were thought to be able to communicate with gods and bring back knowledge from other realms that gave insight into earthly matters. If someone had a natural talent for these communications, they would further their practice by using various tools to assist them with their communications and visions. Seers were sought out to speak of omens and weather, to make decisions on whether or not to go into battle, or even when to plant seeds for the year's harvest. This gave the oracles and seers a very powerful position with leaders, often being hired to see into the future of a reigning king or war general.

In the Middle Ages, divination is ridiculed by the Christian church and considered an evil practice. This is often seen as hypocritical since church fathers and their practices were very similar to divinatory techniques. Even kings and queens used hired seers and magicians to help time their decisions and celebrations. John Dee comes to mind as a powerful magician that used astrology and divination to help Queen Elizabeth I with her reign, even somewhat being attributed to have been a huge part of England's powerful status for centuries leading right up to today.

So, we may not be trying to build a world-renowned empire with our practices, but how can we use these techniques to empower ourselves in the 21st century?

Practice

There are a number of ways to practice forecasting, and some people may be more gifted than others, but all people are capable of using these abilities to help themselves or others. Consider anytime you've run into a divinatory practice. Perhaps you've seen a needle tied to a thread held above a pregnant woman's belly to forecast the gender of the child, or maybe you've driven past a palm reader's shop while driving through the city. These common practices often get passed off as only for fun, but if performed correctly and with passion, they can reveal secrets of the world that are some of the most valuable gifts known to man.

Some people may be able to simply meditate on a subject and get a clear vision of what's to come; this is rare but not unheard of. For our intents and purposes, we will assume we are starting from scratch. First, let's look into some preparatory techniques to prepare the mind for messages and insight.

Meditation

Meditation as seen a rise in popularity in recent decades, this practice is some of the most simple and powerful actions you can take to control your mind and emotions. Plus, it's free and requires no tools.

There are endless amounts of meditation techniques available online, but for the most part, simply sitting and letting the thoughts come and go as they please is enough to gain insight into the power of meditation.

Here's one simple practice:

1. Sit comfortably and quietly in a place with very little distraction
2. Breathe deeply and exhale, counting one.
3. Do ten deep breaths and then count backward to one again.
4. Continue this until you no longer need to count.
5. Notice how the thoughts disappear and you are only focused on breath.
6. Continue as needed until you are in a clear mindset

This seems simple, because it is, the more you practice this, the easier it is to get into that 'zone' where your mind is free of clutter. This 'zone' is the place you want to be during any divinatory practice. The clear-headedness is needed for any information to come through that isn't your brain simply throwing images at you. This works especially well before a tarot session.

Music and Sound

Some people have trouble closing out the distractions around them; this is where music or white noise comes in. By having trance-inducing music, you can block out distractions and more easily enter into the zone. Consider Indian sitar music and its droney and repetitive layers; this is specifically designed to create a distraction-free atmosphere for meditation and insight.

There are many apps and videos online that have white noise or drone sounds to induce a trance state, while in a trance you may more readily find the answers you're seeking and gain the insight you seek. You may even wish to use an instrument such as bells or singing bowls to create the sounds yourself.

Mantras and chants go well with these practices as well; if you simply hum your own noise, you may find yourself in a trance-like state. Some prefer to use affirmations or Indian style mantras such as the OM sound to add to their meditation practice.

Yoga and Movement

Yoga, dance and other arranged movement can also induce a trance-like state. Having planned motions that are complex or repetitive will allow the mind to free itself from day to day worries and needs. This is a great technique to combine with music as well.

Yoga postures and stances help to keep the body healthy as well as the mind. The more content you are with your health, the easier it will be to enter the zone, less worry, the more one-pointedness.

Fasting

Many people have had success and incredible transformative experiences by fasting. Simply choosing a fitting day, perhaps astrologically timed, to only drink water will put the body in a heightened state of awareness, making insight and trance more easily accessible. Do your research on fasting and always listen to your body, if you are uncomfortable, then eat some fruits or other raw foods.

Combined Practice

So, we now have a few preparatory practices to increase the potency of our practice. These techniques listed above are perfect for getting the mind and body ready for forecasting and divination. If we take these practices and combine them with numerology, astrology and tarot, we have a powerful combination of techniques to add to our lives and increase our success and prosperity.

What cannot be stressed enough is that for you to get the most out of these forecasting techniques is you need to listen. Being able to tell the difference between your own thoughts and cosmic insight is key to a successful practice. By practicing the preparatory techniques above and readying the mind, we will find insight and the answers we seek much easier. No one throws down some cards and gets everything they want; it comes with passion and determination, dedication and humility, and overall comes with love, for yourself and the universe.

Let's take what we have now learned and combine it all together into a formidable practice and philosophy.

Geographical House Divisions and the Four Elemental House- Also Called Trinities

Geographical House Divisions

Geographical divisions are very general descriptions and are easily overruled by other factors in the chart. They can be useful, but only for a general feel for the chart, requires seven or more Planets to influence the native.

Northern - Houses 1 to 6 - subjective and avoidant, the native shows tendencies to withdraw from others, enjoys working and operating successfully away from the public eye.

Southern - Houses 7 to 12 - objective, optimistic and embracing, the native enjoys plunging into life, they are happy, gregarious, enjoy public recognition and praise.

Eastern - Houses 10 to 3 - controlling and leading, a strong presentation and bearing, the native likes to take charge and they make their own breaks in life. The 12th House may weaken this tendency if overemphasized.

Western - Houses 4 to 9 - impressionable and pessimistic, often wanting others to do everything for them, a weakness which may be seen as being overly gullible. Easily influenced by others but very charming and social, people love to invite them to parties.

This House division corresponds to the four Elements of the twelve zodiac Signs and require four or more Planets to have a strong influence.

Fire Houses -1, 5 & 9 - Life / Personal - these Houses represent your vitality and self-expression through your individual creativity and actions. These people are idealists, adventurers and local heroes who show us that it is possible to be spiritual and human at the same time. An over-emphasis on these Houses can lead to its negative characteristics: narcissistic, self-centered and childish behavior. No longer the heroes we worship, they can become the bullies we fear.

Earth Houses - 2, 6 & 10 - Wealth / Work - these people are interested in and concerned with material possessions. They are dedicated to completing a task and are reliable in work and play. They are not necessarily money-oriented, but they understand the usefulness and power of financial and material security. Often, they are the ones who hold the community together through their wise use of time and energy. These natives teach us how to go about creating security in our lives. If this element dominates the chart, it is possible that its negative characteristics will show, such as being lazy, indulgent, greedy, hoarding and accumulating possessions at the expense of others. Once idolized for their sensible lifestyles and work ethics, they become the target of unhappy tenants, students and staff.

Air Houses - 3, 7 & 11 - Relationship / Social -these natives are people-oriented, they need to connect and share, and Facebook is filled with Air Signs. Often seen at parties, talking on the phone and at the negotiating table, these people may whither if they don't have someone to talk to. They are communicators, we can learn a lot from them about planning, strategy and relating to one another for the betterment of humanity. An unhealthy focus on these House qualities can lead to worry, meaningless meetings, endless texts and grandiose thinking. We respect our leaders who exhibit good communication skills, but when they fail us, we feel manipulated.

Water Houses - 4, 8 & 12 - Psychic / Psychological - a focus on these Houses shows emotional sensitivity. These natives may benefit from some form of counseling or mentoring to help them understand and cope with their sensitivity and psychic ability. As said before, sensitive/psychic people often dwell in their inner world and require grounding. This is often through specific meditation techniques and any form of physical, mental and emotional discipline. These are our inspirational dreamers. Too much emphasis on these Houses can lead to an over-sensitive individual who requires constant reassurance and nurturing. They can experience severe mood swings, but usually it is directed inwards, at them. These natives often quietly self-destruct: they become recluses; they are not the noisemakers of the other elemental Houses.

Conclusion

Numerology has been used for years, and it is a highly valuable tool that can help you discover more about yourself and how you can navigate your life in alignment with who you truly are. By tapping into your numbers and learning how to read your chart you can explore the vast world of you through a totally new perspective!

If you want to go beyond reading your own chart and really getting deeper into the different numbers and how they can be read in other ways, I encourage you to continue studying numerology. You will likely be surprised to find out that there is so much to learn! You can also start connecting your numerology practice to your astrology or tarot practice, or even using numerology to lead you into a healthy astrology or tarot practice to help you discover even more about yourself.

The more that you invest in understanding yourself through crafts like numerology, the easier it is for you to develop yourself along this journey. It is important to understand that tools like numerology are only meant to be used as a guide and not as a strict rule book in your life. As you read through your chart and reflect on it, remember that you may find areas where you do not resonate with your chart simply because you are a unique individual. You may find that you can find an even deeper resonance by going back to the double-digit number before the single digit number to help you resonate even deeper. In other numbers, you may completely identify with the primary number and find that it tells you plenty. To summarize, there is so much to be learned about yourself through numerology, but the ultimate learning comes from reflecting on it and seeing how it actually relates to you in your lifetime. This way, you can learn not only about numerology, but about yourself, too.

It is a good idea to write your chart down on paper or in a document so that you can reflect back on it whenever you need to. Many people find that their charts become valuable to them at many points in life, and they reference back to it frequently. As a result, they are able to get great information about how they can move through different phases of their life, what they can expect from the people around them, and how they make better decisions. Regularly reflecting back on your chart can be a valuable opportunity for you to move in alignment with your true soul, which is the biggest benefit of numerology.

At the end of the day, the more you can come into alignment with yourself through tools like numerology, the more balanced your life is going to become. The key here is to understand your tendencies and patterns and realize that being empowered with this information means that you can start making more informed decisions. Numerology is not about being locked into a specific pattern or "doomed" to a certain lifestyle, but instead it is about learning how-to live-in flow with you in this lifetime.